THE EARLY CHRISTIAN FATHERS

THE EARLY CHRISTIAN FATHERS

A selection from the writings of the Fathers
from St. Clement of Rome to St. Athanasius

Edited and translated by
HENRY BETTENSON

OXFORD UNIVERSITY PRESS
London   Oxford   New York

Oxford University Press

LONDON OXFORD NEW YORK
GLASGOW TORONTO MELBOURNE WELLINGTON
CAPE TOWN IBADAN NAIROBI DAR ES SALAAM LUSAKA ADDIS ABABA
DELHI BOMBAY CALCUTTA MADRAS KARACHI LAHORE DACCA
KUALA LUMPUR SINGAPORE HONG KONG TOKYO

ISBN 0 19 283009 0

First published by Oxford University Press, London, 1956

First issued as an Oxford University Press paperback, 1969

Reprinted 1974

*Printed in Great Britain
by Richard Clay (The Chaucer Press), Ltd,
Bungay, Suffolk*

Contents

Introduction

The aim of this book is to illustrate, from the writings of those authors on whom tradition has bestowed the name of *Fathers of the Church*, the process of development in Christian thought, life, and worship during the period which culminated in the acceptance of the Christian faith by the Emperor Constantine, and, what that acceptance made possible, the first oecumenical formulation of doctrine at the *Council of Nicaea*, which begins the era of conciliar definitions. It is a period in which the Church is seen defending and explaining its teaching and practice against misrepresentation by the pagans; striving to safeguard its tradition from distortion by those within the society, or who claimed to be within it; coming to terms (for good or, it may be, for bad) with its environment in the world; working out the implications of the Apostolic faith and devotion, and translating the faith into the language of Hellenistic thought; and consolidating its organization and its forms of worship.

Clement of Rome

The title of *Apostolic Fathers* is by custom applied to certain writers of the age generally known as 'sub-apostolic' who were thought of as the immediate successors and disciples of the Apostles. They are represented here by St. Clement of Rome and St. Ignatius of Antioch.

The letter from the Church at Rome to the Church of the Corinthians which tradition ascribes to a certain Clement is in itself anonymous, but there is no reason to doubt the ascription. Who that Clement was is a question to which three considerable answers have been given. There is, first, that Clement who was a fellow labourer of St. Paul, one of his 'fellow workers whose names are in the book of life'.[1] Origen and Eusebius saw in him the author of the letter; a possible but unlikely conjecture. Then there is Titus Flavius Clemens, cousin of the Emperor Domitian and consul with the Emperor in A.D. 95, who at the close of his consulship was arrested, together with his wife Domitilla, on the charge of 'atheism' and 'Jewish practices'. He was put to death; his wife was banished. Now Domitilla was probably a Christian; the

[1] Phil. iv. 3.

cemetery at Rome which bears her name may well have been her gift to the Church: and many scholars have assumed that the consul also was a believer (Streeter suggested[1] that he might be the 'most excellent Theophilus' of the Lucan preface), and that he wrote the letter to the Corinthians. But it seems certain that our author was not a Roman by race; and it is more than doubtful if the consul could have been a professed Christian. The third suggestion is that the writer was a freedman of the household of Clemens and Domitilla; and this seems most plausible: but the further suggestion that he was a Jew by race has the flimsy basis of a reference in chapter 4 to Jacob as 'our father'; it is contradicted by the whole tone of the epistle.

The official list of popes gives the succession Peter, Linus, Cletus (or Anacletus), Clement. We may suppose our Clement to have been in some sense a bishop; and the traditional dates of Pope Clement, 90–100, would cohere with the internal evidence of the letter. For the Neronian persecution is apparently referred to as an event of the past; but the Church has suffered further disasters. We need not doubt that this points to the troubles of Christians under Domitian; and the situation presupposed in the sections concerning the ministry—the Apostles have passed away, as have also some of their successors—is that of a generation after Nero's principate. A.D. 94 is a likely date.

The letter was occasioned by news reaching Rome of faction within the Church at Corinth, leading to the deposition of certain blameless presbyters; evidently the Corinthian Christians had not changed much since the time when St. Paul had been moved by reports of schisms to write 1 Corinthians. The Roman Church now intervenes because of Christian concern over this distressing situation, not because it claims authority over other churches. Since Corinth was a Romanized city after its refounding as a colony in 44 B.C. the Roman believers may well have had a particular concern about the fortunes of the Church in that place.

For us the importance of the epistle lies in the picture it presents of the Roman Church at the end of the first century. A comparison of Clement with the other Apostolic Fathers reveals a wide variety of types of thought and ways of life in the early Church; the curious exegetics of *Barnabas*, the theological crudities of *Hermas*, the fervid sacerdotalism of Ignatius; and it is a comparison which may serve to show the emergence of the characteristic Roman Christianity. Here we find no ecstasies, no miraculous 'gifts of the Spirit', no demonology,

[1] In *The Four Gospels*, 1924, pp. 534 ff.

no preoccupation with an imminent 'Second Coming'. The Church has settled down in the world, and is going about its task 'soberly, discreetly and advisedly'; Christians pray for their secular rulers, and for a spirit of submission to authority, even in time of persecution. For his theology the writer accepts the monotheism common to Judaism and Stoicism (he employs both scriptural and Hellenic phraseology); to which he adds, without any feeling of tension, the Christology of Paul and *Hebrews*; he has little to say of the Holy Spirit. One would assume that he had small interest in theological speculation; rather he is concerned with the organization of the Christian community, its ministry, and its liturgy: and what he says about the ministry is of great interest to us, though notoriously uncertain of interpretation. Above all, Clement is a moralist. The Christianity he portrays is

a moral movement, firmly set in a clear consciousness of knowing the living God, and living a redeemed life in Christ. Compared with other religions, it was the religion of inwardness and the Spirit, and at the same time a brotherhood, as comprehensive as human life and as deep as human need. . . . If we compare what the Roman church has here written with what we know of town and community life, the societies, schools, etc., of that time, the tremendous difference strikes us at once, and we remember the words of the Apostle Paul to the Philippians: 'ye are children of God without blemish in the midst of a crooked and perverse generation, among whom ye are seen as lights of the world'.[1]

Ignatius

Ignatius, Bishop of Antioch, was condemned to death in his own city, and taken to Rome, expecting to be thrown to the wild beasts in the amphitheatre. Apart from what we can discover from his letters, we know nothing of him. We infer from the fate which he anticipated that he was not a Roman citizen, for citizens were exempt from such indignity; we gather from his letters that he was converted in adult life. The date of his death is unknown; Eusebius gives 108, while John Malalas (*c.* 600) assigns it to 115, on the occasion of Trajan's visit to Antioch. It is not a fact beyond all doubt that Ignatius actually suffered matryrdom; for by the fourth century his bones were assumed to have been buried in his episcopal city; and if this tradition is true he could scarcely have been torn to pieces by the beasts at Rome.

[1] Harnack, quoted by Dr. Lowther Clarke in the introduction to his *First Epistle of Clement*, 1937, p. 44.

On the long journey from Syria Ignatius was taken, closely guarded, through districts of Asia Minor where there were many churches. At Laodicea there was a choice of roads; the southern route leading through Tralles, Magnesia, and Ephesus, while the route chosen reached Smyrna by way of Philadelphia and Sardis. It appears that messages were sent from Laodicea to the Christian communities on the southern road, who had been expecting to greet the hero on his way to martyrdom, and they sent delegates to Smyrna to meet him there and convey their sympathy and admiration. At Smyrna there was a pause in the journey, while the party awaited a ship, and Ignatius had time to write letters of thanks and exhortation to the brethren at Ephesus, Magnesia, and Tralles. At the same time he took the opportunity to write to the church at Rome, warning the brethren of his impending arrival and imploring them not to try to win for him the mistaken kindness of a reprieve. From Smyrna the guards took him by sea to Troas, where another pause enabled Ignatius to write to the churches of Philadelphia and Smyrna; and to send a personal letter to Polycarp, Smyrna's bishop. These were letters of thanks for the kindness they had shown him.

The chief themes of the letters are: warnings against the Docetic heresy (which denied the reality of Christ's human nature, and therefore of his sufferings); and, more insistent, the exhortation to unity, with the emphasis on the authority of the bishop, and, under him, of the clergy.

Ignatius affirms the true corporeity of the Redeemer, and the reality of his human sufferings; with equal clarity he maintains his true divinity. 'He was truly born, truly ate and drank; was truly persecuted under Pontius Pilate; he was truly crucified and he truly died.'[1] 'Son of Mary, and Son of God, first passible, then impassible, Jesus Christ our Lord.'[2] He is the *Logos* who reveals the Father; he bestows immortality through his death and resurrection, though Ignatius does not attempt to explain how this is effected; the Spirit is the *charisma* of Christ; and Christianity is Christ in us. Of his theology Dr. Sanday says:

Ignatius uses language which is not always in keeping with the rules of the later theology (e.g. 'blood of God'. 'suffering of God'): but the striking thing about him is the way in which he seems to anticipate the spirit of the later theology; the way in which he singles out as central the points which it made central, and the just balance which he observes between them. He has a broad and simple view of the mission of the Son by the Father, which is more like that

[1] *Trall.* 9.   [2] *Eph.* 7.

of the prologue to the Fourth Gospel than anything else. . . . It is to the credit of Ignatius that he writes like one who still feels the immense personal impression of the life of Christ.[1]

The theme of unity and submission to ecclesiastical authority, represented primarily by the bishop, appears in letter after letter. Unity is the very condition of Christianity: without the bishop there is no Church; without the bishop there can be no baptism, no *agape*, no Eucharist: the bishop presides at common worship; if presbyters officiate, they do so as his delegates. There is no word of any *charisma* of the Spirit; no mention of prophecy, nor of any other 'gifts'. There is one authority, and one primary ministry, the 'monarchical episcopate'. Those who regard this 'prelacy' as an unfortunate development, as the intrusion of a rigid sacerdotalism into the Christian brotherhood, naturally tend to find in Ignatius' reiterations the signs of something like a neurotic obsession with episcopacy, or at least of an hysterical anxiety to enforce a novel conception of the ministry which he, perhaps egotistically, feels to be all-important: and they can point to his positive craving for martyrdom as evidence of a sort of spiritual exhibitionism. On the other side it is urged that a time of persecution is not the suitable occasion for introducing experiments, but rather for rallying round the old loyalties; that Ignatius seems to have been a leader loved and trusted in Asia Minor as well as in Syria; that he was calling on the faithful to close their ranks in the face of danger from persecution and from erroneous teaching.

There is no denying a certain shrillness in the voice of Ignatius; a tone very different from the level steadiness of Clement. 'Ignatius is a mystic with heart red-hot and nerves strained to the breaking-point.'[2] Battifol says of him: 'His letters, written in an abrupt and nervous style, over-loaded with metaphors, incoherent, popular, and lacking every Hellenic grace, are yet endowed with such pathetic faith, and such passionate joy in martyrdom with such an overwhelming love of Christ, that they are one of the finest expressions of the Christianity of the second century.'[3]

The Didache

In 1875 Bryennios, Metropolitan of Serrae, who later became Patriarch of Nicomedia, was working in Constantinople in the library of the

[1] *Christologies Ancient and Modern*, pp. 10 f.   [2] Clarke, op. cit., p. 43.   [3] Article 'Ignatius' in *Dictionary of Christian Biography*.

Greek Patriarch of Jerusalem when he found a manuscript dated 1056 which contained copies of the Epistles of Clement, Barnabas, and Ignatius, and a document purporting to set out the *Teaching of the Apostles*, which has become generally known as the *Didache*, from the first word of its Greek title. This document was published in 1883, and caused no small stir; for it seemed likely to turn upside-down the received ideas of the early history of the ministry. On the face of it the treatise was of a very early date, before itinerant prophets had been displaced by a settled permanent ministry; when episcopacy was not yet the universal form of church government, and 'bishop' was synonymous with 'presbyter'; when the *agape* was still conjoined with the Eucharist; when liturgy and theology were still in an early stage. Most scholars inclined to a date in the first century, some arguing for as early as 60, or at any rate not later than 100.[1] Lightfoot placed it at the very beginning of the second century, at latest. But others soon began to express doubts about its genuineness. It was admittedly 'pseudepigraphical' in claiming to be the 'teaching of the Apostles'; and the sceptics went beyond the supposition that it represented the practice of the early Church—or of a particular early church—in the first or second century, regarded by that community as based on the Apostolic instructions; they held it to be a deliberate piece of archaeologizing, a later generation constructing a fancy picture of life in the primitive Church. Dr. Charles Bigg[2] attributed it to the fourth century, regarding it as a Montanist pamphlet, put out during Julian's persecution. The place accorded to prophets in the document has led many[3] to give to it a Montanist provenance, though few seem to have followed Bigg in bringing it down so late. Dr. Armitage Robinson thought it an artificial production of the latter part of the second century, believing that the 'Two Ways', which forms its first part, is based on *Barnabas*. Others suppose that it genuinely represents conditions in some remote backwater of the Church, which may either have preserved features of primitive church life, or have slipped into eccentricities. It would probably be safe to say that there is now a general tendency to regard the treatise as an archaizing work, of the later second century. Certainly there has been little acceptance of Streeter's suggestion, that it reflects the conditions of the early church at Antioch, one of the great centres of Christianity.

There is more general agreement in supposing a Syrian provenance.

[1] C. H. Turner, *Studies in Church History*, chap. 1.   [2] *Doctrine of the Twelve Apostles*, 1898.
[3] e.g. Hilgenfeld and Connolly.

It is the first example of the 'Church Orders'; and they, except for the *Apostolic Tradition* of Hippolytus, are probably all either Syrian or Egyptian; the two which are in part derived from the *Didache* (the *Didascalia* and the *Apostolic Constitutions*) are almost certainly Syrian; and internal evidence favours Syria rather than Egypt as the land of origin.[1]

The importance of Apostles and Prophets in the Church as pictured in the document seemed, when it was first published, to support the theory of a 'charismatic ministry' in the early Church, a ministry called directly by God through the bestowal of special spiritual gifts, or *charismata*. On the basis of the *Didache*, together with the lists of 'gifts' in 1 Cor. xii. 28 ff. and Eph. iv. 11 ff. Harnack evolved his theory of the early ministry. He held that in the first century there were two ministries: that of preaching, which was universal and 'charismatic'; and that of administration, the ordained ministry of bishops (a title convertible with 'presbyters') and deacons, exercising a local authority. The 'universal' ministry was, he held, by far the more important in the early days; and in the *Didache* we see a state of transition; the local ministry is beginning to take over the authority of the 'charismatic'. But there is really no warrant for all this, either in Scripture or in this document, whatever view is taken of its date or of its representative character. The lists in the epistles are not enumerations of ministers but of 'gifts', several of which might be displayed by the same man; there is no suggestion in the New Testament of a ministerial authority derived from the gift of prophecy, nor of any distinction between 'charismatic' and ordained ministries; in fact, ordination is spoken of as conveying a charisma (2 Tim. i. 6). And the *Didache* does not show a threefold ministry of apostles, prophets, teachers, but describes itinerant prophets who teach, and who may be called apostles.

As for the passages about the Eucharist in the *Didache*; it seems improbable that chapter xiv is a mere duplication of the instructions in chapters ix and x. It is much more likely that the earlier passage refers to the *agape*, the latter to the Eucharist proper.

Diognetus

The *Epistle to Diognetus* is by custom ranked among the Apostolic Fathers; but it has more affinity with the Apologists, those writers

---

[1] e.g. the corn 'sown on the mountains'; the availability of baths for baptism; the implied abundance of rivers; the apparent absence of slavery and capitalism.

whose concern it was to explain and defend Christianity before the pagan world. The main concern of the Church in earliest days had been the winning of converts and the guidance of the infant Christian communities; defensively, the Christian leader's first task had been to repel Jewish attacks. But by the turn of the century Christianity was becoming a considerable element in many cities of the Roman Empire; its rapid growth began to arouse distrust and perplexity, and to provoke repressive measures. Thus arose the need for apologetic; to show the reasonableness of the new faith, and, if possible, to state it in terms comprehensible and acceptable to the educated man of the Roman world; to claim toleration for Christians as people of blameless lives, willing to be exemplary citizens because of their faith, not in spite of it, if only they might be excused the customary religious observances of the pagan empire.

The chief aim of this epistle is to demonstrate the attractiveness of the Christian way of life. Its theology is vague, and the apologetic of the early chapters, with its commonplace attack on Jewish and pagan worship, is unimpressive. But the elegance of its style and the sincere nobility of much of its thought, particularly in the setting forth of the redemption, cannot be denied. Lightfoot called it 'the noblest of early Christian writings', and it has won high praise from most of those who who studied it; and yet it was unknown to Eusebius; it is not noticed by any ancient or medieval writers; and the sole authority for the text is a late medieval manuscript which was destroyed by fire in Strassburg during the Franco-Prussian war. This neglect is puzzling; perhaps its anonymity lost it a place among the Apostolic Fathers, while other Apologists had put up a more trenchant and systematic defence; and its theological imprecision did not commend it to a later age as an authority on doctrine.

Its authorship admits a wide—sometimes a wild—conjecture. Clement, Apollos, Justin, Quadratus, Marcion, 'Aristides' have all been suggested on quite inadequate grounds. Connolly argued with some plausibility for Hippolytus, who has been called the residuary legatee of the unclaimed literature of the second century. It has even been conjectured that it might be a fifteenth-century essay in the manner of Justin. The earliest date suggested is the reign of Trajan; the latest (discounting theories of forgery) the beginning of the fourth century. There seems to be now a general inclination towards the middle of the second century; and the tone of the letter, with its merely inchoate theology, the absence of any doctrine of the Spirit, and the lack of any traces of institutionalism, supports an early date. Nothing is known of its place of origin; nor of the identity of Diognetus, who may well be a literary fiction; for the document is an 'epistle' rather than a true letter, an apologetic treatise in epistolary form.

Justin

The most famous of the Apologists proper is utterly lacking in the elegance and charm of the writer to Diognetus. Justin was born of gentile parents towards the end of the first century in Flavia Neapolis (the ancient Sichem, now called Nablus) in Samaria. In his *Dialogue with Trypho* he tells of his early passion for philosophy; how he betook himself to a Stoic teacher (who showed no interest in theology); then to a Peripatetic (who displayed too lively a concern for his fees); thence to a Pythagorean (but he demanded a too intensive course of preliminary study). Dissatisfied with these tutors, Justin put himself under a Platonist and found his doctrines more congenial. Then, in mature life, he was converted to Christianity, apparently at Ephesus, and rejoiced at finding the goal of his long search. But he still thought of himself as a philosopher, and when, soon after his conversion, he removed to Rome and set up as a teacher he still wore, says Eusebius, the distinctive cloak which was the accepted academical dress of the professor of philosophy; a garb which would accord well with the claim of his *Apology* that Christianity is the fulfilment of the philosophic quest; Christ did not come to destroy the Academy, the Lyceum, and the Stoa. Tradition holds that in the reign of Marcus Aurelius, about A.D. 165, Justin met the death which earned him the title afterwards affixed as a kind of surname.

He seems to have been a prolific writer, and his reputation has attracted many spurious attributions; but only two books have come down to us which are certainly his; the *Apology* addressed to the Emperor Antoninus Pius and his adopted sons, with its supplement (the so-called '*Second Apology*'), and the *Dialogue with Trypho*. The dialogue, ostensibly a report of an argument with a Jew whom Justin met at Ephesus soon after his conversion, is of interest in the evidence it provides for contemporary Jewish Christianity, and in the Procrustean methods by which Justin forces the Old Testament to supply prefigurations of the New. But for us Justin is more important as an apologist whose chief aim is to obtain justice for Christians by defending them against pagan calumny. Though more doctrinal than the other Apologists, he is not really a theologian; rather he is a philosopher—of a somewhat superficial kind—and a moralist, for whom Christianity is rational truth and a noble way of life. He is one of the first to strive to reconcile Christianity and Hellenic thought, by asserting that while the Church has the complete truth there are truths of philosophy as well, which, because they are true, must be due to the working of the same *Logos* who revealed all truth in his incarnate life, who is both the creative Word and (as the Stoics also taught) the Divine Reason. Hence arises Justin's one original contribution to Christian thought, the conception of the 'Spermatic Logos'. Before the coming of Christ men had been enabled to attain to bits and pieces of the truth through the possession of 'seeds' of the Divine Reason; at Christ's coming the whole *Logos* took shape and was made man. It is this liberal attitude to pagan thought which is Justin's chief importance, not any contribution to technical theology. He shows us an educated man of the second century, seeking to commend the faith to others of like interest and the same background of culture. He is no profound thinker, and no stylist; his works are rambling and diffuse; woolly as well in texture of language as of thought.

So far we have met with Apostolic Fathers and Apologists. The next two writers bear the title of Catholic Fathers, bestowed in virtue of their position as defenders of the faith of the main tradition of the Church against Gnostic heresy, some account of which must now be given.

Gnosticism

'Gnostic' is a term used to cover a wide range of notions, and there is no general agreement about the precise limits of its denotation; it refers in fact to a type of thought rather than to a specific heresy. The word is derived from the Greek for knowledge (*gnosis*); and it is characteristic of the Gnostic that he lays claim to the possession of esoteric truth about God and his relation to the world of matter, and to men in their material bodies. Such a relation is a problem for the type of outlook from which Gnosticism emerges, for that outlook is fundamentally dualistic, making a clean break between spirit and matter, between God and the world. Harnack saw in Gnosticism the 'acute Hellenisation of Christianity', but it seems to be more oriental than

Greek; and it is pre-Christian in origin, coming into conflict with the Faith when this amorphous Eastern syncretism tries to take Christianity into its system and to expound the teaching of Christ in terms of oriental theosophy. To the Gnostic the Christianity of the gospels was milk for the spiritual nursery; the mature man needed a diet more intellectually satisfying, a diet which Gnosticism offered to supply. It was clearly impossible that Absolute Spirit should have direct contact with matter, either in creation or in revelation; still more incredible was the notion that God could become man. The world could only have indirect relation to God by means of a chain of beings, of graduated spirituality. Hence in Samaria Simon Magus, we are told, taught that from the One there issued Thought, and from Thought came various ranks of Angels, and by them the world was made: at Antioch, at the beginning of the second century, Saturninus ascribed creation to seven Angels, of which Jehovah was one: while the lunatic fringe of Syrian Gnosticism was represented by the Ophites, who revered the Serpent of Genesis iii as being man's helper against the inferior creator-god, the Demiurge: and the Cainites took their name from the character whom they held to be the first hero in Scripture, for they went to the extreme of exegetical topsy-turvydom, assuming that all biblical judgements, like dreams, 'go by contraries', and applying this canon of popular oneirocriticism throughout the Scriptures. In Alexandria Basilides interposed 365 heavens between the Supreme Being and the material world, and taught that the disorder of the world was healed when Nous descended from the Supreme upon the son of Mary, and this deified man was taken up to heaven without suffering, while Simon of Cyrene died on the cross. Carpocrates held that the world's disorder was the fault of the Angels of creation, who spoilt the divine plan by their officious introduction of law (especially the law of property) and morality (especially sexual morality); so that a return to anarchy and communism would set men free from the infinite succession of birth and rebirth and the bondage of matter. But the greatest of the Gnostics was Valentinus, an Egyptian who taught in Rome in the middle of the second century. His cosmological fantasy presents a dizzy scheme of 'Aeons', ultimately derived from the Supreme Being, and composing the 'Pleroma', the fullness of the Divinity—apparently a poetical symbolism of the attributes of the Supreme. These Aeons are arranged in pairs, male and female, each pair producing a subordinate pair, until Will and Wisdom gave birth to the abortion Achamoth, who is the source of confusion, which is restored to order by two pairs of Aeons,

Christ and Spirit, Definition and Cross. Finally, Jesus comes into being as the last of the Aeons, and Achamoth produces three types of men; the Carnal (the pagans, who are irredeemable), the Psychic (ordinary Christians who are capable of restoration), and the Pneumatic (the spiritual Valentinians, who need no redemption).

'We are dealing in the last resort with the products of human fancy, a fanciful world "moulded to the heart's desire", in which the religious imagination was not tied down to historical facts preserved in an authoritative book. In these days I venture to think that we are not sufficiently grateful to the orthodox Catholic theologians who clung so doggedly to the literal truth of the Scriptures.' This is the verdict of Dr. Burkitt,[1] although he took the favourable view of Valentinus that he was a Christian seeking to interpret the Faith in terms acceptable to Hellenistic culture.

Irenaeus

The refutation of such vertiginous fancies, the overthrow of 'the base-less fabric of this vision', and the affirmation of the apostolic tradition and the scriptural revelation was the purpose of the great work of Irenaeus. Little is known of his life. He was born in Asia Minor about 130, and as a youth he saw and heard Polycarp of Smyrna. Later he came to Gaul, and in 177 as a presbyter of Lyons he took to Pope Eleutherus the letter of the confessors of the Gallican churches—which he may have written. In the same year he succeeded Pothinus as Bishop of Lyons. Tradition attributes his death (some say by martyrdom) to the first years of the next century.

The work generally known as *Adversus Haereses* really bears the title *The Refutation of False Gnosis*; and the first two books give a detailed exposure of Gnostic fantasies; books iii and iv expound Christian teaching; the fifth and last book treats of the resurrection and the con-summation of history—including an account of the millenarian hope which Irenaeus shared with Papias and Justin, and others who took the Apocalypse as their map of the future. Irenaeus is chiefly concerned to establish the 'Apostolic Tradition', the Church's 'Rule of Faith', against the Gnostic claim to the possession of a secret tradition. And he insists that this Rule is guaranteed as being the teaching of the great sees, whose succession can be traced back to the founding Apostles. Against

[1] *Church and Gnosis*, p. 63.

the claim to an unwritten esoteric doctrine he opposes the authority of Scripture: the New Testament is now for the first time quoted as Scripture; and the gospel canon is closed, for does not nature itself teach us that there must be four gospels, and no more than four? Thus against the novelties of Gnosticism he opposes the traditional Faith, the established succession of bishops, and the guaranteed revelation in the gospels. 'Although the expression The Catholic Church, which came into vogue towards the end of the second century, does not occur in the writings of Irenaeus, the thing itself is constantly before him, that is, the conception of the one true Church spread over the earth, and bound together by the one true faith, in contrast to the manifold and variegated and apostate forms of heresy.'[1]

Irenaeus may justly be called the first biblical theologian; for him the Bible is not a collection of proof-texts as it is for the Apologists, but a continuous record of God's self-disclosure and his dealings with man, reaching its culmination in the person and work of Christ. His Christology is not systematically expounded; Irenaeus was not a systematic thinker. But the chief points are clear: Christ is the *Logos*, the complete revelation of the Father's love; in opposition to the Gnostic notion of emanation Irenaeus affirms the eternal co-existence of the *Logos* with the Father, thus developing the teaching of the prologue of the Fourth Gospel. But he employs Pauline as well as Johannine ideas; Christ is the second Adam who restores mankind to the position lost by the Fall, or rather he enables man to fulfil the potentialities possessed by Adam at his creation; for man was not created perfect and immortal, but capable of perfection and immortality. This redemptive work, by which Christ 'joins the end to the beginning', that is, restores man to God, is one of the meanings of the famous doctrine of 'recapitulation'. The word is Pauline—or deutero-Pauline—from Ephesians i. 10. But on the whole, though Irenaeus makes use of Pauline phrases and images, his doctrine of redemption is 'Eastern' or 'incarnationist'. He speaks of Christ's victory over Satan, of ransom, of sacrifice, but these conceptions do not seem to be brought into relation with one another, or with the dominant theme of salvation through Christ's incarnation and our incorporation in him. This, at least, is how it appears to most commentators. But Bishop Aulén, in his important book *Christus Victor*, finds in Irenaeus a consistent statement of the 'classical' theory of the Atonement, doing justice to every aspect of the work of Christ regarded as an act of God, and free from the forensic notions of the later 'Western' view.

[1] Lipsius in *D.C.B.* art. 'Irenaeus'.

Tertullian

Irenaeus followed the example of the Apologists in seeking to expound Christian teaching in terms acceptable to Greek thought; thus contributing to what Harnack termed 'the dilution of Christianity by Hellenism', but what others have seen as the legitimate and indeed necessary development of the Johannine teaching on the *Logos* who enlightens every man. The other great 'Anti-Gnostic Father' was a man of very different temper and outlook. Tertullian was born at Carthage about the middle of the second century, the son of a pagan centurion. He was educated for the law, and was a well-established pleader when in 193 he was converted to Christianity by witnessing the courage of Christians facing torture and death for the Faith. It is not certain if he was ever ordained; and in 203 he left the Great Church to join the Montanists, a sect of enthusiasts who asserted that the new era of the Paraclete had begun with them and was being manifested in the gift of the 'New Prophecy', bringing a new revelation to interpret and extend the Gospel, if not to supersede it, and to impose a more rigorous moral standard. Starting in Phrygia, this movement spread to Africa, where Tertullian found it congenial to his fiery spirit and his austere morality.

Tertullian was uncompromising by nature; and he would resist to the uttermost any attempt to contaminate the faith by association with pagan thought. Was not philosophy the parent of Gnostic error? 'What has Athens to do with Jerusalem? What harmony can there be between the Academy and the Church?'[1] Tertullian is at one with Irenaeus in insisting that the Church's teaching is based on Scripture interpreted by the Church according to the tradition delivered by the Apostles to the churches and preserved by the succession of bishops. Against the Gnostics Tertullian emphasizes the humanity of Christ and the reality of his sufferings with the vehement paradox which is characteristic of him. His most famous passage is generally misquoted: 'The Son of God died; it must needs be believed because it is absurd. He was buried and rose again; it is certain because it is impossible.'[2] One erratic thinker whose views were refuted at length by Tertullian has usually been classed with the Gnostics, and he was so classed by Irenaeus. But although, like the Gnostics, he was a dualist, his dualism is so different from theirs and has so different an origin, that this traditional classification introduces confusion. This teacher was Marcion, who came from

[1] *De Praescr. Haer.* vii.   [2] *De Carne Christi*, 5.

Pontus to Rome in 140 and won a reputation as a theologian. Unlike the Gnostics, his interests were not in cosmology, but in ethics and the exegesis of Scripture. He carried the Pauline contrast between the Law and the Gospel to the point of denying any compatibility between the Old and the New Testaments, and went on to postulate two Gods: the God of the Old Testament, a God of justice who is the Creator, the Demiurge (and here he is akin to the Gnostics), is inferior to the supreme God of the New Testament who is the God of love. Jesus, as the agent of the good God, came to destroy the work of the Demiurge. Marcion also joins company with the Gnostics in denying the reality of Christ's humanity, and in supposing that man's aim should be to free himself from enslavement to matter by ascetic discipline. Naturally he rejected the whole of the Old Testament and made a selection of his own from the New Testament Scriptures consisting of the greater Epistles of Paul and an edited version of Luke's Gospel. Tertullian devoted five books to the refutation of this type of teaching. But it was more easy to demonstrate the absurdity of Marcion's doctrine than to solve in detail the problems raised by many passages in the Old Testament. Indeed, until literary and historical criticism led to the conception of a progressive revelation there was no real solution but only an escape by the liberal use of allegory.

Another type of erroneous teaching combated was that of the 'Monarchians', who professed to be the champions of monotheism in a pagan world: one school upholding the unity of God by declaring Christ to be a man on whom the power of the Spirit descended, who are therefore called Dynamic Monarchians; while another school, the Modalist Monarchians, saw in Christ and the Spirit merely temporary modes of God's manifestation. These latter were represented at Rome by Praxeas and Noetus, and against Praxeas Tertullian wrote a treatise in which he laid down the lines of the later Trinitarian doctrine by the use of the terms 'substance' and 'person' to express distinction in the unity of the Godhead. This is not to assert that Tertullian anticipates Nicene orthodoxy; for him the Son 'comes into being', 'there was a time when the Son did not exist'. He does not attain to the conception of the eternal coexistence which we find in Irenaeus.

In his *Apology*, written in 197, soon after his conversion, Tertullian writes as a lawyer, pleading that the persecution of Christians is illegal, and that the laws against Christians are a denial of human rights. Like other Apologists, he rebuts the allegations of unnatural vice levelled against the Christians, but he does it in more detail, with a wealth of irony. He does not shrink from a piece of dubious special pleading in his assertion—which became a commonplace with Christian writers—that only bad emperors had oppressed the Church: he even claims that Marcus Aurelius favoured Christians; a claim which would have seemed curious to Justin, and to Pothinus and his fellow martyrs in Gaul.

Clement of Alexandria

Alexandria was the chief intellectual centre of the Hellenistic world; it was also the metropolis of Greek-speaking Jewry and the head-quarters of Jewish apologetic. The Septuagint, which was partly apologetic in intention, was produced there, and Philo had there carried on his indefatigable labours with the aim of accommodating Jewish religion to Greek learning. The same kind of activity was pursued there by Christian teachers, and at one extreme it gave rise to Gnostic aberrations; more central was the work of the catechetical school for the instruction of converts, of which the first known head was the Sicilian, Pantaenus. He was succeeded by Clement, whose name has been thought to indicate descent from the Titus Flavius Clemens who has already been mentioned. He was born in the middle of the second century, educated probably at Athens, and succeeded Pantaenus in 190. In 203, on the outbreak of the persecution of Severus, he retired from Alexandria, and apparently never returned: tradition held that he eventually suffered martyrdom, and for long he was venerated as a saint; but he has never received official canonization.

The aim of his writings is to rescue learning from the disrepute into which Gnosticism had brought it, by setting up the ideal of a 'true Gnosis', in opposition to Gnosis falsely so-called. He develops the Johannine theme of Justin, that the *Logos* is the source of all spiritual and intellectual enlightenment; that Greek philosophy, as well as Jewish prophecy, was a preparation for Christ. His teaching is contained in three main works, which correspond to the three stages of initiation into the Christian Mysteries. The *Protrepticus* ('Exhortation to the Greeks') sets out the superiority of the Christian revelation; the *Paidagogus* ('Tutor') represents Christ as instructing the convert in matters of outward conduct as a preliminary to the reception of the true doctrine; and this doctrine is given in the *Stromateis* ('Miscellanies'—literally 'patch-work') in which the Christian philosophy is somewhat desultorily expounded. There was also a fourth major work, the *Hypotyposes* ('Outlines'), giving commentaries on various parts of Scripture; but of this only fragments have survived.

Clement is not an important theologian nor a profound thinker; 'a warm-hearted rambling man with large but somewhat woolly mind and a poetical enthusiasm showing itself in an eloquence which his Greek readers would recognize to be of the proper literary quality'.[1] But his warmth and liberal vision are endearing, and F. D. Maurice found him 'that one of the Old Fathers whom we should all have reverenced most as a teacher and loved most as a friend'.[2] Westcott sees his particular interest as a figure in an age of transition. 'Doctrine was passing from the stage of oral tradition to written definition. Thought was passing from the immediate circle of the Christian revelation to the whole domain of human experience. Life in its fullness was coming to be apprehended as the object of Christian discipline.'[3] We have seen that the Gnostics made play with their claim to an esoteric tradition. Clement claims to be the 'true Gnostic' dependent upon an unwritten tradition, entrusted by the Lord to his Apostles and handed down from father to son (not, in Clement, from bishop to bishop). This tradition he identifies with the 'Ecclesiastical Rule', his term for what Irenaeus and Tertullian call the 'Rule of Faith'; which he regards not as an independent source of teaching but as a key to the understanding of the Church's doctrine; not as co-ordinate with Scripture in authority but as a guide to its exegesis. Dr. Hanson, in his recent study of Clement's use of this term,[4] shows that it includes at least three elements: private speculations, often of a Gnostic type; doctrinal speculations inherited from Alexandrian teachers, which he believed to be ultimately derived from the Lord; and what the Fathers called the *didascalia*, the Church's interpretation of her faith in teaching and preaching.[5]

Typical of Clement's Gnosticism is his contrast between faith and knowledge. Faith is for him the foundation of elementary Christian belief on which knowledge is built, the knowledge which in its perfection is the contemplation of God, and the consequent recovery of the divine likeness in man. Every man has the *image* of God in him, which is to be transformed into the *likeness*; this image is man's reason, whose source is the *Logos*, who therefore is at work as well in Hellenic thought as in Jewish religious intuition. God has spoken 'at sundry

[1] E. Bevan, *Christianity*, 1932, p. 76.   [2] *Lectures on Ecclesiastical History*, 1854, p. 239.   [3] Art. 'Clement of Alexandria' in *D.C.B.*   [4] In *Origen's Doctrine of Tradition*, 1954, chap. iv.   [5] *v.* G. L. Prestige, *Fathers and Heretics*, 1940, Lecture 1.

times and in divers manners' not only 'through the prophets' but
through the philosophers also. The true Gnostic should unite all the
truth which is the gift of the one divine *Logos*. 'Towards this great unity
of all science and all life Clement himself strove; and by the influence
of his writings he has kept alive in others the magnificent promises
included in the teachings of St. Paul and St. John, which by their very
grandeur are apt to escape apprehension. He affirmed, once for all, upon
the threshold of a new age, that Christianity is the heir of all past time,
and the interpreter of the future.'[1]

Origen

Clement's work was carried on, and to some extent obscured, by the
prodigious labours of his pupil, Origen. Origen was born of Christian
parents; he is the first of the Fathers of whom a Christian home and
boyhood is recorded. His father was martyred in 203, and Origen himself was only prevented from courting the same fate by the shrewd
action of his mother, who hid the clothes of the youthful aspirant to
the martyr's crown, rightly judging that modesty would get the better
of zeal. After his father's death he supported himself and the family by
teaching, and enjoyed the patronage of a wealthy lady, while enduring
as best he could the companionship of a Gnostic protégée of his patron,
apparently a person of eclectic tastes, like some of her sisters of the
present age, who find themselves able to combine a professed mem-
bership of the Church with an interest in theosophy, or in 'Christian
Science'. But soon Origen, at the age of eighteen, was called to take
Clement's place as head of the catechetical school. He sold his secular
library to purchase an exiguous annuity of about a shilling a day, which
sufficed, so simple were his wants, to make him independent of fees.
He learnt Hebrew in order to study the Old Testament in the original
tongue, and started on the labours which resulted in his *Hexapla*; he
made himself familiar with pagan philosophy, and attended the lectures of Ammonius Saccas, the Neoplatonist, under whom Plotinus
studied a year later.

The school grew rapidly; but in 215 his successful labours were interrupted by the massacre at Alexandria known as the 'Fury of Cara-
calla', and he withdrew to Caesarea, where he was honoured by the
invitation of the Palestinian bishops to expound the Scriptures in

[1] Westcott, op. cit.

Church; an unusual distinction for a layman, which shows the extent
of his reputation. His own bishop, Demetrius, took offence at this and
recalled him in 216. An important consequence of this return was the
conversion of a wealthy heretic named Ambrose, who encouraged
him to embark on the work of authorship which made him one of the
most prolific writers of antiquity. Ambrose went further; he set up
an efficient book-producing organization, with seven shorthand-
writers and seven copyists, besides expert calligraphers. Among the
first 'titles' of this publishing-house were the *De Principiis* and the
earlier part of the great *Commentary on St. John's Gospel*. Origen's influence increased, till he became 'the unofficial representative, arbiter,
and peacemaker of the Eastern church'. Then, about 230, he fell foul
of his bishop by receiving ordination, while on a visit to Greece, at the
hands of his old friends, the bishops of Caesarea and Jerusalem. The
action was uncanonical; for no bishop was allowed to ordain a man
from another's jurisdiction: besides that, Origen had in early life placed
a barrier to his ordination when, in a moment of zeal which he afterwards regretted, he interpreted Matthew xix. 12 with a literalness surprising in one who was to be the chief exemplar of allegorical exegesis.
Demetrius had before been piqued by the Caesarean engagements of
his subordinate, and now he was not unjustifiably incensed at this
breach of ecclesiastical order. Origen was condemned at Alexandria
and banished, and later Demetrius obtained his condemnation at Rome,
though the East as a whole seems to have ignored these disciplinary
measures. From 230 to his death in 254, a death hastened by the torture
he endured in the Decian persecution, Origen made Caesarea his home
and headquarters. Thither Ambrose transferred his publishing machi-
nery, and thence treatises and commentaries, and, towards the end of
his life, volumes of sermons, poured in a never-failing stream.

Origen was, first, a great teacher, and his pupil, Gregory Thauma-
turgus, has left an account of his methods and of the power he exercised. 'No subject was barred, nothing was kept from us. . . . We were
allowed to make ourselves familiar with all kinds of doctrine, from
Greek and Eastern sources, on spiritual or secular subjects, ranging
freely over the whole field of learning.' The master taught, 'in words
which inspired us as well by their humility as by their confidence that,
as the eye seeks light, and the body craves food, so our mind is informed by nature with a longing to know the truth of God and the
causes of phenomena'. 'He kindled in our hearts the love of the divine
Logos, the supreme object of love, who by his unspeakable loveliness

draws all irresistibly to himself.' The minds of his pupils were so fired that 'the only object worthy of our pursuit seemed to be philosophy, together with our teacher of philosophy, that divinely-inspired man', the aim of whose teaching was that the pupil should 'make himself like God in purity of mind, that he may draw near to God and abide in him'.

It would be impossible here to attempt any account of Origen's vast theological output, or to estimate his importance in the many fields in which he worked. He has been called the first great scholar of the Church, the first great preacher, the first great devotional writer, the first great commentator, the first great dogmatist. We may glance at his labours in two fields; in biblical studies and exegesis, and in doctrine.

In his work on the Bible Origen shows little of critical acumen, even for his age; he has nothing like the ability displayed in this regard by Dionysius of Alexandria in his discussion of the authorship of the Apocalypse; neither does he evince any interest in the establishment of the true text in places where he quotes variant readings from different manuscripts. The important thing is that he recorded so many variations, and so called the attention of others to problems that he himself was little concerned to solve. One great pioneer work he did achieve. Because of the problems raised by the innumerable discrepancies between the Septuagint version and the received Hebrew text, Origen proposed himself the preparation of a monumental comparative edition of the Bible, setting out in parallel columns the Hebrew text, a transliteration into Greek characters, Aquila's slavishly literal version, Symmachus' Greek translation, the Septuagint, and Theodotion's revision of the LXX: making six columns, and this gives it the title *Hexapla* ('sixfold'). So colossal a work (it took a quarter of a century to complete) could hardly expect a wide circulation; and it survives only in fragments. Its importance lies in the novelty of a sound method. Other biblical works of Origen include expositions, in either commentaries or homilies, of almost every book of the Bible. Though they may often exasperate the modern reader by repetition, by diffuseness, by the lack of any sense of proportion and of any historical sense, by fantastic speculations, there are in them so many flashes of penetration, there is so much of nobility of thought, so candid a facing of difficulties, such a determination to *interpret* the Bible, rather than to use it as a repository of 'proof-texts', that 'it is due to Origen, more than to any any other single master, that one of the most extensive branches of

Christian literature, that of biblical interpretation, and one of the principal divisions of Christian thought, that of biblical theology, were established for all time in the centre of the activity of the Church'.[1]

Origen defined the method of biblical interpretation which had already been employed by Chrstian writers, and which Clement had briefly touched on. Scripture, says Origen, is like a man, in that it is composed of body, soul, and spirit. The body of scripture is its literal meaning, which is comprehensible to the simple: the soul is the moral meaning, clear to any believer when it is pointed out to him: the spirit is the spiritual or allegorical sense. It must be admitted that Origen says very little about the 'moral' meaning; but since his illustration—the Pauline reference of the unmuzzled ox to the right of ministers to support by the people—seems to imply that it consists in the particular application of some general principle illustrated by the text, the moral meaning will in most instances emerge directly from the literal. In any case Origen is mainly concerned with the allegorical method, revealing the hidden spiritual meaning, the device whereby the difficulties and inconsistencies of the scriptures, and even what are, from a Christian standpoint, the immoralities, can be harmonized with the Faith. It is not a method for today; though something very like it appears in the present vogue of 'typology'. But in earlier ages 'it made it possible for intelligent Christians to believe the Bible . . . and by saving the Bible it gave security to the historical foundation of the Christian faith'.[2] And even today it is the only method by which many of the Psalms can be used intelligently as the vehicles of Christian devotion.

In the *De Principiis* ('On First Principles') Origen produced the first synthesis of philosophical theology. Previous writers had written on particular topics and chiefly in refutation of various aberrant teachers, or had given a necessarily superficial account of the Church's tenets for the purposes of apologetic. Clement had attempted something like a general account of the Christian 'Gnosis'; but it was not in his nature to be systematic. Origen's work is based on the scriptural revelation and on the deliverances of human reason. On matters which were treated neither by Scripture nor by Christian tradition he feels free to speculate. In many respects his dogmatic system was inadequate or erroneous by the standard of the later judgement of the Church: in particular he seems to stress the distinctions in the Trinity at the expense of the Unity; to subordinate the Son too definitely; and to limit the activity of the Spirit. But he was a pioneer; and Athanasius and the

[1] Prestige, op. cit., p. 54.   [2] Ibid., pp. 58 f.

Cappadocians, whose theology was expressed in the great doctrinal
formulas, owed far more to him than did Arius and his like, who
claimed to be the heirs of Origen in virtue of a few oddments they col-
lected from the store which he left behind.

Cyprian

Among the writers of the early Church are three who first won a reputation in the law-courts. Minucius Felix, the Apologist, displays in
his *Octavius* the persuasive arts of the pleader: Tertullian is the vehement advocate, master of epigram and the biting phrase; while
Cyprian's legal training and experience must have helped to develop
in him those abilities which made him a great ecclesiastical statesman
and administrator. In some of his letters we may find an impetuous
advocacy recalling the manner of his fellow-citizen Tertullian whom
he called 'the Master' ('Give me the Master', he would say, when he
wished to consult his writings). But in the main his qualities were not
so much those of the bar, as of the judicial, or the front, bench. Cyprian
was a leading member of the Carthaginian bar before his conversion in
246, a man of wealth and good social position. Two years after his
baptism he was elevated to the bishopric, apparently by popular
acclaim; a rapid rise which testified to his reputation, but was not cal-
culated to endear him to all his fellow presbyters. Two years after his
consecration the persecution of Decius broke out, and Cyprian went
into hiding for a year. Then he returned to rule his diocese ably and
firmly until his martyrdom during Valerian's persecution in 258.

His qualities of statesmanship were put to the proof by three problems which arose during his episcopate. First there was the question of
the treatment of those who had lapsed under pressure and had offered
sacrifice. Many of these claimed re-admission to the Christian society
on the strength of certificates signed by 'confessors', those who had
suffered imprisonment or torture and had faced death for their Faith,
or by those who had achieved martyrdom. The notion had grown
up that these heroes of the Church were empowered to dispose of their
superfluous merit to weaker brethren who might thus gain remission
of the consequences of their failure; it was in some sense an anticipation of the late medieval system of indulgences. The authorities thus
faced a dilemma; to honour these drafts on the confessors' spiritual
account might seem too facile a condonation of weakness; to refuse

them would be a slight on the prerogative of those whom the Church delighted to honour. Cyprian's position was especially unenviable: his rapid promotion had aroused resentment; his withdrawal during the persecution could be misinterpreted. The cause of the *lapsi* and the confessors was championed by one Novatus, a presbyter, who took his case to Rome, where he became a stimulant to the schism of Novatian, who had been elected anti-pope. Since Novatian had at first taken a moderate line on the question at issue between Novatus and his bishop, until Novatus, the supporter of laxity in Africa, egged him on to adopt a rigorist position in defiance of Pope Cornelius, it would appear that the real dispute was between bishop and presbyter on the question of authority in the Church. Cyprian's policy was to ignore the *libelli* and consider each case on its merits, imposing penance on the *lapsi* before re-admission, and permanently inhibiting lapsed clergy from the exercise of their ministry. The same decision was taken by a Roman council under Cornelius. In 252, under the threat of renewed persecution, a general amnesty was proclaimed for all those under penance.

In this matter Cyprian had interpreted, if he had not directed, the mind of the leaders of the Church. In the second matter of controversy —the question of the admission of those baptized by heretics—his policy was endorsed neither by Rome nor by the later practice of the whole Church. Cyprian maintained that heretical baptism was invalid, since baptism was an act of the Church, and heretics were, by definition, outside the society; 'no man can have God as his Father unless he has the Church as his Mother'. Stephen, the new Bishop of Rome, opposed the practice of rebaptism, and excommunicated those who adhered to it. For a time the Eastern and African churches continued their custom, while the West followed Stephen: and in the end the Western view prevailed, and received conciliar sanction at Arles, in 314. Yet, though his policy was abandoned, Cyprian's behaviour in the dispute has generally been contrasted favourably with Stephen's conduct. 'Cyprian did right in a wrong cause (as it hath since been judged), and Stephen did ill in a good cause: as far then as charity is to be preferred before a true opinion, so far is Cyprian's practice a better precedent for us, and an example of primitive sanctity, than the zeal and indiscretion of Stephen.'[1]

Since the position of Novatus and his like was fundamentally, as we have seen, a challenge to episcopal authority, while the baptismal controversy concerned the nature of the Church, Cyprian was impelled to

[1] Jeremy Taylor, *The Liberty of Prophesying*, 2, 23,

develop his theory of the Church and its ministry: and herein is his chief importance in the history of Christian thought, for this was the first complete statement on this subject, though it may be claimed that most of what Cyprian has to say had already been said or implied by Ignatius and Irenaeus. In his treatise *On the Unity of the Church* [1] Cyprian discusses the nature of that unity and the place of the bishop in the Christian community. The Church's unity, he affirms, is derived from the unity of the one God in Trinity; it finds its expression and safeguard in the unity of the episcopal college. For episcopal authority is corporate, being represented in each place by the local bishop, who exercises there the plenitude of the collegiate authority of the whole body; he cannot be overruled, in that place, by the majority of his fellow bishops, although disputed matters are to be submitted to the judgement of the whole college. It seems certain that this doctrine was suggested by the collegiate nature of magistracies under the Roman constitution; it is eminently the product of a lawyer-statesman.

Athanasius

The terminus proposed for these selections is the formula of the Faith promulgated by the Council of Nicaea: but that formula did not win immediate and universal acceptance—it was really the product of a minority accepted under pressure by some of the delegates and received without enthusiasm by many of the 'neutrals'—and a bitter struggle was waged for half a century between Arianism of varied shades and the supporters of Nicaea under their champion, Athanasius, from whose writings the points at issue are illustrated. The implications of this Faith and its technical terms were discussed and finally settled by the three great Cappadocian Fathers, Basil and the two Gregorys, who consolidated positions won by Athanasius.

Athanasius was born in Alexandria in about 296, and received a good grounding in secular learning and made himself well versed in the Scriptures. At an early age he attracted the notice of Alexander, the bishop, who made him his companion and secretary, and later ordained him deacon. In 319 Arius, the popular and able rector of a suburban parish, was accused of teaching that Jesus Christ was neither truly God nor truly man; and for this combination of unitarianism and paganism

---

[1] The problems of the 'interpolations' in the text are briefly treated in a note on the extract given.

—the doctrine of one God in lonely transcendence together with the worship of one who was less than God—he was condemned and deposed in 321. Yet he persisted in his teaching and was active in propaganda and intrigue, claiming the support of the writings of Origen, Dionysius of Alexandria, and Lucian, the martyr presbyter of Antioch. Certainly there were passages in Origen—where he stresses the subordination of the Son—and in other earlier writers, which, taken by themselves, could be interpreted in an Arian sense; just as there were many passages in Scripture which the Arians delighted to quote as proof-texts of their doctrine.

In 325 Constantine summoned the first Oecumenical Council at Nicaea, a council which, though predominantly Eastern in composition, represented the whole Church and at the suggestion of a Western bishop, Hosius of Cordova, adopted the term *homoousion*, 'of the same substance', to describe the essential unity of the Father and the Son. To the formula of Nicaea all but the extreme Arian wing subscribed. Athanasius attended the council as secretary and adviser of his bishop, and when Alexander died, three years afterwards (or later), his trusted deacon succeeded him, to meet the troubles which the dying bishop had foretold. They were not long in gathering: Eusebius of Nicomedia, the leader of the Arians at the council, had accepted the Nicene formula; but scarcely had the bishops dispersed when he busied himself in the intrigues in which he took such pleasure and displayed so much skill and assiduity. He demanded the recall of Arius, obtained the ear of Constantine, and induced him to press the demand. Athanasius refused; fantastic charges were trumped up against him, and in 335 a council at Tyre decreed his deposition, and the Emperor sent him into honourable exile at Trèves, where his eldest son had his court. On the death of the great Emperor two years later Athanasius was restored to his see, which had been left vacant since his departure; but Eusebius was still busy, and he prevailed on Constantius, Emperor of the East, to foist another bishop on Alexandria. For the second time Athanasius went into exile, making his way to Rome, where he was welcomed with every show of respect by Constans, Emperor of the West, who, seeing the danger of schism in the Empire, interceded with his brother and achieved the restoration of Athanasius in 346. Four years later Constans was murdered; Constantius became sole Emperor, and a Western council at Milan was coerced to condemn Athanasius, who spent the next seven years in hiding, sometimes in his episcopal city, but chiefly among the monks in the desert. Yet from his hiding-places the bishop continued to direct his flock; the monks distributed his writings; and it was in this period that he produced his *Orations against the Arians*, to support the acceptance of the Nicene Faith in Asia Minor.

The 'royal-hearted' exile, the 'invisible patriarch', was always effectively governing his church, consoling or stimulating the faithful, keeping in his hands a network of correspondence, dispatching messages and orders which would be received as loyally as if brought by a deacon of the Alexandria throne. And with that marvellous power of self-adaptation prominent among the Pauline qualities which Dean Stanley has so well pointed out in this majestic character, Anthanasius made these six years of seclusion available for literary work of the most substantial kind, both controversial and historical. The books which he now began to pour forth were apparently written in cottages or caves, where he sat, like any monk, on a mat of palm-leaves, with a bundle of papyrus beside him, amid the intense light and stillness of the desert, which might harmonise with his meditations and his prayers.[1]

Constantius died in 361, and Julian succeeded, Athanasius was re-called to his see (the intruded Arian bishop, George of Cappadocia, having been imprisoned and then lynched); and his first concern was to reconcile the 'conservative' party, the 'Origenists', to the Nicene formula. He achieved this aim at a synod of Alexandria in the next year; but after eight months the Emperor expelled him from Egypt, and he spent over a year on the run. Recalled by Jovian, he was again exiled after two years, in 365. This fourth and last exile was only of four months' duration; he was brought back in response to popular clamour throughout Egypt, and enjoyed seven years of peace and honour until his death in 373.

The chequered history of Athanasius, with its alternations of honour and exile, bound up as it was with the personalities and predilections of successive Emperors, and beset by intrigue, is paralleled in the pro-cession—a bemused observer might call it a phantasmagoria—of councils and formulas during these fifty years, wherein creed and counter-creed, extreme manifesto and attempted compromise, tumbled after each other in bewildering sequence. The final triumph of the Nicene faith, and its ratification at the Council of Constanti-nople in 381, is due to Athanasius more than to any other man. With unflagging energy he defended the formula of the *homoousion*, as ex-pressing this truth, that if Christ is God, then he must be God in the same sense as God the Father is God; divinity is one 'substance'. To believe in the godhead of the Son in any other sense is to introduce

[1] W. Bright in *D.C.B.*, art. 'Athanasius'.

paganism with its ranks of divinities, semi-divinities, demi-semi-divinities. How then can we maintain that the Father is God, the Son God, and the Spirit God, and yet safeguard Christian monotheism? The final working-out of the terminology by the Cappadocians developed the teaching of Athanasius. There is but one substance in the Trinity, one essential 'stuff' of godhead. But the revelation in Scripture, and in Christian experience as witnessed in the Church's worship, shows us three distinct 'persons', three *hypostases* or objective realities, having relations with each other, and, severally yet not independently, with man. Both 'Monarchianism', in its modal form of Sabellianism, and 'Emanationism', as taught by Arius, would have paganized Christianity: Sabellianism by reducing to a mere apparition the revelation of God in Christ; Arianism by separating the Redeemer from the Creator, by making the Son a creature and thus looking for salvation to one who was less than Almighty God. Athanasius, 'single-hearted, and sometimes single-handed, had saved the Church from captivity by pagan intellectualism. Indeed he had done more. By his tenacity and vision in preaching one God and Saviour he had preserved from dissolution the unity and integrity of the Christian faith.'[1]

[1] Prestige, op. cit., p. 76.

Note on References, etc.

The translations throughout are the Editor's.

References to the works of the Fathers are given according to the customary titles, Latin ones being used where there are no standard English titles. See also List of Works Cited, pp. 301 ff.

. . . indicates the omission of some words of the original.

. . . [Isa. liii. 1–12]: biblical references given thus indicate that the omitted words reproduce, wholly or substantially, the passage of Scripture referred to.

LXX = Septuagint (i.e. the earliest Greek version of the Jewish Scriptures). Unless otherwise stated it may be assumed that quotations from the O.T. and Apocryphal books are from the LXX; the symbol is inserted only to explain the use of a text different from that of current English versions (A.V., R.V., &c.) based on the Hebrew.

Ps. xxi (22), &c., indicates a quotation from a Psalm in the LXX where the numbering differs from the current English versions (e.g. Ps. xxi (LXX) = Ps. 22 (Heb., B.C.P., A.V., &c.); but these double references are given only when there is a difference of text between LXX and current versions.

Clemens Romanus (Clement of Rome)

Bishop of Rome, end of first century.—EDITION: J. B. Lightfoot in
The Apostolic Fathers (ed. J. R. Harmer, 1891).

I. The Person and Work of Christ

(a) The Pattern of Humility

Christ is with those of humble mind, not with those who exalt themselves over his flock. The sceptre of the majesty of God, that is, our Lord
Jesus Christ, did not come with the pride of pretension and arrogance—
though he had the power—but in humility of mind, just as the Holy
Spirit said of him: 'Lord, who has believed our report? . . .' [Isa. liii.
1–12 *and* Ps. xxi (22) 5–8).[1] You see, beloved brothers, what is the
pattern given to us; for if the Lord was thus humble in mind, how are
we to behave, when we through him have come under the yoke of
grace?   [*First*] *Epistle to the Corinthians,* xvi

(b) Enlightenment

[Ps. 1 *is quoted, ending,* 'The sacrifice of praise will glorify me, and
there is the way by which I shall show him the salvation of God'] This
is the way, beloved, in which we found our salvation, Jesus Christ, the
high priest[2] of our offerings, the protector and helper of our weakness.
Through him let us gaze fixedly into the heights of heaven.[3] Through
him we see as in a mirror[4] the spotless and excellent face of God:
through him the eyes of our hearts were opened: through him our
senseless and darkened mind springs up to the light: through him the
Ruler willed that we should taste the immortal knowledge . . . [Heb.
i. 3, 4, 7, 5, 13]

                                                                    Ibid. xxxvi

(c) A Sacrifice for Us

In love the Ruler took us to himself. Because of the love he had towards
us, Jesus Christ our Lord gave his blood for us by the will of God, his
flesh for our flesh, his life for our lives.   Ibid. xlix

---

[1] The O.T. is quoted, not the gospel story of the Passion.   [2] Echoing Hebrews, like
much in the rest of the chapter, and in the whole work. But to Clement the high priesthood of Christ is connected with the liturgy rather than the atoning death.   [3] Cf. Acts
i. 10.   [4] Cf. 2 Cor. iii. 18.

(*d*) *The Chance of Repentance*

Let us fix our gaze on the blood of Christ and recognize how precious
it is to his Father, because it was shed for our salvation and offered the
grace of repentance to the whole world. Let us pass in review all the
generations and learn that from generation to generation the Lord has
given a chance of repentance to those who are willing to turn to him
. . . [*e.g. Noah and Nineveh*]   [*First*] *Epistle to the Corinthians*, vii

The ministers of God's grace [*sc. the prophets*] have spoken through the
Holy Spirit about repentance . . . [*quotations from Ezekiel and Isaiah*]
                                                           Ibid. viii. 1

[*The story of Rahab*]. By the scarlet thread they showed prophetically
that through the blood of the Lord there shall be redemption for all
those who believe and hope in God . . .   Ibid. xii

II. Sanctification—Justification

(*a*) *By Works*

Since we are the portion of the Holy one let us practise what belongs
to holiness. . . . Let us put on concord, being humble in mind, disciplined, keeping ourselves from gossip and slander, being justified by
works, not words . . .   Ibid. xxx

(*b*) *By Faith*

They all [*sc. the patriarchs*] were honoured and glorified, not through
themselves or their works or their righteous behaviour, but through
God's will. And we also, who have been called in Christ Jesus through
his will, are not justified through ourselves or through our own wisdom or understanding or piety, or our actions done in holiness of
heart, but through faith, for it is through faith that Almighty God has
justified all men that have been from the beginning of time: to whom
be glory for ever and ever. Amen.   Ibid. xxxii

III. The Holy Spirit and the Trinity

The doctrine of the Spirit is only inchoate. There are these passing references:

A full out-pouring of the Holy Spirit came upon [*you*] all . . .
                                                           Ibid. ii. 2

Have we not one God and one Christ and one Spirit of Grace shed upon us?   Ibid. xlvi. 6

As God lives and the Lord Jesus Christ lives, and the Holy Spirit, the faith and hope of the elect . . .   Ibid. lvii. 2

The ministers of God's grace [sc. the O.T. prophets] spoke through the Holy Spirit about repentance . . .   Ibid. viii. 1

You will give us joy and gladness if you obey what we have written through the Holy Spirit . . .   Ibid. lxiii. 2

There is no reference to ecstatic manifestation nor to Christian prophets such as we find in Paul's first letter to Corinth. The Holy Spirit inspires godly men under the old and the new dispensations.

IV. The Church and Ministry

(a) Christ's Army

Let us therefore, brethren, enthusiastically accept military service, in obedience to his perfect commands. Let us observe those who serve in the army under our military authorities, and note their discipline, their readiness, their obedience in carrying out orders. Not all of them are prefects, or tribunes, or centurions, or commanders of fifty, and so on; but each man in his rank carries out the orders of the emperor or the leaders. 'The great cannot exist without the small, nor the small without the great'[1] . . . [based on 1 Cor. xii. 12–26]   Ibid. xxvii

(b) Spiritual Gifts

Let our whole body be preserved in Christ Jesus, and let each man be subject to his neighbour, as he has had his place assigned by his spiritual gift. Let the strong not neglect the weak; let the weak respect the strong. . . . Let the pure in flesh [sc. the ascetic] refrain from boasting of it, knowing that it is Another who supplies his self-discipline. Let us consider, brethren, of what stuff we are made;[2] out of what tomb and darkness our fashioner and creator brought us into his world, having prepared his benefits before we were born. Having all these things from him we ought in all respects to give him thanks; to whom be glory for ever and ever. Amen.[2]   Ibid. xxxviii

---

[1] This looks like a proverb. There is a very similar saying in Plato, Laws 902 E, 'Great stones without small, make a bad wall.'   [2-2] The solemn phrases, the concluding doxology, and the verb 'give thanks', εὐχαριστεῖν, suggest a liturgical source.

(c) The Clergy and the Laity

The Lord has commanded that the offerings and services should be performed with care, and done at the fixed times and seasons, not in a haphazard and irregular fashion. . . . The high priest has been given his own special services, the priests have been assigned their own place, and the Levites have their special ministrations enjoined on them. The layman is bound by the ordinances of the laity.[1]

[First] Epistle to the Corinthians, xl

Let each one of you, my brothers, give thanks[2] to God in his own order, with a good conscience, not transgressing the fixed rule of his service, and with solemn reverence. It is not in every place that the various sacrifices . . . are offered, but in Jerusalem only; and even there not in every place but before the shrine at the altar[3] . . .   Ibid. xli

(d) The Apostles and their Successors

The Apostles received the gospel for us from the Lord Jesus Christ: Jesus the Christ was sent from God. Thus Christ is from God, the Apostles from Christ: in both cases the process was orderly, and derived from the will of God. The Apostles received their instructions; they were filled with conviction through the resurrection of our Lord Jesus Christ, and with faith by the word of God; and they went out full of confidence in the Holy Spirit, preaching the gospel that the Kingdom of God was about to come. They preached in country and town, and appointed their first-fruits, after testing them by the Spirit, to be bishops[4] and deacons of those who were going to believe. And this was no novelty, for indeed a long time ago the Scripture had mentioned bishops and deacons; for there is somewhere this passage: 'I will set up their bishops [overseers] in righteousness and their deacons [ministers] in faith.'[5]

(xliii) Is it any wonder if those who in Christ were entrusted by God with such a work appointed the aforesaid persons? Seeing that the blessed Moses also, 'a faithful servant in all his house',[6] noted down in

[1] The regulations of Leviticus are applied to Christian worship. There is probably no direct equation; high-priest, priest, Levite = bishop, priest, deacon: this is a later inference. 'Layman' (λαϊκός) is first found here, marking the clear distinction of ministers and people. [2] εὐχαριστείτω, 'celebrate the eucharist': another reading is εὐαριστείτω, 'be pleasing', which is perhaps more appropriate to the laity. [3] Therefore there must be one assembly and one place of worship in Corinth. [4] 'Bishops' and 'presbyters' seem to be interchangeable terms in Clement. [5] Isa. lx. 17, but not LXX, which has, 'I will give your rulers in peace and your overseers (ἐπισκόπους) in righteousness.' The Hebrew gives, 'I will make your officers peace and your taskmasters righteousness.' [6] Heb. iii. 5, cf. Num. xii. 7.

the sacred books all that had been enjoined upon him. . . . For when
jealousy arose about the priesthood and the tribes were disputing which
of them should be adorned with that glorious name, he commanded
the twelve tribal chiefs to bring rods inscribed with the name of each
tribe . . . [*The story of Aaron's rod*, Num. xvii]. Do you suppose that
Moses did not know beforehand what was going to happen? To be
sure he knew it. But he acted thus to prevent disorder in Israel, that the
name of the true and only Lord might be glorified: to whom be glory
for ever and ever. Amen.

(xliv) Our Apostles also knew, through our Lord Jesus Christ, that
there would be strife on the question of the bishop's office. Therefore,
for this reason, since they had complete foreknowledge, they appointed
the aforesaid persons and later made further provision that if they[1]
should fall asleep, other tested men should succeed to their ministry
[λειτουργία]. Therefore, when men who were appointed by the
Apostles, or afterwards by other men of repute,[2] with the approval of
the whole church,[3] have done their service blamelessly to the flock
of Christ with humility of heart, in a peaceful and gentlemanly way,
and have had a good report from all sides for long periods, we consider
it unjust to depose them from their ministry. For it will be no trivial
sin on our part if we depose from the bishop's office those who have
in a blameless and holy manner offered the gifts.[4] Happy the presbyters[5] who have gone on their way before this, for they obtained a ripe
and fruitful departure; since they need not fear that anyone should remove them from their appointed place. For we see that you have displaced certain men of honourable behaviour from a ministry which
they had honoured without reproach.   Ibid. xlii–xliv

V. Liturgy

Specimens of Liturgical Style

Let us run towards the goal which from the beginning has been handed
down to us, the goal which is peace; and let us fix our gaze on the
Father and Creator of the whole universe, and let us cling to his

---

[1] Presumably referring to the bishops; but grammatically it might refer to the Apostles.
[2] Those, apparently, who succeeded to the Apostles, exercising a general authority in the
Church. Cf. the position of Timothy and Titus in the Pastoral Epistles. The 'bishop's'
ministry was local.   [3] i.e. the *local* church, clergy, and laity.   [4] In the Eucharist.
[5] Presbyters seem here to be clearly identified with bishops.

splendid and superlative gifts of peace, and to his benefits. Let us see him in our mind, and contemplate with the eyes of the soul his for-bearing will. Let us observe how unmoved by anger he is in relation to his whole creation.

(xx) The heavens roll on under his direction and are subjected to him in peace. *Day and night* fulfil the course prescribed by him, without hindering each other. *The Sun and moon and the chorus of stars* revolve within their appointed limits according to his ordinance in peace, with-out any deviation. The earth brings forth according to his will at the proper seasons, and produces food in abundance for men and beasts and all things that exist upon the earth, without dispute and without alter-ing any of his decrees. The unsearchable depths of the abysses and the inexplicable judgements of the underworld are held in constraint by the same ordinances. The basin of the boundless sea, gathered together, in accordance with his act of creation, 'into its meeting-places',[1] does not transgress the barriers set round it, but does as he commanded it.

The ocean which man cannot pass, and the worlds beyond it, are directed by the same ordinances of the Ruler. Spring and summer, autumn and winter give way to one another in peace. *The winds in their different quarters* fulfil their service unhindered in their proper season. *Perpetual springs*, created for enjoyment and health, unfailingly offer their breasts, designed to secure life for men. And the smallest of creatures meet in concord and peace. All those the great Creator and Ruler commanded to be in peace and concord; he benefits all, and especially he benefits us who have taken refuge in his mercies through Jesus Christ our Lord, to whom be glory and majesty for ever and ever. Amen.   [*First*] *Epistle to the Corinthians*, xix–xx

This chapter, with its solemn liturgical rhetoric, is probably based on the *anaphora* of the old Roman liturgy. The pattern of the thanksgiving is that of the 'Clementine Liturgy' of the *Apostolic Constitutions*, and the phrases in italics are found there (see Brightman, *Liturgies Eastern and Western*, pp. 15, 16). The tone of the passage is Old Testament or Stoic rather than specifically Christian.

Let us think of the whole host of angels, how they stand by and serve his will. For the Scripture says: 'Ten thousand times ten thousand were doing service to him, and they cried out, Holy, holy, holy, Lord Sabaoth; the whole creation is full of his glory'.[2] Then let us, gathered together in awareness of our concord, as with one mouth shout earn-estly to him that we may become sharers in his great and glorious

---

[1] Gen. i. 9 (LXX).   [2] Isa. vi. 3.

promises. For the Scripture says, 'No eye has seen, no ear has heard, it has not entered man's heart, how many things God has prepared for those who patiently await him.'[1] Ibid. xxxiv

This passage clearly has a liturgical reference. εἰς τὸ αὐτὸ συναχθέντες—'gathered together', is technical for the Christian assembly—*synaxis*. The Christians of Rome and Corinth join in the *Sanctus* with 'the whole company of heaven', as they 'do their service' (λειτουργοῦσιν—'liturgize').

[*Grant to us Lord*] that we may hope in thy name, the primal origin of all creation, and open the eyes of our hearts to know thee . . . the only benefactor of spirits and God of all flesh . . . observer of men's works, helper of those in peril, saviour of the despairing, creator and overseer (ἐπίσκοπος) of every spirit. Thou increasest the nations on earth, and didst choose out of all men those who love thee through Jesus Christ, thy beloved servant, through whom thou didst instruct, sanctify, honour us. We beseech thee, Master, to be our helper and protector. Save the afflicted among us; have mercy on the lowly; raise up the fallen; appear to the needy; heal the ungodly; restore the wanderers of thy people; feed the hungry; ransom our prisoners; raise up the sick; comfort the faint-hearted . . .

(lx) . . . Thou who art righteous in judgement . . . good in the things that are seen and faithful among those who trust in thee, merciful and pitiful; forgive our sins and failings. . . . Grant concord and peace to us and all that dwell on the earth, as thou didst grant to our fathers, when they called upon thee in holiness, with faith and truth, so that we may be saved, being obedient to thy almighty and excellent name, and to our governors and rulers on earth. (lxi) Thou, Master, hast given them the authority of kingship by thy magnificent and ineffable power, that we, recognizing the glory and honour which thou hast given them, may submit ourselves to them, in no way opposing thy will. Grant them, Lord, health, peace, concord, stability, that they may without stumbling administer the government which thou hast given them. For thou, heavenly Master, King of Ages, givest honour and glory to the sons of men, and authority over things that are on earth. Do thou, Lord, direct their counsel, according to what is good and well-pleasing in thy sight, that, administering in peace and gentleness with godliness the authority thou hast given them, they may obtain thy favour. O thou who alone canst do these good things for us,

[1] Cf. 1 Cor. ii. 9.

and things far exceeding these, we praise thee through the high-priest
and protector of our souls, Jesus Christ, through whom be glory and
majesty to thee, both now and for all generations and for ever and ever.
Amen.   [*First*] *Epistle to the Corinthians*, lix–lxi

VI. Eschatology

(a) The End and the Judgement

Let that passage of Scripture[1] be far from applying to us, where it
says: 'Wretched are the double-minded who doubt in their soul, and
say, We have heard these things also in our fathers' time, and look, we
have grown old and none of them has happened to us. Silly fools, compare yourselves to a tree. Take a vine: first it drops its leaves; then a
shoot comes, then a leaf, then a flower, after that the sour fruit, then
the fully ripe grapes.' You see that in a short time the fruit of the tree
reaches maturity. In truth his will shall be fulfilled quickly and suddenly. The Scripture bears witness, when it says: 'He shall come
quickly and not linger, and the Lord will come suddenly to his temple,
even the Holy One whom you expect.'[2]   Ibid. xxiii

Since all things are seen and heard, let us fear him and abandon hideous
desires for evil deeds, that we may be sheltered by his mercy from the
coming judgements.[3] For where can any of us escape from his mighty
hand? What world will receive anyone who deserts from his service?
For the Writing[4] says in one place: 'Where shall I go' &c. . . . [Ps.
cxxxix. 7 f.] Whither shall anyone go away, or where shall anyone run
away from him who embraces the whole universe?[5]   Ibid. xxviii

(b) The Resurrection: The Analogy of Nature

Let us observe, beloved, how the Ruler is continually displaying the
resurrection that will be, of which he made the first fruits when he
raised the Lord Jesus Christ from the dead. Let us look, beloved, at the
resurrection which happens regularly. Day and night show us a resurrection; the night goes to sleep, the day rises: the day departs, night

[1] Perhaps from the *Book of Eldad and Modad* which Hermas (*Vis.* ii. 3) quotes with reference
to coming tribulation. [2] Isa. xiii. 22; Mal. iii. 1. [3] This may refer to tribulations in this
world, which Clement expects: 'We are in the same arena as the martyrs' (vii. 1). But the
context seems eschatological. [4] Not γραφή (Scripture) but γραφεῖον, i.e. one of the 'Writings', the third division of the Hebrew Bible, the others being the Law and the Prophets.
This is the earliest extant use of the technical term. [5] 'A Stoic rather than Jewish conception of God' (W. K. L. Clarke).

comes on. Let us take the crops. How does the sowing happen, and in what way? 'The sower went out' and cast each of his seeds into the ground. These fall dry and bare on to the ground and decay. Then from the decay the mightiness of the Ruler's providence raises them up, and many grow from the one and bear fruit. Ibid. xxiv

(c) *The Legend of the Phoenix*

Let us look at the marvellous sign which takes place in the East, in the district of Arabia. There is a bird called the phoenix. It is the only one of its kind, and it lives for five hundred years. And when it reaches the time of its dissolution, the time for it to die, it makes for itself a coffin of incense and myrrh and other spices, which when the time is up it enters and dies. But with the decay of its flesh a worm is produced, which is nourished from the moisture of the dead creature and grows wings. Then, when it has grown into a fine specimen, it takes up the coffin in which are the bones of its progenitor and flies with them from Arabia to Egypt, to the city called Heliopolis. And in the day-time, in view of all, it flies to the altar of the Sun and lays them on it, and then sets off back again. The priests then examine the records, and find that it has come after an interval of exactly five hundred years. (xxvi) Do we then think it a great marvel if the Creator of the universe is to effect the resurrection of those who served him in holiness with the confidence of a good faith, seeing that he shows us the magnificence of his promise even by a bird? . . . Ibid. xxv–xxvi

The legend of the Phoenix is related in Herodotus ii. 73 and Tacitus, *Annals*, vi. 28.

VII. The Christian Life

How blessed and marvellous are the gifts of God, beloved. Life in immortality,[1] splendour in righteousness, truth in boldness, faith in confidence, discipline in holiness: all these are in our understanding. What, then, are the things prepared for those endure? The Creator and Father of the Ages,[2] the all-holy one himself knows their number and beauty[1] . . . Ibid. xxxv

[1-1] Hellenic rather than biblical ideas (cf. xix. 3, 'Who is able to express the beauty of God'). [2] 'Aeons'—either 'ages' or supernatural beings (as in Gnostic speculations).

VIII. Scripture and Gospel

Let us be humble-minded, my brothers, and get rid of all conceit and
vanity and foolishness and anger, and let us do as Scripture bids us; for
the Holy Scripture says, 'Let not the wise man boast in his wisdom,
neither let the strong boast in his strength, nor the rich in his riches,
but if a man boasts let him boast in the Lord, to seek him out and to do
judgement and righteousness.'[1] Especially remembering the words of
the Lord Jesus, which he spoke teaching kindness and forbearance.[2]
This is what he said: 'Show mercy, that you may receive mercy; forgive, that you may be forgiven; as you treat others, so you will be
treated; as you give, so will it be given to you; as you judge, so will you
be judged; as you show kindness, so will kindness be shown to you.
Measure for measure, you shall receive what you bestow.'[3]

With this commandment and these instructions let us keep ourselves
firm to proceed in obedience to his holy words, in humility of mind.
For the Holy Word says: 'Upon whom shall I look, except upon the
man who is meek and quiet and trembles at my oracles.'[4]

[First] Epistle to the Corinthians, xiii

IX. Peter and Paul, Apostles and Martyrs

Let us come to an end of those ancient examples [*of jealous persecution*],
and come to the athletes of most recent times; let us take the noble
examples of our generation. Through envy and jealousy the greatest
and most righteous 'pillars' were persecuted and engaged in the con-
test unto death. Let us have the good Apostles before our eyes. Peter
through wicked jealousy endured not one or two hardships but many,
and after having thus borne witness went on to the place of glory
which was his due. On account of envy and strife Paul gave an example of the prize of endurance: seven times imprisoned, driven into

---

[1] 1 Sam. ii. 10; Jer. ix. 23 f. [2] This suggests a collection of sayings of the Lord, perhaps
arranged under topics, as 'Kindness'. The introductory formula (used again in xlvi and in
Polycarp ii. 3, cf. Acts xx. 35) may point to catechetical instruction. The *verba Christi* are
not yet 'Scripture', a term reserved for the O.T. Cf. xlvi: '. . . Remember the words of
Jesus our Lord. He said: 'Woe to that man! It would have been good for him if he had
not been born, rather than cause one of my elect to stumble; it would have been better for
him to have a millstone hung round him and be sunk in the sea, than to have seduced
one of my elect!' Here Clement is either rearranging *verba Christi*, or using another source
than the Gospels. The latter seems more likely. (See Lowther Clarke, *First Epistle of
Clement*, pp. 32 f.) [3] A catena of Matt. v. 7, vi. 14, vii. 1 f.; Luke vi. 31, 36–38. [4] Isa.
lxvi. 2.

exile, stoned; he preached in the East and the West, and won noble renown for his faith. He taught righteousness to the whole world and went to the western limit of the earth.[1] He bore witness before the rulers, and then passed out of the world and went on to the holy place, having proved himself the greatest pattern of endurance.

(vi) With these men of holy life was assembled a great host of the elect,[2] who suffered on account of envy, with many indignities and tortures, and have provided for us a most noble example.   Ibid. v–vi

---

[1] i.e. Spain, cf. Rom. xv. 24.   [2] Presumably in the Neronian persecution. Tacitus (*Ann.* xv. 44) says that 'a vast multitude' suffered indignities and tortures.

Ignatius

Bishop of Antioch. Martyred (?) *c.* 115.—EDITION: J. B. Lightfoot in *The Apostolic Fathers* (ed. J. R. Harmer, 1891).

I. To the Ephesians

(a) Exhortation to Unity and Obedience

I hope that, if I am worthy, I may find continual satisfaction in you. Now it is right that you should in every way glorify Jesus Christ who glorified us; that being perfectly united in obedient submission to the bishop and the presbytery, you may be sanctified in all respects. (iii) . . . I exhort you to be in harmony with the thought of God; for Jesus Christ, our inseparable life, is the Father's thought, and in the same way the bishops who are established in the farthest parts of the earth share in the thought of Jesus Christ. (iv) Hence it is right for you to be in harmony with the thought of God. And so you are. For your reverend presbytery, which is worthy of God, is tuned to the bishop, as strings to a lyre: and thus in your concord and harmonious love Jesus Christ is sung. . . .

(v) For if I in a short time had such intercourse with your bishop, intercourse not in the fashion of this world but in the Spirit, how much more do I congratulate you who are closely attached to him as the church is attached to Jesus Christ and as Jesus Christ to the Father, that all may be harmonious unity. Let no one be deceived. A man who is not within the sanctuary is deprived of the bread of God. For if the prayer of 'one or two'[1] has such power, how much more that of the bishop and all the church. Therefore a man who does not come to the assembly is arrogant, and has separated himself; for the Scripture says, 'God resists the proud'.[2] Let us then be very careful not to resist the bishop, that through our submission to the bishop we may belong to God.

(vi) And in proportion as a man sees his bishop keeping silence, let him stand in greater awe of him. For when anyone is sent by the master of the house as his steward,[3] we ought to receive him as him who sent him. Clearly then we should regard the bishop as the Lord himself . . .

To the Ephesians, ii–vi

[1] Cf. Matt. xviii. 19. [2] Prov. iii. 34, quoted Jas. iv. 6, 1 Pet. v. 5. [3] Cf. Matt. xxi. 33 ff.; John xiii. 20; Matt. x. 40.

(b) The Incarnation

Avoid heretics like wild beasts; for they are mad dogs, biting secretly. You must be on your guard against them; their bite is not easily cured. There is only one physician [*who can cope with it*], a physician who is at once fleshly and spiritual, generate and ingenerate, God in man, true life in death, born of Mary and of God, first passible then impassible, Jesus Christ our Lord.   *Ibid.* vii

(c) The Eucharist as a Bond of Peace

Therefore be eager for more frequent gatherings for thanksgiving [*eucharist*] to God and for his glory. For when you meet frequently the forces of Satan are annulled and his destructive power is cancelled in the concord of your faith. There is nothing better than peace, in which all hostility is abolished, whether it comes from the powers of heaven or the powers of earth.   *Ibid.* xiii

(d) The Power of the Cross

My spirit[1] is abased in self-surrender[1] because of the cross, which is an offence to the unbelievers, but to us salvation and eternal life. 'Where is the clever man?' 'Where is the expert debater?'[2] Where is the boasting of the so-called sensible people? For our God, Jesus the Christ, was conceived by Mary according to God's plan,[3] of the seed of David but also of the Holy Ghost; he was born and was baptized, that by his Passion he might cleanse water.   *Ibid.* xviii

(e) The Defeat of Sin and Death

The virginity of Mary and her child-bearing was hidden from the prince of this world; so likewise was the death of the Lord—three mysteries that are to be proclaimed with a shout, which were effected in the quiet of God. How then were they revealed to the ages?[4] A star shone in heaven, brighter than all other stars;[5] its light was unspeakable, and its strangeness caused amazement; and all the other stars, with

---

[1]-[1] Literally, 'My spirit is *scum*'—the last word, περίψημα, is that translated 'off-scouring' in 1 Cor. iv. 13, where, as here, the reference is probably to human 'scape-goats' at Athens, taken from the lowest criminals—hence applied to a self-devoted victim.   [2] 1 Cor. i. 20.   [3] The divine 'economy' or 'dispensation', with particular application to the Incarnation as the central act in God's 'management of his household'.   [4] The 'aeons'. In Col. i. 26, Eph. iii. 9 'a mystery hidden from the ages' the meaning is probably temporal, 'from the beginning of time'. Here past and present are perhaps personified. But 'aeons' may have the Gnostic meaning, 'supernatural powers'.   [5] Romantic exaggerations about the star of the Nativity are found in the *Protevangelium* and other extra-canonical sources.

the sun and moon, became a chorus for that star, which outshone them all; and all were troubled to know whence came this strange appearance, so unlike them. From that time onward all magic [1] was abolished and every spell; the ignorance of wickedness vanished, the ancient kingdom was destroyed; for God was displayed in human form to bring 'newness of eternal life'. [2] Then what had been completed in the purpose of God began to be enacted: hence the whole universe was stirred, because the destruction of death was being undertaken.

(xx) If Jesus Christ should deem me worthy, through your prayers, and if it should be his will, I intend [3] to write you a second pamphlet in which I shall proceed to expound the divine plan [4] of which I have begun to treat, with reference to the new man, Jesus Christ, which consists in faith towards him and love towards him, in his passion and resurrection; especially if the Lord should make some revelation to me. Meet together in common—every single one of you—in grace, in one faith and one Jesus Christ (who was of David's line in his human nature, son of man and son of God) that you may obey the bishop and presbytery with undistracted mind; breaking one bread, which is the medicine of immortality, our antidote to ensure that we shall not die but live in Jesus Christ for ever.   *To the Ephesians*, xix–xx

II. To the Magnesians

(a) *Exhortation to Unity under the Church's Ministers*

I advise you, be eager to act always in godly concord; with the bishop presiding as the counterpart of God, the presbyters as the counterpart of the council of the apostles, and the deacons (most dear to me) who have been entrusted with a service [*diaconate*] under Jesus Christ, [5] who was with the Father before all ages and appeared at the end of time. Therefore do all of you attain conformity with God, and reverence each other; and let none take up a merely natural attitude towards his neighbour, but love each other continually in Jesus Christ. Let there be nothing among you which will have power to divide you, but be united with the bishop and with those who preside, for an example and instruction in incorruptibility.

(vii) Thus, as the Lord did nothing without the Father [6] (being united with him), either by himself or by means of his Apostles, so you must

As symbolized by the visit and homage of the Magi. [2] Rom. vi. 4. [3] Apparently unfulfilled. [4] 'economy'. [5] Or 'the ministry of Jesus Christ' (who 'came not to be ministered to, but to minister [διακονῆσαι]'). [6] Cf. John viii. 28.

do nothing without the bishop and the presbyters. And do not try to think that anything is praiseworthy which you do on your own account: but unite in one prayer, one supplication, one mind, one hope; with love and blameless joy. For this is Jesus Christ, and there is nothing better than he. Let all therefore hasten as to one shrine, that is, God, as to one sanctuary, Jesus Christ, who came forth from the one Father, was always with one Father, and has returned to the one Father.

To the Magnesians, vi–vii

(g) Christ the Fulfilment of the Prophecies

Do not be led astray by strange doctrines and ancient unprofitable myths.[1] For if we are still living according to Judaism to this day, then we are admitting that we have not received grace.[2] For the divinely inspired prophets lived in expectation of Jesus Christ: and therefore they were persecuted, being inspired by his grace so that unbelievers might be convinced that there is one God who has displayed himself through Jesus Christ his Son, who is his Word that proceeds from silence, who in all respects was pleasing to him who sent him.

(ix) Now if those who were accustomed to the ancient practices [*sc. of Judaism*] attained to a new hope, abandoning the keeping of sabbaths and making the Lord's day the centre of their lives, the day on which our life also rose through him and through his death, which some men deny—that mystery by which we attained belief, and therefore we endure, that we may prove to be disciples of Jesus Christ our only teacher—if this is so, how shall we be able to live apart from him? For even the prophets were his disciples through the Spirit and expected him as their teacher.[3] And therefore when he came, whom they rightly awaited, he raised them from the dead.[4]   Ibid. viii–ix

(c) Unity and Obedience

Be eager to be firmly established in the precepts of the Lord and of the Apostles, 'that you may be prospered in all that you do'[5] in flesh and spirit, in faith and love, in the Son and Father and Spirit, in the beginning and the end, with your right reverend bishop and the worthily-woven chaplet[6] of your presbytery, and with the godly deacons. Be

---

[1] Cf. 1 Tim. iv. 7; Titus i. 14.   [2] Cf. Gal. v. 4.   [3] Cf. 1 Pet. i. 11.   [4] i.e. by the *descensus ad inferos*, to which Ignatius also refers in *Philad*. v and ix; cf. 1 Pet. iii. 19, iv. 6. This belief was cherished in the early Church; Justin, *Dial*. 72, Irenaeus, e.g. v. 31, Tertullian, *De An*. 55, Clement of Alexandria, *Strom*. ii. 9, vi. 6.   [5] Cf. Ps. i. 3.   [6] In the assemblies of the early Church the bishop sat in the centre, surrounded by the presbyters.

submissive to the bishop and to one another, as Jesus Christ was to the
Father, and the Apostles to Christ and the Father, that there may be a
union both of flesh and spirit.   *To the Magnesians*, xiii

III. To the Trallians

(a) Obedience to the Ministers

When you are submissive to the bishop as to Jesus Christ, it is clear to
me that you are not living as ordinary men but according to Jesus
Christ, who died for us that you might escape death through faith
in his death. It is therefore necessary that you should do nothing without the bishop; and that is your practice. Submit yourselves also to the
presbytery, as to the Apostles of Jesus Christ, our hope: for if we live in
him we shall be found in him. And those who are deacons of the
mysteries of Jesus Christ must please all men in all ways. For they are
not deacons [*ministers*] of food and drink, but servants of the church of
God; therefore they must guard against reproach as they guard against
fire.

(iii) Likewise let all men respect the deacons as they reverence Jesus
Christ, just as they must respect the bishop as the counterpart of the
Father, and the presbyters as the council of God and the college of
Apostles; without those no church is recognized.   *To the Trallians*, ii–iii

(b) A Warning against Schism

Be on your guard against such men [*sc. Docetic heretics*]. And this will
be your case if you are not self-assertive and if you are inseparable from
Jesus Christ and from the bishop and the institutions of the Apostles.
He who is within the sanctuary is pure: he who is outside is not pure;
that is, he who acts independently of bishop and presbytery and
deacons. Such a man is not pure in his conscience.   Ibid. vii

(c) The Reality of Christ's Human Nature

Turn a deaf ear to any speaker who avoids mention of Jesus Christ who
was of David's line, born of Mary, who was truly born, ate and drank;
was truly persecuted under Pontius Pilate, truly crucified and died
while those in heaven, on earth, and under the earth beheld it; who
also was truly raised from the dead, the Father having raised him, who
in like manner will raise us also who believe in him—his Father, I say,
will raise us in Christ Jesus, apart from whom we have not true life.
                                                              Ibid. ix

IV. To the Romans

(a) Greetings. The Glory of the Roman Church

To the church . . . which has the chief seat in the place of the district of the Romans, worthy of God, worthy of honour, worthy of congratulation, worthy of praise, worthy of success, worthy in purity, having the chief place in love, keeping Christ's law, bearing the Father's name: I salute that church in the name of Jesus Christ, the Father's Son. To those who in flesh and spirit are at one with his every command, filled with the grace of God without distraction, and strained clear from every extraneous pollution, abundant greetings of unalloyed joy in Jesus Christ our God.   *To the Romans*, opening

(b) 'Do not seek to save me'

I am afraid that your affection for me may do me harm; for it is easy for you to do what you will, but hard for me to attain to God, unless you are kind to me [*sc. by not intervening on my behalf*].

(ii) I would have you please God and not man, as, to be sure, you are doing. For I shall never have such another opportunity as this to attain to God; while you, if you keep silent, will win the credit of the noblest possible achievement. For if you are silent and leave me to my doom, then am I a word of God; but if you set your hearts on my physical existence, I shall again be a mere cry. This is the only favour I ask; that I may be poured as a libation while an altar is still ready; so that you may form a choir and sing to the Father, in Jesus Christ, because God has deigned to allow the bishop from Syria to appear in the West, having summoned him from the East. It is glorious to have my sunset from the world but towards God, that I may have my sunrise to him.

(iii) You never grudged anyone; you instructed others. For myself, I only wish that the lessons you give should hold good. Only pray that I may have courage, inwardly and outwardly . . .   *Ibid.* ii–iii

(c) His Longing for Martyrdom

I die for Christ of my own choice, unless you hinder me. I beseech you not to show 'inopportune kindness'[1] to me. Let me be given to the wild beasts, for by their means I can attain to God. I am God's wheat,

[1] A Greek proverb says, 'Inopportune kindness is as bad as enmity.'

and I am being ground by the teeth of the beasts so that I may appear as pure bread.[1] Rather coax the beasts, that they may become my tomb, and leave no part of my body behind, that I may not be a nuisance to anyone when I have fallen asleep. Then shall I be truly a disciple of Jesus Christ, when the world shall not even see my body. Entreat the Lord for me that through these instruments I may appear as a sacrifice to God. I do not lay injunctions on you, as Peter and Paul did. They were Apostles; I am a convict. They were free; I am a slave, up till now: but if I suffer, then am I a freedman of Jesus Christ, and shall rise free in him. Now I am learning in my bonds to abandon all desire.

(v) From Syria to Rome I am 'fighting with wild beasts',[2] by land and sea, by night and by day, being bound among ten leopards, I mean the squad of soldiers, who become worse in return for their gratuities. But through the wrongs they do me I become more of a disciple, 'yet I am not justified on this account'.[3] I hope I may have profit of the wild beasts that have been got ready for me: and I pray that they may prove expeditious with me: and I will coax them to eat me up expeditiously, and not refuse to touch me through cowardice, as they have done in some cases. Why, if they refuse though I am willing, I will force them to it. I ask your indulgence; I know what is for my good; now I am beginning to be a disciple: may nothing, of things visible and invisible, grudge my attaining to Jesus Christ. Let all come, fire and cross and conflicts with beasts, hacking, cutting, wrenching of bones, chopping of limbs, the crushing of my body, cruel chastisements of the devil laid upon me. Only let me attain to Jesus Christ.

(vi) . . . My birth pangs are at hand. Bear with me, my brothers. Do not hinder me from living: do not wish for my death. Do not make the world a present of one who wishes to be God's. Do not coax him with material things. Allow me to receive the pure light; when I arrive there I shall be a real man. Permit me to be an imitator of the Passion of my God . . .

(vii) I write to you while alive, yet longing for death; my desire[4] has been crucified and there is not in me any sensuous fire, but living water bounding up in me,[5] and saying inside me, 'Come to the Father'. I have no pleasure in food which is destined for corruption,[6] nor in the

---

[1] Lightfoot suggests a reference to the Pentecostal loaves of fine flour (Lev. xxiii. 17) of which 'no part was allowed to be left' (Josephus, *Antiquities*, iii. 10, 6).   [2] I Cor. xv. 32.
[3] I Cor. iv. 4.   [4] i.e. (almost certainly) 'my carnal desire' (so Lightfoot). But Bigg (Bampton Lectures, 1886, pp. 6 sqq.) defends Origen's interpretation, 'My Love is crucified.' (Origen, *In Canticum Canticorum*, prologue.)   [5] Cf. John, iv. 10 f.   [6] Cf. John vi. 27.

delights of this life. I desire the bread of God, which is the flesh of Christ who was of the seed of David; and for drink I desire his blood which is incorruptible love.   *To the Romans*, iv–vii

V. To the Philadelphians

(*a*) *Unity and Schism*

All who belong to God and Jesus Christ are with the bishop; and all who repent [*sc. of schism*] and come into the unity of the Church will also belong to God, that they may be living according to Jesus Christ. Make no mistake, my brothers. If anyone follows a man who causes a schism he 'does not inherit the kingdom of God'.[1] And any man who goes in for strange doctrine dissociates himself from the Passion.

To the Philadelphians, iii

(*b*) *The Eucharist the Centre of Unity*

Take great care to keep one Eucharist.[2] For there is one flesh of our Lord Jesus Christ and one cup to unite us by his blood;[3] one sanctuary, as there is one bishop, together with the presbytery and the deacons, my fellow-servants. Thus all your acts may be done accordingly to God's will.   Ibid. iv

(*c*) *The Beginnings of the New Testament*

I have my refuge in the gospel[4] as in the flesh of Jesus, and in the Apostles[4] as the presbytery of the Church. Yes, and we loved the prophets because their preaching looked forward to the Gospel . . .

Ibid. v

(*d*) *Ignatius as a Prophet*

When I was among you I cried out (I spoke with a loud voice, with God's voice): 'Give heed to the bishop and the presbytery and the deacons.' There were some who suspected that I said this on previous information about the division caused by certain persons. But he in whom I am bound is witness that I was not informed by human agency. It was the Spirit that preached, saying, 'Never act without the

---

[1] 1 Cor. vi. 9.   [2] The first use of this word for the sacrament.   [3] Cf. 1 Cor. x. 16 f.
[4-4] Either the Gospel(s) and the Epistles (Westcott), or (more likely, in view of Irenaeus's other uses of τὸ εὐαγγέλιον) the gospel message expounded by the Apostles (Lightfoot). In any case we have here evidence of some authoritative scriptures of the New Testament.

bishop. Keep your body as the temple of God. Love union; shun divisions. Be imitators of Jesus Christ, as he was of his Father.'

To the Philadelphians, vii

(e) The Old Testament and the Gospel

I hear certain persons [*sc. Judaizers*] saying, 'Unless I find it in archives[1] I will not believe it in the Gospel.' And when I replied, 'It *is* in the Scriptures', they answered, 'That remains to be proved.' But as for me, Jesus Christ *is* the archives, the inviolable archives are his cross, death and resurrection, and faith through him.   *Ibid.* viii

VI. To the Smyrnaeans

(a) Salvation through the Death of Christ, Human and Divine

I perceived that you are settled in unshakable faith, nailed, as it were, to the cross of our Lord Jesus Christ, in flesh and spirit, and with firm foundations in love in the blood of Christ, with full conviction with respect to our Lord that he is genuinely of David's line according to the flesh, son of God according to the divine will and power, really born of a virgin and baptized by John that 'all righteousness might be fulfilled'[2] by him, really nailed up in the flesh for us in the time of Pontius Pilate and the tetrarchy of Herod—from this fruit of the tree, that is from his God-blessed passion, we are derived—that he might 'raise up a standard'[3] for all ages through his resurrection, for his saints and faithful people, whether among Jews or Gentiles, in one body of his Church. (ii) For he suffered all this on our account, that we might be saved. And he really suffered, as he really raised himself. Some unbelievers say that he suffered in appearance only. Not so—they themselves are mere apparitions. Their fate will be like their opinions, for they are unsubstantial and phantom-like.   *To the Smyrnaeans*, i–ii

(b) The Physical Resurrection

For I know and believe that even after his resurrection he was in a physical body; and when he came to Peter and his companions he said, 'Take hold and feel me, and see that I am not a bodiless phantom.'[4] And

---

[1] *Sc.* the Old Testament; so, plausibly, Lightfoot. Others make it an appeal to primitive evangelical documents against a later contaminated 'Gospel'. [2] Matt. iii. 15. [3] Isa. v. 26, &c., cf. John xii. 32. [4] Cf. Luke xxiv. 36 f. Jerome ascribes this form of the saying to the *Gospel according to the Hebrews*. But Eusebius, who knew that gospel, is unable to place it, and Origen, who also knew it, ascribes the saying to the *Teaching of Peter* (Jerome, *De Viris Illustribus*, i. 11, 16; Eusebius, *Hist. Eccl.* iii. 36; Origen, *De Principiis*, praef. 8).

immediately they touched him and believed, when they had had contact with his flesh and blood. Therefore also they despised death and
proved superior to death. And after his resurrection he ate and drank
with them as being in a physical body, though in spirit he was united
with the Father.

(iv) If these acts of our Lord were mere appearance, then so are my
bonds. Why then have I exposed myself to death, fire, sword, wild
beast? Ah, but 'near the sword near God',[1] in the presence of wild
beasts, in the presence of God. Only let it be in the name of Jesus Christ
so as to share his Passion. I endure all things, since he gives me the
power who is perfect man.[2]   Ibid. iii–iv

They [sc. the Docetists] have no concern for love, none for the widow,
the orphan, the afflicted, the prisoner, the hungry, the thirsty. They
stay away from Eucharist and prayer, because they do not admit that
the Eucharist is the flesh of our Saviour Jesus Christ[3] which suffered for
our sins, which the Father raised up by his goodness.   Ibid. vi

(c) Unity under the Ministry. The Supreme Authority of the Bishop

Shun divisions, as the beginning of evils. All of you follow the bishop,
as Jesus Christ followed the Father, and the presbytery as the Apostles;
respect the deacons as the ordinance of God. Let no one do anything
that pertains to the church apart from the bishop. Let that be considered
a valid Eucharist which is under the bishop or one whom he has dele-
gated. Wherever the bishop shall appear, there let the people be; just as
wherever Christ Jesus may be, there is the catholic[4] Church. It is not
permitted to baptize or hold a love-feast[5] independently of the bishop.
But whatever he approves, that is also well-pleasing to God; that all
your acts may be sure and valid.   Ibid. viii

Later, the Eucharist was separated from it, as appears from Pliny (Ep. x. 96),
contemporary with Ignatius. Cf. Didache, quoted on the next page.

[1] A similar saying is attributed to Christ by Origen and Didymus, 'He who is near me is
near the fire, he who is far from me is far from the kingdom.' Gregory Nazianzen ascribes
to Peter the saying, 'The soul in distress is near to God' (Orig., Hom. in Jer. xx. 3;
Didymus, In Pss., on lxxxviii. 8; Greg. Naz. Ep. 20 and Orat. xvii. 5).   [2] Cf. Rom. viii.
17, Phil. iv. 13, 2 Tim. ii. 10, Eph. iv. 13.   [3] Tertullian has a similar argument against
Marcion, and Irenaeus against those who deny the resurrection (Tert. Adv. Marc. ix. 40,
Iren. IV. xviii. 5).   [4] i.e. the universal Church. This is the first extant application of the
epithet, but it does not yet bear the later technical meaning of the Catholic Church as
opposed to heretical or schismatic sects.   [5] The Agape, the common meal of Christians
in which in Apostolic times the Eucharist was embedded (1 Cor. xi. 17 ff.).

The Teaching of the Apostles (The Didache)

First or second century.—EDITION: J. B. Lightfoot in *The Apostolic Fathers* (ed. J. R. Harmer, 1891).

The Worship and Ministry of the Church

The first six chapters expound the 'Two Ways', of life, and of death.

(a) Baptism

Baptize thus: having first recited all these things, baptize 'in the name of the Father, and of the Son, and of the Holy Ghost',[1] in running water. If you have no running water, baptize in other water; if you cannot baptize in cold water, use warm. If you have neither, pour water on the head thrice 'in the name of the Father, and the Son, and the Holy Spirit.' Before baptism, the baptizer and baptized should fast, and any others who can: and you must order the baptized to fast for a day or two. *Didache*, vii

(b) The Thanksgiving[2]

Give thanks in this manner. First, over the cup: 'We give thanks to thee, our Father, for the holy vine of thy son David, which thou hast made known to us through Jesus thy Son: thine be the glory for ever.' Then over the broken bread: 'We give thanks to thee, our Father, for the life and knowledge which thou didst make known to us through Jesus thy Son: thine be the glory for ever. As this broken bread was scattered upon the mountains and was gathered together and became one, so let thy Church be gathered together from the ends of the earth into thy Kingdom: for thine is the glory and the power through Jesus Christ for ever and ever.'

Let none eat or drink of this Eucharist[3] of yours except those who have been baptized into the name of the Lord. For on this point the Lord said, 'Do not give what is holy to the dogs.'[4]

(x) And when you have had enough give thanks in this form. 'We give thanks to thee, holy Father, for thy holy name, which thou hast

---

[1] Matt. xxviii. 19.   [2] Whether this *eucharistia* is the Eucharist or the thanksgiving at the Agape is a matter of dispute among scholars.   [3] Or 'thanksgiving' (if the reference is to the Agape).   [4] Matt. vii. 6.

made to dwell in our hearts, and for the knowledge and faith and immortality which thou didst make known to us through Jesus thy Son: thine be the glory for ever. Thou, almighty Master, didst create all things for thy name's sake; thou didst give food and drink to men for their enjoyment, so that they might give thanks to thee; and on us thou didst bestow spiritual food and drink and eternal life through thy Son. Above all we give thanks to thee because thou art mighty; thine be the glory for ever. Remember, O Lord, thy Church, to deliver it from all evil and "to make it perfect in thy love":[1] and "gather it together from the four winds"[2]—the sanctified Church into thy Kingdom, which thou didst prepare for it:[3] for thine is the power and the glory for ever.

'Let grace come and this world pass away. Hosanna to the God of David. If any man is holy, let him come: he who is not, let him repent. Maran atha.[4] Amen.'

But allow the prophets to give thanks as much as they will.

Ibid. ix–x

(c) Apostles and Prophets

Regarding apostles and prophets act according to the instruction of the gospel. Let every apostle who comes to you be received as the Lord. But he shall stay only one day; and a second day, in case of special need. If he stays for three days he is a false prophet. When the apostle goes away let him receive only bread, to suffice until he finds his next lodging: if he asks for money he is a false prophet. You must neither test nor examine a prophet who speaks in the spirit: for 'every sin shall be forgiven, but not this sin'.[5] But not everyone who speaks in the spirit is a prophet; he is only a prophet if he has the ways of the Lord. The false and the genuine prophet will be known therefore by their ways. Every prophet who orders a table in the spirit does not eat of it: if he does, he is a false prophet. If a prophet teaches the truth but does not practise what he teaches, he is a false prophet. On the other hand, when any prophet has been tested and found genuine, if he does some act as an outward symbol of the Church,[6] and yet does not instruct you to follow his example, he shall not be judged by you; for so did the prophets of old also, and he has his judgement with God.

Ibid. xi

---

[1] 1 John iv. 18.　[2] Matt. xxiv. 31.　[3] Matt. xxv. 34.　[4] 1 Cor. xvi. 22. 'The Lord is coming', or 'has come', or 'Come, O Lord'.　[5] Matt. xii. 31.　[6] This curious expression, ποιῶν εἰς μυστήριον κοσμικὸν ἐκκλησίας, has not been satisfactorily explained. 'If he doeth ought as an outward mystery typical of the church' (Lightfoot-Harmer)—probably some dramatic symbol of the mystical union of Christ with his Bride.

If any genuine prophet desires to settle among you he is 'worthy of his upkeep'.[1] . . . Therefore you shall take and give to the prophet the first-fruit of the produce of the wine-vat and of the threshing-floor, and of oxen and sheep; for they are your chief priests. If you have no prophet, give them to the poor. If you make bread, take the first-fruit and give it according to that commandment. In the same way when you open a jar of wine or oil, take the first-fruit and give to the prophets; and take the first-fruit of money and clothing and every possession, as seems good to you, and give it according to the commandment.   *Didache*, xiii

(d) *The Eucharist*

On the Lord's Day assemble together and break bread and give thanks, first making public confession of your faults, that your sacrifice may be pure. If any man has a quarrel with a friend, let him not join your assembly until they are reconciled, that your sacrifice may not be defiled. For this is the sacrifice spoken of by the Lord: 'In every place and time offer me a pure sacrifice . . .' [Mal. i. 11, 14].   *Ibid.* xiv

(e) *The Ministry*

Appoint therefore for yourselves bishops and deacons worthy of the Lord; mild men, who are not greedy for money, men who are genuine and approved; for they perform for you the service of the prophets and teachers. So do not look down on them; they are your men of rank, along with the prophets and teachers.   *Ibid.* xv

[1] Matt. x. 10.

The Epistle to Diognetus

Second or third century.—EDITION: J. B. Lightfoot in
The Apostolic Fathers (ed. J. R. Harmer, 1891).

(a) The Three Questions of Diognetus

Right honourable Diognetus, I see that you are exceedingly eager to
know about the religion of the Christians, and are inquiring about
them clearly and carefully: you ask who is the God in whom they trust,
and in what manner they worship him, so that they disdain the world
and despise death, and do not count as gods those whom the Greeks
regard as gods, nor observe the superstition of the Jews; and you ask
what is the intimate affection they have for one another; and why it is
that this new race or new culture has come into human life now and
not before this. I welcome this eager interest.

Ep. to Diognetus, i

(b) The Mistaken Worship of Pagans and Jews

. . . See of what substance or form they are whom you declare and
consider to be gods . . . [*There follows a conventional diatribe against
idolatry on the lines of* Isa. xl. 19–20, xliv. 9–20; Ps. cxv. 4–8.]

Ibid. ii

Next I suppose that you are particularly desirous of hearing why
Christians do not worship in the same fashion as Jews. Now seeing that
the Jews abstain from the above-mentioned kind of worship and claim
to worship one God as ruler of the universe, they lay claim to the
right conception; but in that they offer this observance in a manner
like those above-mentioned, they are completely in error: for the
Greeks present an example of folly in offering to things without sense
or hearing; if the Jews considered that in making their offerings to
God they imply his need of them they would probably deem their
activity to be stupidity rather than piety. For 'he who made the heaven
and the earth and all that is in them'[1] and supplies us all with what we
need could not himself need any of the things which he himself provides for those who suppose themselves to be giving.

    [(iv) *The absurdity and impiety of Jewish dietary laws, sabbath, cir-
cumcision, &c.*]

Ibid. iii, iv.

[1] Acts xiv. 15.

(c) The Christian Way of Life—in the World but not of it

Christians are not distinguished from the rest of mankind by country
or language or customs. . . . This doctrine has not been discovered by
them through any inventive faculty or the careful thought of preten-
tious men;[1] they are not champions of a man-made principle,[2] as
some are. While they live in cities both Greek and oriental, as falls to
the lot of each, and follow the customs of the country in dress, food,
and general manner of life, they display the remarkable and confessedly
surprising status of their citizenship. They live in countries of their own,
but as sojourners. They share all things as citizens; they suffer all things
as foreigners. Every foreign land is their native place, every native
place is foreign. . . . They pass their life on earth; but they are citizens
in heaven. They obey the established laws, but they out-do the laws
in their own lives. They love all men;[3] and are persecuted by all. They
are not understood, and condemned. They are put to death, and yet
made alive . . . [&c., on the lines of 2 Cor. vi].   Ep. to Diognetus, v

(d) Christians are 'the Soul of the World'

In general, we may say that Christians are in the world what the soul
is in the body. The soul is dispersed throughout the parts of the body,
Christians throughout the cities of the world. The soul inhabits the
body, but does not belong to the body: Christians inhabit the world,
but 'do not belong to the world'.[4] The soul is invisible and is kept in
custody in the visible body;[5] Christians are observed, since they are in
the world, but their religion remains unseen. The flesh hates the soul
and though it suffers no wrong it fights against it, because it is hindered
from indulging in its pleasure: so too the world hates Christians,
though suffering no wrong from them, because they oppose its
pleasures. The soul loves the body which hates it: Christians love those
that hate them. The soul is locked up by the body,[5] but it sustains the
body: Christians are detained as it were in the custody of the world:
but they sustain[6] the world. The immortal soul inhabits a mortal
tenement; Christians sojourn among things doomed to corruption,
awaiting the incorruption which is in heaven. When the soul is ill
treated in respect of food and drink it is improved: Christians under

---

[1] Referring probably to Rabbinic subtleties.   [2] Greek philosophy.   [3] A rather slight
answer to Diognetus's second question.   [4] Cf. John xv. 14; xvii. 11, 14, 16.   [5] Cf. Plato,
'the soul is bound in the body' (Phaedo 82 E), 'we men are in a kind of custody'—the word
used by our author— (ib. 62 B, quoting Orphic 'mysteries').   [6] Cf. Matt. v. 13. Justin,
Apol. i. 45. God delays the end of the world because of the virtues of Christians.

daily punishment flourish all the more.[1] This is the high rank to which
God has appointed them; and it is not permitted to seek exemption.

(e) The Incarnation of the Word

As I said, it was no worldly discovery which was committed to them,
nor is it a human invention which they claim to preserve with such
care; nor have they been entrusted with the administration of mysteries
devised by man. No, it was in truth God himself, the all-ruling, all-
creating, invisible God who himself from heaven established among
man the truth, and the holy and incomprehensible word,[2] and fixed it
in their hearts, not, as one might guess, by sending to men some subordinate, some messenger or ruler, one of those who administer the
affairs of earth or of those entrusted with the management in heaven;
but he sent the very artificer and craftsman of the universe, by whom he
created the heavens, by whom he shut the sea within its bounds; whose
secret designs all the elements faithfully observe, from whom the sun
has received the measures of its daily courses to observe, whom the
moon obeys when he bids her shine by night, whom the stars obey as
they follow the course of the moon; by whom all things have been
disposed and defined and subjected . . . he it was whom he sent to
them. . . . Well, did he send him, as a man might suppose, to rule as
tyrant, to inspire terror and astonishment? No, he did not. No, he sent
him in gentleness and mildness: as a king sending his royal son, he
sent him as God: but he sent him as to men, as saving them; as per-
suading, not exercising force (for force is no attribute of God). He sent
him as summoning men, not prosecuting them; as loving, not judging.
For he will send him as judge; and 'who shall stand at his appearing?'[3]
. . . [a lacuna in the MS.] thrown to wild beasts, that they may deny the
Lord, and yet not overcome. Do you not see that as more of them are
punished, so others abound the more? These things do not seem to be
the works of man: they are the power of God; they are the proofs of
his presence.

(viii) What man had any knowledge at all of the character of God,
before Christ came? Or do you accept the empty nonsense talked by
plausible philosophers, some of whom said that God was fire (giving
the name of God to their future destruction!), others said he was
water, others some other of the elements created by God. . . . No man

---

[1] Cf. Tertullian *Apol.* 50, below, p. 166.   [2] Ambiguous, because of the ambiguity of
λόγος—(a) reason, (b) word (teaching), (c) Word. Probably (b) is here the main thought,
though the adjectives are more apt to (c).   [3] Mal. iii. 2.

has seen him or recognized him; but God revealed himself: and he revealed himself through faith, by which alone it is granted to see God. For God, the master and creator of the universe . . . was shown to be not only loving to men but also long-suffering. Yes, such as he always was and is and will be: kind, and good, and free from anger, and true; and he alone is good. And when he had conceived a great and unutterable scheme he communicated it only to his Son. Well then, all the time that he kept and guarded his wise counsel in a mystery he seemed to have no care or thought for us. But when he revealed it through his only Son, and made clear what he had prepared from the beginning, he offered us all things at once—to partake of his benefits, and to see and understand[1] things which none of us would ever have expected.

Ep. to Diognetus, vii-viii

(f) The Atonement

[2]In time past he allowed us to be carried along by our inordinate impulses . . . not because he was pleased with our sins, but because of his forbearance; not because he approved of the season of wickedness, but because he was creating the present season of righteousness, so that we who in the past had been convicted as unworthy of life on the basis of our own works might now be made worthy of the agency of God's kindness; and now that we had shown clearly that of ourselves it was impossible for us to enter into the kingdom of God, we might be made able by God's power . . . he himself took upon him our sins, himself gave his own Son as a ransom for us. . . . For what could cover our sins but his righteousness? In whom was it possible for us, lawless and impious as we were, to be justified, save only in the Son of God? Oh, sweet exchange and unsearchable act of creation . . . that the lawlessness of many should be hidden in the one righteous, and the righteousness of one should justify many who were lawless.   Ibid. ix

(g) The Imitation of God's Love

Having this knowledge [*of God's nature*] with what joy do you suppose you will be filled? How will you love him who so loved you first? Why, in loving him you will be an imitator of his kindness. And do not marvel that a man can imitate God. By the will of God he can. True happiness consists not in exercise of power over one's neighbours,

[1] Or, retaining the MS. reading, 'do things &c.'; cf. end of chapter vii, above.   [2] The answer to Diognetus's third question.

nor in wishing to get the better of one's weaker fellows, nor in riches, nor in using force on one's inferiors. It is not in such things that a man can imitate God. No, such things are outside God's magnificence. But any man who takes upon himself his neighbour's load, who is willing to use his superiority to benefit one who is worse off, who supplies to the needy the possessions he has as a gift from God and thus becomes a god to his beneficiaries—such a man is an imitator of God. Then though actually on earth you will see that God has his commonwealth in heaven; then you will begin to speak the mysteries of God; then you will love and admire those who are being punished for their refusal to deny God; then you will condemn the deceit and error of this world, when you know what is the true life in heaven, when you despise the apparent death in this world, and fear the real death, which is reserved for those who shall be condemned to the eternal fire.

Ibid. x

Justinus (Justin Martyr)

Martyred *c.* 165.—EDITION: *Apologies*, A. W. F. Blunt (Cambridge Patristic Texts, 1911).

The Defence and Explanation of Christian Faith and Practice

(a) Heathen Gods are Demons

This is the truth of the matter. In days of old evil spirits appeared in various guises and defiled women and corrupted boys, and made a show of such horrors that those who did not judge actions by the light of reason were struck with amazement. Such men were seized with dread and failed to understand that they were wicked spirits: instead they called them gods and addressed them all by the titles which each demon bestowed on himself. When Socrates tried to bring these matters to the light and to rescue mankind from those demons by the critical application of sound reasoning, then those very demons used the agency of man who delighted in wickedness to secure his execution for atheism and impiety, alleging that he was introducing novel supernatural powers. They are active against us on just the same lines. For not only was the truth of those matters established by Socrates among the Greeks by the application of reason (*logos*), but also among the barbarians by the Word (*logos*) himself who took the form and was made man, and received the name of Jesus Christ. Taught by him, we aver that these demons are not only not good, but wicked and unholy demons whose actions are inferior to those of mere men who set their hearts on virtue.   *Apologia I*, v

(b) The God whom Christians Worship

Thus we are called atheists. And we admit that in respect of such supposed gods as those we *are* atheists: but not in regard to the most true God, the Father of righteousness and moderation and the other virtues, the God who is without a trace of evil. Him we worship and adore, and his Son, who came from him and taught us of these things, and the host of other good angels who attend on God and are of god-like nature, and the Spirit of prophecy. These we worship with reason and truth.   Ibid. vi

(c) He admits to his Fellowship those who choose to imitate his Goodness

We see that God provides all things, and we do not suppose that he stands in need of the material offerings of men. But we are taught, and believe with conviction, that he accepts only those who imitate those virtues of the divine character, such as moderation, righteousness, and love of man; such qualities as are the essential properties of God, who had no name ascribed to him: we are taught that he, being good, made all things in the beginning out of formless matter, for the sake of mankind; and if by their deeds men show themselves worthy in respect of his purpose, we believe that they are admitted to his society, to reign with him, released from corruption and suffering. For as he made us at the beginning from non-existence, so we suppose that those who choose what is pleasing to him are, in virtue of that choice, admitted to immortality and fellowship with God. For our original birth was not a matter of our choice; but the pursuit of those objects which he desires us to pursue, exercising choice through the rational powers which he has bestowed on us—to this he persuades us, and leads us to faith.

Ibid. x

(d) We worship the Creator, revealed by his Son

We are not atheists, for we worship the Creator of the universe (while asserting, according to our instructions, that he needs no blood, nor libations, nor incense) with the word of prayer and thanksgiving . . . expressing our thanks to him in words, with solemn ceremonies[1] and hymns, for our creation, for all the means of health, for the properties of things in their variety, and for the changing seasons: praying that through faith in him we may be born again in incorruption. Every man of sense will admit all this to be true of us. The master who taught us this worship, and who was born to this end, was crucified under Pontius Pilate, procurator of Judaea in the reign of Tiberius Caesar. We are sure that he is the Son of the true God, and hold him the second in order, with the Spirit of prophecy in the third place. I shall show that the honour which we pay is rational.

Ibid. xiii

(e) The Christian and the State

The Lord said, 'Pay to Caesar what belongs to Caesar; to God, what belongs to God.'[2] Therefore we render worship to God alone, but in

---

[1] Probably the Eucharist (= thanksgiving).   [2] Matt. xxii. 21.

all other things we gladly obey you, acknowledging you as kings and rulers of earth, and praying that in you the royal power may be found combined with wisdom and prudence.   *Apologia I*, xvii

(*f*) *The Incarnation of the Word*

[*Justin has mentioned parallels to Christian beliefs in pagan mythology—sons of gods and miraculous births.*] My purpose is to establish that our beliefs, which we have received from Christ and the prophets who preceded him, are the sole truth and are anterior to all these chronicles; and that we claim acceptance not because our teaching coincides with theirs, but because it is the truth. And the truth is that Jesus Christ alone has been begotten as the unique Son of God, being already his Word, his First-begotten, and his Power. By the will of God he became man, and gave us this teaching for the conversion and restoration of mankind. Before he came as man among men certain inventors of fables, acting for those evil spirits of whom I have spoken, made use of poetry to publish their myths as fact.   *Ibid.* xxiii

(*g*) '*Christians before Christ*'

It is unreasonable to argue, in refutation of our doctrines, that we assert Christ to have been born a hundred and fifty years ago, under Cyrenius, and to have given his teaching somewhat later, under Pontius Pilate; and to accuse us of implying that all men born before that time were not accountable. To refute this, I will dispose of the difficulty by anticipation. We are taught that Christ is the First-born of God, and we have explained above that he is the Word [*reason*] of whom all mankind have a share, and those who lived according to reason are Christians, even though they were classed as atheists. For example; among Greeks, Socrates, and Heraclitus; among non-Greeks, Abraham, Ananias, Azarias, and Misael, and Elias, and many others.   *Ibid.* xlvi

(*h*) *The Sign of the Cross*

This passage is the earliest example of Christian symbolism, and may be compared with the symbolism of early Christian art.

Think for a moment, and ask yourself if the business of the world could be carried on without the figure of the cross. The sea cannot be crossed unless this sign of victory—the mast—remains unharmed. Without it there is no ploughing: neither diggers nor mechanics can do their work without tools of this shape. The human figure is distinguished from that of brute beasts solely by having an upright posture and the ability to extend the arms; and also by the nose through which the creature gets his breath, which is set at right angles to the brow, and displays just the shape of the cross. It was said through the prophet, 'The breath before our face is the Lord Christ'.[1] And the standards in use among you display the power of this figure (I mean the legionary ensigns[2] and trophy-poles[3] which accompany your processions everywhere as symbols of power and dominion), though you are unconscious of the fact: and you set up the images of deceased emperors on such a figure,[4] and call them 'gods' in the inscriptions.   Ibid. lv

(j) Baptism

I shall now explain our method of dedicating ourselves to God after we have been created anew through Christ. . . . All who accept and believe as true the things taught and said by us, and who undertake to have the power to live accordingly, are taught to pray and entreat God, fasting, for the forgiveness of their former sins, while we join in their prayer and fasting. Then we bring them to a place where there is water, where they are regenerated in the same way as we were: for they then make their ablution in the water in the name of God the Father and Lord of all, and of our Saviour Jesus Christ and of Holy Spirit.   Ibid. lxi

(k) The Eucharist

When we have thus washed a man who has accepted the teaching and has made his profession of faith, we bring him to those who are called brethren, where they are assembled, to offer prayers in common for ourselves, for the person thus illuminated, and for all others everywhere, with might and main; that we, who have learnt the truth, may be granted to prove, through our deeds also, good citizens and keepers of the commandments, that we may obtain eternal salvation.

At the end of prayers we embrace each other with a kiss. Then bread is brought to the president of the brethen, and a cup of water and wine: this he takes, and offers praise and glory to the Father of all, through the name of his Son and of the Holy Spirit; and he gives thanks at length for our being granted these gifts at his hand. When he has finished the prayers and the thanksgiving[5] all the people present give

---

[1] Lam. iv. 20 (LXX).   [2] Eagles with outstretched wings.   [3] With cross-bars from which depended captured arms.   [4] Either on the cruciform legionary standard; or in pictures of apotheosis, borne heavenwards on outstretched wings.   [5] 'Eucharist'.

their assent with *Amen*, a Hebrew word signifying 'So be it'. When the president has given thanks[1] and all the people have assented, those whom we call 'deacons' give a portion of the bread over which thanksgiving has been offered, and of the wine and water, to each of those who are present; and they carry them away to those who are absent.

(lxvi) This food is called Eucharist [*thanksgiving*] with us, and only those are allowed to partake who believe in the truth of our teaching and have received the washing for the remission of sins and for regeneration; and who live in accordance with the directions of Christ. We do not receive these gifts as ordinary food or ordinary drink. But as Jesus Christ our Saviour was made flesh through the word of God, and took flesh and blood for our salvation; in the same way the food over which thanksgiving has been offered[2] through the word of prayer[3] which we have from him—the food by which our blood and flesh are nourished through its transformation—is, we are taught, the flesh and blood of Jesus who was made flesh.   *Apologia I*, lxv–lxvi

(l) Christian Worship

After these things we always remind each other of them; and those of us who have means assist all who are in want, and we visit each other continually; and for all that we receive we bless the Maker of all things through his Son Jesus Christ and through Holy Spirit. And on the day which is called the Sun's Day there is an assembly of all who live in the towns or the country; and the memoirs of the Apostles or the writings of the prophets are read, as much as time permits. When the reader has finished the president gives a discourse, admonishing us and exhorting us to imitate these excellent examples. Then we all rise together and offer prayers: and, as I said above, on the conclusion of our prayer, bread is brought, and wine and water; and the president similarly offers up prayers and thanksgivings to the best of his power, and the people assent with *Amen*. Then follows the distribution of the Eucharistic gifts[4] and the partaking of them by all; and they are sent to the absent by the hands of the deacons. The well-to-do who wish to give, give of their own free choice and each decides the amount of his contribution. This collection is deposited with the president, who gives aid to the orphans and widows and all who are in want through sick-

---

[1] Or has celebrated the Eucharist.   [2] 'eucharisted bread'.   [3] Or, 'the prayer of the word (*or* Word)'; or, 'prayer to the Word who came from him.'   [4] '*eucharisted* things'—'things over which thanks have been offered'.

ness or any other cause: he is also the protector of those in prison, of strangers from abroad, in fact, of all in need of assistance.

We hold our common assembly on the Sun's Day because it is the first day, on which God put to flight darkness and chaos and made the world; and on the same day Jesus Christ our Saviour rose from the dead; for they crucified him on the day before Saturn's Day, and on the Sun's Day, which follows Saturn's, he appeared to his Apostles and disciples and taught them these things, which we have handed on to you for your consideration.   Ibid. lxvii

(m) The Name of God

The Father of all has no name given him, since he is unbegotten. For a being who has a name imposed on him has an elder to give him that name. 'Father', and 'God', 'Creator', 'Lord', 'Master', are not names but appellations derived from his benefits and works. His Son (who alone is properly called Son, the Word who is with God and is begotten before the creation, when in the beginning God created and ordered all things through him) is called Christ because he was anointed and God ordered all things through him. The name Christ also contains an unknown significance, just as the title 'God' is not a name, but represents the idea, innate in human nature, of an inexpressible reality.
                                                        Apologia II, v

(n) The Logos and the Philosophers

For myself, when I learned the wicked travesty by which the evil demons had disguised the divine teachings of the Christians, in order to deter others from them, I laughed at the spreaders of false reports, at the travesty, and at the popular opinion. I confess that I prayed and strove with all my might that I might prove a Christian: not because Plato's teachings are contrary to Christ's, but because they are not in all respects identical with them: as is the case with the doctrines of the others, the Stoics, the poets, and the prose authors. For each, through his share in the divine generative Logos, spoke well, seeing what was akin to it; [1] while those who contradict them on the more important matters clearly have not obtained the hidden wisdom and the irrefutable knowledge. Thus, whatever has been spoken aright by any men belongs to us Christians; for we worship and love, next to God, the Logos which is from the unbegotten and ineffable God; since it was

[1] Or 'what was suited to his capacity'.

on our behalf that he has been made man, that, becoming partaker of our sufferings, he may also bring us healing. For all those writers were able, through the seed of the Logos implanted in them, to see reality darkly. For it is one thing to have the seed of a thing and to imitate it up to one's capacity; far different is the thing itself, shared and imitated in virtue of its own grace.   *Apologia II*, xiii

Irenaeus

c. 130–200. Bishop of Lyons *c.* 177–200.—His great work *Adversus Haereses* is extant only in a Latin version, though fragments of the original Greek are quoted by later authors, and there are considerable remains of a Syriac, and some fragments of an Armenian translation. The Latin version was made soon after the original— it was used by Tertullian—and follows the Greek with an illiterate fidelity.

EDITIONS: *Adversus Haereses*, W. W. Harvey (1857): references to the chapters and sections of Massuet (given in Harvey's edition); *Demonstration of the Apostolic Preaching* (translation), J. A. Robinson (1910).

I. God

(a) The Unity of God

The Father of all is far removed from the emotions and passions which are common to men. He is simple, uncompounded, without diversity of parts; wholly identical and consistent; since he is all understanding, all spirit, all thought, all hearing, all seeing, all light, and the whole source of all that is good. *Adversus Haereses*, II. xiii. 3

It is best for us to begin with the first and greatest principle, that is with God the Creator . . . and to show that there is nothing above him or beyond him. It was of his own decision and free act that he made all things, not moved by anything; since he is the only God, the only Lord, the only Creator, the only Father, the only Sovereign, and it is he who bestows existence on all things. How could there be any other Totality [*plerôma*] beyond him: or another Principle or Power or another God? For God who is the totality of all these must needs include all things in his infinite being, while he himself cannot be included by any other thing. If there is anything outside him he is then not the totality of all things, nor does he contain all things. Ibid. i. 1

(b) The Nature of God: his Justice, Goodness, and Wisdom

Marcion divides God into two, and calls one God good, the other just; and in so doing he destroys the divinity of both. For he who is just is not God if he is not also good; for if he lacks goodness he is not God; while he who is good without being just is similarly deprived of divinity. And how can the Father of all men be called wise if justice is not attributed to him? . . . God is therefore good and merciful and patient, and saves those whom he ought to save; nor does his goodness fail because it operates with justice, nor is his wisdom lessened. For he saves those whom he ought to save, and judges those who deserve judgement; and his justice is not displayed harshly, since without doubt his goodness goes before and leads the way.

Adversus Haereses, III. xxv. 3

When the Spirit of Rebellion [*apostasia*] unjustly held sway over us, and, though we were by nature the property of God omnipotent, unnaturally alienated us from God, and made us his own disciples; than the all-powerful Word of God, who never fails in justice, acted justly even in dealing with the Spirit of Rebellion. For it was by persuasion, not by force, that he redeemed his own property . . . for thus it behoved God to achieve his purpose: with the result that justice was not infringed, and God's original handiwork was saved from perishing.

Ibid. v. i. 1

This is the Creator: in respect of his love, our Father, in respect of his power, our Lord; in respect of his wisdom, our Maker and Designer.

Ibid. v. xvi. 3

(c) *The Knowledge of God*

We cannot know God in his greatness, for the Father cannot be measured. But by his love (for this it is which leads us to God through the agency of his Word) we ever learn, in obeying him, that this great God exists, and that he himself by his own will and act disposed, ordained, and governs all things.   Ibid. IV. xx. 1

Through his love and infinite kindness God comes within the grasp of man's knowledge. But this knowledge is not in respect of his greatness or his true being; for no one has measured that or grasped it. Rather do we know him in this way; that we recognize that he who made all things and fashioned them, and breathed into his creatures the breath of life, who nourishes us through his creation, who establishes all things by his Word and binds them together by his Wisdom; that he is the one true God.   Ibid. III. xxiv. 1

(d) *God's Design for Man*

In the beginning God fashioned Adam, not because he had need of man, but that he might have a being on whom to bestow his benefits. . . . Nor did he order us to follow him because he needed our service, but because he thus conferred on us salvation. . . . Our service of God does not afford God anything, nor has he need of human obedience; but he has granted, to those who follow him and serve him, life and incorruption and eternal glory. He confers benefits on his servants because of their service, and on his followers because of their following. But he receives no benefit from them; for he is rich and complete, lacking nothing.

Ibid. IV. xiv. I

So also God from the beginning fashioned man with a view to displaying his bounty. He chose the patriarchs with a view to their salvation; he prepared a people, teaching them, obstinate as they were, to follow God; he set up prophets on the earth, thus accustoming man to hear his Spirit and have fellowship with God. He indeed had need of none; but to those who had need of him he granted his fellowship; and for those who were pleasing to him he drafted a plan of salvation, like an architect; and to those who saw him not in Egypt he gave guidance; to those who were restless in the wilderness he gave the Law which suited their needs; to those who entered into the good land he presented a worthy inheritance; for those who return to the Father he kills the fatted calf and gives them the best robe;[1] in many different ways he restores man to harmony and salvation. For this reason John says in the Apocalypse: 'His voice was like the voice of many waters.'[2] The 'many waters' represent the Spirit of God; and in truth they are many, because the Father is rich and great. Through all these waters the Word passed and gave assistance ungrudgingly to those who submitted to him, prescribing laws suitable for every condition.

Ibid. IV. xiv. 2

II. Man

(a) Man's Imperfection and Progress

'Could not God have displayed man perfect from the beginning?' If anyone asks this, he must be told that God is absolute and eternal, and in respect of himself all things are within his power. But contingent things have their beginning of being in the course of time, and for this reason they must needs fall short of their maker's perfection; for things which have recently come to birth cannot be eternal; and, not being eternal, they fall short of perfection for that very reason. And being newly created they are therefore childish, and immature, and not yet

[1] Luke xv. 22 ff.   [2] Rev. i. 16.

fully trained for an adult way of life. And so, just as a mother is able to offer food to an infant, but the infant is not yet able to receive food unsuited to its age; so God himself could have offered perfection to man at the beginning, but man, being yet an infant, could not have taken it.   *Adversus Haereses*, IV. xxxviii. I

God made man lord of the earth . . . but he was small, being but a child. He has to grow and reach full maturity . . . God prepared a place for him better than this world . . . a paradise of such beauty and goodness that the Word of God constantly visited it, and walked and talked with man; prefiguring that future time when he would live with man and talk with him, associating with men and teaching them righteousness. But man was a child; and his mind was not yet fully mature; and thus he was easily led astray by the deceiver.

Apostolic Preaching, xii

All created things which through the bountiful goodness of God receive increase and persist on and on, shall gain the glory of the Eternal, for God bestows what is good without stint. In that they have beginning they are not eternal; but in that they endure through long ages they shall gain the quality of eternity, God freely granting them to endure for ever.

And thus God is first in all respects: he only is eternal, and before all and the cause of the being of all things; all other things remain in subjection to God. And subjection to God is incorruptibility; and continuance in incorruptibility is the glory of eternity. Through such obedience and discipline and training, man, who is contingent and created, grows into the image and likeness of the eternal God. This process the Father approves and commands; the Son carries out the Father's plan, the Spirit supports and hastens the process; while man gradually advances and mounts towards perfection; that is, he approaches the eternal. The eternal is perfect; and this is God. Man has first to come into being, then to progress, and by progressing come to manhood, and having reached manhood to increase, and thus increasing to persevere, and by persevering be glorified, and thus see his Lord. For it is God's intention that he should be seen: and the vision of God is the acquisition of immortality; and immortality brings man near to God.

Adversus Haereses, IV. xxxviii. 2–3

With this doctrine of immortality as a thing to be acquired by created man contrast *Apostolic Preaching*, xv, where it is said that before the Fall man was by nature immortal:

God set man certain limits, so that, provided he kept God's commandment, he should remain in his original immortality: otherwise he
should become mortal and dissolve into the earth from which he was
created.

(b) Man's Education

We were not made gods at our beginning, but first we were made
men, then, in the end, gods. God does this out of the purity of his goodness so that none may think him envious or ungenerous. 'I have said,
You are gods, and all of you children of the Highest.'[1] So he speaks, but
since we are not able to bear the power of divinity, he goes on to say,
'But you will die like men.' Thus he expresses both the generosity of his
giving, and our weakness, and the fact that we are possessed of free will.
For because of his kindness he bestowed his gift upon us, and made
men free, as he is free. Because of his foresight he knew men's weakness,
and the results of that weakness; but because of his love and his goodness he will overcome [the weakness of] the nature of created man. It was
necessary that [the weakness of men's] nature should first be shown and
afterwards be overcome, and mortality be swallowed up by immortality, corruptibility by incorruptibility,[2] and man become conformed to
the image and likeness of God, having received the knowledge of good
and evil.   Ibid. IV. xxxvii. 4

Man received the knowledge of good and evil. Now this is good: to
obey God, to believe in him, and keep his commandments; and this is
the life of man. Just as not to obey him is evil; and this is the death of
man. Thus when God showed his kindness, man learnt the good of
obedience and the evil of disobedience; his mind perceived by experience the distinction between good and evil, so that he might
exercise his own decision in the choice of the better course. . . . How
could he be trained in the good, without the knowledge of its contrary? For an object apprehended by experience has a surer effect than
any theoretical inference. For just as the tongue by means of taste gains
experience of sweet and bitter, and the eye by vision distinguishes black
and white, and the ear through hearing learns to distinguish sounds;
so the mind experiences good and evil, and by accepting the discipline
of the good becomes more determined in preserving the good by
obedience to God. First the mind discovers that disobedience is evil
and bitter; and by penitence it spits it out. Then it learns by realization

[1] Ps. lxxxi (82). 6, 7.   [2] 2 Cor. v. 4; 1 Cor. xv. 53–54.

what sort of thing is contrary to goodness and sweetness; and thereafter
it does not attempt even to taste of disobedience to God. But if a man
shuns this acquaintance with good and evil, and this two-fold apprehension, he causes his own death although he does not know it.

How then will any be a god, if he has not first been made a man?
How can any be perfect when he has only lately been made man?
How immortal, if he has not in his mortal nature obeyed his Maker?
For one's duty is first to observe the discipline of man and thereafter to
share in the glory of God.   *Adversus Haereses*, IV. xxxix. 1–2

It was for our benefit that the Lord allowed all these things [*sc. evil and
opposition to his purposes*], that we may be trained by means of them, and
learn to be circumspect, and so persevere in complete love of God when
we have been taught by reason to love him. God shows his kindness in
dealing with man's rebellion; for man is educated by means of it, as
the prophet says: 'Your desertion shall correct you.'[1] God directs all
things to achieve the end of man's perfection and man's edification;
and to display his own character, so that his goodness may be demonstrated and his righteousness fulfilled, and that the Church may be
conformed to the image of his Son, and man may at length reach
maturity, becoming ripe, through these experiences, for the vision and
enjoyment of God.   Ibid. IV. xxxvii. 7

God suffered Jonah to be swallowed by a whale, not that he should
thus utterly perish, but that he should be vomited out and be the more
obedient to God and glorify him the more for this unlooked-for
deliverance, and that he should bring the Ninevites to sincere repentance. . . . In the same way God suffered man to be swallowed by a
great whale, namely the author of man's transgression, not that he
should thereby perish, but because he designed and made ready for him
a scheme of salvation . . . that, receiving from God unlooked-for salvation, man may rise from the dead and glorify God . . . and not consider his immortality as his own by nature, as if he were naturally like
God . . . and that he may always be thankful to God because from
him he has obtained the gift of immortality.   Ibid. III. xxi. 1

(c) Flesh, Soul, and Spirit

There are three elements of which, as we have shown, the complete
man is made up, flesh, soul, and spirit; one of these preserves and
fashions the man, and this is the spirit; another is given unity and form

[1] Jer. ii. 19.

by the first, and this is the flesh; the third, the soul, is midway between the first two, and sometimes it is subservient to the spirit and is raised by it: while sometimes it allies itself with the flesh and descends to earthly passions. . . . All who fear God and believe in the coming of his Son, and through faith establish in their hearts the Spirit of God, are rightly given the name of men. They are purified and spiritual, and live for God, because they have the Spirit of the Father, who cleanses man and lifts him up to the life of God. *Ibid. v. ix. 1*

Soul and spirit can be constituents of man; but they certainly cannot be the whole man. The complete man is a mixture and union, consisting of a soul which takes to itself the Spirit of the Father, to which is united the flesh which was fashioned in the image of God . . . men are spiritual not by the abolition of the flesh . . . there would then be the spirit of man, or the Spirit of God, not a spiritual man. But when this spirit is mingled with soul and united with created matter, then through the outpouring of the Spirit the complete man is produced; this is man made in the image and likeness of God. A man with soul only, lacking spirit [?Spirit], is 'psychic'; such a man is carnal, unfinished, incomplete; he has, in his created body, the image of God, but he has not acquired the likeness to God through the spirit [?Spirit].[1]
Ibid. v. vi. 1

(d) Man's Freedom and God's Design

'How often did I wish to gather together your sons and you refused?'[2] In saying this the Lord made plain the ancient law of man's freedom; for God from the beginning made man free. Man had his own power of decision, just as he had his own life, so that he might freely fall in with God's intention, without compulsion from God. For God does not use force, but his intention is at all times for man's good; and therefore his design for all is good. He equipped man with the power of choice, as he also equipped the angels (for angels are rational beings); that those who obey might deservedly possess good, the good which is given by God but whose retention depends on themselves. . . . If it was by nature that some are bad and others good, the latter would not be praiseworthy for their goodness, which would be their natural equipment; nor would the bad be responsible, having been so created. But in fact all have the same nature, with the power of accepting and

---

[1] Irenaeus does not clearly distinguish between 'spirit of man' and 'Spirit of God' bestowed on man. It is often impossible to know which he means. It is indeed doubtful if he himself knew.   [2] Matt. xxiii. 37.

achieving good, and the power likewise of spurning it and failing to achieve it. Therefore it is just that among men in a well-ordered community the good are praised . . . and the evil are called to account; and this is all the more true in respect of God's dealings with men. . . . If it were not in our power to do, or refrain from doing, what cause had the Apostle, and, which is more important, what cause has the Lord himself, to counsel to do some things and refrain from others? But because man is from the first possessed of free decision, and God, in whose likeness he was made, is also free, man is counselled to lay hold of the good, the good which is achieved in fullness as a result of obedience to God. And not only in actions but in faith also God has preserved man's free and unconstrained choice. For he says, 'Let it happen to you according to your faith',[1] thus showing that faith is something which a man has as his own, as he has his own power of decision.   *Adversus Haereses*, IV. xxxvii. 1

(e) *Man's Sin*

In the first Adam we offended God by not performing his command; in the second Adam we have been reconciled, becoming 'obedient unto death'.[2]   Ibid. v. xvi. 3

As through a conquered man our race went down to death, so through a conqueror we ascend to life.   Ibid. v. iii. 1

As through a tree we were made debtors to God, so through a tree we receive the cancellation of our debt.   Ibid. v. xvii. 3

Light does not fail because men have blinded themselves; it remains, with its own properties, while the blinded are plunged in darkness through their own fault. The light does not force itself on any man against his will; nor does God constrain a man, if he refuses to accept God's working [*i.e. by which God brings man to perfection*]. Therefore all who revolt from the Father's light, and who transgress the law of liberty, have removed themselves through their own fault, since they were created free and self-determining. God, with his perfect foreknowledge, has prepared for each class a fitting habitation; to those who seek the light of immortality and hasten towards it he graciously grants the light for which they long: for the others who spurn the light . . . and, as it were, blind themselves, he has prepared darkness. . . . Submission to God is eternal rest . . . those who flee from it have

[1] Matt. ix. 29.   [2] Phil. ii. 8.

a habitation which their flight deserves. Now since all good things are
with God, those who of their own decision flee from God defraud
themselves of every good . . . and incur a just judgement.

Ibid. IV. xxxix. 3

Fellowship with God is light and life . . . separation from God is
death.   Ibid. v. xxvii. 2

Men, being created by God, are by nature sons of God; but they are
not sons in their deeds. (3) For as among men disobedient sons, disowned by their fathers, are by nature their sons but are alienated in
law, since they are no longer heirs of their natural parents: in the same
way, with God, those who disobey him are disowned and have ceased
to be sons.   Ibid. IV. xli. 2–3

God questions Adam and Eve [*after their disobedience*] in such a way that
the guilt might be brought home to the woman; and goes on to
examine her so that the guilt might be transferred to the serpent. . . .
The serpent he did not question, knowing him to be the prime mover
in the transgression; but he first pronounced a curse on the serpent, to
proceed to a milder rebuke of the man. For God detested man's
seducer; but he showed a gentle pity for the man who had been
seduced; and this was the reason why he cast man out of Paradise and
removed him far from the tree of life; not, as some do not scruple to
assert, that he grudged him the tree of life, but because he pitied him.
Therefore he sought to prevent him continuing in transgression for
ever, and to prevent the sin in which he was involved from being
eternal, and the evil without end or remedy. So he put a stop to his
wickedness by interposing death and making his sin to cease . . . so
that man by dying to sin should begin to live to God.

Ibid. III. xxiii. 5

The devil was jealous of the man, God's creation, and tried to create
enmity between man and God. Therefore God removed from his
company him . . . who introduced sin; but man he pitied, who had
thoughtlessly, though wickedly, allowed himself to disobey. And in
pity God turned the enmity on the devil himself.   Ibid. IV. xl. 3

. . . It was the ground that God cursed, not Adam. And he cursed the
serpent; and the fire was 'prepared for the devil and his angels',[1] not
originally for man.   Ibid. III. xxiii. 2

---

[1] Matt. xxv. 41.

In contrast with such passages as the above, Irenaeus elsewhere asserts that divine likeness in man was lost by the Fall, that men choose their own condemnation, and that death is the penalty of sin.

We lost, in Adam, the privilege of being in the image and likeness of God.   *Adversus Haereses*, III. xviii. 1

In times past it was said that man was made after God's image; but this image was not displayed. For as yet the Word was invisible, after whose image man had been made; and for this reason it was easy for him to lose the likeness.   Ibid. v. xvi. 2

Eve by her disobedience brought death upon herself and on all the human race: Mary, by her obedience, brought salvation.

Ibid. III. xxii. 4

III. Christ and his Incarnation

(a) His Generation

If anyone asks us how the Son was 'produced' from the Father, we reply that no one understands that 'production' or 'generation' or 'calling' or 'revelation' or whatever term anyone applies to his begetting, which in truth is indescribable. Valentinus[1] does not understand it, nor Marcion,[1] nor Saturninus,[1] nor Basilides,[1] nor angels, nor archangels, nor principalities nor powers. Only the Father knows who begat him, and the Son who was begotten. Thus, since his generation cannot be described, no sensible man exerts himself to talk of 'begettings' and 'productions', or undertakes to explain what is indefinable. All men certainly know that a word is 'emitted' from the mind; and so those who have thought out the term 'emissions' have not hit on anything important, nor have they discovered some hidden mystery in applying to the only-begotten Word of God a meaning which is a matter of common knowledge. They call him indescribable and unnamable and then, as if they had assisted at his birth, they talk largely about 'the production and generation of his first begetting', and liken him to a word 'emitted' by human speech. But we shall not go astray if we say about him, as about matter, that God 'produced' him. For we have learnt from Scripture that God is the first source of all. But whence or how he 'emitted' material substance the Scriptures have not revealed.

[1] Teachers among the 'heretics' against whom Irenaeus was writing.

And it is not our duty to indulge in conjecture and make guesses about infinite things which concern God. The knowledge of such matters is to be left to God.   Ibid. II. xxviii. 6

(b) The Logos

'Christ', says Paul, 'is the end of the Law, to obtain justification for every believer.'[1] How could Christ be the end of the Law unless he were also its beginning? For he who brought the end wrought the beginning also. It is he himself who says to Moses, 'I have surely seen the affliction of my people in Egypt, and I have come down to rescue them.'[2] From the beginning he was accustomed, as the Word of God, to descend and ascend for the salvation of those who were in distress.

Ibid. IV. xii. 4

(c) The Word reveals the Father

Since he 'who effects all operations in all'[3] is God, his true nature and immensity cannot be discovered or described by his creatures. But he is by no means unknown to them. For through his Word all his creatures learn that there is one God, the Father, who controls all things, and gives existence to all. As the Gospel says, 'No one has seen God; except that the only begotten Son who is in the Father's bosom, has himself described him.'[4] Thus the Son makes the Father known from the beginning. For he has been with the Father from the beginning: and he has shown to mankind the visions of the prophets, the different kinds of spiritual gifts, and his own ministry, and the glorification of the Father in due sequence and order, at the fitting time for man's profit. For when there is due sequence there is consistency, and where there is consistency, there is the choice of the opportune time, and the choice of the opportune time brings benefit for man. But for this reason the Word was made the minister of the Father's grace to man, for man's benefit. For man he wrought his redemptive work,[5] displaying God to man, and man to God. He safeguarded the invisibility of the Father, lest man should ever become contemptuous of God, and that man should always have some goal to which he might advance. At the same time he displayed God in visible form to men through his many acts of mediation,[6] lest man should be utterly remote from God and so cease to be. For the glory of God is a living man; and the life of man is the

---

[1] Rom. x. 4.   [2] Exod. iii. 7.   [3] 1 Cor. xii. 6.   [4] John i. 18.   [5] dispositiones.   [6] per multas dispositiones = διὰ πολλὰς οἰκονομίας. Dispositio is commonly a translation of οἰκονομία in Irenaeus and οἰκονομία ('economy') usually means God's dealing with man.

vision of God. For if the manifestation of God in creation gives life to all who live on earth, much more does the revelation of the Father through the Word bestow life on those who see God.

Adversus Haereses, IV. xx. 6

The Son always co-exists with the Father and has revealed the Father from of old, from the beginning.   Ibid. II. xxx. 9

The name of God or Lord is given only to him who is God and Lord of all; who said to Moses 'My name is I AM. And you shall say to the Israelites, 'HE WHO IS has sent me to you.'[1] The name of God and Lord is given also to his Son, Jesus Christ our Lord, who makes men the sons of God if they believe in his name. And the Son says to Moses, 'I have come down to rescue this people.'[2] For it is the Son who descended and ascended for the salvation of men. Thus through the Son who is in the Father, and has the Father in himself, HE WHO IS has been revealed. The Father bears witness to the Son; the Son proclaims the Father. So Isaiah says, 'I am witness, says the Lord God, and so is the child [servant] whom I have chosen, that you may know and believe and understand that I AM.'[3]   Ibid. III. vi. 2

God makes all things in measure and order, and with him nothing is without proportion. He was right who said that the immeasurable Father is measured in the Son; for the Son is the measure of the Father, since he contains the Father.   Ibid. IV. iv. 2

Through the creation the Word reveals God the creator; through the world, the Lord who made the world; through the handiwork, the artificer; through the Son, the Father who begat him. All alike confess this [*sc. by the fact of their existence*]; but all do not believe. By Law and Prophets the Word proclaimed himself and the Father: and the whole people alike heard; but all did not believe. And through this same Word, made visible and tangible, the Father was displayed, although all did not believe in him. Yet all saw the Father in the Son; for the Father is the invisible of the Son, the Son the visible of the Father.[4]

Ibid. IV. vi. 5

(d) The Divine and Human Nature of Christ

There is one God, who by his Word and Wisdom made and ordered all things. . . . His Word is our Lord Jesus Christ who in these last

---

[1] Exod. iii. 14.   [2] Exod. iii. 8.   [3] Isa. xliii. 10.   [4] This sentence is not susceptible of any close rendering in English. The Latin version represents the Greek τὸ ἀόρατον γὰρ τοῦ Υἱοῦ Πατήρ, τὸ δὲ ὁρατὸν τοῦ Πατρὸς Υἱός.

times became man among men, that he might unite the end with the beginning, that is, Man with God. Therefore the prophets who received from this same Word their prophetic gift, proclaimed his advent in the flesh, by which was effected the mingling and uniting of God and man according to the Father's pleasure. For the Word of God foretold from the beginning that God would be seen by men and would live with them on earth and converse with them; that he would be present with his creatures to bring salvation to them and to be perceived by them; that he would free us 'from the hands of those who hate us', that is, from the whole spirit of transgression; and would make us 'serve him all our days in holiness and righteousness';[1] that man, taking to himself the Spirit of God, should pass to the glory of the Father.

Ibid. IV. xx. 4

Our Lord Jesus Christ, the word of God, of his boundless love, became what we are that he might make us what he himself is.

Ibid. v. praef. (*ad fin.*)

As he was man that he might be tempted, so he was the Word that he might be glorified. The Word was quiescent, that he might be capable of temptation, dishonour, crucifixion, and death; while the manhood was swallowed up[2] [*in the Godhead*] in his victory, his endurance . . .[3] his resurrection and ascension.

Ibid. III. xix. 3

If anyone asks why it is that the Lord had made it plain that 'the Father alone knows the hour and the day',[4] although he has communion with the Son in all things, he could not at present find an answer more suitable or more proper or less perilous than this; that we may learn from our Lord himself (our one true teacher) that the Father is above all. As he says, 'the Father is greater than I'.[5] Our Lord has proclaimed that the Father is superior in respect of knowledge to the intent that we should leave to God complete knowledge and questions such as this, so long as we are subject to the conditions of this world.

Ibid. II. xxviii. 8

---

[1] Luke i. 72-75. [2] So the Latin version. But the Greek preserved (?correctly) in the *Eranistes* of Theodoret (III, Ἀπαθής, ed. Schultz, IV. 232) has συγγενομένου (sc. τοῦ Λόγου) τῷ ἀνθρώπῳ, 'the Word coming to the man's aid'. (See Harvey's edition of Irenaeus, vol. ii. p. 104.) [3] The Latin has no equivalent to the word χρηστεύεσθα which appears in Theodoret. This should mean 'performance of acts of kindness' (sc. miracles); but the context seems to be the Passion and triumph. [4] Matt. xxix. 36. [5] John xix. 28.

IV. The Atonement

(a) 'God was in Christ reconciling the World'

God became man, and it was the Lord himself who saved us.

Adversus Haereses, III. xxi. 1

[*In answer to the Ebionites*] . . . How can they be saved unless he was
God who wrought their salvation on the earth? And how shall man
pass to God unless God has passed into man?[1] How shall man be freed
from the generation of death,[2] except he pass into a new birth, wonderfully and unexpectedly given by God, for a token of salvation, a birth
from a virgin, receiving a re-birth through faith?[2] How can men
receive adoption by God if they remain as they are by human birth in
this world?   Ibid. IV. xxxiii. 4

(b) He shared our Sufferings; we share his Victory

If he did not really suffer there was no grace [*sc. in his forgiveness of his
tormentors*] . . . and when we begin to endure real suffering he will
clearly be leading us astray in exhorting us to endure scourging and to
turn the other cheek, if he did not first endure the same treatment in
reality; . . . in that case we should be 'above our master'. . . . But as
he, our Lord, is our only true master, so he is truly the good and
suffering Son of God, the Word of God the Father made the son of
man. For he strove and conquered. He was as man contending on
behalf of the father[3] and through obedience cancelling the disobedience. He bound the strong one and set free the weak, and gave salvation to his handiwork by abolishing sin. For he is our most holy
Lord, the merciful lover of the human race. (7) He united man to God,
as we have said. Had he not as man overcome man's adversary, the
enemy would not have been justly overcome. Again, had it not been
God who bestowed salvation we should not have it as a secure possession. And if man had not been united to God, man could not have
become a partaker of immortality. For the mediator between God and
man had to bring both parties into friendship and concord through his
kinship with both; and to present man to God, and make God known

[1] So the Latin version. The Greek (in Theodoret, *Eranistes*, II, Ἀσύγχυτος gives πῶς
ἄνθρωπος χωρήσει εἰς Θεὸν εἰ μὴ ὁ Θεὸς ἐχωρήθη εἰς ἄνθρωπον; where ἐχωρήθη must mean
'had been contained in man', which suggests that the first εἰς should be omitted, 'How
could man receive God, had God not been received into man'.   [2-2] The Latin here (the
Greek is not extant) is obscure and seems defective.   [3] So the Latin text, *pro patribus*; but
pro fratribus, 'on behalf of his brethren', would make better sense.

to man. In what way could we share in the adoption of the sons of God unless through the Son we had received the fellowship with the Father, unless the Word of God made flesh had entered into communion with us? Therefore he passed through every stage of life, restoring to each age fellowship with God. . . . The Law, being spiritual, merely displayed sin for what it is; it did not destroy it, for sin did not hold sway over spirit, but over man. For he who was to destroy sin and redeem man from guilt had to enter into the very condition of man, who had been dragged into slavery and was held by death, in order that death might be slain by man, and man should go forth from the bondage of death. For as through the disobedience of one man, who was the first man, fashioned out of virgin soil, many were made sinners; so it was necessary that through the obedience of one man, who was the first to be born of a virgin, many should be justified and receive salvation.

Ibid. III. xviii. 6–7

(c) Rebellion Restored by Obedience

The Word, the maker of all things, overcame the devil through man, displayed him as a rebel and subjected him to man.[1] . . . That, as through rebellion he lorded it over man, so by man's return to God his rebellion might be made impotent.

Ibid. v. xxiv. 4

The rebellious angel has his power destroyed by this answer ['Thou shalt worship the Lord thy God and him only shalt thou serve', Matt. iv. 10]; he is exposed for what he is and is overcome by the Son of man who keeps God's command. For since in the beginning he persuaded man to transgress his Maker's command he therefore had him in his power; for his power lies in disobedience and rebellion, and by those he bound man.

Ibid. v. xxi. 3

(d) Ransom—Redemption—Blood

He who was powerful Word and also truly man redeemed us by his own blood by a rational transaction,[2] and gave himself as a ransom for these who had been taken into captivity . . . attaining his purpose not by force . . . but by way of persuasion . . .

(2) The Lord redeemed us by his blood and gave his life for our life, his flesh for our flesh, and poured out the Spirit of the Father to unite

---

[1] Luke x. 19. [2] *rationaliter*—as opposed to an arbitrary exercise of omnipotence. But the meaning is uncertain.

us and reconcile God and man, bringing God down to man through the Spirit, and raising man to God through his incarnation, and by his coming truly and surely conferring on us immortality by means of our fellowship with God.   *Adversus Haereses*, v. i. 1–2

But the main teaching of Irenaeus is of propitiation by the life and obedience of Jesus Christ rather than particularly by his Passion. The mediating work is the Incarnation.

. . . The Lord restored us to friendship through his incarnation, becoming the 'mediator between God and man'.[1] On our behalf he propitiated the Father, against whom we had sinned, and cancelled our disobedience by his obedience, restoring us to fellowship with our Maker and submission to him.   Ibid. v. xvii. 1

(e) The Sanctification of each Stage of Life

He was thirty years old when he came to be baptized. Then, having reached the required age for a teacher, he came to Jerusalem, that all should have a fair opportunity to hear his teaching. He did not appear to be other than what he really was, as they say who hold that his appearance was illusory. No; he appeared as he really was. Thus as teacher he was of a teacher's age; he did not reject humanity nor go beyond its limitations; he did not abrogate his laws for humanity in his own case: rather he sanctified each stage of life by [*making possible*] a likeness to himself. He came to save all through his own person; all, that is, who through him are re-born to God; infants, children, boys, young men and old. Therefore he passed through every stage of life. He was made an infant for infants, sanctifying infancy; a child among children, sanctifying childhood, and setting an example of filial affection, of righteousness and of obedience; a young man among young men, becoming an example to them, and sanctifying them to the Lord. So also he was a grown man among the older men, that he might be a perfect teacher for all, not merely in respect of revelation of the truth, but also in respect of this stage of life, sanctifying the older men, and becoming an example to them also. And thus he came even to death, that he might be 'the first-born from the dead, having the pre-eminence among all [or *in all things*]',[2] the Author of Life, who goes before all and shows the way.   Ibid. II. xxii. 4

[1] 1 Tim. ii. 5.   [2] Col. i. 18.

(f) The 'Recapitulation' of Man in Christ

The only-begotten Word, who is always present with the human race, united and mingled with his handiwork, according to the Father's pleasure, and incarnate, is himself Jesus Christ our Lord, who suffered for us, and rose again for us, and is to come again in the glory of the Father to raise up all flesh to manifest salvation, and to apply the rule of just judgement to all who were made by him. Thus there is one God the Father, as we have demonstrated, and one Christ Jesus our Lord who came[1] in fulfilment of God's comprehensive design[1] and consummates all things in himself.[2] Man is in all respects the handiwork of God; thus he consummates man in himself: he was invisible and became visible; incomprehensible and made comprehensible; impassible and made passible; the Word, and made man; consummating all things in himself. That, as in things above the heavens and in the spiritual and invisible world the Word of God is supreme, so in the visible and physical realm he may have pre-eminence, taking to himself the primacy and appointing himself the head of the Church, that he may 'draw all things to himself'[3] in the due time.   Ibid. III. xvi. 6

The Lord leads into the Paradise of Life those who obey his teaching, 'consummating[4] in himself all things, things in heaven and things on earth'. 'Things in heaven' are spiritual things, 'things on earth' refers to his dealings with man. He 'consummated all things in himself' by joining man to Spirit and placing Spirit in man. He himself became the source of Spirit, and he gives Spirit to be the source of man's life. For it is through Spirit that we see and hear and talk.[5]

(xxi. 1) He effected the consummation [restoration],[4] and declared

---

[1-1] *per universam dispensationem:* see note 6, page 75, above.   [2] *Recapitulation.* This is a notion with which Irenaeus is specially associated. The Greek verb ἀνακεφαλαιόω occurs twice in the New Testament, Rom. xiii. 9—all the commandments are 'summed up' in the commandment to love one's neighbour—and Eph. i. 10—the Father 'consummates' all things in Christ. In Irenaeus the word has several meanings or shades of meaning: (i) the idea of consummation: Christ as the true man, fulfilling the divine purpose, with the closely related idea of 'restoration' of what man had been at the Fall; this seems to be most frequently in his mind when he uses the phrase, as in v. xxi. 1, quoted infra. (ii) Sometimes, however, he employs it in a sense somewhat like that in Romans, as in III. xxiii. 3 (p. 82)—the Lucan genealogy shows our Lord 'recapitulating' the whole human race—and III. xxiii. 1—Christ's work as a 'recapitulation' of God's plan of salvation— where a compendious action is described. (iii) In v. xix. 1 by his obedience 'on the tree' the Lord 'recapitulates' (cancels) the disobedience 'connected with a tree': cf. III. xxi. 10, quoted (p. 83) below. (iv) In one place (v.xxix. 2) all wickedness is said to be 'concentrated' in the Beast of Revelation, a meaning very like the first.   [3] John xii. 32.
[4] Eph. i. 10, ii. 15 f. See n. 1 above.   [5] See n., p. 71.

war on our enemy, and crushed him who in the beginning had led us
captive in Adam. . . . The victory over the enemy would not have
been rightly won had not his conqueror been born as man from a
woman. For it was through a woman that the devil held sway over
man from the beginning, when he set himself to be man's adversary.
Therefore the Lord confesses himself to be the Son of man, restoring in
himself that original man from whom is derived that part of creation
which is born of woman; that as it was through a man that our race
was overcome and went down to death, so through a victorious man
we may rise up to life: and as through a man death won the prize of
victory over us, so through a man we may win the prize of victory
over death. (2) Nor would the Lord have made an end[1] in his own
person of that original enmity between man and the serpent . . . had he
come from another father.   *Adversus Haereses*, v. xx. 2 (*ad fin.*)–xxi. 2

The Word existed in the beginning with God and through him all
things were made. He was always present with the human race, and in
the last times, according to the time appointed by the Father, he has
been united with his own handiwork and made man, capable of
suffering. Thus we can set aside the objection, 'If Christ was born at a
certain time it follows that he did not exist before that.' For we have
shown that the Son of God did not then begin to be: he existed always
with the Father. But he was incarnate and made Man; and then he
summed up[2] [?consummated] in himself the long line of the human
race, procuring for us a comprehensive salvation, that we might re-
cover in Christ Jesus what in Adam we had lost, namely, the state of
being in the image and likeness of God.   Ibid. III. xviii. 1

. . . God (the Word) restored[2] in himself man, his ancient handiwork,
that he might do to death sin, strip death of its power and give life to
man . . .   Ibid. III. xviii. 7 (*ad fin.*)

He restored[2] in himself his ancient handiwork. As through one man's
disobedience sin gained entrance, and death obtained power as a result
of sin; so through the obedience of one man righteousness was introduced and he causes life to flourish in men, who before were dead.
And as Adam was first made from untilled soil and received his being
from virgin earth (since God had not yet sent rain and man had not yet
cultivated the ground)[3] and was fashioned by the hand of God, that is

[1] Eph. I. 10, ii. 15 f. See n., p. 81.   [2] 'recapitulated': see note above, p. 81.   [3] cf.
Gen. ii. 5.

by the Word of God, 'by whom all things were made'[1] . . .; so he who
existed as the Word restored[2] in himself Adam, by his birth from Mary
who was still virgin, a birth befitting this restoration of Adam.[3]

Ibid. III. xxi. 10

Luke shows that the genealogy which traces the lineage from our
Lord back to Adam comprises seventy-two generations. Thus the end
is joined with the beginning and we are shown that it is he who has
summed up[2] in himself all the nations descended from Adam who are
dispersed throughout the world, and all men of different languages.
Together with Adam he has summed up all generations . . .

Ibid. III. xxii. 3

V. The Holy Spirit

(a) The Holy Spirit in the Church

We receive our faith from the Church and keep it safe; and it is as it
were a precious deposit stored in a fine vessel, ever renewing its vitality
through the Spirit of God, and causing the renewal of the vessel in
which it is stored. For this gift of God has been entrusted to the Church,
as the breath of life to created man, to the end that all members by
receiving it should be made alive. And herein has been bestowed on us
our means of communion with Christ, namely the Holy Spirit, the
pledge of immortality, the strengthening of our faith, the ladder by
which we ascend to God. For the Apostle says, 'God has set up in the
Church Apostles, prophets, teachers'[4] and all the other means of the
Spirit's working. But they have no share in this Spirit who do not join
in the activity of the Church. . . . For where the Church is, there is
the Spirit of God; and where the Spirit of God is, there is the Church
and every kind of grace. The Spirit is truth. Therefore those who have
no share in the Spirit are not nourished and given life at their mother's
breast; nor do they enjoy the sparkling fountain that issues from the
body of Christ.

Ibid. III. xxiv. 1

(b) The Giver of Life and Light, 'who spake by the Prophets'

God was seen prophetically through the Spirit in those days [i.e. in
the Old Testament], but by adoption through the Son, while in the

---

[1] John i. 3.   [2] 'recapitulated'; see note above, p. 81.   [3] The stress on the Jesus-Adam
parallel suggests that ἀνακεφαλαιόω here means something like 're-enact', 'reproduce'.
Christ the second Adam restores man to original righteousness by 're-enacting' Adam in
obedience.   [4] 1 Cor. xii. 28.

Kingdom of Heaven he will be seen in his own being as Father.[1] The
Spirit prepares man for the Son of God, the Son leads man to the Father,
the Father gives immortality for eternal life, which comes to each man
as a result of the vision of God. (6) As those who see the light are in the
light and share in its brightness, so those who see God are in God and
share his brightness. The brightness gives them life; and thus those
who see God receive life. And for this reason he who cannot be
grasped or comprehended or seen makes himself seen, comprehended
and grasped by those who believe, that he may give life to those who
grasp and see him by faith. . . . True life comes from partaking in
God; and to partake in God is to know him and to enjoy his goodness.
. . . This was symbolically revealed through the prophets, that God
will be seen by men who bear his Spirit and always look for his coming.
. . . For some of them saw the Spirit of prophecy and his activities
poured out in all kinds of spiritual gifts: others saw the coming of the
Lord and the ministry[2] which is his from the beginning, through which
he fulfilled the Father's will in Heaven and on earth. Others saw the
glory of the Father revealed in ways suited to the times and to themselves who saw and to those who then heard and those who were to
hear of them thereafter. So God was revealed; for by all these ways God
the Father is displayed. The Spirit works, the Son fulfils his ministry,
and the Father approves; and man is thus brought to full salvation.

Adversus Haereses, IV. xx. 5 (*ad fin.*)–6

(c) The Renewal of the Image of God

Already we receive some portion of his Spirit, for our perfecting and
for our preparation for immortality, as we gradually become accustomed to receive and bear God. This is what the Apostle calls a 'first
instalment'[3] . . . which dwells in us and makes us even now spiritual,.
and thus our 'mortality is swallowed up in immortality'.[4] . . . And this
comes about not by getting rid of the material body but by sharing in
the Spirit. . . . If because we have the 'first instalment' we cry 'Abba,
Father',[5] what will happen when on rising we see him face to face? . . .
What will be the effect of the whole grace of the Spirit which will be
given to men by God? It will make us like him and will perfect in us
the Father's will; for it will make man in the image and likeness of
God.   Ibid. v. viii. 1

---

[1] *paternaliter*, contrasted with *prophetice* and *adoptive*.   [2] *administrationem* = (?) οἰκονομίαν,
mediating work': see note 6 on p. 75.   [3] Eph. i. 14.   [4] 2 Cor. v. 4.   [5] Rom. viii. 5.

See above on Man, sub-section (*c*), p. 70 sq. (*Adv. Haer.* v. ix. 1): Irenaeus continues:

Where the Spirit of the Father is, there is the living man . . . flesh possessed by the Spirit, forgetful of itself, assuming the quality of Spirit, made conformable to the Word of God . . . (3) . . . Receiving the Spirit, we walk in newness of life, in obedience to God. Without the Spirit of God we cannot be saved.   Ibid. v. ix. 2–3

Through the Spirit we rise to the Son; through the Son we rise to the Father.   Ibid. v. xxxvi. 2

The Spirit of remission of sins, whereby we are brought to life.
                    Ibid. IV. xxxi. 2

(d) Word—Wisdom—Spirit

We have shown at length that the Word, that is the Son, was always with the Father. And God tells us, through the mouth of Solomon, that Wisdom, that is the Spirit, was with him before the whole creation: 'The Lord established the earth by his Wisdom . . .' [Prov. iii. 19] and again, 'The Lord created me for his works as the beginning of his ways; he established me before the ages' . . . [Prov. viii. 22 ff.]
                    Ibid. IV. xx. 3

(e) Son and Spirit (Word and Wisdom) in Creation

Throughout the Word and the Spirit God made, ordered, and governs all things, and gives them being.   Ibid. I. xxii. 1

Man is a blend of soul and flesh. He was fashioned in the likeness of God and was formed by the hands of God, that is, by the Son and the Spirit, to whom he said, 'Let us make man.'[1]   Ibid. IV. praef. 3

Angels did not make us or fashion us. Angels could not have made the image of God, nor could any other have done this but the Word of God, nor a power much less than the Father of all. In carrying out his intended work of creation, God did not need any help from angels, as if he had not his own hands.[2] For he has always at his side his Word and Wisdom, the Son and the Spirit. Through them and in them he created all things of his own freee will. And to them he says, 'Let us make man . . .' [Gen. i. 26].   Ibid. IV. xx. 1

[1] Gen. i. 26.   [2] For the 'hands of God' cf. under The Trinity (*Adv. Haer.* v. i. 3) below, p. 88.

(f) *From the Father through the Son*

[*The Spirit the 'giver of life' and every good gift, as well natural as spiritual*]
. . . The Word . . . bestows the Spirit on all . . . on some by way of
creation, the gift of being; on some by way of adoption, the gift of
rebirth as sons of God.   *Adversus Haereses*, v. xviii. 1

The Lord had pity on the Samaritan woman[1] . . . and promised her
living water . . . for he had in himself water 'springing up to produce
eternal life'.[2] The Lord received this as a gift from the Father, and he
gives it to those who share in him, sending out the Holy Spirit into the
whole world.

(2) The Lord entrusted to the Holy Spirit the human race which had
'fallen into the hands of thieves'. He had pity on it and bound up its
wounds, and gave two royal *denarii*, so that we receiving through the
Spirit the image and inscription of the Father and the Son may make
profit of the *denarius* entrusted to us and pay it to the Lord with
increase.[3]   *Ibid*. III. xvii. 1–2

(g) *The Descent of the Spirit on the Son*

[*Attacking the Gnostic distinctions between Jesus the man and Christ the
supernatural 'aeon'*] . . . For it is not true that Christ then [*sc. at the baptism*]
descended on Jesus: nor are Christ and Jesus two distinct persons, but
the Word of God, the Saviour of all and the Ruler of heaven and earth,
is Jesus. He took flesh; he was anointed by the Father with the Spirit
and became Jesus Christ [*i.e. Jesus the Anointed*] as also Isaiah says 'there
shall spring forth a rod from the root of Jesse, and a flower shall come
up from this root, and the Spirit of God shall rest upon him, the spirit
of wisdom and understanding' . . . [Isa. xi. 1–4]; and again Isaiah, fore-
telling his anointing, and the end for which he was anointed, says,
'The Spirit of God is upon me, wherefore he has anointed me, and sent
me to preach good tidings to the lowly' . . . [Isa. lxi. 1–2]. Therefore
the Spirit of God descended on him; the Spirit of him who through the
prophets had promised that he would anoint him, in order that we
might receive of the abundance of his unction and be saved.

                                                 Ibid. III. ix. 2

Cf. III. xviii. 3 quoted under 'Trinity', p. 88.

[1] The Samaritan woman is allegorized as a type of the heathen world.   [2] John iv. 14.
[3] Cf. Luke x. 35; Matt. xxv. 16.

God promised through the prophets to 'pour out this Spirit upon his servants and handmaidens in the last days, that they may prophesy'.[1] And the Spirit descended from God on the Son of God, made son of man, and with him became accustomed to dwell among the human race and to 'rest on'[2] men and to dwell in God's creatures, working the Father's will in them, and renewing them from their old state into the newness of Christ.   Ibid. III. xvii. I

See also under VI. The Trinity, below.

VI. The Trinity

(a) General

The Word of God, present with his handiwork from the beginning, reveals the Father to all to whom he wills, when the Father wills and how he wills. Thus in all and through all there is one God the Father and one Word, one Son, and one Spirit, and one salvation to all who believe in him.[3]   Ibid. IV. vi. 6 (ad fin.)

The Father [in creation] has service abundant and inexpressible. For in all things he is served by his Son and the Holy Spirit, his [the Son's?][4] similitude, his Word and Wisdom; to whom all angels render service and are subject.   Ibid. IV. vii. 3

(b) The Functions of the Three Persons

The Spirit prepares man for the Son of God; the Son leads man to the Father; the Father gives man immortality ... (6) ... Thus God was revealed: for in all these ways God the Father is displayed. The Spirit works, the Son fulfils his ministry, the Father approves.
                    Ibid. IV. xx. 4 (ad fin)–6

... The Spirit supplies knowledge of the truth and has made known the ways[5] of the Father and the Son towards man.
                    Ibid. IV. xxxiii. 7

---

[1] Joel ii. 29.   [2] Isa. xi. 2.   [3] The reading here is not quite certain. As it stands, there is probably a correlation, Father : Word : : Son : Spirit, as in Origen de Princ. I. iii. 5 (Greek, quoted by Justinian), see below, p. 239; and cf. Basil, adv. Eunom. v: εἰκὼν μὲν Θεοῦ Χριστὸς ... εἰκὼν δὲ τοῦ Υἱοῦ τὸ Πνεῦμα, cf. de Sp. Sanct. 64; and see the next extract.
[4] The Latin figuratio sua should in strict syntax mean 'his (the Father's) similitude'. But the translator's syntax is eccentric, and it seems likely that sua refers to the Son. The Greek αὐτοῦ would be ambiguous. See the previous note.   [5] οἰκονομίαι: see note 6, p. 75 above.

[*Man's progress to God*] . . . The Father decides and commands; the Son carries out the Father's plan; the Spirit supports and hastens the process . . .   *Adversus Haereses*, IV. xxxviii. 3

The Lord redeems us . . . and pours out the Spirit of the Father to unite God and man. . . . (3) . . . The Word of the Father and the Spirit of God, united with the material substance of Adam, God's primal handiwork, had made man living and perfect, receptive of the perfect Father. . . . For Adam of old had experienced the 'hands'[1] of God; for it was to them that the Father said, 'Let us make man in our image and likeness.'[2] Therefore in the end ('not as a result of the flesh, nor of the will of man',[3] but of the good pleasure of the Father) his 'hands' brought man to full life, that the second Adam should be 'in the image and likeness of God'.   Ibid. v. i. 2–3

The Father supports Creation and his Word; the Word, supported by the Father, bestows the Spirit on all, as the Father wishes. . . . So there is revealed the one God the Father, 'above all, through all, in all'.[4] Above all is the Father, and he is the head [?source] of Christ; through all, the Word; and he is the head [?source] of the Church; in all, the Spirit, and he is the 'living water'[5] which the Lord bestows on all that rightly believe, and love and know him.   Ibid. v. xviii. 1

Through the Spirit man ascends to the Son, through the Son to the Father.   Ibid. v. xxxvi. 2

In the name of Christ ['the Anointed'] is implied the anointer, the anointed and the unction. The Father is the anointer; the Son, the anointed; the Holy Spirit the unction. As the Word declares through Isaiah: 'The Spirit of God is upon me, because he has anointed me'.[6]
                                   Ibid. III. xviii. 3 (*sub fin.*)

(c) A Curiosity of Typology

Rahab received the three spies, who were spying out the whole land; signifying the Father and the Son, with the Holy Spirit.
                                        Ibid. IV. xx. 12

---

[1] See above, p. 85.   [2] Gen. i. 26.   [3] John i. 13.   [4] Eph. iv. 6.   [5] John vii. 39.   [6] Isa. xli. 1. Cf. above under The Holy Spirit, p. 86.

VII. The Church

(a) The Notes of the Church—Succession—Tradition—Scripture

By 'knowledge of the truth' we mean: the teaching of the Apostles; the order of the Church as established from the earliest times throughout the world: the distinctive stamp of the Body of Christ, preserved through the episcopal succession: for to the bishops the Apostles committed the care of the church which is in each place, which has come down to our own time, safeguarded without any written documents, by the most complete exposition [*i.e. the Creed*], which admits neither increase nor diminution [*of the tradition*]: the reading of the Scriptures without falsification, and consistent and careful exposition of them, avoiding temerity and blasphemy: and the special gift of love, which is more precious than knowledge, more glorious than prophecy, surpassing all other spiritual gifts.[1]   Ibid. IV. xxxiii. 8

(b) The Permanence of the Catholic Church—An Allegory

The following extract is the end of an elaborate and somewhat inconsistent allegory. Lot stands for the Father; his seed for the Holy Spirit; his two daughters for the 'two congregations', the Jewish and the Christian Church; and then his wife for the Church.

... Lot's wife remained in Sodom; for she was no longer mortal flesh, but a permanent statue of salt. ... The Church, which is 'the salt of the earth',[2] is thus left in the ends of the earth, suffering the accidents of man's condition. Whole limbs are from time to time removed, but the statue of salt continues: it is the support of the faith, and strengthens the sons of God and sends them on to their Father.

Ibid. IV. xxi. 3

(c) Tradition and Succession in the Church

When the heretics are refuted from the Scriptures they turn to accusing the Scriptures themselves, as if there were something amiss with them. They impugn the authority of Scripture on the ground of 'inconsistency' and because, they say, only those who have the tradition can discover the truth; and the tradition has been handed down by word of mouth, not by the written word. This, according to them, is Paul's meaning when he says, 'But wisdom we speak among the mature; but

[1] Cf. Eph. iii. 19 and 1 Cor. xiii.   [2] Matt. v. 13.

it is a wisdom that does not belong to this world.'[1] Each of these heretics claims that this wisdom is what he himself has discovered by himself—or rather invented. Thus the truth is really found only with them, at one time with Valentinus, at another with Marcion, then with Cerinthus, with Basilides, or with some other opponent of the faith. . . . (2) But when on our side we challenge them by an appeal to that tradition which derives from the Apostles, and which is preserved in the churches by the successions of presbyters,[2] then they oppose tradition, claiming to be wiser not only than the presbyters but even than the Apostles, and to have discovered the truth undefiled. The Apostles, they say, mingled with the Saviour's words matter belonging to the Law; and, besides this, the Lord himself uttered discourses some of which derived from the Demiurge,[3] some from the Intermediate Power, some from the Highest. Whereas they themselves know the hidden mystery without doubt, contaminations, or admixture. Which is a most insolent blasphemy against their Creator. Thus it comes about that they agree neither with Scripture nor with tradition . . .

(iii. 1) Those who wish to see the truth can observe in every church the tradition of the Apostles made manifest in the whole world. We can enumerate those who were appointed bishops in the churches by the Apostles, and their successors down to our own day. They never taught and never knew of such absurdities as those heretics produce. For even if the Apostles had known hidden mysteries and used to impart them privately and secretly to 'the mature', they would have transmitted those secrets above all to those to whom they were entrusting the care of the churches. For they would especially wish those men to be 'mature' and irreproachable, seeing they were handing over to them their own office of doctrinal authority. In them unblemished character would be the greatest blessing, their failure utter calamity. But it would be excessively tedious, in a book of this kind, to give detailed lists of the successions in all the churches. Therefore we will refute those who hold unauthorized assemblies—either because of false self-importance, or pride, or blindness and perversity—by pointing to the tradition of the greatest and oldest church, a church known to all men, which was founded and established at Rome by the most renowned Apostles Peter and Paul. This tradition the church has from

---

[1] 1 Cor. ii. 6. *perfectus* = τέλειος, perfect, mature, complete; probably with the associated idea of 'fully initiated' (τελῶ = initiate).   [2] i.e. bishops, who are often termed 'presbyters' indiscriminately in the first centuries.   [3] The Gnostic creator, distinct from the Father.

the Apostles, and this faith has been proclaimed to all men, and has come down to our own day through the succession of bishops. For this church has a position of leadership and authority; and therefore every church, that is, the faithful everywhere, must needs agree[1] with the church at Rome; for in her[2] the apostolic tradition has ever been preserved by the faithful from all parts of the world. (2) The blessed Apostles, after they had founded and built the church [*at Rome*], handed over to Linus the office of Bishop. Paul mentions this Linus in his epistles to Timothy.[3] He was succeeded by Anacletus, after whom Clement was appointed to the bishopric, third in order from the Apostles.[4] He not only had seen the blessed Apostles, but had also conferred with them, and had their preaching still ringing in his ears, and their tradition still before his eyes. In this he was not alone; for many still survived who had been taught by the Apostles. Now while Clement was bishop there arose a considerable dispute among the brethren in Corinth. And the church at Rome sent a very weighty letter to the Corinthians, to urge them to reconciliation, to renew their faith, and to tell them of the tradition recently received from the Apostles. . . . (3) Euarestus succeeded Clement; Alexander followed Euarestus; then Sixtus [Xystus] was appointed, the sixth in order from the Apostles; then Telesphorus, who had a glorious martyrdom; then Hyginus; then Pius; after him Anicetus; he was succeeded by Soter; and now Eleutherus occupies the see, the twelfth from the Apostles. In this order and succession the Apostolic tradition in the church and the preaching of the truth has come down to our time. . . .

(4) And then Polycarp, besides being instructed by the Apostles and acquainted with many who had seen the Lord, was also appointed for Asia by the Apostles as bishop in the church in Smyrna. Even I saw him in my early manhood; for his was a long life, and he was a great age when he suffered a martyrdom full of glory and honour and departed this life, having taught always the doctrine he had learned from the Apostles, which the church has handed down, which is the only true doctrine. All the churches throughout Asia testify to this, and the successors of Polycarp down to this day. These are witnesses to the truth far more trustworthy and reliable than Valentinus and Marcion and other such misguided persons. Polycarp, when staying at Rome in the time of Anicetus, converted many of the before-mentioned

[1] *convenire*, perhaps 'resort to'. [2] *in qua*, perhaps translating ᾗ 'inasmuch as'. If ἐν ᾗ, referring to Roman Church, the faith is regarded as preserved by the communication of Rome with the other churches. But it may refer back to *omnem ecclesiam* in the sense 'the whole Church'. [3] 2 Tim. iv. 21. [4] But see p. 138.

heretics to the Church of God, declaring that he had received this one and only truth from the Apostles, the truth which has been handed down by the Church. There are some also who heard him relate that John, the Lord's disciple, went to the baths at Ephesus; and rushed out, without taking a bath, when he saw Cerinthus inside, exclaiming, 'Let us get away before the baths fall in; for Cerinthus is in there, the enemy of the truth.' This same Polycarp once was confronted by Marcion, who said: 'Do you know who I am?' To which Polycarp replied, 'I know you for Satan's eldest son.' Such a dread of heresy had the Apostles and their disciples that they shunned even verbal communication with those who perverted the truth. . . . The church in Ephesus which Paul founded and where John dwelt until the time of Trajan is also a genuine witness to the Apostolic tradition.

Adversus Haereses, III, ii–iii

The Church although scattered through the whole world even to the ends of the earth has received the faith from the Apostles and from their disciples. This is the faith in one God the Father almighty, who has made heaven and earth and sea and all that is in them: and in one Christ Jesus, the son of God, who was made flesh for our salvation, and in the Holy Spirit who through the prophets proclaimed God's ways with man,[1] and the coming[2] [*of Christ*], the birth of a Virgin, and the suffering and the resurrection from the dead, and the ascension into heaven in the flesh of the beloved Christ Jesus, our Lord, and his coming from heaven in the glory of the Father to consummate[3] all things, and to raise up all flesh of all mankind. . . . Since the Church has received this preaching and this faith, as we have said, although she is scattered through the whole world, she preserves it carefully, as one household: and the whole Church alike believes in these things, as having one soul and heart, and in unison preaching these beliefs, and teaches and hands them on as having one mouth. For though there are many different languages in the world, still the meaning of the tradition is one and the same. And there are no different beliefs or traditions in the churches established in Germany, or in Spain, or among the Celts, or in the East, or in Egypt or Libya, or those established in the centre of the earth.[4] But just as the sun, God's creature, is one and the same in all the world, so the preaching of the truth shines everywhere and enlightens all men who wish to come to the knowledge of the

---

[1] οἰκονομίαι, see note on p. 75.   [2] The Latin version gives the singular, 'the Advent': the Greek has 'comings', perhaps rightly, referring to the two comings here mentioned. [3] να”κεφαλαιοῦσθαι: see note 2, p. 81.   [4] Italy?—or Palestine?

truth. And the talented theologian among those in authority in the churches will not say anything different from these beliefs (for 'no one is above his teacher'[1]): nor will the feeble divine diminish the tradition.   Ibid. I. x. 1–2

(d) Spiritual Gifts in the Church

Those who are truly his disciples receive grace from him and put this grace into action for the benefit of other men, as each has received the gifts from him. Some drive out devils . . . some have foreknowledge of the future . . . others heal the sick through the laying on of hands . . . and even the dead have been raised up before now and have remained with us for many years. Why, there is no numbering of the gifts which all over the world the Church has received from the Lord, and put into action day by day, in the name of Christ Jesus who was crucified under Pontius Pilate, for the benefit of the nations, without deceit and without payment. For as the Church has received freely from the Lord, so it freely serves mankind.   Ibid. II. xxxii. 4

(e) The Church of the Gentiles—an Allegory

The marriage of Moses to an Ethiopian woman whom he made a woman of Israel prefigured the grafting of the wild olive on to the true olive to share in its fruitfulness.[2] For he who was born in the flesh as the Messiah was sought for by his own people to be slain, but escaped death in Egypt, that is, among the gentiles, and sanctified the infants there, and hence brought into being a church in that land . . . The marriage of Moses was a type of the mystical marriage of Jesus, and the Ethiopian bride signifies the church of the Gentiles. And those who revile and slander that church shall not be clean, but shall be lepers and be cast out from the camp of the just.   Ibid. IV. xx. 12

Cf. the allegory of Rahab, p. 88, of Lot's wife, p. 89. Elsewhere (*Adv. Haer*. IV. xxi. 3) Irenaeus has an elaborate allegory of Jacob and Esau, starting from Rom. ix. 10–13. Jacob the younger supplants Esau; the Christian Church succeeds the chosen people. Esau attacks Jacob; the Jews persecute the Church. Jacob has twelve sons when sojourning in Egypt; Christ has twelve Apostles while sojourning on earth. The various sheep were the reward of Jacob; the various races of the Church were Christ's reward. Jacob endured for Rachel (the younger sister); Christ for the Church. 'For with God nothing is empty of meaning, nothing without symbolism.'

[1] Matt. x. 24.   [2] Cf. Num. xii. 1 and Rom. xi. 17.

(*f*) Heresy and Schism

It is our duty to obey those presbyters[1] who are in the Church, who have their succession from the Apostles, as we have shown, who with their succession in the episcopate have received the sure spiritual gift of truth according to the pleasures of the Father. The others, who stand apart from the primitive succession, and assemble in any place whatever, we ought to regard with suspicion: either as heretics, and unsound in doctrine; or as schismatics, conceited and self-assured; or else as hypocrites, acting thus for the sake of gain and vanity. All these have fallen away from the truth.   *Adversus Haereses*, IV. xxvi. 2

The spiritual disciple truly receives the Spirit of God. . . . 'He will judge all men, while he will be judged by none'.[2] . . .

(7) He will judge those who produce schisms, who have no trace in them of the love of God, and who have an eye to their own profit rather than to the unity of the Church. Such men for any trivial cause cleave and divide the great and glorious Body of Christ, and do their best to destroy it; they speak peace but bring about war; they 'strain out the gnat while they swallow the camel'.[3] No amendment can come from them to cancel the harm of schism.   Ibid. IV. xxxiii. 1, 7

VIII. The Sacraments

(*a*) Baptism

As dry flour cannot be united into a lump of dough, or a loaf, but needs moisture; so we who are many cannot be made one in Christ Jesus without the water which comes from heaven. And as dry earth does not produce fruit unless it receives moisture; so we, who are at first 'a dry tree',[4] would never have yielded the fruit of life without the 'willing rain'[5] from above. For our bodies have received the unity which brings us to immortality, by means of the washing [*of Baptism*]; our souls receive it by means of [*the gift of*] the Spirit. Thus both of these are needed, for together they advance man's progress towards the life of God.   Ibid. III. xvii. 2

(*b*) The Eucharist

From all this [*sc. the prophetic denunciation of sacrificial cults*] it is clear that what God required of them for their salvation was not sacrifices

[1] i.e. bishops: see note on p. 90.   [2] 1 Cor. ii. 15.   [3] Matt. xxiii. 24.   [4] Isa. lvi. 3.   [5] Ps. lxvii. 10 (68.9).

and holocausts, but faith, obedience, and righteousness. So God taught his will in Hosea: 'I desire mercy rather than sacrifice, and knowledge of God above holocausts', and our Lord gave them the same warning.[1] . . . And he also counselled his disciples to offer to God the firstfruits of his creatures, not because he needed these gifts, but so that they should not be unfruitful nor unthankful. This he did, when he took bread, of the natural creation, and gave thanks, and said, 'This is my body'. Likewise the cup of wine, belonging to the creation of which we are part, he declared to be his blood, and explained as the new oblation of the New Testament. This oblation the Church receives from the Apostles and throughout the whole world she offers it to God, who supplies as our nourishment the firstfruits of his gifts in the New Testament. Concerning this, Malachi thus prophesied: 'I will not receive sacrifice at your hands. . . . In every place incense is offered in my name, and a pure sacrifice; for my name is great among the gentiles. . . .'[2] By this he quite clearly means that the former people will cease to offer to God, but in every place a 'sacrifice' will be offered, and that a 'pure' sacrifice;[3] while his name is 'glorified among the gentiles'.

Ibid. IV. xvii. 4

There are oblations there [sc. among the Jews] and oblations here; sacrifices among the chosen people, sacrifices in the Church. Only the kind of sacrifice is changed, for now sacrifice is offered not by servants but by sons. There is one and the same Lord; but there is a character appropriate to a servile oblation, and a character appropriate to the oblation of sons, so that even by means of the oblations a token of liberty is displayed.

Ibid. IV. xviii. 2

We are bound to make our oblation to God and thus to show ourselves in all things grateful to him as our Creator. . . . And it is only the Church which offers a pure oblation to the Creator, presenting an offering from his creation, with thanksgiving. The Jews do not offer such an oblation, for their 'hands are full of blood';[4] for they did not receive the Word through whom the offering is made to God. Neither do any of the congregations of the heretics. For some of them say that the Father is a different being from the Creator;[5] so that in offering to the Father gifts taken from this created world they represent him as coveting another's possessions. While those who say that our created world was made 'of decay, ignorance, and passion' sin against their

---

[1] Hos. vi. 6; Matt. xii. 7. [2] Mal. i. 14. [3] This text is similarly interpreted by Justin, Tertullian, Chrysostom, Augustine, and others. [4] Isa. i. 15. [5] See pp. 10 ff.

Father in offering to him the fruits of 'ignorance, passion and decay'; a
gesture rather of insult than of gratitude. How can they consistently
suppose that the bread over which thanks have been given is the body
of their Lord, and that the cup is the cup of his blood, if they allege
that he is not the son of the Creator of the world—that is, his Word,
through whom the tree bears fruit, the springs flow, and the earth
yields 'first the blade, then the ear, then the full corn in the ear'?[1]
(5) Again, how can they say that flesh passes to corruption and does not
share in life, seeing that flesh is nourished by the body and blood of
the Lord? Let them either change their opinion, or refrain from making
those oblations of which we have been speaking. But our opinion is
congruous with the Eucharist, and the Eucharist supports our opinion.
We offer to him what is his own, suitably proclaiming the communion and unity of flesh and spirit.[2] For as the bread, which comes
from the earth, receives the invocation[3] of God, and then it is no longer
common bread but Eucharist,[4] consists of two things, an earthly and a
heavenly; so our bodies, after partaking of the Eucharist, are no longer
corruptible, having the hope of the eternal resurrection.

(6) We make, then, our offering to him, not as if he stood in need of
anything, but giving thanks to his sovereignty and sanctifying his
creation. . . . He takes to himself our good endeavours to the end that
he may repay us with his good things . . . [Matt. xxv. 34–36]. The
Word himself gave commandment to his people that they should make
oblations, although he needed none, that they might learn to serve
God. For that reason he wishes us to offer our gifts at the altar continually, without ceasing. There is therefore an altar in heaven; for
thither our prayers and oblations are directed.

Adversus Haereses, IV. xviii. 4–6

Therefore Paul says to the Corinthians, 'I gave you milk to drink, not
solid food, for you were not able to bear it',[5] that is, 'You have been
taught about the coming of the Lord as man, but as yet the Spirit of
the Father does not rest upon you because of your weakness'; 'for
since', he says, 'there is envy and strife among you, are you not living
according to your lower nature, as merely human?'[6] He is saying that

---

[1] Mark iv. 28.   [2] The Greek of John Damascene reads, 'proclaiming our communion
and unity, and confessing the resurrection of flesh and spirit', but the additional words
spoil the sense and are probably interpolated.   [3] ἐπίκλησις, the technical word for the invocation of the Spirit at the consecration. (The text of Damascene has ἔκκλησις, almost
certainly an error.)   [4] Cf. Justin Mart. *Apol.* i. 66, above, pp. 61–62.   [5] I Cor. iii. 2.
[6] Ibid., verse 3.

the Spirit of the Father is not yet with them, because they are not fully developed and their common life is imperfect. Thus the Apostle has power to give them 'solid food' – for when the Apostle laid hands on people they received the Holy Spirit, which is the food of life—but the Corinthians were not capable of receiving the Spirit, because the senses of their soul were still weak and not yet trained towards God. In the same way, God had power to give man perfection from the beginning; but man, being newly made, was incapable of receiving it, or, if he received it, to take it in, or, if he took it in, to retain it. Therefore the Son of God, being perfect, shared in man's infancy, not on his own account, but because of man's childishness, adapting himself to man's capacity.   Ibid. IV. xxxviii. 2

Utterly foolish are those who despise the divine scheme for man; who deny the salvation of the flesh and scorn the notion of re-birth, alleging the flesh incapable of immortality. If the flesh is not to be saved, then the Lord did not redeem us by his blood, nor is the 'cup of blessing [cup of the Eucharist] the partaking of his blood',[1] nor is the 'bread which we break the partaking of his body'.[1] . . . (3) We are his members, and are nourished by means of his creation (and he himself provides his creation for us, 'making the sun to rise and sending rain as he wills'[2]); therefore the drink, which is part of his creation, he declared to be his own blood; and by this he enriches our blood: and the the bread, which comes from his creation, he affirmed to be his own body; and by this he nourishes our bodies. Whenever then the cup that man mixes and the bread that man makes receive the word of God, the Eucharist becomes the body of Christ and by these elements the substance of our flesh receives nourishment and sustenance. How then can they allege that flesh is incapable of the gift of God, which is eternal life, seeing that the flesh is fed on the flesh and blood of the Lord and is a member of him?   Ibid. v. ii. 2–3

IX. The Resurrection

(a) The Intermediate State

If the Lord followed the normal course of death that he might be the 'firstborn from the dead', and stayed till the third day in 'the lower parts of the earth', and then rose in his physical body to show the marks of the nails to his disciples, and thus ascended to the Father; this must

[1] 1 Cor. x. 16.   [2] Matt. v. 45.

needs overthrow the contention that this world of ours is the under-world, and that the 'inner man' leaves this body here and ascends into the region above the heavens. For the Lord 'departed in the midst of the shadow of death'[1] where are the souls of the departed, and then arose in bodily form and after his resurrection was taken up [*into heaven*]. Therefore it is clear that the souls of his disciples, for whom the Lord performed this, will depart into an unseen region, set apart for them by God, and will dwell there until the resurrection which they await. Then they will receive their bodies and arise entire, that is, in bodily form as the Lord arose, and thus will come into the presence of God. *Adversus Haereses*, v. xxxi. 2

(b) Corporal Resurrection

What is restored to life is not something other than that which dies; just as that which is lost is not something different from that which is found. It was the sheep that was lost which the Lord came to find. What then was it which perished? Clearly it was the substance of flesh, which lost the breath of life. . . . The Lord came to restore this flesh to life, that 'as in Adam all die', as possessing merely sensual life, we may live 'in Christ', as having spiritual life, putting away not the handiwork of God but the lusts of the flesh, and receiving the Holy Spirit.

Ibid. v. xii. 3

If men think only of the weakness of the flesh, and do not consider the power of him who raises it from the dead, they ignore the might of God. . . . For God fails in power if he does not give life to mortality and bring corruptibility to incorruption. But we ought to infer God's power in all these things from a consideration of our beginning; God took clay from the earth, and fashioned man. Now to bring man to being, to make a living and rational creature, of bones, muscles, veins and all the rest of man's economy, which as yet did not exist; this was a task far harder, far more incredible, than to restore this creature when it had been created and then re-dissolved into the earth, having returned to those elements out of which man was first created. If God gave existence, when he so willed, to those who did not exist, much more will he restore those who have come into being to the life which he gave them, if he so wills. The flesh which at the beginning was the subject of God's art will be found capable of receiving and assimilating God's power. Ibid. v. iii. 2

[1] Ps. xxii (23), 4. 'depart' = $\pi o \rho \epsilon \upsilon \theta \hat{\omega}$ = 'journey' ('walk', A.V. & P.B.).

(c) The Restored Creation

Some men hold beliefs which are imported from heretical discourses; they are ignorant of the ways of God's working and of the mystery of the resurrection of the just and of their kingdom, which is the beginning of immortality, the kingdom by which such as have proved worthy are gradually accustomed to receive God. For this reason it is necessary to say something on this subject and to explain that in the restored creation the righteous must rise first at the appearing of God to receive their promised inheritance, promised by God to the fathers, and to reign therein; after that follows the judgement. For it is only right that they should receive the reward of their endurance in that created order in which they suffered hardship or affliction and were in all manner of ways tested by suffering; that they should be brought to life in that created order in which they were put to death for the love of God; and to reign where they had endured bondage. For God is 'rich in all things'[1] and all things are his. Therefore this created order must be restored to its first condition and be made subject to the righteous without hindrance; and this the Apostle shows in the Epistle to the Romans, when he says, 'The earnest expectation of the creation awaits the revelation of the sons of God' . . . [Rom. viii. 19–21].

Ibid. v. xxxii. 1

[*Quoting* Matt. xxvi. 29, 'I will no more drink the fruit of the vine until I drink it new in my Father's kingdom.'] He will certainly himself renew the inheritance of the earth and restore the mystery of the glory of his sons: as David says, he 'shall renew the face of the earth'.[2] He promised to 'drink of the fruit of the vine' with his disciples[3] and he thus indicated two things; the inheritance of the earth in which the new fruit of the vine will be drunk, and the physical resurrection of his disciples. For it is the body which arises new which receives the new drink. We cannot understand him as drinking the fruit of the vine when he has taken his place with his followers in the region above the heavens: and those who drink it are not disembodied: for to drink wine belongs to the body rather than the spirit.

Ibid. v. xxxiii. 1

(d) The Millennium

This blessing [*sc. of Isaac*, Gen. xxvii. 27–29] indisputably refers to the time of the kingdom, when the righteous shall rise from the dead and reign; when creation, renewed and liberated, shall produce food of

[1] Rom. x. 12.   [2] Ps. ciii (104). 30.   [3] Matt. xxvi. 29.

every kind in abundance, thanks to the dew of heaven and the fertility of the earth. The presbyters[1] who saw John, the Lord's disciple, recall hearing from him that the Lord taught about this time in these words; 'The days will come in which vines shall grow, each with ten thousand shoots, each shoot with ten thousand branches, each branch ten thousand twigs, each twig ten thousand clusters, each cluster ten thousand grapes; and each grape when pressed shall yield twenty-five measures[2] of wine. And when any of the saints shall take hold of one of the clusters, another cluster shall call out, "I am a better cluster; take me, and bless the Lord through me". Likewise a grain of wheat shall yield ten thousand ears, each ear ten thousand grains, each grain ten pounds of pure white flour. And fruits, seeds, and grass shall yield in like proportion. And all the animals, enjoying these fruits of the earth shall live in peace and harmony, obedient to man in entire submission.'

(4) The authority for these sayings is Papias, who belonged to an earlier generation, who heard John speak and was a companion of Polycarp. This passage comes from the fourth of his five books.[3] He adds, 'These things are credible to believers. And when the traitor Judas was sceptical and asked, "How will the Lord effect such produce?", the Lord said, "Those who come to that era shall see" ' ... [*Irenaeus proceeds to reject an allegorical interpretation of* Isa. xi. 6–9].

                                        Adversus Haereses, v. xxxiii. 3–4

(e) 'Many Mansions'

When this present fashion of the world has passed away, and man has been renewed and has grown ripe for immortality, so as to be no longer capable of growing old, then there will be the 'new heaven and the new earth';[4] they will be new and in them man will abide always new, and in fellowship with God. . . . Then, as the elders say, those who are found worthy to dwell in heaven shall go thither; while others shall enjoy the delights of paradise; others possess the splendour of the city.[5] For the Saviour will be seen in every place according to the worthiness of the beholders.

(2) They say that this is the distinction between the dwellings of those who yield a hundred-fold, sixty-fold, and thirty-fold:[6] the first

[1] Since Irenaeus refers in § 4 to Papias, the plural in the Latin is probably an error; but the plural also occurs in xxxvi. 1.   [2] About 225 gallons.   [3] Eusebius, III. 39, gives the title Τῶν Λογίων Κυριακῶν Ἐξήγησις ('Exposition of the Dominical Oracles'—i.e. of 'authoritative writings relating to the Lord Jesus Christ, giving an account of his deeds as well as his sayings, i.e. Gospels, though not necessarily our canonical Gospels'—H. J. Lawlor and J. E. L. Oulton, *Eusebius*, ad loc.)   [4] Rev. xxi. 1.   [5] i.e. the New Jerusalem.   [6] Cf. Matt. xiii. 8.

shall be taken up to heaven, the second shall dwell in paradise, the third shall inhabit the city. It was for this reason the Lord said, 'In my Father's house are many dwelling-places'. [1] For all things belong to God, and he provides for all a fitting habitation. As his Word says, 'The Father has appointed to all, according as each is or shall be worthy'. [2] And this is the triple couch [3] on which those who have been invited to the marriage recline to feast. The presbyters who were disciples of the Apostles tell us of this arrangement and disposition of those who are saved; and by such degrees they advance, and first by the Spirit ascend to the Son, and by the Son to the Father; the Son in due course yields up his work to the Father as the Apostle says [*citing* 1 Cor. xv. 25–28].

Ibid. v. xxxvi. 1–2

X. Faith and Revelation

The Lord has taught us that no one can know God unless he is taught by God; that is, without God's help he cannot be known. But it is the will of the Father that he should be known; for he is known by those to whom the Son reveals him. And the Father has revealed the Son to this end, that he may be displayed to all through the Son and that those who believe in him and are justified may be received into immortality and eternal refreshment. Now to believe in him is to do his will. Those who do not believe and therefore shun his light he will rightly shut up in the darkness which they themselves have chosen. Therefore the Father has revealed himself to all, making his Word visible to all: and on his part the Word showed the Father and the Son to all since he was seen by all. And thus there is a just judgement of God; for all alike saw, but all did not alike believe.   Ibid. IV. vi. 4

XI. Natural Religion

The law of nature, by which the natural man is justified, [4] which, even before the giving of the Law, was kept by those who were justified by faith and pleased God, this law the Lord did not annul but extended and fulfilled as is shown by his own words [Matt. v. 21 *et seq.*].

Ibid. IV. xiii. 1

[1] John xiv. 2.   [2] Either a traditional *verbum Christi* current among those millenarian presbyters (cf. the quotation in Papias, above); or a reference to the seats 'on the right hand and the left', Matt. xx. 23; or, less likely, to the Parable of the Talents.   [3] The *triclinium*, on three sides of a Roman dinner-table, consisting of *lectus summus, lectus medius, lectus imus*.   [4] Cf. Rom. ii. 17.

XII. The Conclusion

The Apostle has proclaimed that 'creation shall be liberated from the bondage of corruption into the liberty of the glory of the sons of God'.[1] And in all and through all the same God the Father is displayed, who fashioned man and promised to the fathers the inheritance of the earth, and 'led out[2] that inheritance' in the resurrection of the righteous, and fulfils his promises in the kingdom[3] of his Son; afterwards bestowing, with fatherly love, things 'which eye has not seen, nor ear heard, nor has it risen into the heart of man'.[4] For there is one Son who accomplished the Father's will: and one human race in which the mysteries [*i.e. divine purposes*] of God are fulfilled, 'whom[5] angels long to see', and are not able to search out the wisdom of God, whereby his handiwork is perfected by being conformed to the Son and incorporated in him; namely that his offspring, the first-begotten Word, should descend into creation, into his handiwork, and be received thereby; that creation, for its part, should receive the Word and ascend to him, rising above the angels, to be made according to the image and likeness of God.   *Adversus Haereses*, v. xxxvi. 3

[1] Rom. viii. 21. [2] *eduxit*. Probably we should read *elegit* 'chose', as in Ps. xlvii. 4. Whatever the reading this seems to be the reference. [3] Lat. *in regnum*, perhaps 'to establish the kingdom'. [4] I Cor. ii. 9. [5] *quem*. Better, 'quae' *which* (mysteries) angels long to see' (I Pet. i. 12).

Quintus Septimius Florens Tertullianus (Tertullian)

Floruit c. 200.—EDITIONS: partly in *Corpus Scriptorum Ecclesiasticorum Latinorum* (Vienna), by various editors. Elsewhere Migne *Patrologia Latina*, i–ii. Latin titles are explained on pp. 301 f.

I. God

(a) Natural Religion

The object of our worship is the one God who created the whole massive structure with all its apparatus of elements, bodies, and spirits: who fashioned it out of nothing through his word, by which he gave the command; through his design, by which he arranged the whole; by his power, by which he could effect his plan, to make it the adornment of his own majesty. Hence the Greeks call the universe the Cosmos (which means 'ornament'). God is invisible, though he is seen; incomprehensible, though manifested by grace; inconceivable, though conceived by human senses. In this lies his reality, and his greatness. But as a general rule, what can be seen, grasped, conceived, is inferior to the eyes which see, the hands which handle, the senses which discover it: while that which is infinite is known only by itself. It is God's infinity which gives us the conception of the inconceivable God; for his overwhelming majesty presents him to man as at once known and unknown. And the height of man's sin is the refusal to recognize him of whom man cannot be ignorant. Do you wish to have proof from all his wonderful works, by which we are preserved and sustained, which minister delight while they inspire us with awe? Do you want proof from the witness of the soul itself? For though the soul be confined in the body's prison, though thwarted by evil influences, though enervated by the lusts and desires of the flesh, though made the servant of false gods; yet when the soul comes to its senses, as it were from a drunken stupor, or awakes from sleep, or recovers from a kind of sickness and is restored to health, then it speaks of God, in the singular; appropriately, since the true God is one. Thus 'Great God', and 'Good God', and 'God grant', are phrases in general use. And the soul bears witness that God is our judge, by such phrases as, 'in the sight of God', 'I commend my cause to God', and 'God will repay me'. What evidence that the soul is naturally Christian! In fact, with such utterances the soul fixes its gaze not on the Capitol but on heaven; recognizing heaven as the abode of God. From him and from thence the soul descended.   *Apologeticus*, 17

(b) The Unity and Nature of God

Either God is one or he does not exist. For it is more fitting to ascribe non-existence than the wrong kind of existence. Now, that you may know that God is one, ask what kind of being God is, and the conclusion is inevitable. In so far as human limitations can define God, this is my definition of his nature, a definition which will be admitted by the general sense of mankind: God is the supreme being,[1] existing in eternity, unborn, uncreated, without beginning, without end. Such are the conditions to be attributed to the eternity which makes God the supreme being; God must have these and similar attributes that he may be supreme in form and mode of being,[2] in power and might. This is a matter of general agreement, for no one will deny that God is the supreme being, unless a man can bring himself to declare that God is an inferior being, which would be to rob him of the quality of deity and so to deny his existence. What, then, will be the postulate of this supreme being? Surely this, that nothing will be equal to it: and this is to say that there will not be another supreme being. . . . The supreme being must be unique.   *Adversus Marcionem*, i. 3

(c) God is substantial

[*The Word is substantial.*] I assert that nothing insubstantial and void could have proceeded from God, since he himself is not insubstantial and void from whom it issued; nor can that lack substance which came forth from so great a substance and created such great substances; for he created all things which were made through him. 'Without him no thing was made';[3] but can he himself be nothing? Is it conceivable that an insubstantial being should have created concrete things; a void, solids; an incorporeal, bodies? For though it may sometimes happen that something can be made whose nature is different from that of the agent of its creation, it is still true that nothing can be created by the agency of what is insubstantial and void. How then can the Word of God be insubstantial and void, that Word who is called the Son of God, and given the name of God? The Scripture says, 'Thou shalt not

---

[1] *summum magnum.*   [2] *forma et ratione.*   [3] John i. 3.

take the name of God for nothing.'[1] This surely is he 'who, being in the form of God, thought it not a prize to be equal with God'.[2] What form was this? Surely in *some*[3] form, not none. For who will deny that God is a body, although 'God is spirit'?[4] For a spirit is a body, of its own kind, in its own form. But these 'invisible things', whatever they are, have their own body and their own form in the presence of God by means of which they are visible to God alone; much less will that be devoid of substance which issued from his substance. Whatever then that substance of the Word was, I call that a person, and claim for that person the name of Son; and I acknowledge him as Son, while maintaining that he is distinct from the Father.   *Adversus Praxean*, 7

(d) Creation

When we try to consider God as known by man, it will be right for us, if the question is raised, 'In what fashion is he known?', to begin from his works, which are prior to man. Thus his goodness will be discovered, and when that is established as a premise it may suggest a way of thinking by which we can understand how the later sequence of events has come about. The disciples of Marcion can thus recognize the goodness of our God, and admit that it is a goodness worthy of God, for the same reasons by which we showed the unworthiness of their god's 'goodness'. To begin with, the matter which is the ground of his being known he did not find in some other being, but created it for himself. This is the first goodness of the Creator: he did not wish to remain hidden for ever; he did not wish that there should be no being to whom God could be made known. For what good is comparable to the knowledge and enjoyment of God? Although the existence of this good was not yet apparent, there being no one to whom it might appear, yet God foreknew the good which was to appear, and therefore charged his supreme goodness with the task of mediating that good. But of course this goodness did not suddenly come into being; it did not arise from some carnal whim or sudden impulse, as if it might be thought of as beginning to exist when it began to be exercised. For if it was this goodness that made the beginning, at the time when it began to be exercised; it did not begin to be when it made the beginning. But it was when the beginning had been made that the temporal order was brought to birth by God's goodness, for the stars and the lights of heaven were fixed to mark and distinguish the passage

---

[1] *in vanum*, 'for a void thing', 'for unreality' (Exod. xx. 7).   [2] Phil. ii. 6.   [3] reading *aliqua*: MSS. *alia*.   [4] John iv. 24.

of time: 'they will be for times and months and years'.[1] Therefore that which created time had no time before time was; just as that which made the beginning had no beginning before the beginning. And so, being thus free from the order of beginning and the measure of time, it must be ranked as existing from the age which has no measure and no limit: nor can it be considered as arising suddenly, or casually or impulsively. It cannot be considered as arising *from* anything; that is, it has no temporal characteristics, but is to be taken as eternal, inherent in God from everlasting. For this reason it is worthy of God, and puts to shame the 'goodness' of Marcion's god; for that god's goodness is subsequent, not only to the beginning of things and the creation of time, but actually to the evil of the creator; but can evil be committed by goodness?   *Adversus Marcionem*, ii. 3

(e) The Goodness of Creation, and of the Law

The world was made up of all kinds of good things, and gives sufficient indication of the great good in store for him for whom all this was provided. Who really was worthy to inhabit God's works but the image and likeness of God himself? And that image was wrought by goodness, and goodness more closely engaged on the task; for the work was done not by a word of command but by the very hand of goodness, with this kind word by way of preface, 'Let us make man in our own image and likeness'.[2] Thus goodness spoke; and goodness fashioned man out of clay to make this wonderful structure of flesh, equipped with so many qualities though formed of one material; goodness breathed into it a soul so that it was not dead but living: goodness set man over all things, to enjoy them, even to name them: goodness added further delights for man, so that, although in possession of the whole globe, he should dwell in the greatest pleasures of all, being transported into paradise, a movement which prefigures the transference from the world into the Church. The same goodness furnished him also with a helper, that there might be nothing in his state that was not good, for 'It is not good for the man to be alone'.[2] Goodness knew that Mary's sex would benefit him and thereafter the Church. Yes, and the Law, which you attack, which you twist for purposes of controversy; that Law was demanded by goodness in the interest of man, that he might cleave to God, lest he should seem to be not left free but cast off and put on an equality with the rest of the animal creation, his servants, which were free from constraint, enjoying the liberty of

[1] Gen. i. 15.   [2-2] Gen. i. 26–ii. 19 *passim*.

contempt: the Law was given that man might glory in the thought that he alone was worthy to receive the Law from God; and that as a rational creature, capable of intelligence and knowledge, he should be constrained by the very liberty he possessed, the liberty of a rational being; for he was subject to him who had subjected all things to man [cf. Ps. viii. 6]. Goodness likewise added a warning to obey the Law, saying, 'On the day that you eat you will die'.[1] For it was a most gracious act of God's goodness, to show the result of transgression lest ignorance of danger should prompt neglect of obedience. Further, if the reason for the Law's imposition was first given, the reason for its observance followed; so that the penalty should be ascribed to the transgression, which he who gave the warning did not wish to happen. Therefore acknowledge the goodness of God so far, shown in the goodness of his works, his blessings, his indulgences, his providences, his gracious laws and warnings.   Ibid. ii. 4

(f) Matter not Eternal

Hermogenes lays down the premise that God made all things either out of himself, or out of nothing, or out of something; his object being to refute the first two possibilities, and to establish the third, namely, that God created out of something, and that something was matter. God could not, he asserts, have created out of himself; because then his creation would have been part of himself; but God cannot be reduced to parts, being indivisible and unchangeable, and always the same, in that he is Lord. Further, anything made of himself would have been something of himself: then his creation and his creating would have to be accounted imperfect, a partial creation and a partial creating. Or if he completely made a complete creation, then he must needs have been at once complete and incomplete; complete, that he might make himself, and incomplete that he might be made of himself. A further serious difficulty; if he existed he could not be created, if he did not exist, he could not create. Again he who always exists cannot *become*, but *is* for everlasting. Therefore he did not create out of himself; that would be inconsistent with his nature. Similarly, he argues that he could not have created out of nothing. He defines God as good, utterly good, and therefore wishing to make all things as good, as utterly good as he himself is . . . but evil is found in his creation, and this is certainly not according to his will . . . therefore we

[1] Gen. iii. 3 (cf. 5).

must assume it came into being as a result of a fault in something, and that something is undoubtedly matter.

(3) He adds another argument; God has always been God, and always Lord. Now he could not be regarded as always Lord, as he is always God, if there had not been something already existing of which he could be accounted Lord. Therefore matter always existed for God to be always Lord of it. . . . *We* maintain that he always has the title of God, but not always that of Lord; for the nature of these two titles is different. God is the title of the *substance*, the divine *nature*: Lord the title of *power*. . . . He became Lord and acquired that name from the time when things came into being over which the power of the Lord was exercised: the position and the title come through the accession of power. God is father and judge: but it does not follow that he is father and judge eternally because he is always God. He could not be father before he had a son; nor judge before sin was committed.

Adversus Hermogenem, 2–3

II. Man

(a) The Corporeal Soul

Tertullian argued in his *de Anima* (chs. 1–8) that the soul is corporeal. He continues as follows:

When we ascribe to the soul a body of a nature and kind peculiar to itself, this peculiarity has determined the other accidents of corporality: either they are found in it, since we have shown the soul to be a body, but even so they are of their own particular kind, corresponding to the special nature of the body to which they belong; or they are not present, but the absence from the soul's body of the usual attributes of bodies is due to the peculiar nature of that body. Yet we will not hesitate to assert that the more usual marks of corporality, which are completely inseparable from that condition, are found also in the soul: such attributes as shape and definition, and the three dimensions of length, breadth, and height, by which scientists measure bodies. . . . We also ascribe to the soul corporeal lineaments, not only from the confidence in its corporality supplied by rational thought, but also from the assurance given by grace through revelation . . . [*A Montanist sister is in the habit of receiving revelations during divine service which she relates to the esoterics after the end of devotions*] 'Amongst other things', she says, 'there was shown me a soul in bodily shape, and the spirit remained in view. It was not insubstantial and void of qualities, but such as to suggest that it might be grasped; it was soft and shining and of the colour of mist, and its shape was in all respects human' . . . Your own common sense will suggest that the soul cannot but be thought of as having human appearance, in fact the outward shape of the particular body which it informed. The consideration of man's origin may lead us to this supposition. For reflect that when God had 'breathed into the face of man the breath of life, and man was made into a living soul'.[1] surely all the breath passed straightway through the face into the inner parts, and was diffused through all the spaces of the body; and at the same time it was compressed by the divine breathing and was moulded by every feature within and hardened, as it were, in a shape. Hence therefore the corporality of the soul was solidified by compression, and its appearance formed by a moulding process. This is the inner man, distinct from the outer, though identical with it as its replica.

It has its own eyes and ears; Paul had to have them to hear and see the Lord.[2] It has also the other members, with which it acts in thoughts and dreams. Thus in the underworld the rich man has a tongue, the poor man a finger, and Abraham a bosom.[3]   *De Anima*, 9

(b) All Souls derive from Adam (Traducianism)

Hence [sc. from instinctive behaviour and 'reflex actions' of plants] we conclude that all the natural properties of the soul are inherent in it as belonging to its substance; and they advance and develop with it from the moment when it acquires its being . . . [Differences due to environment and individual history]. It is clear how great are the influences which dispose the soul's nature in such various ways that men commonly think of natures. However, they are not distinct species but accidents of the one nature and substance, namely that which God bestowed on Adam and made the matrix of all.   Ibid. 20

Thus from the one man comes all this abundance of souls, since nature observes the command of God, 'Increase and grow into a multitude'.[4] For in the very preface to the one operation, 'Let us make man',[5] the whole of posterity is spoken of by the use of the plural, 'and let *them* have authority over the fish of the sea'. And quite naturally; the seed contains the assurance of the crop.   Ibid. 27 (ad fin.)

[1] Gen. ii. 7. [2] Cf. 2 Cor. xii. 1-4. [3] Cf. Luke xvi. 22 ff. [4] Gen. i. 28 et passim.
[5] Gen. i. 26.

(c) Freedom

We define the soul as born of the breath of God; immortal, corporeal, having shape, simple in substance, susceptible of the functions proper to it, developing in various ways, having freedom of choice, affected by external events, mutable in its faculties, rational, dominant, capable of presentiment, evolving in plurality from one archetype. *De Anima*, 22

[*Attacking the determinism of the Gnostic Valentinians*] . . .These heretics say that nature cannot be changed . . . because 'a good tree does not bear bad fruit, nor a bad tree good fruit; and can one reap figs from thorns or grapes from thistles?'[1] If this is so, God will not be able 'to raise up sons of Abraham from stones' nor will the 'offspring of vipers' be able to 'produce fruits of repentance'.[2] . . . But the sayings of Scripture will not prove inconsistent. A bad tree will not yield good fruit without grafting, and a good tree will give bad fruit if not tended. Stones will become sons of Abraham if trained into Abraham's faith: the 'offspring of vipers' will 'produce fruits of repentance' if they expel the poison of malignity. This will be the power of the grace of God, more powerful surely than nature, having under it in us the free power of choice, which is called 'self-determination'. This faculty belongs to our nature and is capable of change; and thus whithersoever it inclines, our nature inclines the same way.   Ibid. 21

(d) Man's Sin and God's Foreknowledge

And now for those questions of yours, you dogs, whom the Apostle turns out of doors,[3] you who bark at the God of truth. These are the bones of your arguments which you chew over. 'If God is good, and has foreknowledge and the power to avert evil, why has he allowed men to be beguiled by the devil and to fall away from obedience to his law into death; seeing that man is God's own image and likeness, yes, and his own substance too, because of the status of his soul? For if he is good, he would not wish such a thing to happen; if prescient, he would not be ignorant that it was to happen; if powerful, he could prevent its happening: every event must be consistent with those three attributes of the divine majesty. If any event is inconsistent it is established beyond doubt that we must believe God to be neither good, nor prescient, nor powerful. For just as with the existence of such a God, good, prescient, and powerful, nothing of this kind would have occurred, so its occurrence proves that God has not these qualities.

[1] Matt. vii. 17.   [2] Matt. iii. 7 ff.   [3] Cf. Phil. iii. 2.

In reply the first task is to defend the attribution to the Creator of those qualities which are called in doubt, viz. his goodness, foreknowledge, and power. I shall not spend much time on this point, since Christ himself has already shown how this is to be done; we must prove these qualities from his works. The works of the Creator bear witness both to his goodness, in that his works are good, as we have shown; and to his power, in that they are so great, and that he creates out of nothing. For even if he made them, as some will have it, out of some pre-existent stuff, still it was creation from nothing in this respect, that they were not that which they now are. In fact his works are as great as they are good, and God's power is such that all things are his, and therefore he is omnipotent. But what shall I say of his foreknowledge? Those great prophets whom it inspired are its sufficient witnesses. Do we have to claim foreknowledge for the author of all things? For clearly it was by this property that he foreknew the whole universe in ordering it, and ordered it in foreknowing it. Certainly he foreknew even the transgression of man; for had he not foreknown it, he would not have imposed that warning, with the threat of death. Thus, if these faculties existed in God, in accordance with which no evil could or should have happened to man, and yet in fact the evil did happen, let us look at the nature of man and see if this was not rather responsible for the occurrence of the evil which could not be due to God. I find that man was established by God as a free being, possessed of the power of choice; for just in this do I observe in him the image and likeness of God, that he is characterized by this condition. For the human race differs in outward appearance and feature: it is not in this respect that man is fashioned in the likeness of God, whose form is always the same. Rather it is in that essential being[1] which he derived from God, that of the soul, which corresponds to the form of God. In that he has been given the characteristic of freedom and power of choice. And that he has this condition is confirmed by the very law which God then established. For a law would only be established for one who had the power of *choosing* the obedience demanded by the law; and the threat of death would only be attached to transgression if man were endowed with freedom to defy the law. Thus in the Creator's latter laws you may discover him 'setting before man good and evil, life and death'.[2] And the whole scheme of man's discipline through God's rules, with God's calls and threats and exhortations, assumes that man is free to choose obedience or defiance.

[1] *substantia.*   [2] Deut. xxx. 15.

(6) . . . In case you should object that man ought not to have been
endowed with a freedom that was to prove his ruin, I will first maintain
the rightness of this endowment to support my argument that he *was*
in fact so endowed and that this was consonant with the nature of God.
I will do this by showing the cogent reason for his being so equipped.
In our God goodness and practical wisdom[1] always work together;
for goodness without wisdom is not goodness: and wisdom without
goodness is not wisdom; unless indeed you can believe in the irrational
good of Marcion's god. And these qualities will be found to support
this endowment of man with freedom. God had to be known; and
there had to be some being worthy of knowing God: and could anything be imagined so worthy as the 'image and likeness of God'? . . .
It would indeed be strange if man had dominion over all the world and
should not first of all have sway over his own mind: should be lord of
others but slave to himself. . . . Therefore in order that man might
have as his own the good which was granted to him by God, that it
might become his own possession and, in a sense, his by nature;[2] he
was equipped at his creation with the power of freewill, as a kind of
dispenser[3] of the good granted to him by God. The result was that
man could, of his own accord, exhibit good as his own possession.
The principle of goodness demanded this; for good is to be performed
voluntarily, that is, of free choice; a freedom which is in accordance
with the purpose of man's creation, but not in bondage to it. Thus man
might be really good, being found good in accordance with his creation but at the same time of his own will; being good as it were of the
proper quality of his own nature. . . .[4] Thus complete freedom of
choice for good or ill was granted to man, that he might be master of
himself consistently, cleaving to good of his own accord, of his own
accord eschewing evil. For it was necessary that man, who is in any case
set under the judgement of God, should make the judgement just, as
being dependent on the merits of his choice—his free choice. Otherwise there would be no equity in the recompense of good and evil to
beings who proved good or evil through necessity and not of choice.

Adversus Marcionem, ii. 5–6

---

[1] *ratio*, 'reason', 'rationality', 'principle'.   [2] 'et fieret proprietas boni in homine et
quodammodo natura', perhaps 'that there might be in man the proper quality, and, in a
sense, nature, of good'.   [3] *libripens*, 'weigher', perhaps 'taskmaster'.   [4] *de proprietate
boni*, perhaps 'good with the proper quality of goodness'.

(e) The Nobility of Flesh

[*Attacking Gnostic heretics who ascribed the creation of the material world, and hence of human flesh, to an inferior divinity.*] Now whatever the supreme God of each of those heretics may be, I should be justified in deriving the dignity of the flesh from him, since he gave consent to its production. For to be sure if he had not consented to its creation he would have forbidden it when he knew that it was taking place. So even according to those heretics the flesh is equally something derived from God. For whatever he has allowed to exist is part of his work . . . [*The rest of the material creation is transient, but not man.*] The other creatures were made for man, and were made inferior to him, and subjected to man by God. It was fitting that all these issued into being at a word of command, by the mere power of the voice; while man, as their lord, was fashioned by God's direct action. . . Notice also that man is properly called 'flesh', which was the earlier designation of man. 'God made clay from the earth into a man.'[1] Now he was man, who before was clay. 'And he breathed in his face the breath of life, and man', that is clay, 'was made into a living soul. . . .' Thus man was first a clay figure, then an entire man. I would call your attention to this in order that you may know that all God's purpose and promises to man are for the benefit not of the soul alone but of the soul and the flesh. . . .

(6) Let me then pursue my purpose, which is to do my best to claim for the flesh all that God conferred upon it in creating it, the flesh which then gloried in the fact that this poor clay had come into the hands of God, whatever they are, and was happy enough at the mere touch. . . . Think of God wholly occupied and absorbed in the task, with hand, sense, activity, forethought, wisdom, providence; and, above all, that love of his which was tracing the features. For in all the form which was moulded in the clay, Christ was in his thoughts as the man who was to be; for the Word was to be made clay and flesh, just as at that time earth was fashioned into man. . . . Some things are privileged to become nobler than their origin . . . gold is earth, as coming from the earth; but when it becomes gold it is a far different substance, more splendid and renowned than the lowly source from which it derives. So it was possible for God to purify the gold of our flesh from the dross of clay and to ennoble its condition.

De Resurrectione Carnis, 5–6

[1] Gen. ii. 7.

(f) The First Sin, through Discontent and Envy

I observe the birth of discontent in the devil himself when in the beginning he was discontented and vexed that the Lord God had subjected the whole of creation to man, his own image. For if the devil had suffered that contentedly[1] he would not have grieved; had he not grieved he would not have envied man: and envy was the cause of his deceiving man. . . . Then when the woman met him I may safely say that as a result of their conversation she was filled with a spirit infected with discontent; for it is certain that she would never have sinned, had she contentedly persisted in obedience to the divine command. Furthermore, she did not stop there, after her private meeting with the devil, but she was too discontented to keep silence in the presence of Adam, though he was not yet her husband and therefore not bound to listen: but she passed on to him what she had imbibed from the evil one. Thus another human perishes through the discontent of the one; and himself soon perished through his own discontent. . . . Here is the primal source of judgement and of sin; hence God is aroused to anger and man is induced to sin. . . . What offence is ascribed to man before the sin of discontent? He was blameless, the intimate friend of God, the husbandman of paradise. But when he succumbed to discontent he ceased to mind the things of God, he ceased to be content with heavenly things. Thenceforth man is bound to the earth, cast out from God's sight, and begins to be easily influenced, as a result of discontent, towards everything that is such as to offend God.   *De Patientia*, 5

(g) The Image and Likeness

[*In Baptism*] death is done away by the washing away of sins: for, of course, the removal of guilt removes the penalty. Thus man is restored to God, into 'his likeness', for he had of old been 'in his image'. The state of being 'in the image of God' relates to his form; 'in the likeness' refers to his eternity: for he receives back that Spirit of God which at the beginning he received from God's inbreathing, but which he afterwards lost through his transgression.   *De Baptismo*, 5 (*ad fin.*)

(h) Inherited Guilt

If the blessing of the fathers was destined to be transmitted to their posterity, before that posterity had done anything to deserve it, why

[1] *patientia*, here translated 'content', has no one equivalent in English, including, as it does 'patience', 'submission', 'discipline'.

should not the guilt of the fathers flow down to their sons, so that the transgression as well as the grace should spread through the whole human race? With this proviso, which was to be uttered later, that 'men shall not say, The fathers have eaten a sour grape and the children's teeth have been set on edge',[1] that is, 'the father shall not take upon himself the transgression of his son, nor the son the transgression of his father, but each man shall be guilty of his own transgression'.[2] This means that after the hardness of the people and the hardness of the law had been overcome, God's justice should then judge individuals and not the whole race. Yet if you would receive the gospel of truth you would discover to whom that saying refers which speaks of 'bringing home to the sons the transgressions of their fathers';[3] namely those who of their own accord applied the saying to themselves with, 'His blood on our head and on the heads of our sons'.[4] God's providence had already heard that, and made that judgement.

Adversus Marcionem, ii. 15

He says that he 'came to save what was lost'.[5] What do you suppose was lost? Man, without doubt. Wholly or partly? Wholly, to be sure: for the sin which was the cause of man's perdition was committed as much by the impulse of the soul, from concupiscence, as by the act of the flesh, in tasting. Thus it gave the whole man a criminal record,[6] and the result was that man deservedly incurred the full sentence of perdition.

De Resurrectione Carnis, 34

We have 'borne the image of the man of earth'[7] by our partnership in sin, participation in death, exile from paradise.   Ibid. 49

We who know the origin of man boldly lay it down that death comes to man not as a natural consequence, but as a consequence of a fault which was not itself natural. Now it is easy to use the word 'natural' of what seems to be attached to our condition, though accidentally, from our very birth. If man had been created expressly for death, then indeed death would be ascribed to 'nature', Further, that he was not created for death is proved by the Law itself which placed him under a conditional threat, and made death an event dependent on man's own choice. In fact, if he had not sinned he would not have died.

De Anima, 52

---

[1] Jer. xxxi. 29. Cf. Ezek. xviii. 2.   [2] Cf. Ezek. xviii. 20.   [3] Exod. xx. 5.   [4] Matt. xxvii. 25.
[5] Matt. xviii. 11.   [6] *elogio transgressionis inscripsit*, a technical term of criminal procedure: *elogium* was the record of offence, sentence, &c., or a warrant for arrest, or an entry on a charge sheet or a dossier.   [7] 1 Cor. xv. 49.

(j) Inherited Taint

Satan . . . we call the angel of evil, the contriver of all error, the corrupter of the whole world. Through him man was beguiled in the beginning to transgress the command of God, and therefore was consigned to death: and in the result he has infected the whole human race by their descent from him, transmitting to them his own damnation.

Testimonium Animae, 3

[*The expression 'children of wrath'*] makes it clear that sins, the lusts of the flesh, unbelief, anger, are imputed to the nature that is common to all men. That is because the devil has taken possession of human nature and infected it by implanting the seed of sin

Adversus Marcionem, v. 17

Let us suppose, with the Psychics,[1] that the early times had licence for all kinds of shamelessness; that the flesh enjoyed itself before the time of Christ—or rather was lost before it was sought by its Lord. It was not yet worthy of salvation, nor fit for the work of holiness. As yet it was ranked 'in Adam', ready to lust after anything attractive, setting its gaze on lower things, retaining its lascivious desires from [?the time of] the fig leaves.   *De Pudicitia*, 6

(k) Corruption begins at Birth. The Flesh is Neutral

All the qualities conferred on the soul at birth are even now obscured and spoiled by him who envied them in the beginning; to prevent their being clearly observed or rightly exercised. For a wicked spirit will be found attached to every man, lying in wait for him at the very gateway of birth; in fact it is invited to be present by all the superstitious practice [*among the heathen*] connected with child-birth. Thus all men are born with idolatry as midwife. . . . (40) So every soul takes its status 'in Adam' until it receives a new status 'in Christ'; until then it is unclean; and sinful, because unclean, receiving shame[2] from association with the flesh. For although the flesh is sinful, and we are forbidden 'to walk according to the flesh',[3] and its 'works' are condemned as 'lusting against the spirit',[4] and on account of the flesh men are censured as 'carnal', which is a disgrace, yet there is nothing disgraceful about the flesh, as such. For by itself the flesh has neither sense nor feeling so as

---

[1] The 'worldly', Tertullian's name for the orthodox Christians who allowed forgiveness of sin after baptism.   [2] Reading uncertain. Some editors insert a negative, which would make the passage more consistent with what follows; 'though not receiving shame'.
[3] Cf. 2 Cor. x. 2.   [4] Gal. v. 17.

to urge or command to sin. How could it? It is merely instrumental. . . .
Thus the flesh is reproached in the Scripture, because the soul cannot
act without it in the practice of lust, gluttony, drunkenness, cruelty,
idolatry, and the other works which are not feelings but actions. In fact,
sinful *feelings* which do not issue in acts are always ascribed to the soul.
'A man who has looked at a woman lustfully has already committed
adultery in his heart.'[1] On the other hand, what can the flesh do apart
from the soul, in the practice of virtue, justice, endurance, modesty? It
would be absurd to attach guilt to the flesh when you may not give it
credit for any goodness of its own. The agent of a crime is brought to
trial that the real culprit may bear a heavier load of guilt by the accusation of his instrument. *De Anima*, 39–40

(*l*) *The Corruption of Man's Nature: not Complete*

Besides the evil in the soul which is brought in by the intrusion of an
evil spirit, there is a prior evil which arises from the corruption of its
origin, an evil in a certain sense natural. For, as we have said, the corruption of nature is another nature, having its own god and father,
namely the author of the corruption. In spite of that there is also in the
soul that original good, the divine and genuine good, which is natural
in the true sense. For what comes from God is not so much extinguished as obscured. It can be obscured, because it is not God: it cannot be extinguished, because it comes from God. So that, as a light,
when its rays are interrupted by some obstacle, still remains; although it
is not seen, if the obstacle be opaque enough: so the good in the soul,
overcome by evil in proportion to the quality of that evil, either has its
light obscured and is not seen at all, or sends out its rays when it finds
a way through. Thus some men are very bad, and some are very good;
and yet all souls are one genus; there is some good in the worst, some
evil in the best. *Ibid.* 41

III. The Incarnation

(*a*) *Derivation from the Father*

But I derive the Son from no other source, but from the substance of
the Father; I describe him as doing nothing without the Father's will,
as receiving all power from the Father; how then can I be abolishing

[1] Matt. v. 28.

from the faith that monarchy[1] when I safeguard it in the Son, as handed down to the Son by the Father? Let this assertion be taken as applying also to the third degree of the Godhead, since I regard the Spirit as having come from no other source, but from the Father, through the Son. Have a care then that it is not rather you who abolish the monarchy in overthrowing its order and mode of working which is arranged in as many persons[2] as God wished. But so surely does the monarchy remain unimpaired, despite the introduction of a trinity, that it has to be restored by the Son to the Father . . . [Ps. cx. 1; 1 Cor. xv. 24, 27–28]. We see then that the Son is no detriment to the monarchy, although it is now vested in the Son, because it remains unimpaired while thus vested, and the Son will restore it unimpaired to the Father. . . . He who has delivered the kingdom, and he to whom he has delivered it, must needs be two.   *Adversus Praxean*, 4

(b) The Eternal Reason—Logos

Before all things existed God was alone. He was himself his own universe, his own place, everything. He was alone in the sense that there was nothing external to him, nothing outside his own being. Yet even then he was not alone; for he had with him something which was part of his own being, namely, his Reason. For God is rational and Reason existed first with him, and from him extended to all things.[3] That Reason is his own consciousness of himself. The Greeks call it *Logos*, which is the term we use for discourse;[4] and thus our people usually translate it literally as, 'Discourse was in the beginning with God', although it would be more correct to regard Reason as anterior to Discourse, because there was not Discourse with God from the beginning but there was Reason, even before the beginning, and because Discourse takes its origin from Reason and thus shows Reason to be prior to it, as the ground of its being.[5] Yet even so there is no real difference. For although God had not yet uttered his Discourse, he had it in his own being, with and in his Reason, and he silently pondered and arranged in his thought those things which he was soon to say by his Discourse. For with his Reason he pondered and arranged his thought and thus made Reason into Discourse by dealing with it discursively. To understand this more easily, first observe in yourself (and you are 'the image and likeness of God') that you also have reason in yourself,

[1] With reference to the 'Monarchians', who claimed that they alone upheld the unity of God, see pp. 122, 123 ff., 134–5, 137. [2] *nominibus*—'names'. [3] Reading *ab ipso ad omnia*. [4] *sermo*, translated in this extract as 'discourse', 'speech'. [5] *substantia*.

as a rational creature; that is, a creature not merely made by a rational creature, but given life from his very being. Notice that when you silently engage in argument with yourselves in the exercise of reason, this same activity occurs within you; for reason is found expressed in discourse at every moment of thought, at every stirring of consciousness. Your every thought is speech; your every consciousness is reason. You cannot but speak it in your mind, and while you are talking you encounter speech as your interlocutor; and that speech has in it the reason which you employ when thinking, when you converse with the speech by which you think when talking. Thus, in a sense, speech is in you as something distinct from yourself; by speech you talk in thinking, and think in talking. How much more fully does this happen in God, for your status is that of image and likeness of him. While he keeps silence he has within himself Reason, and, in that Reason, Discourse . . . which he made distinct from himself by reason of its activity within him.

(6) This mode of operation of the divine consciousness is revealed in the Scripture also under the title of Wisdom. . . . Notice that Wisdom speaks, as created as a second person: 'The Lord created me as the beginning of his ways, for his works' . . . [Prov. viii. 22]. That is, he created and begat his own consciousness. . . . When God first willed to create . . . he first produced the Word, which had within it its own inseparable Reason and Wisdom, so that all things might come to be through that by which they had been pondered and arranged, yes, and already made, in God's consciousness; all they lacked was to be openly apprehended and grasped in their own forms and concrete existences.[1]

(7) This then is the time when the Word takes upon itself its outward manifestation and dress, that is, sound and utterance, when God said 'Let there be light'. This was the entire nativity of the Word, when it proceeded from God, who created it for thinking with the title of Wisdom . . . and begot it to put the thought into effect . . . then the Word makes God his Father, since by proceeding from him he became the first-begotten Son: first-begotten, as begotten before all things; only-begotten, as begotten uniquely from the womb of his heart, as the Father bears witness in, 'My heart has thrown up a good Word'[2] . . . 'So', you say, 'you suppose that the Word is a concrete existent,[1] made up of spirit, wisdom, and reason.' Indeed I do. You refuse to consider him as a concrete, independent existent.[1] . . . 'For what is a

[1] substantia. [2] Ps. xlv. 1.

word', you will say, 'except sound and a noise produced by the mouth, and (as the grammarians tell us) pulsations of air, conveying an intelligible meaning when heard, but apart from that a mere insubstantial something, without body?' . . . [*the 'corporeity' of God, and therefore of his Word, quoted above*, pp. 104–5].   *Adversus Praxean*, 5–7

(c) 'Projection—Sun and Ray—Spring and River

[*Valentinus taught the 'projection',* προβολή, *of aeon from aeon, and the Logos doctrine may seem something of this kind.*] But with Valentinus the 'projections' are far removed from their author . . . with us, 'the Son alone knows the Father', 'has declared the Father's bosom',[1] 'has heard and seen all things in the Father's presence', . . . [*a cento of similar quotations*] 'For who knows the things that are in God, except the Spirit which is in him'.[2] Now the Word is formed by Spirit, and spirit is, so to speak, the body of the Word.[3] Therefore the Word is always in the Father; 'I in the Father'[4] and 'with the Father' . . . [John i. 1] and never separated or apart from the Father . . . [John x. 20]. This will be the 'projection' of truth, the safeguard of unity, by which we say that the Son was 'produced' from the Father, but not separated from him. For God produced the Word, as the Paraclete also teaches, as a root produces the shoot, a spring the river, the sun a ray: for these manifestations are 'projections' of those substances from which they proceed. I would not hesitate to call a shoot 'the son of a root', a river 'the son of a spring', a ray 'a son of the Sun'. For every original source is a parent, and what is produced is its offspring. Much more is this true of the Word of God, who has received the name of Son as his proper designation; but the shoot is not detached from the root . . . [&c.) nor is the Word detached from God. Thus in accordance with those analogies I confess that I speak of two, God and his Word, the Father and his Son. For root and shoot are two, but conjoined . . . [&c]. Everything that proceeds from anything must needs be another thing, but it is not therefore separate. When there is one other, there are two; where there is a third, there are three. The Spirit makes the third from God and the Son, as the fruit from the shoot is the third from the tree, the canal from the river the third from the source, the point of focus of a ray third from the sun. But none of those is divorced from the

---

[1] Tertullian, like some other early writers, interprets John i. 18 as 'the Son who is in the Father's bosom has declared it (*sc.* the bosom, i.e. his inward thoughts and nature)'.
[2] Cf. 1 Cor. ii. 11.   [3] 'Sermo spiritu structus est . . . sermonis corpus spiritus.' The point is lost in English; 'speech (the Word) is constructed by breath (the Spirit) . . . breath (spirit) is the body of speech (word)'.   [4] John xiv. 11.

origin from which it derives its own qualities. Thus the Trinity derives from the Father by continuous and connected steps; and it in no way impugns the monarchy while it preserves the reality of the 'economy'.[1]

Ibid. 8

(d) Distinction without Division

The Son is not other than the Father by separation from him but by difference of function, nor by division but by distinction: for the Father and the Son are not identical but distinct in degree. For the Father is the whole substance [of deity], while the Son is derivative and a portion of the whole. He himself confesses, 'The Father is greater than I am'.[2] And in the psalm it is sung that he has been subordinated by the Father 'a little on this side of the angels'.[3] So the Father is other than the Son, as being greater, as he who begets is other than the begotten, the sender than the sent, the creator than the agent of creation.   Ibid. 9

At first, when the Son was not yet manifest, God said, 'Let there be light, and light came into being'.[4] And the Word himself was straightway the 'true light which lights every man coming into this world',[5] and through him the light of the world came to be. Thenceforward God willed to create, and created, through the Word, with Christ as his assistant and minister.   Ibid. 12

(e) The Word in the Old Dispensation

[Revelations and theophanies in the Old Testament, and all God's dealings in judgement, were mediated by the Son.] For it was the Son who descended from time to time to have converse with men, from Adam to the patriarchs and prophets; in vision, in dream, 'in a looking-glass, in an enigma',[6] always preparing from the beginning that course which he was to follow out to the end.[7] Thus he was always learning, even as God, to have intercourse with men on earth, being none other than 'the Word' who was to be 'made flesh'. Now he was learning this in order that he might prepare the way of faith for us, to make it easier for us to believe that the Son of God has descended into the temporal world, seeing that we know that something of the kind had been done in times past. 'These things were written', as they were also done, 'on

---

[1] οἰκονομία, i.e. God's way of dealing with man and revealing himself.   [2] John xiv. 28.
[3] Ps. viii. 5.   [4] Gen. i. 3.   [5] John i. 9.   [6] 1 Cor. xiii. 12.   [7] Reading uncertain. Perhaps in fine, 'in the end', would consort better with 'from the beginning' and with 'the ends of the ages' (i.e. the consummation of history), below. And cf. Adversus Marcionem, ii. 27, 'ediscens . . . a primordio . . . quod erat futurus in fine'.

our behalf, on whom the ends of the ages have come.'[1] Thus already
he experienced human emotions . . . [*questioning, repenting, being angry,
&c., in the Old Testament*].   *Adversus Praxean*, 16

(f) The Two Natures

Therefore, learn with Nicodemus that 'what is born in flesh is flesh;
and what is born of the Spirit is spirit'.[2] Flesh does not become spirit,
nor spirit flesh; they can clearly exist in one person. Jesus consisted of
flesh and spirit; of flesh as man, of spirit as God. The angel at the time
proclaimed him Son of God, in respect that he was Spirit, keeping for
the flesh the title Son of Man. Thus also the Apostle confirms that he
was composed of two realities,[3] when he designated him the 'mediator
of God and man'.[4]   *Ibid.* 27

All that you demand as worthy of God will be attributed to the Father
who is invisible, inapproachable, serene—in fact what I may call the
God of the philosophers. All that you cavil at as unworthy will be
ascribed to the Son, who is seen, heard, approached; the agent and
servant of the Father, who combines[5] in himself man and God; God
in his works of power, man in his weaknesses, so that he may confer on
humanity as much as he withdraws from divinity; in fact, all that, to
your thinking, is my God's disgrace, is the mystery[6] of man's salvation.
God lived with men as man that man might be taught to live the divine
life: God lived on man's level, that man might be able to live on God's
level: God was found weak, that man might become most great. If
you disdain a God like this, I doubt if you can wholeheartedly believe
in a God who was crucified. But how perverse is your attitude towards
both the modes of the Creator. You call him judge, and you reprobate
as cruelty the strictness of the judge which matches the deserts of the
cases. You demand a God of supreme goodness; and then, when his
gentleness accords with his kindness and associates with man in lowli-
ness to suit man's poor capacities, then you cry this down as weakness.
You are satisfied neither with a great nor with a modest God; neither
with the judge nor with the friend.   *Adversus Marcionem* ii. 27

(g) The Son, in his Suffering, Distinct from the Father
[*The Monarchians who equate Christ with the Father make the Father die
on the Cross.*] This is blasphemy. Let it not be spoken. Let it suffice to say

---

[1] I Cor. x. 11.   [2] John iii. 6.   [3] *utriusque substantiae*.   [4] I Tim. ii. 5.   [5] *miscente*,
'mingling'—but the literal translation would be misleading.   [6] *sacramentum*, perhaps
'symbol' or 'bond' (both these meanings found in Cyprian).

that Christ the Son of God died; and died because it is contained in Scripture. For when the Apostle proclaims that Christ died, he feels the heavy responsibility of the assertion, and adds, 'according to the Scriptures', so as to soften the harshness of the pronouncement and to avoid presenting an obstacle to the hearer. Yet since in Jesus two natures are established, a divine and a human, while it is agreed that the divine is immortal, the human nature mortal, it is clear that when the Apostle says that 'Christ died', he is speaking in respect that he is flesh and man and son of man, not in that he is Spirit and Word and Son of God. He says that Christ, 'the anointed', died and thus makes it clear that what died was that which was anointed, that is, his flesh. . . . Therefore the Father did not suffer with the Son. Indeed they are afraid of direct blasphemy against the Father, and hope to alleviate by conceding that the Father and the Son are two persons, if, as they say, 'the Son suffers while the Father suffers with him'. Even here they are stupid. For to 'suffer with' is to suffer. If the Father cannot suffer he cannot 'suffer with' . . . It is as impossible for the Father to 'suffer with' as it is for the Son to suffer in respect of his divinity. 'But in what way did the Son suffer, if the Father did not suffer with him?' The answer is; the Father is distinct from the Son [in his humanity] not from [the Son in] his divinity. If a stream is contaminated . . . this does not affect the source, although there is no separation between source and stream.

Adversus Praxean, 29

(h) The Word Clothed in Flesh

[*Some Monarchians*] attempt to distinguish two beings in one person, the Father and the Son, saying that the Son is the flesh, that is, the man, Jesus; while the Father is the spirit, that is, God, Christ. Thus those who strive for the identity of the Father and Son are now beginning to divide them, rather than to make them one. . . . This sort of 'monarchy' distinguishing Jesus from Christ, they perhaps learnt from Valentinus. But . . . their 'Father' is described as Word *of* God, Spirit *of* God. . . . Who was the God born in flesh? The Word, and the Spirit, who was born with the Word in accordance with the Father's will. Therefore the Word was in flesh; but we must ask *how* the Word 'was made flesh', whether by transformation into flesh or by being clothed therewith. The latter, surely. We must believe that God's eternal nature precludes change or transformation. Transformation involves the destruction of what originally existed: what is transformed ceases to be what it was and begins to be something else. But God does not cease to be, nor can he be other than what he is: and the Word is God, and 'the Word of the Lord remains for ever',[1] that is, it continues in the same form. . . . It follows that his incarnation means that he comes to be in flesh and through flesh is manifested, seen, and handled. Other considerations demand this interpretation. For if he was incarnate by transformation and change of substance, Jesus would then be one substance made of two, of flesh and spirit, a kind of mixture, as electrum is an amalgam of gold and silver. Thus he would come to be neither gold (i.e. spirit) nor silver (i.e. flesh), sincet he one element is changed by the other and a third thing is produced. Then Jesus will not be God, since he ceases to be the Word, which was made flesh; nor will he be flesh, that is, man; for that which was the Word is not flesh in the true sense. Thus out of the two a thing is produced which is neither one nor the other, but a third something, very different from either. . . . We see a twofold mode of being,[2] not confused but conjoined in one person, Jesus, who is God and man. . . . And the proper quality of each substance remains so intact that the spirit carried out in him his own activities; the powers and works and signs: while the flesh underwent the experiences proper to it; hunger, when it met the devil; thirst, when with the Samaritan woman; weeping, for Lazarus; troubled even unto death; and, at the last, the flesh died.

Adversus Praxean, 27

(j) Jesus Forsaken by the Father

You find him crying out in his suffering, 'My God, my God, why hast thou forsaken me?'[3] Then, either the Son was suffering, forsaken by the Father, and the Father did not suffer; or, if it was the Father who was suffering, to what God was he crying? But this was the cry of flesh and soul (that is, of man), not of the Word and the Spirit (that is, not of God); and it was uttered for the very purpose of showing the impassibility of God who thus forsook his Son in delivering his humanity to death. This was the Apostle's meaning when he wrote, 'If the Father did not spare his Son':[4] and before him Isaiah declared, 'The Lord hath delivered him up for our sins'.[5] He forsook him in not sparing him, he forsook him in delivering him up. Yet the Father did not forsake the Son, for the Son entrusted his spirit into the Father's hands. In fact, he

---

[1] Isa. xlv. 8. [2] *duplex status*. [3] Matt. xxvii. 46. The Monarchians interpreted this as marking the departure from the man Jesus of the Christ-God. Early orthodox interpreters often came very near to this acceptation, e.g. Hilary of Poitiers, 'The voice of the human body proclaims the departure of the Word' (*Comm. in Matt.* 33, quoted in E. Evans, *Tertullian's Treatise against Praxeas*, 1948). [4] Rom. viii. 32. [5] Isa. liii. 6 (LXX).

thus entrusted it, and straightway died. For while the spirit remains in the flesh it is utterly impossible for the flesh to die. Thus to be forsaken by the Father was death to the Son. The Son therefore both dies at the Father's hand and is raised up by the Father according to the Scriptures.   Ibid. 30

(k) No Shame in Human Birth

[*Marcion's disparagement of the human body, and especially human birth, as unbecoming to the Son of God.*] At any rate Christ loved man, man who is solidified in the womb, amongst all the uncleanness, who issues through the parts of shame, who is reared by means of all the indignities of infancy. For his sake Christ descended, for his sake he preached, for his sake 'he humbled himself even unto death, the death of the cross'.[1] Certainly he loved him whom he redeemed at so great a cost. . . . Therefore in loving man he loved the process of birth also, and his flesh. Nothing can be loved apart from that through which it has existence. Take away the process of birth, and then show me the man: take away the flesh and show me whom Christ redeemed. If these constitute the man whom God redeemed, how can you represent them as humiliating to him, seeing that he redeemed them? Or unworthy of him, seeing that he would not have redeemed them, had he not loved them? He reforms our birth by a new birth from heaven; he restores our flesh from all that afflicts it; he cleanses it when leprous, gives it new light when blind, new strength when paralysed, when possessed by demons he exorcizes it, when dead he raises it to life. Is there then any humiliation in being born in flesh . . .?

(5) . . . Was not God really crucified? Did he not really die after real crucifixion? Did he not really rise again, after real death? If not, then Paul's determination was mistaken, 'To know nothing among you save Jesus crucified';[2] mistaken too his insistence on his burial, his emphasis on his resurrection. Then our faith also is mistaken, and our hope in Christ a mere illusion. . . . Spare us the one and only hope of the whole globe; for you are destroying the indispensable glory[3] of the faith. All that is unworthy of God is for my benefit. I am saved if I am not ashamed of my Lord. For he says, 'If anyone is ashamed of me, I shall be ashamed of him'.[4] Nowhere else do I find grounds for shame which may prove me, through 'despising shame',[5] to be nobly shameless

[1] Phil. ii. 8.   [2] 1 Cor. ii. 2.   [3] *decus*; another reading, *dedecus*, would give a paradox typical of Tertullian, 'the indispensable *shame* of our faith'.   [4] Matt. x. 33.   [5] Heb. xii. 2.

and happily foolish. The Son of God was born: shameful, therefore there is no shame. The Son of God died: absurd, and therefore utterly credible. He was buried and rose again: impossible, and therefore a fact. . . . Thus the quality of the two modes of being displayed the humanity and the divinity: born as man, unborn as God; in one respect carnal, in the other spiritual; in one respect weak, in the other exceedingly strong; in one respect dying, in the other living. The proper qualities of the two conditions, the divine and the human, are attested by the equal reality of both natures: with the same faith the Spirit and the flesh are distinguished; the works of power attest the Spirit of God;[1] the sufferings, the flesh of man . . . If the flesh with its sufferings was a figment, then the Spirit with its mighty works was unreal. Why do you cut Christ in half with a lie? He was wholly truth. Believe me, he preferred to be born than to be in part a lie.

De Carne Christi, 4–5

IV. The Atonement

The atonement by incarnation—reminiscent of the 'recapitulation' doctrine of Irenaeus—is expounded in the treatise *Adversus Marcionem*, ii. 27 (above, p. 122). The incarnation and passion as a demonstration of love is argued in *De Carne Christi*, 4 (above, p. 125 sq).

(a) The Eve–Mary antithesis

The devil had taken captive the image and likeness of God; but God restored it by a parallel process. For the word which was the architect of death found its way into the ear of Eve while she was still virgin: correspondingly the Word of God, which was the builder of life, had to be introduced into a virgin, that what had gone to destruction through the female sex should by the same sex be restored to salvation. Eve believed the serpent, Mary believed Gabriel; the one sinned by believing, the other by believing effaced the sin. But did Eve conceive nothing in her womb from the devil's word? She certainly did. For the devil's word was the seed for her, so that thereafter she should give birth as an outcast, and give birth in sorrow. And in fact she bore a devil who murdered his brother; while Mary gave birth to one who should in time bring salvation to Israel, his own brother after the flesh and his own murderer. Thus God sent down into the womb his Word,

---

[1] i.e. the Spirit of his divinity. 'Spirit' is used by Tertullian of the divine nature.

the good brother, that he might wipe out the memory of the wicked brother. It was necessary that Christ should come forth for man's salvation from that place into which man had entered when already condemned.   Ibid. 17

Cf. the antithesis in Irenaeus, above, pp. 82–3.

(b) Satisfaction

Tertullian's is the first recorded use of the term *satisfactio* in this context. But by it he means reparation by penitence and good works: it does not refer to the work of Christ.

[*Of sin after repentance.*] A man who by repentance of his sins had begun to make satisfaction to the Lord, will give satisfaction to the devil by repenting of his repentance; and will be the more hateful to God, the more acceptable he is to God's rival.   *De Poenitentia*, 5

The king of Babylon, when he had been an exile from human form for seven years in squalor and filth,[1] recovered his kingdom by offering the sacrifice of the patience of his body and (what is more to be desired by man) gave satisfaction to God.   *De Patientia*, 13

[*The prodigal*] recalls God, his Father, makes satisfaction to him by returning, and receives his original clothing, namely that status which Adam lost by transgression.   *De Pudicitia*, 9

[*The object of fasting*] is that a man should make satisfaction to God by means of the ground of his offence, namely the prohibition of food, and thus by a reverse process should, by abstinence, revive the salvation which he had extinguished by gluttony, when he rejected the many things that were allowed for the sake of one which was forbidden.
                                                     De Ieiunio, 3

(c) Ransom

In our prescribed prayer, when we say to the Father, 'Lead us not into temptation' (and what temptation greater than persecution?), since we ask from him exemption from temptation, we acknowledge that it comes from him. For the following clause is, 'But deliver us from the evil one', that is to say, 'Do not lead us into temptation by handing us over to the wicked one'. For then we are delivered from the devil's hands, when we are not handed over to him for temptation. The legion

[1] Cf. Dan. iv. 25 ff.

of the devil had had no power over the herd of swine, had he not obtained it from God; so far is he from having power over God's sheep. I may affirm that even the bristles of the pigs were then numbered with God, not to speak of the hairs of the saints. If the devil seems to have any rights as his own it is over those who do not belong to God, the nations having been accounted by God 'a drop from a bucket, as dust of the threshing floor, as spittle',[1] and so thrown open to the devil 'with vacant possession' as it were. But he has not power, of his own right, over those of God's household; for the examples of his power attested in Scripture show on what occasions and for what purposes this authority is given. The right to tempt [test] is granted for the purpose of proving . . . [e.g. Job] or reprobation, like the authority given to an executioner . . . [e.g. Saul, 1 Sam. xvi. 4] or of restraining . . . [e.g. Paul, 2 Cor. xii. 7] . . . The Apostle also 'handed over Phygellus and Hermogenes to Satan that they might be corrected so as not to blaspheme'.[2] You see then that the devil, so far from having power in his own right, rather receives it at the hands of God's servants.

De Fuga in Persecutione, 2

Man's ransom, then, does not imply that the powers of evil have acquired any rights over man, so that the ransom should be paid to them. For Tertullian ransom is a metaphor for rescue, conveying also the idea of cost to the rescuer as in the next passage.

[*May a Christian buy off persecution?*] To ransom with money a man whom Christ redeemed with his own blood, is not this unworthy of God and his ways of dealing with man? For he 'spared not his own Son'[3] . . . 'he was led as a sheep to slaughter', &c.[4] . . . and delivered up to 'death, the death of the cross'.[5] And all this that he might win us away from our sins. The sun made over the day of our purchase, our release was effected in the underworld, our contract made in heaven;[6] the eternal gates were raised up, that the king of glory might enter, who has bought man from the earth, nay, from the underworld, to set him in heaven. What kind of man, then, is he who strives against Christ, nay, who depreciates and soils the merchandise which he acquired at so great a price, the price of his most precious blood? Why, it were better to flee than to be reduced in price, for that is what happens if a

---

[1] Isa. xl. 15 (LXX).   [2] 2 Tim. i. 15.   [3] Rom. viii. 32.   [4] Isa. liii. 7.   [5] Phil. ii. 8.
[6] There is some obscurity here, but the metaphors are all commercial: *sol cessit diem emptionis* has perhaps a pun on *cessit*, the sun 'retired' at the crucifixion, *emancipatio apud inferos* is clearly connected with some form of the 'Harrowing of Hell' myth, *stipulatio in coelis* just possibly refers, by contrast, to Isa. xxviii. 15, 'with hell have we made a contract'.

man puts on himself a lesser value than did Christ. And the Lord ransomed him from the angelic powers who rule the world, from the spirits of iniquity, from the darkness of this world, from eternal judgement, from everlasting death: while you are bargaining for him with an informer, or soldier, or some petty thief of an official, on the sly,[1] as if you were passing stolen goods; whereas it is man whom Christ redeemed, yes, and set at liberty, before the eyes of all the world . . .

Ibid. 12

(d) The Death of Christ Essential

[*The Gnostic Apelles asserted that Christ assumed 'angelic' flesh, and therefore did not need to be born.*] No angel ever descended for the purpose of being crucified, of experiencing death, of being raised from the dead. If there was never such a cause for angels to be embodied, there you have the reason why they did not receive flesh through the process of birth. They did not come to die, therefore they did not come to be born. But Christ was sent to die, and therefore he had of necessity to be born, that he might be able to die; for it is the rule that only that dies which is born. Nativity and mortality are connected by a mutual bond.

De Carne Christi, 6

He who did not really suffer did not suffer at all; and a phantasm could not suffer. Thus the whole work of God is overthrown. The death of Christ, which is the whole essence and value of the Christian religion, is denied.

Adversus Marcionem, iii. 8

V. The Holy Spirit

(a) His Relation to Father and Son

For the statement that the Holy Spirit is derived from the Father through the Son see *Adversus Praxean*, 8 (above, pp. 120-1).

The Son promises that after his ascension to the Father he will request the Father for the Paraclete also, and he will send him; and note that he is 'another'. Now we have already stated[2] in what sense he is 'other'. Further, 'He will take of mine, as I of what is the Father's.'[3] Thus the connexion of Father and Son, of Son and Paraclete, makes three who cohere in a dependent series. And these three are one *thing*,

---

[1] lit. 'under the fold of the toga'. [2] Especially in chapter 9, quoted above, p. 121. 'Other' means 'distinct', not 'divided'. [3] John xiv. 16, xvi. 14 f.

not one person;[1] in the same way as the saying 'I and the Father are one thing'[2] refers to unity of essential being,[3] not to singularity of number . . .   *Adversus Praxean*, 25

(b) Spirit Apparently Identified with Word

He who was to be born of a virgin was announced by the angel himself, as destined to be Son of God: 'The Spirit of God shall come upon thee and the power of the Highest shall overshadow thee, therefore that which shall be born of thee shall be called a holy thing, the Son of God.'[4] They [sc. the Monarchians[will wish, indeed, to cavil even here, but 'truth will prevail'.[5] 'Of course', they say, 'the Son[6] of God is identical with God, and the power of the Highest is the Highest.' And they have no compunction about supplying an implication which, if correct, would have been stated in Scripture. For on whose account did the angel scruple to say quite openly, 'God shall come upon thee, and the Highest shall overshadow thee'? But in saying, 'The Spirit of God', although the Spirit of God is God,[7] still he is not directly called God, and therefore he wishes a portion of the whole godhead to be understood, which was to receive the name of Son. Spirit of God here must be the same as the Word. For just as when John says, 'The Word was made flesh',[8] we understand the Spirit also where the Word is mentioned, so also here we recognize the Word when the Spirit is named. For the Spirit is the substance of the Word, and the Word is the activity of the Spirit,[9] and the two are a unity.[10]   *Ibid.* 26

Other passages also seem to identify the Word and the Spirit; and two of them are quoted below. But 'Spirit' in Tertullian may mean the Third Person, or the divinity common to the whole Trinity, since 'God is Spirit'. There is doubtless some confusion in his thought: and in the last passage this is aggravated by his curious interpretation of Luke i. 35, and his desire to harmonize it with John i. 14.

The Spirit of God and the Word of God and the Reason of God, the Word of Reason and the Reason of the Word and the Spirit [of the Word],[11] Jesus Christ who is both. . . .[12] Jesus Christ has been approved

---

[1] *tres unum sunt, non unus.*   [2] John x. 30.   [3] *substantiae unitatem.* I Cor. iii. 8, where 'planter and waterer' are said to be *unum*, suggests that Tertullian's exegesis is fanciful. It is certainly anachronistic.   [4] Luke i. 35.   [5] I Esdras iv.41: *magna est veritas et praevalet* (sic).   [6] The argument seems to require 'the Spirit of God'.   [7] Reading uncertain. MSS. have *etsi spiritus dei*, which is just intelligible 'though he is Spirit of God'. The emendation translated, *etsi spiritus dei deus*, was suggested by Fulvius Ursinus in the sixteenth century.   [8] John i. 14.   [9] See note 3, p. 120.   [10] *unum*, 'one thing'.   [11] The bracketed words should apparently be supplied.   [12] Presumably 'Spirit and Word-Reason (i.e. Logos)'.

as the Spirit of God, the Word of God, the Reason of God; the Spirit, by which he had power; the Word, by which he taught; the Reason, by which he came.   *De Oratione*, 1

We are sure that Christ always spoke in the prophets, as the Spirit of the Creator . . . who from the beginning was heard and seen in the Father's name, as the Father's representative . . . the Word and Spirit, that is the Christ of the Creator . . . the Son and Spirit and substance of the Creator.   *Adversus Marcionem*, iii. 6

[*God speaks in the plural, 'Let us make man'*] because already there was attached to him his Son, a second person, his own Word; and a third, the Spirit in the Word.   *Adversus Praxean*, 12

[*The ascended Christ who is to come in glory*] has meanwhile poured out the gift which he has received from the Father, the Holy Spirit, the third name of divinity, the proclaimer of the one monarchy, and at the same time the interpreter of the economy[1] (if a man will accept the discourses of his New Prophecy[2]) and the 'leader unto all truth',[3] the truth which is in the Father and the Son and the Holy Spirit, according to the Christian revelation.[4]   Ibid. 30 (*ad fin.*)

(c) Montanism and the Holy Spirit

[*At the Transfiguration*] Peter 'did not know what he was saying'.[5] How was that? Was it because of mere aberration, or in accordance with the rule (as we have maintained[6] in support of Prophecy) that a state of ecstasy, of being 'out of one's mind', accompanies the operation of grace? For a man who is 'in the spirit', especially when he beholds the glory of God and when God speaks through him, must inevitably lose consciousness, overshadowed as he is by the Divine Power.[7]
                                      Adversus Marcionem, iv. 2

The Paraclete has 'many things to teach'[8] which the Lord reserves for him, according to his pre-arranged plan. First, he will bear witness to Christ and our belief about him, together with the whole design of God the Creator; he will glorify him and remind us of him; and then when the Paraclete has thus been recognized in the matter of the primary rule of faith, he will reveal many things which relate to discipline.

[1] i.e. God's ways in relation to men. [2] i.e. Montanism. [3] John xvi. 13. [4] *sacramentum*— 'mystery', 'teaching'. [5] Luke ix. 33. [6] Jerome mentions a lost work of Tertullian 'On Ecstasy', in six books. [7] Cf. the story of a Montanist ecstasy in *de Anima* 9, above, pp. 108–9. [8] John xvi. 13.

These revelations will be attested by the consistency of their proclamation; although they are new, in the sense that they are only now revealed, and burdensome, because they are not at the moment being
borne: but still they are the demands of the same Christ, who said that
he had many more things which were to be taught by the Paraclete,
things just as burdensome to men today as to those [*disciples*] by whom
they were not yet being borne.   *De Monogamia*, 2

(d) The New Discipline of the Paraclete

[*In forbidding remarriage*] the Paraclete introduces no novelty: he defines
what he has hinted at, he makes demands which he has hitherto for-
borne. If you think over these matters you will easily reach the conclusion that since the Paraclete could have forbidden marriage altogether, much more had he the right to proclaim against remarriage,
and that it is the more credible that he should have restrained what he
might properly have abolished. You will realize this if you can understand what Christ wishes. In this matter you ought to recognize the
Paraclete as your 'advocate' [*i.e. your supporter*], in that he excuses your
weakness the necessity for complete continence ... (4) ... We have
proved this point, that the discipline of monogamy[1] is nothing new
nor a thing imported into Christianity, but rather an ancient and characteristic discipline of Christians; so that you must regard the Paraclete
as rather a restorer than an innovator.   Ibid. 3 (*ad fin.*)–4

Christ abolished the commandment of Moses ... why then should
not the Paraclete have cancelled the indulgence granted by Paul ... ?[2]
'Hardness of heart'[3] held sway until the coming of Christ; let weakness
of the flesh bring its reign to an end with the coming of the Paraclete.
The New Law abolished divorce ... the New Prophecy abolished
second marriage.   Ibid. 14

The Lord has sent the Paraclete for this very purpose, that discipline
might progressively be guided, ordered, and brought to perfection
by his representative, the Holy Spirit. ... The province of the Holy
Spirit is just this; the guidance of discipline, the interpretation of Scripture, the reformation of the intellect, the advance towards better
things. All things have their proper time and await their due season. ...
So righteousness was at first rudimentary, when nature feared God;
then by means of the Law and the Prophets it progressed to infancy;

---

[1] i.e. the right to marry once only.   [2] Cf. 1 Cor. vii. 9, 39.   [3] Matt. xix. 8.

thereafter through the Gospel it reached the fervour of adolescence; and now through the Paraclete it is being established in maturity.

De Virginibus Velandis, 1

(e) Montanism and the Church of the Spirit

Now what of that church of yours, wordly man?[1] This power [*of 'binding and loosing'*] will attach to spiritual powers, to an apostle or prophet as far as they show the personal qualities[2] of Peter. For the Church is properly and primarily the Spirit, in whom is the trinity of the one divinity, the Father, Son, and Holy Spirit. The Spirit makes the assembly of the Church, which the Lord established in three persons. And thus the whole number of those who have leagued together in this faith is given the status of the Church by the Church's author and consecrator. Therefore the Church will indeed remit sins; but it will be the Church of the Spirit, by the agency of a spiritual man, not the Church as a number of bishops. For the right of judgement belongs to the Lord, not the servant; to God himself, not to the priest.

De Pudicitia, 21

(f) Examples of 'New Prophecy'

But, you say, the Church has power to remit sins? I have the more reason for acknowledging and asserting this, in that I find the Paraclete saying, through the New Prophets, 'The Church has power to remit a sin; but I will not do it, lest they commit other sins'. Ibid.

That was an illuminating remark which the Paraclete made through the prophetess Prisca about those people [*who deny bodily resurrection*], 'They are things of flesh, and they hate the flesh'.

De Resurrectione Carnis, 11

VI. The Trinity

(a) 'Economy'

We have always believed (and all the more so now, as better instructed through the Paraclete, the 'leader into all truth') in one only God, yet

---

[1] 'Psychic': see note, p. 116. [2] *secundum personam Petri*: cf. earlier in the same chapter, 'Whence do you claim for the Church the right [*to remit "capital" sins*]? Is it because the Lord said to Peter, "On this rock, &c. . . ."'? Do you presume that this power of "binding and loosing" has flowed down to you, i.e. to all the church which is closely related to Peter? How absurd you are, in overthrowing and changing the manifest intention of the Lord who conferred this on Peter *as a person (personaliter)'* . . . [*examples from Acts ii–xv*].

[handwritten marginalia: Economy]

[handwritten marginalia: gnostic word in later times, H.S. proceeds from Father]

subject to the 'dispensation' (which is our translation of 'economy') that the one only God has also a Son, his own Word who has proceeded from himself. . . . The perversity [*of Praxeas*] considers that it has possession of the pure truth in thinking it impossible to believe in the unity of God without identifying the Father, the Son, and the Holy Spirit; failing to see that the one may be all in the sense that all are of one, that is through unity of substance; while this still safeguards the mystery of the 'economy', which disposes the unity into a trinity, arranging in order the three persons, Father, Son, and Holy Spirit, though these are three not in quality,[1] but in degree, not in substance but in form, not in power but in manifestation;[2] of one substance, one quality, one power, because God is one and from him those degrees and forms are assigned in the name of Father, Son, and Holy Spirit. How they admit of plurality without division the following discussions will show.   *Adversus Praxean,* 2

(b) The Distribution of the Monarchy

Now all the simple people (I will refrain from calling them thoughtless and morally deficient)—and they are always the majority of believers—are dismayed by the idea of 'economy'. For the rule of faith brings them from the polytheism of the world at large to the one and only God, and they do not understand that while believing the unity of God they must believe it together with his 'economy'. They assume that the plurality and distribution of the trinity imples a division of the unity; but the truth is that the unity in deriving the trinity from itself is not destroyed thereby, but dispensed. And so they make a to-do about our 'preaching of two or three gods', and claim that they are worshippers of One God: not seeing that a unity unreasonably contracted produces heresy, while a trinity reasonably distributed constitutes the truth. 'We maintain the monarchy,' they say. And the Latins, even the manual labourers, produce the phrase 'sole-sway',[3] with such elocution that you are might suppose their comprehension of monarchy as accurate as their pronunciation. But while the Latins are eager to enunciate 'monarchy', even the Greeks refuse to understand the 'economy'. Whereas if I have collectd any small store of the two languages I am aware that 'monarchy' means simply the rule of one individual; but that monarchy, because it is the rule of one, does not preclude the

---

[1] *status.*   [2] *species, perhaps* 'concrete individuality'.   [3] reading uncertain. MSS. 'ita solium ipsum vocaliter exprimunt Latini, et tam opifices.' I retain *solium,* which most editors alter to *sonum,* but accept Rigault's conjecture *etiam opifices.*

monarch, who enjoys that rule, from having a son . . . or administering his monarchy by agents of his own choosing. I could go further,
and say that no sovereignty is so much the possession of one person, to
such a degree a *mon*archy, as not to be administered through other
closely related persons, whom it has looked out for itself as its function-
aries. And if the possessor of monarchy has a son, the monarchy is not
straightway divided, it does not cease to be a monarchy, if the son also
is brought in as partner in it; it continues to belong primarily to him
by whom it is shared with the son, and continues to be a monarchy
when it is held by two who are so united.[1] Therefore, if the divine
monarchy is administered by so many legions and armies of angels . . .
[Dan. vii. 10] it does not therefore cease to be the rule of one. . . . It
would be strange then if God should seem to undergo division and
dispersion in the assignment of Son and Holy Spirit to second and
third place, having their share in the substance of the Father; a division
and dispersion which he does not suffer in that crowd of angels, alien
as they are from his substance. Do you consider that the component
parts of monarchy, its outward proofs, its instruments, and all that
gives a monarchy its strength and prestige—do you consider these are
destructive of it, as the rule of one? Of course not. I wish you would
concern yourself with the *sense* and not with the *sound* of a word. You
should realize that the destruction of a monarchy means the imposition
of another rule of its own rank and quality, and consequently a rival to
it: when another God is brought in, in opposition to the Creator . . .
[*as with Marcion*].   Ibid. 3

See also *Adversus Praxean*, 8 (quoted above, pp. 120–1).

All the Scriptures give clear proof of the Trinity, and of its distinctions;
and it is from these that our principle is deduced, that speaker and
spoken of and spoken to cannot be thought of as one and the same,
since neither perversity nor deception is consonant with God . . . [*e.g.*
Isa. xlii. 1, xlix, 6, lxi. 1, &c.]. Notice also the Spirit speaking from the
standpoint of a third person, concerning the Father and the Son. 'The
Lord said unto my Lord', &c. . . . [*and* Isa. xlv. 1, liii. 1]. These are
only a few examples, but the distinction of the Trinity is quite clearly
displayed. For there is the Spirit himself, who utters the statement: the
Father, to whom he speaks: the Son, of whom he speaks. . . .
                                                                Ibid. 11

---

[1] reading *unitis* (*conj.* Engelbrecht) for MSS. *unicis*.

[*In Gen.* i. 26 *and* iii. 22, *God uses the plural* 'Let us make . . .', 'in our image', 'as one of us'.] There was attached to him the Son, a second person, his Word; and a third person, the Spirit in the Word: therefore he used the plural in speaking. . . . In whose company was he making man? And in whose likeness? With the Son, who was to put on human nature; with the Spirit, who was to sanctify man: he was speaking with these as his ministers and agents, as a result of the unity of the Trinity. In fact the text which follows distinguished the persons; 'and God made man; he made him in the image of God'. Why not 'in his own image' if the maker was one sole person? . . . He had, as his model, the Son who was to become man, a man more genuine and real, and who thus caused the man, who was at that time to be formed out of clay, to be called his image, as 'the image and likeness of the real'.[1] . . . [*Tertullian proceeds, with some inconsistency*] There you have [*in creation*] two beings, one saying, 'Let it be made', the other creating, I have already explained how you must take 'other', in the sense of 'person' not of 'substance', as marking distinction, not division. Yet although I always maintain one substance in three coherent persons, still I am bound to call the giver of a command 'other' than the executor; the sense of the texts demands this.　　　　　　　　　　　　　　　　　　　　*Adversus Praxean,* 12

We who by the grace of God have insight into the situations and contexts of the Scriptures (especially as we are disciples not of men but of the Paraclete) declare that there are two beings, the Father and the Son (and even three, with the Holy Spirit) according to the principle of 'economy', which introduces plurality, lest (and this is your perverse conclusion) it be believed that the Father was born and died; an inadmissible belief, since it is not part of the tradition. Yet we have never given vent to the phrases 'two Gods', or 'two Lords'; not that it is untrue that the Father is God, the Son is God, the Spirit is God; each is God. But we believe this inasmuch as in time past [*i.e. in the Old Testament*] two were proclaimed as Gods and two as Lords, so that when Christ came he should be acknowledged as God and be called Lord, because he is the Son of him who is God and Lord. . . . But when Christ came and was recognized by us as that same person who in time past had made plurality in the godhead, being made a second from the Father and a third with the Spirit, and when the Father was made more fully manifest through him; then the name of God and Lord was restored to unity. . . .　　　　　　　　　　　　　　　　　　　Ibid. 13

[1] Heb. ix. 24.

When he says, 'I am not alone, but I and the Father who has sent me',[1] does he not show that there are two persons, two and at the same time inseparable? In fact, the whole of his teaching was this, that there are two, inseparable.   Ibid. 22

[*When Christ prayed to the Father*] You have here the Son on earth, the Father in heaven. This is not separation, but the divine disposition. Now we know that God is within the depths, and exists everywhere[2] but in might and power; and the Son being indivisible from the Father is everywhere with him. Yet in the 'economy' the Father willed that the Son should be found on earth, himself in Heaven.   Ibid. 23

   See also *Adversus Praxean*, 25 (above, pp. 129–30).

Thus as the Word of God is not God himself, whose Word he is, so also the Spirit, though called God, is not God himself, whose Spirit he is. Nothing is identical with its possessor. Clearly when something is 'from someone', and so is his, as coming from him, it can be something of the same quality as its source and possessor. Therefore the Spirit of God is God, and God's Word is God, as coming from God, but it is not identical with God from whom he is. That which is God of God, as a concrete existent[3] will not be God himself, but God in the sense of being of the substance of God himself, as a concrete existent,[3] as a portion of the whole; much less will the power of the Highest, . . . a mere attribute, be identical with the Highest.   Ibid. 26

   See also *Adversus Praxean*, 29 (above, pp. 122–3).

[*Monarchianism is mere Judaism*] God willed to make a new revelation[4] so that his unity might be believed in a new way, through the Son and the Spirit; so that God, who had in the past been proclaimed through the Son and the Spirit, without being thus understood, might now be openly recognized in his own proper names and persons.   Ibid. 31

VII. The Church

(a) The Apostolic Tradition

Jesus Christ our Lord . . ., while he lived on earth, himself declared what he was, what he had been, what was the Father's will which he was carrying out, what was the conduct he laid down for man: all this

---

[1] John viii. 16.   [2] Cf. Ps. cxxxix. 8.   [3] *substantiva res.*   [4] *sacramentum.*

he declared either openly to the people or privately to the disciples, from whom he chose twelve leading ones to be his close companions, appointed as leaders of the nations . . . [*The Apostles*] first bore witness to the faith in Jesus Christ throughout Judaea and founded churches there: and then went out into the world and published to the nations the same doctrine of the same faith. In the same way they established churches in every city, from which the other churches borrowed the shoot of faith and the seeds of doctrine, and are every day borrowing them so as to become churches. It is because of this that these churches are reckoned as apostolic, as being the offspring of apostolic churches. Every kind of thing must needs be classed with its origin. And so the churches, many and great as they are, are identical with that one primitive Church issuing from the Apostles, for thence they are all derived. So all are primitive and all apostolic, while all are one. And their unity is proved by the peace they share, by the title of 'brethren', by the mutual bond of hospitality; privileges which have no other ground than the one tradition of the same revelation.

Hence then the ruling which we lay down; that since Jesus Christ sent out the Apostles to preach, no others are to be accepted as preachers but those whom Christ appointed. . . . Now the substance of their preaching, that is, Christ's revelation to them, must be approved, on my ruling, only through the testimony of those churches which the Apostles founded by preaching to them both *viva voce* and afterwards by their letters. If this is so, it is likewise clear that all doctrine which accords with these apostolic churches, the sources and origins of the faith, must be reckoned as truth, since it maintains without doubt what the churches received from the Apostles, the Apostles from Christ, and Christ from God. . . . We are in communion with the apostolic churches because there is no difference of doctrine. This is our guarantee of truth. But if any of these heresies are so bold as to insert themselves into the apostolic age that they may therefore appear to have been handed down from the Apostles, because they existed under the Apostles, we can say: 'Let them display the origins of their churches; let them unroll the list of their bishops, in unbroken succession from the beginning, so that the first bishop of theirs shall prove to have as his precursor and the source of his authority one of the Apostles or one of the apostolic men, who without being an Apostle continued with the Apostles. This is how the apostolic churches report their qualifications; as the church of the Smyrnaeans relates that Polycarp was appointed by John, the church of the Romans that Clement was set up by Peter.[1] Similarly, the other churches also point to those whom they regard as transmitters of the apostolic seed, since they were appointed to their bishoprics by Apostles. Even if these heresies should devise such a pedigree, it will be no help to them. For their very teaching, when compared with that of the Apostles, will proclaim by its diversity and contrariety that it originates neither from an Apostle nor from an apostolic man; for the Apostles would not have diverged from one another in doctrine; no more would the apostolic man have put out teaching at variance with that of the Apostles. . . . This test will be applied to those churches of a later date, which are daily being founded. Though they cannot therefore produce an Apostle or an apostolic man for their founder, still, if they unite in holding the same faith, they equally are reckoned apostolic because of the kinship of their teaching. . . . If you would care to exercise your curiosity in the business of your salvation, make a tour of the apostolic churches, in which to this day the actual thrones of the Apostles preside in their stead, where their authentic writings are read, reproducing the voice of each of them and recalling their faces. If Achaea is nearest to you, there you have Corinth: if you are not far from Macedonia, there is Philippi and the Thessalonians. If you can make your way to Asia, there you have Ephesus: while if you are close to Italy, there you have Rome, where we [*in Africa*] have our authority ready to hand. How fortunate that Roman church, on which the Apostles poured out all their teaching and their blood as well; where Peter matched the Lord's passion, where Paul was crowned with a death like John's [*the Baptist's*]; where John the Apostle, after being plunged in blazing oil[2] without suffering hurt, was 'relegated'[3] to an island. Let us see what she has learnt, what she has taught, what tokens of friendship[4] she has passed on to the African churches also. *De Praescriptione Haereticorum*, 20, 21, 32, 36

(b) The Apostolic Lineage

In fine, if it is agreed that what is earlier is truer, and what is there from the beginning is earlier, and that what issues from the Apostles is from the beginning; it will equally be agreed that what has been held

[1] Contrast Irenaeus, pp. 90–1.   [2] Tertullian seems to be the earliest authority for this traditional exploit, commemorated in the Western Church on 6 May, *St. John ante portam Latinam*.   [3] The technical term for exile to a particular place, here the island of Patmos.   [4] *contesseraverit: tesserae* were tokens interchanged between friends. Above (p. 138) Tertullian speaks of *contesseratio hospitalis* between churches. But there is probably another suggestion: *tessera* also means 'watchword', i.e. the Christian creed (the Greek equivalent being σύμβολον, the technical word for the creed).

sacred in the churches of the Apostles is that which has been handed
down from the Apostles. Let us see what 'milk' the Corinthians have
imbibed from St. Paul, by what rule the Galatians have been corrected, what the Philippians read, and the Thessalonians, and the
Ephesians; yes, and what the Romans proclaim, our nearest neighbours,
for to them Peter and Paul bequeathed a gospel signed with their own
blood. We have also churches which are fosterlings of John. For although Marcion rejects the Apocalypse, still the succession of bishops
when traced back to the source will be established with John as founder.
In this way the noble lineage of other churches also is recognized.

Adversus Marcionem, iv. 5

I have preferred [*the authority of*] those churches which were founded
either by the Apostles themselves or by apostolic men. . . . We cannot
reject a custom which we cannot condemn, for it is not imported from
outside, since it is not those outside who have this custom, but men
with whom we share peaceful relations and the name of brotherhood.
We share with them one faith, one God, the same Christ, the same
hope, the same mysteries[1] of the font; in short, we are one Church.
And so whatever belongs to our brothers is ours too . . .

De Virginibus Velandis, 2

Contrast with all this the Montanist doctrine of the 'Spiritual Church', above
p. 133.

(c) The Rule of Faith of the Roman Church

There is only one rule of faith, unchangeable and unalterable: that of
believing in one only God, omnipotent, the creator of the world; and
his Son Jesus Christ, born of the Virgin Mary, crucified under Pontius
Pilate; on the third day raised again from the dead; received into
heaven; now sitting at the Father's right hand; who will come to
judge living and dead, through the resurrection also of the flesh.

De Virginibus Velandis I

Now with us the rule of faith is this: it is believed that God is one, who
is none other than the creator of the world, who produced all things
from nothing by his Word, . . . that Word is called his Son; he was
seen by the patriarchs and ever heard in the prophets; and lastly was
brought down by the spirit and power of the Father into the Virgin
Mary, and made flesh in her womb, and born of her, and lived as

[1] *sacramenta.*

Jesus Christ; that thereafter he proclaimed the new law and the promise of the kingdom of heaven; that he performed works of power; was crucified; on the third day rose again; was snatched up to heaven; and sat down at the Father's right hand; that he sent as his representative the power of the Spirit to guide believers; and he will come with glory to take the saints to the enjoyment of life eternal and of his promises, and to sentence the profane to everlasting fire, after the raising up of both kinds, with the restoration of the flesh.

De Praescriptione Haereticorum, 13

Let us see what the Roman church has passed on to the African churches. It acknowledges one God, the creator of the whole order of things; and Jesus Christ of the Virgin Mary, Son of God the Creator; and the resurrection of the flesh. Ibid. 36

We believe one only God . . . , who has a Son, his Word, who proceeded from himself, by whom all things were made; he was sent by the Father into a virgin, and was born of her, man and God, Son of man and Son of God, named Jesus Christ; he suffered, died, was buried, according to the Scriptures; was raised again by the Father; and taken back to heaven; and sits at the Father's right hand; who will come to judge living and dead; who thereafter, according to his promises, has sent from the Father the Holy Spirit, the Paraclete, the sanctifier of the faith of those who believe in the Father, the Son and the Holy Spirit.

Adversus Praxean, 2

(d) Christian Worship

At this point I shall reveal the real activities of the Christian 'faction'; I have refuted the allegations of evil; I shall now display its virtuous practices. We are a body united by a common religious profession, by a godly discipline, by a bond of hope. We meet together as an assembly and congregation that as an organized force we may assail God with our prayers. Such violence is acceptable to God. We pray also for emperors, for their ministers and those in authority, for man's temporal welfare, for the peace of the world, for the delay of the end of all things. We are compelled to refresh our memories of our sacred writings, if any special feature of the present time requires warning or reconsideration. In any case we nourish our faith with these holy utterances, we stimulate our hope, we establish our confidence; and at the same time we strengthen our discipline by the inculcation of the precepts. In the

same place also exhortations, rebukes, and godly censures are administered. For judgement is passed with great seriousness, as is natural with
men who are convinced that they are in the sight of God: and you have
the most impressive anticipation of the judgement to come when a man
has so sinned as to be banished from participation in prayer and meeting and all sacred intercourse. Our presidents are approved elders, and
they obtain that honour not by purchase but by their tested character;
for there is no price attached to any of the things of God. Though we
have a kind of money-chest, it is not for the collection of official fees,
as if ours were a religion of fixed prices. Each of us puts in a small
donation on the appointed day in each month, or when he chooses, and
only if he chooses, and only if he can; for no one is compelled and the
offering is voluntary. This is as it were the deposit fund of kindness.
For we do not pay out money from this fund to spend on feasts or
drinking parties or inelegant 'blow-outs', but to pay for the nourishment and burial of the poor, to support boys and girls who are orphan
and destitute; and old people who are confined to the house; and those
who have been shipwrecked; and any who are in the mines, or banished
to islands, or in prison, are pensioners because of their confession, provided they are suffering because they belong to the followers of God.

But it is principally the practice and application of such affection as
this that puts a brand of disgrace upon us with certain people. 'See',
they say, 'how they love one another'; for they themselves hate one
another. 'See how ready they are to die for each other'; for they will
more readily kill each other. They find fault with us too because we
call each other 'brother'. And the reason for their calumny is just this,
I feel sure; that among them every name of relationship is assumed in
mere affectation. . . .[1]

What wonder then if a love so great is expressed in a common feast.
I say this because you jeer at our humble meals as being extravagant
as well as infamously criminal. . . . The name of the feast explains the
reason for it; it is called by the Greek name for love [agape]. . . . Before
reclining they taste first of prayer to God; enough is eaten to satisfy
hunger; as much is drunk as befits the temperate. They take their fill
by the standards of those who remember that even during the night
they have to worship God; their conversation is that of men who know
that God hears them. After washing of hands and the lighting of lamps

[1] Perhaps 'as a cloak for wickedness'. Clement of Alexandria (*Stromateis*, ii. 9) and
Minucius Felix (ix) tell us that Christian brotherly love and the appellations 'brother' and
'sister' gave rise to gross slanders about Christian conduct. The sinister suggestion of
frater and *soror* is attested in Petronius and Martial.

individual members are invited to stand out and sing[1] to the best of their ability either from the sacred scriptures or something of their own composing; which gives a test of how much they have drunk. The feast ends, as it began, with prayer. . . . Who has ever been harmed by our assemblies? We are in our meeting just what we are when we are dispersed; we are the same as a body as we are as individuals; we hurt no one; we bring sorrow to no one. When the decent and the good meet together, when the kindly and the pure assemble, that should not be called a faction but a solemn assembly.

Apologeticus, 39

VIII. The Sacraments

(a) Sacraments in General

So violent are the designs of perversity[2] for shaking faith, or even for utterly preventing its reception, that it attacks faith on the very principle on which it is based. For there is really nothing which so hardens men's minds as [*the contrast between*] the simplicity of the divine works which are seen in the act, and the magnificence which is promised in the effect: so that in this matter just because there is such simplicity, such absence of display, or of any novel elaboration, in fact an absence of any costly trappings, when a man is plunged and dipped in water to the accompaniment of a few words, and then rises again not much cleaner, if at all; just because of this it seems to men incredible that eternal life should be won in this manner. . . . We also marvel; but we marvel because we believe. Incredulity marvels, but does not believe. For it marvels at the simple acts as if they were ineffectual, at the magnificent results as if they were impossible. And though you may be quite right about this simplicity, the divine pronouncement has sufficiently answered both objections by anticipation. 'God has chosen the foolish things of the world to confound its wisdom'[3] and 'Things very difficult with men are easy with God'.[4] For if God is both wise and powerful (and even those who ignore him do not deny this) he has good reason for deciding to use, as the materials of his working, the opposites of wisdom and power, that is, foolishness and impossibility. For every virtue has its ground in the things which call it forth.

De Baptismo, 2

[1] Perhaps 'lead in prayer and thanksgiving'. Cf. *Didache*, (above, p. 57) where after the Eucharist (? *Agape*) a prophet may give thanks *extempore*; and Justin, *Apology I*, lxvii (above, p. 62), where the 'president' gives thanks' 'to the best of his power'.   [2] This becomes quasi-technical for 'heresy', or 'irreligion'.   [3] 1 Cor. i. 27.   [4] Matt. xix. 26.

It is utterly impossible for the soul to attain salvation unless it has believed while in the flesh; so truly does salvation hinge on the flesh. In
fact, when the soul is admitted to God's company it is the flesh which
makes that admission possible. The flesh indeed is washed that the soul
may be cleansed; the flesh is anointed that the soul may be consecrated; the flesh is signed [*with the cross*] that the soul too may be fortified; the flesh is shadowed by the imposition of hands that the soul
also may be enlightened by the Spirit; the flesh feeds on the body and
blood of Christ that the soul may be nourished on God. They are united
in this service; they cannot be separated in their reward.

De Resurrectione Carnis, 8

(b) Baptism, including Unction

[*Answering the objection that the Lord did not baptize.*] His disciples used
to baptize as his ministers, as John the forerunner had baptized before,
and with the same baptism of John. Let no one think it was with another baptism, for there is no other except that of Christ, which came
later; for to be sure the baptism of Christ could not be then given by
his disciples, inasmuch as the glory of the Lord was not yet fully completed, nor the efficacy of the font established through the passion and
resurrection; because our death cannot be annulled except by the Lord's
passion, nor can our life be restored without his resurrection.

De Baptismo, 11

Necessary to Salvation

. . . [*In former times salvation was by faith alone.*] Granted that in former
days, before the Lord's passion and resurrection, there was salvation
through bare faith; still, now that faith has been enlarged to include
belief in his birth, passion, and resurrection, there is an enlargement
added to the mystery,[1] namely, the sealing of baptism: the clothing,
as it were, of the faith which before was bare.   Ibid. 13

Does not bestow the Holy Spirit

Not that in the waters we gain the Holy Spirit; but when we have been
cleansed in water under the influence of the angel[2] we are made ready
for the Holy Spirit. Here also a type has gone before: for in this way
John was beforehand the forerunner of the Lord 'preparing his ways';
in the same way the angel who presides over baptism 'makes the paths

---

[1] *sacramentum*, perhaps here meaning 'means of grace'.   [2] A reference to the pool of
Bethesda, John v. 1–9.

straight' for the Holy Spirit who is to come after, by the washing away of sins, which faith obtains when sealed in the Father, the Son and the Holy Spirit.   *Ibid.* 6

The Holy Spirit, according to Tertullian, is given by Unction and Imposition of Hands—see below, p. 147.

The Seal of Preceding Repentance

The sinner must weep over himself *before* receiving pardon, because the time for penitence is the time when he is in danger and fear. Now I do not deny that the divine benefit of the abolition of sins is utterly sure to those who are about to enter the water; but we have to exert ourselves in order to reach that point. For if your repentance is so faithless, who will afford you the sprinkling of any kind of water? It is indeed easy to approach it by stealth and by your assertions to deceive the man who is appointed to perform this office; but God takes care of his treasure and does not allow the unworthy to take it by surprise. . . . That washing is the sealing of faith, and the faith is begun and commended by faithful penitence. It is not for this that we are washed, that we may cease from sin, since in heart we have been washed already. . . . Otherwise, if we cease from sin as a result of the waters of baptism, we put on innocence of necessity, not of freewill. Now whose is the more excellent kind of goodness: that of the man who *cannot*, or of the man who *will* not, be evil? Of him who is ordered to be free from wickedness, or of him who delights to be free? And so the hearers [*catechumens*] ought to desire baptism, not to claim it hastily. For he who desires it, honours it; he who claims it hastily, disdains it . . . the former longs to deserve it, while the latter promises it to himself as his due . . .

De Poenitentia, 6

Contrast with these last passages the statement in *Adversus Marcionem*, i. 28 that the benefits of baptism are remission of sins, deliverance from death, regeneration, the attainment of the Holy Spirit.

Should not be administered rashly and not to infants

But those whose duty it is to baptize know that baptism is not to be bestowed rashly . . . [*the Ethiopian* (Acts vii) *was a special case and so was Saul of Tarsus* (Acts ix)] . . . And so it is more salutary to delay baptism according to the state and character of each person; but especially in the case of infants. For why is it necessary for sponsors also to be involved in danger, who may fail to fulfil their promises through mortality and may be disappointed by the development of a bad character [*in the child*]? The Lord indeed says, 'Forbid them not to come to me'.[1] 'Let them come', then, when they are growing up: let them come if they are learning, if they are being taught whither they are coming; let them become Christians when they are able to know Christ. Why does the age of innocence hasten to the remission of sins? ... For no less reason the unwed should be deferred; for temptation is waiting for them alike in the case of virgins because of their maturity, as in the case of the widowed because they are without partners. Let them wait until they marry, or until they are strengthened for continence. Those who understand the importance of baptism will rather fear its attainment than its delay; unimpaired faith is certain of salvation.

De Baptismo, 18

Note that this is connected with Tertullian's views on post-baptismal sin: see p. 153.

Heretical Baptism is Invalid

Heretics have no fellowship in our discipline; for clearly their debarment from our communion witnesses that they are outsiders; ... they and we have not the same God, or the same Christ, nor one baptism, because not the same ... [*Referring to* Eph. iv. 5 ff., *misquoted* 'one God, one baptism, one church in the Heavens'.]   Ibid. 15

The Ceremonies of Baptism

The minister: see *De Baptismo*, 17, quoted, p. 149, below.
The time:

The Passover affords a more solemn day for baptism; for then it was the Lord's passion, into which we were baptized, was completed ... [*symbolism of 'man bearing a pitcher of water'*] ... After that, Pentecost ... But every day is the Lord's: every hour, every time, is suitable for baptism; if there is a difference in the *solemnity*, there is no distinction in the *grace*.   Ibid. 19

The preparation:

Those who are to enter upon baptism must pray with repeated prayer, fasts and kneelings and vigils; and with confession of all their past sins.
Ibid. 20

[1] Mark ix. 39.

The consecration of the water:

[*The primeval 'hovering' of the Spirit typifies the baptism.*] Thus the nature of water, sanctified by the Holy One, receives the power of sanctifying . . . therefore it makes no difference whether a man be washed in sea, freshwater stream or spring, lake, or tub. . . . All waters . . . after the invocation of God attain the sacramental power of sanctification; for the Spirit straightway comes down upon them from the heavens and is upon the waters sanctifying them by his own power; and being thus sanctified they are imbued at the same time with the power of sanctifying. . . . The spirit and the flesh share in guilt. Therefore when the waters have been as it were medicated through the intervention of the angel[1] the spirit is physically washed and the body spiritually cleansed in the same waters.   Ibid. 4

Renunciation and trine immersion:

In the presence of the congregation and under the hand of the president we solemnly swear that we renounce the devil and his pomp and his angels. Then we are thrice immersed, making somewhat fuller reponses than those appointed by the Lord in the Gospel. Then we are taken up[2] and taste first a mixture of milk and honey. And for a week from that day we abstain from our daily ablutions.   *De Corona*, 3

Unction and Laying on of Hands

After this when we have come out of the font, we are thoroughly anointed with consecrated oil.   *De Baptismo*, 7

Thereafter the hand is laid upon us, invoking and inviting the Holy Spirit through the act of blessing.   Ibid. 8

(c) The Eucharist

[*Interpreting the parable of the prodigal son.*] He receives the ring for the first time when on interrogation he sets his seal to the covenant of faith and so thereafter feeds on the richness[3] of the Lord's body, that is, on the Eucharist.   *De Pudicitia*, 9

[*Symbolic interpretation of the goats of the Day of Atonement; the one driven out standing for Christ in his Passion*] while the other goat offered for sins and then given to the priests of the temple for a meal bears witness to his

[1] Cf. John v. 4; and p. 144, above.   [2] *suscepti:* a Roman father 'took up' his child to acknowledge it as his own.   [3] Literally 'fatness'—the 'fatted calf'.

second manifestation, whereby after all sins have been atoned the
priests of the spiritual temple, that is, the Church, might enjoy as it
were a kind of sacrificial feast.　　　　　*Adversus Marcionem*, iii. 1

But the same figure in *Adversus Judaeos*, 14 seems to refer to the 'second
coming' in the sense of the final consummation, and that is perhaps the meaning
here.

The flesh feeds on the body and blood of Christ that the soul may be
fattened on God.　　　　　　　　　*De Resurrectione Carnis*, 8

'Give us this day our daily bread' we should understand in a spiritual
sense. Christ is our bread because Christ is our life and bread is life.
'I am the bread of life', he says; and a little before, 'The word of the
living God which descended from heaven, that is bread'.[1] Moreover,
his body is acknowledged as being in the bread: 'This is my body'.
　　　　　　　　　　　　　　　　　　　　De Oratione, 6

We take the sacrament of the Eucharist . . . in meetings before day-
break and only from the hand of the presidents. We make oblations
for the dead, and for birthdays, on the anniversaries . . . We are concerned to prevent any of our wine or bread being dropped to the
ground.　　　　　　　　　　　　　　　　　*De Corona*, 3

[*The dangers when a Christian woman has a heathen husband.*] Your husband will not know what it is that you taste secretly before you partake
of food.[2] Even if he knows that it is bread he does not believe it to be
that which it is said to be.[3]　　　　　　　　　*Ad Uxorem*, ii, 5

The Body of Christ—Literally interpreted

[*The faithful grieve*] that a Christian should touch the Lord's body
with hands which have supplied bodies for demons. . . . What wickedness! The Jews laid hands on Christ but once; these men offer violence
to his body every day.[4]　　　　　　　　　　　*De Idololatria*, 7

The Sacrifice

Many people think that they ought not to take part in the prayers of
sacrifice [*i.e. the Eucharist*] on station days [*i.e. fast days*], on the ground
that the fast must then be broken by reception of the Lord's body.

---

[1] John vi. 33, misquoted.　[2] *ante omnem cibum*, which might mean 'before every meal'.
[3] Or 'does he not believe it to be what it is said to be?', referring to heathen calumnies
about the Eucharist.　[4] This may be evidence of daily communion; but more probably
it is rhetorical for 'repeatedly'.

Are we to suppose that the Eucharist cancels a devotion vowed to God? Does it not rather bind it to God? Will not your fast be the more solemn if you have stood at God's altar? When the Lord's body has been received and reserved[1] both points are secured—participation in the sacrifice and performance of the duty.   *De Oratione*, 19

Apparently Symbolic Interpretation

[*The discourse in* John. vi. 53–63.] He makes the word of his discourse to be the giver of life, because that word is spirit and life; he says the same of his flesh, because 'the Word became flesh'. Therefore for the sake of obtaining life we must hunger for the word, devour it with our hearing, chew it over with our intellect, digest it with our faith . . .

De Resurrectione Carnis, 37

He took the bread and distributed it to the disciples, making it his own body by saying, 'This is my body'; that is, the symbol[2] of my body . . . [Jer. xi. 19 (LXX), '*Let us cast wood into his bread*', *a mysterious prophecy (sacramentum) of the crucifixion.*]   *Adversus Marcionem*, iv. 40

. . . bread, by which he represents[3] his own very body.   Ibid. i. 14

IX. The Ministry

On the *episcopal succession* see the passage from *De Praescriptione Haereticorum*, 32, quoted p. 139, above.

(a) The Bishop in Baptism

The supreme priest (that is, the bishop) has the right of conferring baptism; after him the presbyters and deacons, but only with the bishop's authority, on account of their honour in the Church;[4] for when this is preserved, peace is preserved. Otherwise the laity also have the right (for what has been received by all alike can be given by all alike; unless only bishops, priests, and deacons have now the name of disciples). The Lord's word[5] should not be debarred from anyone. . . . But how much more is the discipline of reverence and humility incumbent on laymen (since it also befits their superiors), so as not to arrogate

---

[1] Perhaps to be taken home; cf. the passage from *Ad Uxorem* above.   [2] 'Modern man means by "symbol" something which is not that which it stands for. In earlier times it denoted something which somehow *was* what it symbolized.'—Harnack.   [3] Probably meaning 're-presents', 'makes present', as elsewhere in Tertullian.   [4] *propter honorem ecclesiae*, perhaps 'for the honour of the Church', i.e. to preserve good order.   [5] i.e. his command to baptize.

to themselves the duty assigned to the bishops. Emulation is the mother of schisms. 'All things are permitted, but not all things are expedient',[1] says the most holy Apostle. Let it suffice, then, to exercise your right in cases of necessity, when the special nature of place, occasion, or of the person concerned compels it . . . [*The spurious* Acts of Paul and Thecla *represent Thecla as baptizing.*] How very likely that one who consistently refused to allow a woman even to learn [1 Cor. xiv. 35] should have granted a female authority to teach and baptize!

De Baptismo, 17

(b) The Clergy and the Laity

[*On second marriage.*] It would be idle for us to suppose that what is forbidden to priests is allowed to the laity. Are not laymen also priests? The Scripture says, 'He has made us a kingdom also, and priests, for his God and Father'.[2] The distinction between the order of clergy and the people has been established by the authority of the Church, and by the honour which is hallowed by the special bench of the order. So that where there is no bench of the ecclesiastical order, you offer and baptize, and are your own priest, by yourself. But where there are three persons, though they be laymen, there is a church. Each man 'lives by his own faith', and 'there is no 'class-distinction' with God'.[3] . . . If then you have the right of priesthood in yourself, in cases of necessity, you must accept also the discipline of the priesthood. Do you offer, do you baptize, being a digamist?[4] How much more heinous is it for a digamous layman to exercise priestly functions, when a digamous priest is inhibited from the exercise of his ministry! . . . It is God's will that we should all be in a fit state to administer his sacraments at any time and in any place.

De Exhortatione Castitatis, 7

With this teaching on the 'priesthood of the laity' contrast the following, written before Tertullian became a Montanist.

(c) Casual Ordinations among Heretics

The appointments of the heretics are careless, frivolous, capricious. Now they set up neophytes, now those engaged in secular pursuits, now apostates from us. . . . Advancement is nowhere easier than in the rebels' camp; just to be there is to be certain of promotion. Thus one

---

[1] 1 Cor. vi. 12.   [2] Rev. i. 6.   [3] Rom. ii. 11, 13.   [4] i.e. a widower who has married again.

man is a bishop today, another tomorrow: a man is a deacon today,
tomorrow a reader: today a presbyter, tomorrow a layman; for they
even attach priestly functions to laymen.

De Praescriptione Haereticorum, 41

(d) Widows

I know for a fact that in another place a virgin not yet twenty years
old has been admitted into the order of widows. If the bishop had been
obliged to give her some relief, he could surely have provided it in
some other way, without such violation of discipline, and have avoided
the scandal in the Church of such a miracle—I might almost say a
monster—as a widow-virgin. And she was all the more a portent in
that she did not veil her head even in her status of widow, thus denying
that she was either a virgin or a widow, although having the rank of a
widow and the name of a virgin. But she sits there unveiled; and for
this she has the same authority as for being there as a virgin; on that
bench[1] to which women are not elected until after the age of sixty, if
they have been married to one husband, and have also borne and
brought up children: this is to ensure that they have been trained by
experience of all human affections to know how to help other women[2]
by advice and consolation, and, apart from that, that they have passed
through all the trials by which feminine virtue can be tested. Thus a
virgin can never gain any honour from that situation.

De Virginibus Velandis, 9

[*A man wanting to marry again*] may perhaps plead that his house is
lonely. As if one wife would supply company for a man when on the
point of flight! He certainly has the right to take a widow;[3] in fact it is
permitted to take more than one 'wife' of this kind.

De Monogamia, 16

But the rights and duties of women were limited:

A woman may not speak, nor baptize, or 'offer' [*sc. the Eucharist*], nor
claim the right to any masculine function, still less to the priestly office.

De Virginibus Velandis, 9

[1] Apparently these orders had their special seats in church; cf. the 'bench of clergy', above,
p. 150.   [2] Widows would thus appear to combine the status of alms-women (cf. 'relief',
above) with that of 'district visitors'.   [3] Did widows act as housekeepers for elderly
widowers? There seems no evidence. Or was it a charitable act to give them a home?

But they might prophesy:

The Apostle shows that women have the right to prophesy, by making a woman wear a veil when prophesying. *Adversus Marcionem*, v. 8

(e) Synods of the Church

Throughout Greece these councils of the representatives of all the churches are held at appointed places. By means of these synods all the more important questions are dealt with by common discussion; and this representation of the whole Christian community is celebrated with great solemnity. *De Jejunio*, 13

I would concede your point if the writing of the 'Shepherd' [*i.e. Hermas*] had won a place in the divine Testament; if it had not been judged apocryphal and spurious by every council of churches—including your own.[1] *De Pudicitia*, 16

X. The Discipline of the Church

(a) Censure and Excommunication

We are a body united by our religious profession, by our godly discipline, by the bond of hope. . . . [*In our assembly for worship*] we have exhortations, admonitions, and godly censure. For judgement is administered by us with great gravity, as is natural with men who are convinced that they are in the sight of God; and you have the most impressive anticipation of the judgement to come when a man has so sinned as to be banished from participation in prayer and meeting and all sacred intercourse. *Apologeticus*, 39

But it will be said that some of our Christians depart from the rules of our discipline: in that case they are no longer reckoned as Christians among us. Ibid. 46

(b) All Sins Remissible

Therefore for all sins, whether committed by the flesh or by the spirit, whether by deed or will, he who has appointed a penalty by means of judgement has also promised pardon by means of penitence. . . . That penitence, O sinner, hasten to embrace as a shipwrecked man clutches at the protection of some plank. When you are sunk in the waves of sin this will raise you up and bear you on to the harbour of the divine mercy. *De Poenitentia*, 4

[1] But in *De Oratione*, xii, 'Hermas' is quoted as if authoritative.

(c) One Repentance after Baptism

Because God foresees these poisons [*sc. the devil's temptations with which he assaults baptized Christians*], although the gate of forgiveness has been shut and fastened with the bolt of baptism, he has still allowed some opening to remain. He has stationed in the vestibule a second penitence to open to them that knock;[1] but only once, because it is for the second time; it can never open again, because the last time it opened in vain.

Ibid. 7

(d) Public Penitence

This second and only remaining penitence is so critical a matter that the testing of it is correspondingly laborious; it is not enough for it to be witnessed by mere admission of guilt; it has also to be carried out in action. This action is more commonly expressed and spoken of under its Greek name, *exomologêsis*, by which we confess sin to the Lord; not indeed as if he were ignorant, but inasmuch as the process of satisfaction is set in motion by confession, and by confession penitence is produced, and by penitence God is appeased. And so *exomologêsis* is a discipline consisting in prostration and humiliation, imposing on the offender such a demeanour as to attract mercy. With regard also to the very dress and food of the penitent this discipline enjoins him to go about in sackcloth and ashes, to cover his body in the squalor of mourning, to cast down his spirit, with grief, to exchange his sins for harsh treatment of himself; to have no acquaintance with any food or drink but the plainest, and this not for his stomach's sake but his soul's; in general, to nourish prayers with fasting, to groan, to weep and moan day and night to the Lord his God, to prostrate himself before the presbyter, and to kneel before God's dear ones;[2] to invoke all the brethren as sponsors of his prayer for mercy. The purpose of this *exomologêsis* is to enhance penitence, to honour God by showing dread of the peril [*of his anger*]; by itself pronouncing judgement on the sinner to act as a surrogate for God's indignation; and by temporal affliction, I would not say to frustrate, but to cancel eternal punishment. Thus in prostrating the sinner it raises him up; in making him squalid it renders him clean; in accusing and condemning him it gives him absolution. Be assured that God will spare you in proportion as you do not spare yourself.

Ibid. 9

[1] Cf. Matt. vii. 7. [2] Or 'before God's altars', reading *aris dei* for MSS. *caris*. But the context seems to require persons.

(e) The Papal Claim to forgive Mortal Sins

That Supreme Pontiff,[1] that Bishop of Bishops, issues an edict; 'I absolve the sins of adultery and fornication for those who have done penance'! . . . Where will this liberality be published? On the doors of houses of vice, I suppose, under the signs of their trade? That kind of 'penance' should be announced at the actual scene of the sin! That pardon should be on view at the place where men will enter in the hope of it! But this edict is read in the churches; it is pronounced in the Church, the Church which is a virgin! Let such a proclamation be far removed from the bride of Christ!

De Pudicitia, 1

And yet you bring the penitent adulterer into the church to beg for readmission into the brotherhood. . . . He is in a hair shirt, covered in ashes, in a condition of shame and trembling: you make him prostrate himself in public before the widows, before the presbyters, seizing the hem of their garments, licking their footprints, catching hold of them by their knees; and for this man you use all your aids to compassion, and you preach like the 'good shepherd' and 'blessed Papa' that you are.

Ibid. 13

(f) Mortal and Venial Sins

There are certain sins of daily occurrence to which we are all liable. For who escapes such sins as unjustified anger, even until after 'the sun has gone down'; or physical violence, or thoughtless slander, or heedless swearing, or breaking promises, or lying—from shame or compulsion? In our business, in our daily tasks, in earning our living, in what we see and hear, how great are the temptations that meet us! So that if there were no pardon for such faults, no one would attain salvation. But for these there will be pardon through the intercession of Christ with the Father. But there are other sins very different from these, as being too serious and ruinous to receive pardon. Such are murder, idolatry, fraud, denial [*sc. of Christ*], blasphemy and, of course, adultery and fornication, and any other violation of 'the temple of God'.[2] Christ will no more intercede for those: he who has been born of God will never commit them: If he has committed them he will not be a son of God.   *Ibid.* 19

The power of binding and loosing given to Peter had no reference to

---

[1] Either Zephyrinus, 202–18, or Callistus, 218–23.   [2] *Adversus Marcionem*, iv. 9 gives seven capital sins: idolatry, blasphemy, murder, adultery, fornication, false witness, fraud.

capital sins. The Lord had bidden him pardon his brother even when he sinned against him seventy times seven times: he surely would not have commanded him after that to bind, that is to retain, any thing, unless it might be sins committed by a man against the Lord, not those against his brother. Since offences against man are forgiven, it is implied that sins against God are not to be remitted. Ibid. 21

(g) The Martyrs' Supposed Authority to Forgive Sins

Let the devil find you fortified and armed with concord: for your peace means war for him. Some who have not this peace in the Church are wont to beg it from the martyrs in prison. Therefore you ought to have it in yourself and to cherish and guard it that you may be able perchance to supply it to others. Ad Martyres, 1

With this contrast a passage written when Tertullian had become a Montanist:

But you now fully bestow this power [sc. of forgiveness] on these martyrs of yours. As each after his 'confession' puts on his mild bonds in this new fashion of custody, straightway the adulterers flock around him; the fornicators come to him; they are most eager to gain access to the prison who have lost the right of entrance to the church. . . . Though the sword be now suspended above the martyr's head; though his body be stretched upon the cross; though he be tied to the stake for the lion's prey; though he be tied to the wheel and the fire heaped beneath him; suppose him, I say, in the secure possession of his martyrdom; yet who permits a man to pardon the sins which have been reserved to God? . . . Let it suffice for the martyr to have purged his own sins; . . . who but the Son of God ever redeemed another's death by his own? De Pudicitia, 22

(h) Christians in the World: Military Service

Now the question is raised whether a believer can betake himself to military service, and whether the military may be admitted to the faith, even private soldiers and all the lower ranks, who are not under the necessity of performing sacrifices or administering capital punishment. There is no congruity between the divine and the human *sacramentum*, between the standard of Christ and the standard of the devil, the camp of light and the camp of darkness . . . the Lord in disarming Peter unbelted every soldier from that time forth.

De Idololatria, 19

But contrast these passages:

We sail with you, we serve in the army with you, and till the ground
with you . . .   *Apologeticus*, 42

Marcus Aurelius in his letters testifies that on a famous occasion the
drought in Germany was dispelled by a shower obtained through the
prayers of the Christians who happened to be in the army. . . .[1]

Ibid. 5

We have filled every place of yours, cities, islands, villages, townships,
market-places, the army camps. . . .   Ibid. 37

(*j*) *Christians and Public Offices*

Therefore that sect [*sc. the Christians*], seeing that it commits none of
these crimes which are generally found in the case of illicit factions,
should not merely receive milder treatment but should be granted the
status of a tolerated faction.[2] For, if I am not mistaken, the motive
for the prohibition of factions is based on a careful regard for public
order, that the community may not be split into parties, a state of things
which might easily result in disturbances in elections, meetings, councils, assemblies, and even in public entertainments, by the contention
of rival interests, especially at a time when men have begun to make
money by offering their services for acts of violence. But with us all
ardour for glory or position has grown cold and we have no compulsion to form associations for this end; nor is anything more alien to us
than political activity. We acknowledge only one universal commonwealth, the whole world.   Ibid. 38

[*Comparison of Christianity and philosophy.*] If I am to dispute about restraint of ambition, look at Pythagoras aiming at despotism at Thurii,
and Zeno at Priene: the Christian does not aspire even to the aedileship.

Ibid. 46

A discussion lately arose whether a servant of God should undertake
the administration of any position of dignity or power, if he could keep
himself unharmed from every kind of idolatry, either by some grace

---

[1] The story of the *legio fulminatrix* is told in Eusebius, *Historia Ecclesiastica*, v. 5, who cites
Tertullian and Apollinaris, Bishop of Hierapolis. An opportune shower is attested by Dio
Cassius, lxx. 8; but the Antonine column credits it to Jupiter Pluvius; and Marcus Aurelius
did not favour the Christians, in spite of Tertullian's claim. There is a full discussion of the
legend in Lightfoot, *Apostolic Fathers*, Part II, i. 471–6.   [2] *factio licita.*

or by his adroitness . . . [as Daniel and Joseph]. Let us believe that it is possible for a man to succeed in going through the show of any office in purely nominal fashion, avoiding sacrifices, or the lending of his authority to sacrifices; without contracting for victims, or assigning the care of temples; nor seeing to the incomes of temples; nor giving public entertainments[1] at his own or at the public expense, or presiding at the giving of them; without proclaiming or announcing any solemnity; without even taking an oath; moreover (and these are matters which belong to the exercise of power) without sitting in judgement when the life or character of anyone was at issue (for you might suffer him to judge about money), without condemning[2] or precondemning[3] in such cases; binding no one, imprisoning no one, torturing no one: if it is credible that this is possible. . . . [connexion of magistrates' dress and insignia with idolatry] . . . All the powers and dignities of this world are not only alien from God but hostile to him.

De Idololatria, 17

The tract De Idololatria deals with the various occupations and practices connected with idolatry which are therefore forbidden to a Christian; they include idol-making, the adorning of temples, astrology, the profession of schoolmaster, swearing by idols, the adorning of houses with lamps and garlands; and even the observance of customary days of the financial year, because connected with heathen divinities.

(k) Monogamy

When by the will of God the husband has died, the marriage is also dead by God's will. Why should you restore what God has brought to an end? . . . How greatly second marriages detract from faith, and what a hindrance they are to sanctity, is declared by the discipline of the Church and the ruling of the Apostle who does not allow the twice married to preside,[4] and does not suffer a widow to be admitted to the order unless she has been 'the wife of one man'.[5]

Ad Uxorem, i. 7

I have heard a very subtle line of argument from the other side. The Apostle, they say, allowed a second marriage inasmuch as it is only the members of the clergy whom he binds with the yoke of monogamy.

---

[1] spectacula are forbidden to a Christian: 'We renounce all your shows . . . There is nothing said or seen or heard among us that has to do with the madness of the circus, the licentiousness of the theatre, the cruelty of the arena, the useless activity of the wrestling school'. Apologeticus, 38, cf. De Spectaculis, passim. [2] i.e. by judgement. [3] i.e. by edict. [4] I Tim. iii. 2. [5] I Tim. v. 9.

For what he enjoins on one class of men he does not enjoin on all. Then if he does not enjoin on all what he enjoins on bishops, are we to suppose that he exempts bishops from what he enjoins on all? Does it not rather apply to all just because it applies to bishops? And to bishops just because it applies to all? For whence are bishops and clergy? Do they not come from the general body of the Church? If all are not constrained to monogamy, whence will monogamists be found to enter the clergy? Or shall we have to institute a separate order of monogamists from which the clergy are to be chosen? But when we are proudly asserting our rights as against the clergy then we are all on the same level, all priests, because 'he makes us priests to God the Father'.[1] When we are challenged to accept the same priestly discipline, we put off our clerical attire and are on a different footing.

De Monogamia, 12

XI. The Last Things

(a) The End of the World

'Thy kingdom come' has the same reference as 'thy will be done'; it means 'come *in respect of us*'. For when does God not reign 'in whose hand is the heart of all kings'[2]? But whatever we desire for ourselves we look forward to with our eyes on him, and we leave in his hands what we wait for from him. And so if the manifestation of the Lord's kingdom is the concern of the will of God and of our earnest expectation, how is it that some pray for some extension in this present age, when the kingdom of God, for whose coming we pray, means the conclusion of this age? We desire the hastening of our reign, not the protraction of our slavery. . . . Yea, thy kingdom come, Lord, with all speed—the [*fulfilment of the*] prayer of Christians, the confusion of the nations, the exultation of the angels. For this we endure torment; nay rather, for this we pray.

De Oratione, 5

Our hope of the resurrection cannot be fulfilled, as I think, before the coming of Christ: and therefore all our prayers yearn for the passing of this age and the end of the world, at the great day of the Lord, the day of his wrath and retribution . . .

De Resurrectione Carnis, 22

With these passages contrast:

There is another and greater reason which constrains us to pray for the emperor, and also for the whole estate of the empire and the

[1] Rev. i. 6; cf. *De Exhortatione Castitatis*, quoted p. 150 above.   [2] Prov. xxi. 1.

welfare of Rome. For a stupendous shock impends over the whole
world and the very ending of the age threatening terrible sufferings;
and this we know is only retarded by the respite won by the Roman
Empire.[1] We have no wish to experience these calamities and as we
pray that they may be delayed we favour the long-continued existence
of Rome.   *Apologeticus, 32*

(b) The Paradox

Faith keeps watch for that day . . . and daily fears that for which she
daily hopes.   *De Anima, 33 (ad fin.)*

(c) Resurrection and Judgement

[*Heathen philosophy and poetry has plagiarized the truths of Scripture:
Scripture is superior because older.*] And so we are also derided because we
proclaim that God is going to judge the world. For just so do the poets
and philosophers place a judgement seat in the underworld. In the same
way if we threaten Gehenna, which is a store of hidden subterranean
fire for purposes of punishment, we are received with howls of derision.
For they likewise have the river Pyriphlegethon in the abode of the
dead. And if we mention paradise, a place of divine delight appointed to
receive the spirits of the saints, cut off from the knowledge of this
work-a-day world by a kind of barrier consisting of that zone of fire,
the Elysian fields have anticipated the Faith. Whence, I ask you, arise
these resemblances to our doctrines in the philosophers or poets? They
are just taken from our sacred doctrines.[2] And our doctrines, as being
earlier, are more trustworthy, and more to be believed, for even these
reflexions of them find credence.   *Apologeticus, 47*

When therefore the end and the boundary which yawns between [*this
age and the next*] is reached in order that the outward fashion of the
world itself may be changed, being quite as temporal [*as this age*] and
spread like a curtain over the eternal order; then the whole human race
will be restored, to receive its due reward for merit or demerit in this
age, and to have this payment for all the immeasurable eternity of everlasting ages. Therefore from henceforth there is no death nor repeated

---

[1] Cf. *De Resurrectione Carnis*, 34 '. . . [2 Thess. ii. 1–7] "The restraining power" must be
the Roman state, whose disappearance and dispersal into ten kings [cf. Rev. xvii. 12] will
introduce Antichrist'. This interpretation was adopted by Cyril of Jerusalem, *Catecheses*,
xvii. 12; Jerome, *Ep.* 121, *ad Algasiam*; Augustine, *De Civitate Dei*, xx. 19.   [2] Similar
claims are made by Justin, *Apology I*, 54; and Clement of Alexandria, *Stromateis*, i. 17
and 21.

resurrection, but from now on we shall be the same, and remain unchanged; the worshippers of God will be with God for ever, clothed
with the proper substance of eternity;[1] but the profane and all who are
not wholly devoted to God,[2] in the punishment of fire which is just as
eternal.   *Apologeticus*, 48

(d) The Intermediate State

With us the underworld is not believed to be a bare cavity or some
kind of cesspool of the world open to the sky; but a vast space in a
deep pit beneath the earth, a hidden depth in the earth's very bowels;
since we read that Christ spent three days 'in the heart of the earth',[3]
that is in the farthest inner recess which is concealed in the very earth,
and hollowed out within it and superimposed on the abysses which
stretch away underneath. Now Christ is God, because he both died as
man according to the Scriptures and was buried according to the same
Scriptures, here also he fulfilled the law of his humanity by complying
with the condition of human death in the underworld; nor did he
'ascend to the heights' of heaven before he had 'descended into the
depths'[4] of the earth that he might make the prophets and patriarchs
partakers of himself. You have to believe that the underworld is a
subterranean region, and elbow off those who are arrogant enough to
suppose that the souls of the faithful are too good for the underworld.
. . . 'But', they say, 'Christ went to the underworld just for this purpose, that we should not go there.' Or, 'What distinction is there between heathen and Christians, if there is the same prison for them when
they are dead?' How then shall the soul rise up to heaven, where Christ
already sits at the Father's right hand, when as yet the command of
God has not been heard by means of the archangel's trumpet, when
those whom the Lord's coming shall find on earth have not yet been
'caught up into the air to meet him', together with 'the dead in Christ
who shall first arise?'[5] Heaven is opened to no man while the earth still
remains intact. I would not say it is shut [*for ever*];[6] for when the earth
passes away the kingdom of heaven will be unbarred. But shall we sleep
in the upper air with the perverts of Plato,[7] or in the lower air with
Arius,[8] or around the moon with the Endymions of the Stoics?[9] 'Why',

---

[1] i.e. the substance of angels: *De Resurrectione Carnis*, 36, 'to pass into the angelic state,
through the putting on of the garment of immortality' (cf. *Ad Uxorem*, i. 1, *De Cultu
Feminarum*, i. 2).   [2] *integri ad deum*.   [3] Matt. xii. 40.   [4] Eph. iv. 8, 9.   [5] 1 Thess. iv. 16, 17.
[6] Reading uncertain.   [7] Cf. Plato, *Phaedrus* 249A.   [8] Arius Didymus, an eclectic
philosopher of the first century, tutor of Augustus, gives this as a Stoic notion.
[9] Posidonius seems to have regarded the lunar regions as the abode of souls: see Cicero,
Tusculan Disputations, i. 42 f.

you say, 'in paradise, whither already the patriarchs and prophets have migrated from the underworld in the train of the Lord's resurrection?' And how then is it that John, when the region of paradise, beneath the altar, was revealed to him in the spirit, was shown no other souls there but those of the martyrs? How is it that the most valiant martyr Perpetua,[1] just before the day of her passion, saw in the revelations of paradise only her fellow-martyrs there? . . .   *De Anima*, 55

'Are all souls then', you say, 'in the realm of the underworld?' Yes, whether you like it or not. And there are punishments there and refreshments. . . . Why cannot you suppose that the soul undergoes punishment or comfort in the underworld, in the interval while it awaits the judgement, either of punishment or reward, with a kind of anticipation? . . . Otherwise, what will happen in that interval? Shall we sleep? But *souls* cannot sleep. . . . Or do you think that nothing happens there? . . . Surely it would be the height of injustice if in that place the souls of the wicked still prospered, and the good still failed of happiness? . . . Therefore since we understand that 'prison', indicated in the Gospel, to be the underworld and interpret 'the uttermost farthing'[2] as meaning every small sin which has to be expiated there in the interval before the resurrection,[3] no one will doubt that the soul in the underworld pays some price, without prejudice to the fulfilment of the process at the resurrection, which also will be carried out through the medium of the flesh.   Ibid. 58

(e) The Resurrection of the Flesh

Look now at these analogies of the divine power [*of re-creation*] . . . Winters and summers, spring and autumn seasons roll round in their course with their own qualities, their own characters, their own fruits. For the earth is schooled by heaven to clothe the trees after they have been stripped, to colour the flowers anew, to cover the earth again with grass, to bring forth the seeds which have been destroyed, and not to bring them forth until destroyed. A wonderful plan! The defrauder becomes a preserver, making away in order to restore, losing in order to safeguard, spoiling in order to renew, reducing in order to

[1] Martyred in Africa, probably in A.D. 202. The story of the vision is given in the *Acta S. Perpetuae*.   [2] Matt, v. 26.   [3] Cf. ibid. 35: '. . . And the Judge deliver you to the angel of execution, and he lead you to the infernal prison, whence you will not be released until you have paid for each small sin in the interval before the resurrection.' In *De Resurrectione Carnis*, 42, we find the same interpretation of the 'uttermost farthing', but in *De Oratione*, 7, the satisfaction seems to be required in this life.

enlarge; for indeed this process restores to us things far richer and finer than those which it brought to an end; by a ruin which is in truth a profit, an injustice which yields a dividend, a loss which is a gain. I might sum it up by saying that renewal is a universal principle. Whatever you meet with has before existed; whatever you have lost returns to existence. All things return after they have disappeared; all things begin when they have ceased to be; they come to an end in order that they may come to be. Nothing perishes but with a view to restoration. Thus the whole order of things, this order of revolution, bears testimony to the resurrection of the dead . . . *De Resurrectione Carnis*, 12

(f) Punishment and Reward of Soul and Body

The whole cause of the resurrection, what, in fact, makes it inevitable, will be found to be this: that the judgement should proceed in a way most fitting to God. How shall this judgement be administered? Consider this question. Will the divine investigation conduct an inquiry, into both man's natures, his flesh as well as his soul? For that which is a fitting object of judgement should also be raised from the dead. . . . We say that the fullness and perfection of judgement must needs be brought about by the re-presentation of the whole man; now the whole man appears as a result of the concretion of the two natures, and therefore he must be produced in the two natures, since it is right that he should be judged entire, since he lived only in his entirety. Therefore, as he lived, so he must be judged, since he has to be judged concerning the life he lived.   Ibid. 14

Indeed the soul is so far from passing through life by itself, that we cannot remove even our thoughts from association with the flesh, although they be merely thoughts, although they do not issue into effect through the agency of the flesh. For whatever goes on in the heart is the activity of the soul in the flesh, with the flesh, and through the flesh. . . . My opponents indeed enumerate the 'sins of the flesh'; therefore the flesh will be held to its punishment. But we retort with the 'virtues of the flesh'; therefore the flesh for its good works will be assigned its reward. And if it is the soul which acts and gives the impulse to every action, it is the part of the flesh to obey. We may not suppose God to be either unjust or remiss; but unjust he would be were he to exclude from reward the flesh which is the accomplice in good works; remiss if he exempted it from punishment as the accomplice of evil deeds . . . (17) . . . Since acts and deserts are inseparably linked, and acts are performed through the flesh, it is clearly not enough for the soul, apart from the flesh, to be rewarded with pleasure or torment for the works of the flesh, even though the soul has a body and members,[1] since these are insufficient for full perception, as they are for complete activity. Therefore the soul suffers in the underworld, having a fore-taste of judgement, as it was to the fore in inciting to sin. But it awaits the flesh, that in the flesh it may expiate its deeds, since to the flesh it entrusted the accomplishment of its thoughts. In fact, this will be the principle of the judgement which has been planned for the last day, that by the production of the flesh for judgement the divine sentence may be carried out entire.   Ibid. 15–17

And so the flesh rises again, in its entirety, in its identity, in its integrity. Wherever it is, it is in safe keeping with God through the most faithful 'mediator between God and man, Jesus Christ',[2] who will restore God to man and man to God, the spirit to the flesh and the flesh to the spirit. Both spirit and flesh he has already allied in his own person; he has brought them together as bride to groom and groom to bride. . . . What you think of as the destruction of the flesh you must understand to be only a withdrawal.   Ibid. 63

(g) Christ's Triumph over his Enemies

But what a spectacle is to come! The advent of the Lord, now acknow-ledged, exalted, triumphant. What exultation of angels that will be, what glory of the saints as they arise! And after that the splendour of the reign of the saints, and the city of New Jerusalem! But there are other sights besides; that last and eternal day of judgement; that day unexpected by the nations, that day they laughed at. . . . What an ample entertainment! What shall I marvel at? What laugh at? . . . When I see all those mighty monarchs, whose reception into heaven was proclaimed, groaning together in lowest darkness . . . the gover-nors, the persecutors of the Lord's name, melting in fires more fierce than those with which they raged against the Christians . . . philoso-phers . . . poets . . . tragedians . . . actors . . . charioteers. . . . But perhaps I may prefer to turn my gaze—and I can never have my fill of gazing—on those who raged against the Lord. 'This is he', I shall say to them, 'the son of the carpenter or the prostitute,[3] the Sabbath-breaker,

---

[1] Cf. Tertullian's doctrine of the soul, *De Anima* 9, quoted pp. 108–9 above.   [2] 1 Tim. ii. 5.   [3] Referring to the calumny that Jesus was 'born of fornication' (John viii. 41) between a Jewess and a Roman soldier named Panthera.

the Samaritan, the man with the evil spirit, this is he whom you bought from Judas, whom you struck with the reed and buffeted, whom you shamed with spitting, to whom you gave drinks of vinegar and gall. This is he whom the disciples stole away in secret, that it might be said that he had risen, or whom the gardener took away, that his lettuces might not suffer because of the crowds coming to visit the tomb!' What praetor, consul, quaestor, or priest will in his generosity give you the chance of seeing and delighting in such entertaiment as this?

De Spectaculis, 30

(h) The Millennium

For we also hold that a kingdom has been promised to us on earth, but before [*we attain*] heaven: but in another state than this, as being after the [*first*] resurrection. This will last for a thousand years, in a city of God's making, Jerusalem sent down from heaven which the Apostle also designates as 'our mother from above'[1] and in proclaiming that 'our *politeuma*', that is, citizenship, 'is in heaven',[2] he surely ascribes it to a heavenly city. Ezekiel knew that city,[3] and the Apostle John saw it,[4] and the Word of the New Prophecy which dwells in our faith witnesses to it so that it even foretold the appearance of the likeness of that city to serve as a sign before its manifestation before men's eyes. In fact this prophecy was just lately fulfilled in the course of the eastern expedition. For it is a fact attested even by the heathen that in Judaea a city was suspended from heaven for a short space in the early morning during a period of forty days. . . . We say that this is the city designed by God for the reception of the saints at the [*first*] resurrection, and for their cherishing with abundance of all goods, spiritual goods to be sure, in compensation for the goods we have despised or lost in this age. For indeed it is right and worthy of God that his servants should also rejoice in the place where they suffered affliction in his name. This is the purpose of that kingdom; which will last a thousand years, during which period the saints will rise sooner or later, according to their degrees of merit, and then when the resurrection of the saints is completed, the destruction of the world and the conflagration of judgement will be effected; we shall be 'changed in a moment' into the angelic substance, by the 'putting on of incorruption',[5] and we shall be transferred to the celestial kingdom.

Adversus Marcionem, iii. 24

[1] Gal. iv. 26.   [2] Phil. iii. 20.   [3] Ezek. xlviii. 30 ff.   [4] Rev. xxi. 2 ff.   [5] I Cor. xv. 52, 53.

XII. Apologetics

All who formerly hated because they did not know the true nature of
the thing they hated, cease to hate as soon as they cease to be ignorant.
From these people Christians are made, for just by finding out they
begin to hate what they used to be and to profess that which they had
hated: and their numbers are as great as they are reputed to be. Men
cry out that the state is beset by Christians; that there are Christians in
the countryside, in the villages, in the islands. That people of both
sexes, of every age and condition, even of high position,[1] are passing
over to the Christian society: this they lament as though it were a
calamity. And yet for all that they are not stimulated to consider
whether there may not be some good in it that they have failed to
notice.   *Apologeticus*, 1

Tiberius, in whose time the Christian faith [*nomen*] came into the
world, having received information from Palestine of the events there
which had revealed the truth of Christ's divinity, brought the matter
before the Senate and gave his vote in favour of setting Christ among
the gods.[2] The Senate rejected the proposal because it had not given
its approval of its own initiative. Caesar maintained his opinion and
threatened the accusers of the Christians that they acted at their peril.
. . . [*The good emperors did not persecute, e.g. story of M. Aurelius quoted
above, p. 156.*]   Ibid. 5

Apologeticus 7 and 8 deal with calumnies about Christian practices.

---

[1] Cf. *Ad Scapulam*, 2: 'almost the majority of every community'; ibid. 4: 'Severus refused
to prosecute some very eminent men and women who were Christians'; 5: 'so many
thousands of men and women of all ages and classes'. Similar claims elsewhere in Tertullian,
and in the other Apologists, doubtless contain elements of rhetorical exaggeration. But
Pliny (*Ep.* x. 96, *ad Traianum*) speaks of 'many people of all classes' who were accused of
Christianity, and Tacitus (*Annals*, xv. 44) of an 'immense number' at Rome in A.D. 64.
And there is no reason to doubt that Flavius Clemens and his wife Domitilla, members
of the imperial family, suffered for their Christian profession (Euseb. *H.E.* III. 18).
[2] Cf. 21: '. . . Pilate, who was a Christian by his own conviction, sent information to
Tiberius, the Caesar of that time. The Caesars would have believed in Christ if either
Caesars had not been necessary for the world, or the Christians could have been Caesars'.
Eusebius, *H.E.* ii. 2, repeats this statement about Tiberius' proposal. But Tertullian
is the only evidence; no other Apologist mentions it, and no modern historian
believes it.

We say before all men, and when torn and bleeding through your tortures we shout aloud 'We worship God through Christ'. Think him a man if you will; through him and in him God wills to be known and worshipped. . . . Inquire, then, if the divinity of Christ be a true belief. If it is such a belief that the acceptance of it transforms a man, it follows that everything found contrary to it should be renounced.

Apologeticus, 26

How often you rage against the Christians, partly because of your inclination, partly in obedience to the laws. How often too the hostile mob pays no attention to you and attacks us with stones and fires, taking the law into its own hands. . . . Yet though we are banded together, though we are so eager to face death, what instance did you ever note of a retaliation for injury? Though, if it were permitted among us to repay evil with evil, we might wreak awful vengeance one night with a few torches . . .   Ibid. 37

[*Against the charge of being unprofitable citizens.*] We are no Brahmins or Indian gymnosophists [fakirs], we are not hermits or anchorites. . . . We remember our debt of gratitude to our Lord God the Creator; and we do not spurn any of the fruits of his works. We dwell with you in the world in the ordinary intercourse of daily life, making use of forum, market, baths, shops &c. . . . We sail the seas with you, we serve in the army; we work on the land, in trade; we join in your occupations, we make our industry available for general use. I do not know why we seem unprofitable in your business, since we live with you and in dependence on you . . . [*But we cannot join in your pagan festivals and ceremonies*].   Ibid. 42

Your cruelty profits you nothing, though it grows ever more ingenious; it is one of the attractions of our sect. As often you mow us down, the more numerous do we become; the blood of the Christians is the seed. Many of your philosophers exhort men to patient endurance of suffering and death. . . . Yet their words have won fewer disciples than those whom Christians have taught by the example of their deeds. The very obstinacy which you censure is the teacher. For who, on beholding that 'obstinacy', is not stirred to find out what is behind it? Who, when he has inquired, does not adhere to our faith? And when he has so adhered he desires to suffer that he may purchase the whole of

God's grace, that he may win complete forgiveness from him by the
price of his own blood. For that act obtains pardon for all sins. Thus it
is that we give thanks on the very spot for your sentences; such is the
opposition between divine and human actions, that when we are condemned by you we are absolved by God.   Ibid. 50

See also above, pp. 155–7.

Titus Flavius Clemens Alexandrinus (Clement of Alexandria)

Floruit *c.* 200.—EDITION: Otto Stählin in *Die Griechischen Christlichen Schriftsteller* ('Berlin Corpus', 1905–9).

1. Alexandrian Allegorism: The Christian Gnostic

(a) 'The Gnostic Tradition'

There are some things which my work will speak in riddles; to some it will display its meaning clearly: some things it will only speak; it will try to say things secretly, to display in a hidden fashion, to show while keeping silence. The tenets of notable heresies will be set out, and the answers to them that must be made by way of introduction to the knowledge that is according to the mystic contemplation, in which we will advance according to the renowned and revered Rule of the Tradition . . . so that we may be ready to listen to the transmission of the Gnostic[1] Tradition. . . .   *Stromateis*, I. i (15, 1)

(b) The Fourfold Interpretation of Scripture

The meaning of the Law [*i.e. the Old Testament*] is to be apprehended by us in four[2] ways; as displaying a type, or establishing a command for the moral life, or giving a prophecy.   Ibid. I. xxvii (179, 1)

(c) Philosophy and Religion

Philosophy was necessary to the Greeks for righteousness, until the coming of the Lord: and even now it is useful for the development of true religion, as a kind of preparatory discipline for those who arrive at faith by way of demonstration. For 'your foot will not stumble',[3] as the Scripture says, if you attribute to Providence all good things, whether belonging to the Greeks or to us. For God is the source of all good; either directly, as in the Old and New Testaments, or indirectly, as in the case of philosophy. But it may even be that philosophy was given to the Greeks directly; for it was 'a schoolmaster',[4] to bring

---

[1] i.e. the tradition of *Christian* 'gnosticism'—the full esoteric knowledge (γνῶσις) of God and of his revelation in Scripture.   [2] The *literal* sense is omitted but assumed. Or the MS. reading should be altered to 'three ways'.   [3] Prov. iii. 28.   [4] Gal. iii. 24.

Hellenism to Christ, as the Law was for the Hebrews. Thus philosophy was a preparation, paving the way for the man who is brought to perfection by Christ.   Ibid. 1. v (28, 1)

If our critics force us to make a distinction by calling philosophy a *contributory* cause towards the apprehension of truth, as being a search for truth, we shall admit it to be a preparatory discipline for the 'gnostic', without making it a *necessary* as opposed to a *contributory* cause, or asserting philosophy to be a *sine qua non*. For almost all of us have received the word about God through faith, without having a secondary education or a training in Greek philosophy, some of us without elementary education. But we have been moved by the power of the divinely inspired, non-Greek philosophy, trained by a self-taught wisdom. . . . And yet philosophy by itself did once justify the Greeks, not indeed to the attainment of complete righteousness, to which it proved a contributory cause, as the first two steps are to one mounting to an upper story, or a primary teacher to the budding philosopher.   Ibid. 1. xx (99, 1)

II. God the Father

Infinite and Inexpressible. Apprehended by Grace and Revelation

Since the first cause of anything is exceedingly difficult to discover, the original and supreme cause is hard to describe—the cause which is the reason for the coming to be and for the continued existence of all things. For how can that be spoken of which is not genus, differentia, species, individual, number, accident, subject of accident? One could not rightly describe him as the Whole, for the whole is a term applied to spatial extension, and he is the *Father* of the whole universe. Nor can one speak of him as having parts; for the One is indivisible, and therefore infinite, not in the sense of being inexhaustible to thought, but of being without dimension or limit. Thus the deity is without form and nameless. Though we ascribe names, they are not to be taken in their strict meaning; when we call him One, Good, Mind, Existence, Father, God, Creator, Lord, we are not conferring a name on him. Being unable to do more, we use these appellations of honour, in order that our thought may have something to rest on and not wander at random.[1]

[1] Cf. the passage of Justin quoted above, p. 63.

These taken singly do not express the being of God, but collectively they indicate the power of the Almighty. Descriptions derive either from qualities of things or from their relations to other things; neither of those is applicable to God. He cannot be comprehended by knowledge, which is based on previously known truths, whereas nothing can precede what is self-existent. It remains that the Unknown be apprehended by divine grace and the Word proceeding from him . . . [cf. Acts xvii. 22, 23].   Stromateis, v. xii (82, 4)

God is undemonstrable and therefore is not an object of knowledge. But the Son is Wisdom and Knowledge and Truth and all that is akin to these, and he admits of demonstration and explanation. All the powers of the Spirit [i.e. the divine nature], gathered together into unity, complete the notion of the Son; but he is not completely expressed by our conception of each of his powers. He is not merely One, as Unity, nor Many, as having parts, but One as All. Hence he is All. For he is the circle of all powers, which in him are rounded and united.

Ibid. iv. xxv (156, 1)

God is one, and beyond one, and above the Monad itself. Therefore the pronoun Thou [referring to John xvii. 21] is emphatic and indicates the one really existing God, who is, and was, and will be; for those three divisions of time are included in the name I AM. . . . The goodness of God is apprehended from his character as Father. . . . His attribute of justice derives from the mutual relationship of the Father and the Son—his Word—who is in the Father.

Paedagogus, i. viii (71)

III. God the Son

(a) The Searcher of Hearts

'The spirit of the Lord is a lamp which searches out the inner chambers of the heart.'[1] And as a man by acting righteously becomes more enlightened, so the shining spirit comes closer to him. Thus 'the Lord draws near to the righteous, and nothing escapes him of our thoughts and of the reasonings we entertain';[2] I mean the Lord Jesus, who by the will of the Almighty is 'the overseer of our heart';[3] whose blood was consecrated for us.   Stromateis, iv. xvii (107, 5)

[1] Prov. xx. 2 (not LXX).   [2] Clement of Rome, i. xxi.   [3] Cf. 1 Pet. ii. 25.

As the sun illumines not only the heaven and the whole world, shining on both land and sea; but also sends his rays through windows and small chinks into the furthest recesses of a house; so the Word, poured out everywhere, beholds the smallest actions of man's life.

Ibid. VII iii. (21)

(b) The Cosmic Logos

Most perfect, most holy, most lordly, most commanding, royal, and beneficent is the nature of the Son, most closely joined to the only Almighty. His is the greatest pre-eminence, which orders all things according to the Father's will, and guides everything aright, working all things by unwearying and unfailing power, beholding the hidden thoughts through its activities. For the Son of God never quits his watch-tower: he is not divided nor severed, nor does he pass from place to place: he is always everywhere, and not circumscribed anywhere. He is wholly mind, wholly the Father's light, all eye, seeing all things, hearing all things, knowing all things, searching out the powers by his power. The whole army of angels and of gods is subject to him, to the Word of the Father who has taken upon himself the holy dispensation[1] because of him who made them subject. Ibid. VIII. ii (5)

(c) Knowledge of Son and of Father

[*Some assert that we have* knowledge *of the Spirit—i.e. the Deity—but* faith *in the Son.*] We must *believe* truly in the Son; that he is the Son, that he came, and how he came, and why; and about his suffering. But we must also have *knowledge* of the person of the Son. But, to begin with, there is no faith without knowledge, nor knowledge without faith. Nor does the Father exist without the Son, for 'Father' immediately implies 'Father of a Son'; and the Son is the true teacher about the Father. And in order that a man may believe in the Son, he must know the Father in relation to whom the Son exists. Again in order that we may come to know the Father, we must believe in the Son, because the Son of God is our teacher; for the Father brings us from faith to knowledge by means of the Son, and knowledge of the Son and the Father which follows the Gnostic Rule – the rule of the genuine 'Gnostic' – is an intuition and apprehension of truth through 'the Truth'.[2]

Ibid. v. i (1)

---

[1] 'Economy', see note 6, p. 75.   [2] Cf. John xiv. 6.

(d) The Logos, the Giver of Life, the Teacher of the Good Life

This Word, the Christ, the cause of our being—for he was in God—
as also of our well-being, has now himself appeared to man. He alone
is both God and man; he is for us the source of all good. From him we
learn the good life and are brought to the life eternal . . . [Tit. ii. 11–
13] . . . This is the 'new song', the Epiphany, which has now shone out
among us, of that Word who was in the beginning, and who was
before the beginning. And now, quite recently, he has been manifested—the Saviour who was before; he has been manifested who was
in Him Who Is, because the Word, who was with God, has appeared
as our teacher, he by whom the universe was created. The Word who
in the beginning gave us life when he fashioned us, as Creator, has
taught us the good life, as our teacher, that he may afterwards, as God,
provide us with life eternal. Not that he now has for the first time pitied
us for our wandering; he pitied us from of old, from the beginning.
But now, when we were perishing, he has appeared and has saved us.

Protrepticus, i (7)

(e) 'Very God'

Believe, O man, in him who is man and God: believe in him who
suffered and is worshipped as the living God; servants, believe in him
who was dead; all men, believe in him who is the only God of all men:
believe and receive salvation for your reward . . .   *Ibid.* x (106)

With unsurpassable speed and unexampled goodwill the divine power,
having shone upon the world, has filled everything with the saving
seed. Such a work in so short a time the Lord would not have achieved
without the divine power assisting. He was despised for his appearance, but is worshipped for his work; he is the purifying, saving, delect-
able Word, the divine Word, who is truly God most manifest, made
equal to the Ruler of all; because he was the Son, and 'the Word was
with God'.   *Ibid.* x (110)

IV. The Trinity

(a) The Unity of Father, Word, and Spirit

O wonderful mystery! The Father of all things is one; the Word of
all things is one; the Holy Spirit is one and the same everywhere.

Paedagogus, I. vi (42)

(b) Praise to the Trinity

Be merciful to thy children, O Instructor, O Father, charioteer of Israel, Son and Father, both one, O Lord. Grant that we, thy followers, observing thy commandments, may make perfect the likeness of thy image; that through his strength we may know the goodness of God and the kindness of his judgement. Bestow on us all good things; that we may live our lives in thy peace, and be transferred to thy city; that we may sail over the waves of sin without storm, and be borne along in calm, night and day, by the Holy Spirit, the inexpressible Wisdom, until we come to the perfect day. That we may give praise and thanksgiving to the only Father: and the only Son; to Son and Father, the Son our instructor and teacher, together with the Holy Spirit: rendering all praise to the One, in whom are all things, through whom all things are one, through whom is eternity, of whom all men are members, and the Ages[1] are his glory; all praise to the Good, the Lovely, the Wise, the Just: to him be glory now and for ever. Amen.

Ibid. III. xii (101)

V. Man

(a) The Fall: Not Connected with Sex

He [*Julius Cassianus, an 'encratite' Gnostic, who attacked marriage*] wrests the saying of Paul 'I fear lest, as the serpent deceived Eve' &c.,[2] to mean that human generation arose from this deceit. But the Lord came, admittedly, to 'what was going astray'[3] but not 'straying' from a higher sphere to birth on earth. For generation is part of the creation of the Almighty, and he would not degrade the soul from a higher state to a worse. Rather it was to us who had strayed in our *minds* that the Saviour came, minds which had been corrupted because through our love of pleasure we disobeyed the commandments. It may be that the first-created man may have anticipated our season[4] and before the time of the grace of marriage desired and sinned.

Stromateis, III. xiv (94, 1)

(b) No Inherited Pollution

Let them say where the new-born child committed fornication, or how that can have fallen under Adam's curse which has not yet

---

[1] The 'Aeons', the Angelic Powers of Gnosticism.   [2] 2 Cor. xi. 3.   [3] Matt. xviii. 12.
[4] The time ordained by God for us, the human race, to be conceived.

performed any action. They should logically go on to say that not only the birth of the body is evil but also that of the soul on which the body depends. When David says, 'I was conceived in sins, and in lawlessness my mother bore me',[1] he refers prophetically to Eve as his mother. But Eve was 'the mother of all living',[2] and if he was conceived in sin in this sense still he is not himself in sin nor is he himself sin.

Stromateis, III. xvi (100, 5)

(c) Sin Due to Ignorance

It is in our power to believe and obey, but the cause of evil one may take to be the weakness of matter and the involuntary impulse of ignorance and unreasonable compulsions which arise from lack of knowledge. The 'Gnostic' rises superior to these.   Ibid. VII. iii (16)

(d) Sin and Responsibility

Involuntary action is not judged, whether due to ignorance or compulsion.   Ibid. II. xiv (60)

Actions which are not the result of free-will are not imputed.

Ibid. II. xv (66)

VI. The Work of Christ

(a) Salvation by the Example of Love in Incarnation and Passion

God is himself love, and because of his love he pursued us, and [*in the eternal generation of the Son*] the ineffable nature of God is father, his sympathy with us is mother. It was in his love that the Father pursued us, and the great proof of this is the Son whom he begot from himself and the love that was the fruit produced from his love. For this he came down, for this he assumed human nature, for this he willingly endured the sufferings of man, that by being reduced to the measure of our weakness he might raise us to the measure of his power. And just before he poured out his offering, when he gave himself as a ransom, he left us a new testament; 'I give you my love'.[3] What is the nature and extent of this love? For each of us he laid down his life, the life which was worth the whole universe, and he requires in return that we should do the same for each other.   *Quis Dives Salvetur*, 37

[1] Ps. l (51), 7.   [2] Gen. iii. 20.   [3] Cf. John xiii. 34.

(b) The Downward and Upward Movement of Salvation. Christianized Gnosticism

[The Son], being the Father's power, easily accomplished all his purposes. He leaves not the smallest thing uncared for by his control; for otherwise the whole would not be well wrought by him. I suppose that from the supreme power comes that careful examination which is applied to all the parts, down to the very smallest; to all the parts, till we reach the supreme controller of the whole universe who governs all things according to his Father's will; while all beings, rank on rank in order, behold the universal salvation; until we arrive at the great High Priest. For from one cause—the source of energy according to the Father's will—depend the first, second, and third orders, and then at the edge of the world of sense [?] is the blessed hierarchy of angels. Below them, ordered in due subordination, are the ranks of beings, from one and through one receiving and conferring salvation, extending to us men. Thus, just as even the smallest piece of iron is moved by the influence of a magnet, which extends through a series of iron rings, so virtuous beings are drawn by the Holy Spirit and are closely united to the first 'mansion', and this influence passes down to the last in order. The wicked . . . neither controlling nor controlled, fall downwards headlong. . . . The divine law is that the man who is set on virtue is raised up.   *Stromateis*, VII. ii (9)

(c) Christ's Human Nature: an Approach to Docetism

The 'Gnostic' is not the kind of man to be involved in any passions save those necessarily incident to his sojourn in the body, as hunger, thirst, and the like. But in the case of the Saviour it would be absurd to suppose that his body demanded these essential services for his stay. For he ate, not because of bodily needs, since his body was supported by holy power, but so that his companions might not entertain a false notion about him, as in fact certain men did later, namely that he had been manifested only in appearance. He himself was, and remained, 'untroubled by passion';[1] no movement of the passions, either pleasure or pain, found its way into him.   Ibid. VI. ix (71)

---

[1] ἀπαθής, the ideal Stoic character, not at the mercy of desires and impulses or external circumstances. Clement does not mean that Christ did not experience human suffering; but either that he could not be seduced by pleasure or pain, or that the Divine nature—the Logos—was incapable of suffering.

(d) Victory over Death

The first man played in paradise, at liberty, since he was the child of God. Then he fell, through pleasure (this being the allegorical meaning of the serpent . . .) and was led astray through his desires. There the child, being a man, disobeyed his Father and dishonoured God. How great is the power of pleasure! Man was free, in his innocence, and then found himself bound by his sins. The Lord, on his part, wished to free him from his fetters, and, himself being bound in the flesh—here is divine mystery—grappled with the serpent and enslaved the tyrant, death; and, wonder of wonders, though man was straying through pleasure, though he was held captive by corruption, the Lord displayed him set at liberty by his outstretched arms. O wondrous mystery! The Lord was laid to rest and man was raised up. Man was cast out of paradise; and now he receives a reward greater than that of obedience, the reward of Heaven. *Protrepticus*, xi (111)

(e) 'Universalism'

The gospel says that 'many bodies of those who had fallen asleep arose'[1] —clearly to a better state—the state of those who have been changed. There was then a kind of general movement and change as a result of the 'dispensation'[2] of the Saviour. One righteous man does not differ from another in respect of his righteousness, whether he be under the Law, or a Greek. For God is the Lord not of the Jews only but of all men, though he is more intimately the Father of those who know him. . . . Those who lived good lives before the Law were reckoned as having faith, and were judged to be righteous. It is clear that those who were outside the Law because they spoke a different language, and yet had lived good lives, even if they were actually in Hades and 'in prison',[3] on hearing the voice of the Lord—either his own voice or that which operated through the Apostles—were converted and believed. For we remember that the Lord is 'the power of God';[4] and power could never be powerless.

Thus, I fancy, the goodness of God is proved, and the power of the Lord, to save with justice and equity displayed to those who turn to him, whether here or elsewhere. For the energizing power does not come only on men here; it is operative in all places and at all times. *Stromateis*, VI. vi (47)

[1] Matt. xxvii. 52. [2] 'Economy'; see note 6, p. 75, above. [3] 1 Pet. iii. 19. [4] 1 Cor. i. 29.

(f) The Deification of Man

'To him who has shall be added';[1] knowledge to faith, love to knowledge, and to love the inheritance. (56) And this happens when a man
depends on the Lord through faith, through knowledge, and through
love, and ascends with him to the place where God is, the God and
guardian of our faith and love, from whom knowledge is delivered to
those who are fit for this privilege and who are selected because of
their desire for fuller preparation and training; who are prepared to
listen to what is told them, to discipline their lives, to make progress by
careful observance of the law of righteousness. This knowledge leads
them to the end, the endless final end; teaching of the life that is to be
ours, a life in conformity to God, with gods, when we have been freed
from all punishment and correction, which we undergo as a result of
our wrong-doings for our saving discipline. After thus being set free,
those who have been perfected are given their reward and their
honours. They have done with their purification, they have done with
the rest of their service, though it be a holy service, with the holy; now
they have become pure in heart, and because of their close intimacy
with the Lord there awaits them a restoration to eternal contemplation;
and they have received the title of 'gods', since they are destined to be
enthroned with the other 'gods' who are ranked next below the
Saviour. Thus knowledge is a short cut to purification, and a ready
way to the acceptable change to a higher state.   Ibid. VII. x (55-56)

If you do not believe the prophets . . . the Lord himself will speak to
you 'who, being in the form of God, thought of his equality with God
not as a prize to be grasped, but abased himself'.[2] This is the God of
compassion, yearning to save man; and the Word himself at this
point speaks to you plainly, putting unbelief to shame; the Word, I
say, of God, who became man just that you may learn from a man how
it may be that man should become God.   Protrepticus, i (8, 4)

(g) Progress to Salvation by Faith, Fear, Love, Knowledge

You have, O men, the divine proclamation of grace; you have heard
also, on the other hand, the threat of punishment. Through these the
Lord saves, guiding man by fear and grace.   Ibid. x (95, 1)

---

[1] Matt. xiii. 12.   [2] Phil. ii. 18.

The first inclination towards salvation is displayed to us as faith, then follows fear and hope and repentance: these, advancing with the help of discipline and endurance, lead us to love and knowledge.

Stromateis, II. vi (31, 1)

For the man who walks by reason the first lesson is the knowledge of his ignorance. A man who is ignorant begins his search, and thereby finds the teacher. Having found him he believes, and having believed he hopes, then loves, and hence is made like to the loved one, eager to be that which he has first come to love.   Ibid. v. vii (17, 1)

The first starting-point is learning with fear, which leads us to abstain from wickedness; the second is hope, which leads us to aim at the best, while love completes the process, as is fitting, by training us in the way of knowledge.   Ibid. IV. vii (54)

(h) Salvation by Enlightenment

The darkness is the ignorance which causes us to fall into sins, being blunted in our perception of the truth. Knowledge is enlightenment, which banishes our ignorance and administers a corrective. The casting away of the worse is the revelation of the better. For what ignorance had bound is released through growing knowledge. And these bonds are done away speedily by faith, on the part of man, by grace from the side of God, when our sins are forgiven by the spiritual medicine of baptism.   *Paedagogus*, I. vi (29)

When a man is reminded of the better, of necessity he repents of the worse.   Ibid. I. vi (32)

The 'Gnostic' is saved, we may suppose, owing to his apprehension of the good and the bad life, for as well in knowledge as in activity he 'exceeds the Scribes and the Pharisees'.[1]   *Stromateis*, VI. xv (115)

The heavenly and truly divine desire comes to men in this way, when the ideal[2] is kindled in the soul itself by the divine Word and is able to shine out; and, best of all, salvation immediately attends on noble willing, will and life being, one might say, yoke-fellows.

Protrepticus, xi (117)

As those who have shaken off sleep are at once awake within, or rather, as those who try to remove a film from the eyes do not supply the sun-

---

[1] Matt. v. 20.   [2] τὸ ὄντως καλόν, suggesting the Platonic 'idea', αὐτὸ τὸ καλόν.

light for the eyes, which is not theirs to supply, but remove hindrances
to vision and leave the eye free to see: so in baptism by the divine
Spirit we get rid of the sins which dim our eyes like a mist, and leave
the eye of the spirit free and unhindered and enlightened. By this eye
alone we behold God, when the Holy Spirit pours into us from Heaven.

Paedagogus, I. vi (28)

The Lord, as God and man, gives us all kinds of profit and help. As
God he forgives our sins; as man he educates us to be free from sin.

Ibid. i. iii (7)

VII. The Church

Catholic and Orthodox

We learn from the Scriptures demonstrably that the heresies have gone
astray, and that only in the true Church is the most accurate knowledge.   *Stromateis*, VII. xv (92)

The 'Gnostic' alone, growing old in the Scriptures, preserves the
orthodox teaching of the Apostles and the Church . . .

Ibid. VII. xvi (104)

There is one true Church, the really ancient Church, into which are
enrolled those who are righteous according to God's ordinance. . . .
The one Church is violently split up by the heretics into many sects. In
essence, in idea, in origin, in pre-eminence we say that the ancient
Catholic Church is the only church. This Church brings together, by
the will of the one God through the one Lord, into the unity of the
one faith which is according to the respective covenants (or rather
according to the one covenant established at various times), those
who were already appointed; whom God fore-ordained, knowing
before the world's foundation that they would be righteous. The pre-
eminence of the church, just as the origin of its constitution, depends
on its absolute unity: it excels all other things, and had no equal or rival.
(108) . . . As the teaching of the Apostles is one, so also is the Tradition . . .

Ibid. VII. xvi (107–8)

VIII. Sacraments

(a) Baptism

Being baptized, we are enlightened: being enlightened, we are adopted as sons: being adopted, we are made perfect; being made complete, we are made immortal. The Scripture says 'I said, You are gods, and are all sons of the Highest'.[1] This work has many names; gift of grace, enlightenment, perfection, washing. Washing, by which we are cleansed from the filth of our sins; gift of grace, by which the penalties of our sins are cancelled; enlightenment, through which that holy light which saves us is perceived, that is, by which our eyes are made keen to see the divine; perfection means the lack of nothing, for what is still lacking to him who has the knowledge of God?

Paedagogus, I. vi (26)

(b) The Eucharist

Faith and Hope—Body and Blood—the Church's Nourishment

We may understand 'milk' [I Cor. iii. 2] as meaning the preaching which has been spread far and wide, 'meat' as the faith which as a result of instruction has been compacted to form a foundation. Faith being more solid than hearing is likened to 'meat', since it provides analogous nourishment in the soul. In another place the Lord also expressed that by a different symbolism, when, in John's gospel, he says 'Eat my flesh and drink my blood'.[2] The metaphor of drinking, applied to faith and the promise, clearly means that the Church, consisting, like a human being, of many members, is refreshed and grows, is compacted and welded together, by both these, faith being the body and hope the soul: just as the Lord was made of flesh and blood.   Ibid. I. vi (38)

Spiritual Food

There is one mother, who is a virgin; this is my favourite description of the Church. This mother alone had no milk, being at once mother and virgin, pure as a virgin, loved as a mother. Those who are called her children are nursed with holy milk, the word suitable for babes. She had no milk because the right and proper milk to nourish this child was the body of Christ, suckling with the word the young brood which the Lord himself brought forth with the pangs of his flesh, which the

---

[1] Ps. vi. 1. Cf. John x. 34.   [2] John vi. 53 ff.

Lord himself swaddled with precious blood. O holy birth! O holy
swaddling clothes! The Word is all things to the infant: father, mother,
tutor, and nurse. 'Eat my flesh', he says, 'and drink my blood.'¹ This
proper nourishment the Lord supplies to us; he offers his flesh and
pours out his blood, and the children lack nothing needful for their
growth.

(43) Strange mystery! We are bidden to put off our old fleshly
corruption, as we leave off our old food, and partake of a new diet,²
that of Christ; to store him, as far as we can, in ourselves and take the
Saviour to our hearts, that we may put in order the affections of the
flesh. You cannot understand? Perhaps you may, if I express it more
generally. Put it this way. 'My flesh' is an allegory for the Holy Spirit,
for the flesh is his handiwork. 'Blood', by analogy, stands for the Word,
for the Word is like rich blood poured into our life. The mixture of
flesh and blood is the Lord, the food of his infants; the Lord is Spirit
and Word. The food—that is the Lord Jesus, that is, the Word of God,
Spirit made flesh—is the sanctified heavenly flesh. This food is the
Father's milk, by which we infants are suckled.   Ibid. I. vi (42–43)

The blood of the Lord is twofold. On the one hand it is physical, the
blood by which we have been redeemed from corruption: on the other
it is spiritual, that by which we have been anointed. To drink the blood
of Jesus is to partake of the Lord's immortality; and the Spirit is the
strength of the Word, as blood is the strength of flesh.

(20) As wine is mixed with water so, by analogy, the Spirit is with
man. The mixture nourishes man to faith; the Spirit guides to immortality. The mingling of both—the drink and the Word [? word] is
called Eucharist, a grace of praise and beauty. Those who partake of it in
faith are sanctified in body and soul, since the Father's will had mystically composed the divine mixture, man, by Spirit and Word. For the
Spirit, in truth, is adapted to the soul which is moved by it, and the
flesh adapted to the Word, the flesh for whose sake the Word became
flesh.   Ibid. II. ii (19–20)

'Milk' [1 Cor. iii. 2] is instruction, regarded as the first nourishment of
the soul, 'meat' is mystical contemplation. The flesh and blood of the
Word are the apprehension of the divine power and essence. 'Taste
and see that the Lord is Christ',³ the Scripture says: for thus he imparts
himself to those who partake of this food in a more spiritual manner;

¹ John vi. 53 ff. ² The Greek word means both 'way of life' and, more narrowly,
'regimen' or 'diet'.   ³ Ps. xxxiii (34), 9, reading *Christos* for *chrêstos* ('kind').

for then, as the truth-loving Plato says, 'the soul nourishes itself'.[1]
For the eating and drinking of the divine Word is the knowledge of
the Divine essence.   *Stromateis*, v. x (67)

'The bread is my flesh', &c. [John vi. 51]. Here the mystical meaning
of bread must be understood. He calls his flesh 'bread', his flesh which
rose through fire, just as the wheat rises up from corruption which
follows sowing, and the wheat[2] is brought together by means of fire,[2]
as a baked loaf, for the joy of the church.   *Paedagogus*, I. vi (46)

IX. The Last Things

(a) Purification by Fire

We say that fire sanctifies . . . the souls of sinners, meaning not the
consuming fire of a furnace, but the reasonable fire which penetrates
the soul which passes through the fire.   *Stromateis*, VII. vi (34)

Doing away with the 'works of the flesh' we clothe our putrified flesh
in incorruption and attain to equality with the angels.   Ibid. II. x (100)

(b) Remedial Punishment

All that is virtuous changes to better habitations; the reason for this
change being the choice of knowledge. . . . But strict chastisements,
through the goodness of the great judge, the overseer, compel [*the
wicked*] through increasing suffering to repent. The punishments are
inflicted through the attendant angels, by means of various previous
judgements and by the general judgement.   Ibid. VIII. ii (12)

If like the 'deaf adders'[3] they will not listen to the song . . . let them be
disciplined at the hand of God, enduring paternal correction before
judgement, until they be ashamed and repent, and not incur the final
condemnation by stubborn unbelief. For there are partial disciplines,
called chastisements, which most of us have incurred who have fallen
into sin, though belonging to the Lord's people. But our chastisement
by Providence has been that of children by a teacher or a father. God
does not take vengeance, which is the requital of evil for evil, but he
chastises for the benefit of the chastised.   Ibid. VII. xvi (102)

---

[1] Cf. Plato, *Protagoras* 313 C.   [2] A play on words: πυρός, 'wheat'; διὰ πυρός, 'through
fire'.   [3] Ps. lviii. 4.

(c) Heaven. Degrees of Attainment

There are various mansions, varying according to the worth of the believers. Solomon says, 'There shall be given to him the chosen grace of faith, and a more delightful portion in the temple of the Lord.'[1] Here the comparative, 'more delightful', indicates the lower portions of the Temple of God (which is the whole Church) but does not go as far as to include the superior division where the Lord is. That those three mansions are chosen abodes is the hidden meaning of the numbers in the gospel, 'thirty, sixty, and a hundred'.[2] The perfect inheritance is theirs who attain 'to the perfection of man',[3] according to the Lord's image. This likeness is not, as some suppose, in respect of the human form; such a notion is impious: nor in respect of virtue . . .; for this also is an irreverent interpretation, for men to suppose the virtue of man to be the same as that of Almighty God. 'It is enough for the learner to be like his teacher'[4] says our Teacher. Thus he who is appointed to adoption and friendship with God, according to the likeness of God, shares in the inheritance of the lords and gods, if he has been made perfect in accordance with the gospel, as the Lord himself taught.[5]   Ibid. VI. xiv (114)

These 'shall rest on the holy hill of God'[6] as David says, the 'holy hill' being the Church in heaven, into which God's philosophers are gathered. Those are the 'Israelites indeed', the 'pure in heart', 'in whom is no guile'.[7] They do not wait during the seven days[8] of rest, but in virtue of their growth in the divine likeness they ascend to the inheritance of the service of the eighth heaven, giving themselves to the undistracted vision of never-satisfied contemplation. But 'there are other sheep, which do not belong to this fold',[9] says the Lord, judged worthy of another 'fold', that is, 'mansion', in proportion to their faith. 'My sheep hear my voice',[10] comprehending the commandments 'gnostically', that is, nobly and worthily understanding them and responding with the actions that result from them. So that when we hear the words, 'your faith has saved you',[11] we do not take him to mean simply that those who believe in any way will be saved, without any resulting actions. This saying was addressed to Jews who lived blameless lives in obedience to the Law and merely lacked faith in the Lord.   Ibid. VI. xiv (108)

[1] Wisd. iii. 14.   [2] Matt. xiii. 8.   [3] Eph. iv. 13.   [4] Matt. x. 28.   [5] Cf. Matt. v. 48.
[6] Ps. xiv (15), 1.   [7] John i. 47; Matt. v. 8.   [8] The seven days of purification, a type of the seven heavens of Jewish and Gnostic speculation.   [9] John x. 16.   [10] John x. 27.   [11] Mark v. 34, &c.

(d) Progress in Likeness to God in his Eternal Activity

On the face of Moses there settled a kind of bloom of glory, because of his righteous acts and his continual converse with God, who spoke to him.[1] So on the righteous soul there steals a kind of divine power of goodness, through the divine visitation, revelation, and directing activity. This power, as it were of an intellectual radiance, like the sun's warm beam, stamps on the soul a kind of visible seal of righteousness, light that is united to the soul through unfailing love, which bears God and is borne by God. Thence the growing likeness to God the Father arises in the 'Gnostic', as far as human nature admits, since he becomes 'perfect, as the Father in heaven'.[2] . . . God does not remain in the goodness of his nature, 'without trouble himself and without giving othes trouble'.[3] He performs his own good works, being and continuing to be in reality the good God and Father, continually occupied in doing good, undeviating in unchanging goodness. For what would be the value of a good being who was not *actively* good?

Stromateis, VI. xii (104, 1)

[1] Cf. Exod. xxxiv. 28.   [2] Matt. v. 48.   [3] Epicurus thus described 'the blessed and immortal'. *Diogenes Laertius*, x. 139.

Origenes Adamantius (Origen)

c. 185–255.—Works referred to by Latin titles (*Comm.* = Commentary, *Ep.* = Epistle, *Hom.* = Homilies). EDITIONS: generally the Benedictine (Delarue) reproduced in Migne and Lommatzsch; *Philocalia,* J. A. Robinson; *Comm. in Ioannem,* A. E. Brooke, with the sections of the earlier editions added in brackets, where they differ. Some in *Die Griechischen Christlichen Schriftsteller*.

Since a large part of Origen is available only in Latin versions, those passages which are not directly translated from the Greek are indicated by signs prefixed to the references, thus:

† Indicates the free, and often theologically 'bowdlerized', versions of Rufinus of Aquilea.

‡ The more faithful translation of Jerome.

★ An unknown translator.

I. God

(a) One, Immaterial, Incomprehensible; Revealed in Creation—and especially in Mind

Therefore, having refuted, to the best of our ability, every interpretation [*sc. of Scripture*] which suggests that anything material is to be understood in God, we say that the true nature of God cannot be comprehended by our thought. For if there is anything that we are able to conceive or understand about God, we are bound to believe him far superior to anything which we conceive. If we saw a man scarcely able to look at a spark of light . . . and we wished to teach him about the brightness and the splendour of the sun; should we not have to tell him 'The sun's splendour is better and grander than all this light which you see, to a degree which cannot be described or imagined'? So, while our mind is shut up within the confines of flesh and blood, and is rendered duller and blunter by its connexion with such material substances; though it be considered far superior to material nature, nevertheless, when it strives towards the immaterial, then it scarcely attains the standing of a spark. . . . (6) . . . Our eyes cannot behold the very nature of light, that is, the sun's own self: but beholding its brightness, or its rays . . . we can consider how great is the source and origin of material light. Now the works of the divine providence and the design of the whole universe are as it were rays of God's nature, in comparison with his very being. Our mind cannot behold God as he is in himself, therefore it forms its conception of the Creator of the universe from the

later
Anselm

beauty of his works and the loveliness of his creatures. . . . God is to be thought of as an uncompounded, intellectual being...a monad and, so to say, a unit, a mind, and the source from whom is the beginning of all intellectual being or mind. . . .

(7, *ad fin*) . . . There is a kinship between the human mind and God; for the mind is itself an image of God, and therefore can have some conception of the divine nature, especially the more it is purified and removed from matter.   † *De Principiis*, I. i. 5–7

(b) Omnipotence

We know that in saying 'everything is possible to God,'[1] 'everything' is understood as not extending to the impossible and the inconceivable. We also assert that shameful things are impossible to God, for if they were it would mean that God is able to cease to be God; for 'if God does anything shameful, he is not God'.[2] But where Celsus lays it down that 'God does not will things unnatural' we make a distinction. If 'evil' is equated with 'unnatural' we agree that God wills nothing unnatural, nor anything that springs from evil, nor anything that happens senselessly; on the other hand it must needs be that what happens according to the design and will of God is not unnatural: what God does is not unnatural, even if it be surprising, or surprising to some people. If we are pressed to be more specific, we shall say that there are things which are *supernatural*, in relation to what is commonly regarded as natural, which God may do, in raising a human being above ordinary human nature and making him change to a nature which is higher and more divine, and in keeping him in this state, provided that the man shows by his conduct that he wishes so to be kept.

Contra Celsum, v. 23

(c) Passibility

When I speak to a man and beg him to have pity on me in some matter, if he is without compassion what I say to him causes him no suffering; but if his feelings are tender and his heart is not hard and callous, then he listens and has pity on me, and his feelings are softened in response to my prayer. Something of this sort I would have you suppose concerning the Saviour. He came down to earth in pity for human kind, he endured our passions and sufferings before he suffered the cross, and he deigned to assume our flesh. For if he had not suffered he would not have entered into full participation in human life. He first suffered, then he came down and was manifested. What is that

[1] Matt. xix. 26.   [2] Euripides, *frag.* 292.

passion which he suffered for us? It is the passion of love. The Father
himself and the God of the whole universe is 'longsuffering, full of
mercy and pity'.[1] Must he not then, in some sense, be exposed to suffering? So you must realize that in his dealing with men he suffers human
passions. 'For the Lord thy God bare thy ways, even as a man bears his
own son.'[2] Thus God bears our ways, just as the son of God bears our
'passions'. The Father himself is not impassible. If he is besought he
shows pity and compassion; he feels, in some sort, the passion of love,
and is exposed to what he cannot be exposed to in respect of his greatness, and for us men he endures the passions of mankind.

‡ *Hom. in Ezechielem*, vi. 6

[*There is joy in heaven over one sinner who repents.*] What I wish to say
may perchance astonish you; it seems that we give cause for rejoicing
and gladness to God and to the angels; we who are placed upon earth
offer to heaven an occasion for gladness and exultation, when we have
our conversation in heaven while we walk upon earth, and doubtless
thus it is that we produce a day of rejoicing for the heavenly powers.
But as our good actions and our progress in virtue produce gladness and
rejoicing for God and the angels, so I feel does our evil way of life
bring about lamentation and mourning not only on earth but also in
heaven; and it may well be that men's sins afflict with grief even God
himself. Is not this a cry of lamentation, 'I repent me that I have made
man on the earth'?[3] And that cry of our Lord and Saviour 'Jerusalem,
Jerusalem . . .' [Matt. xxiii. 37]. And do not think that only of the
men of old is it said that 'they stoned the prophets'. Nay, even I at this
day, if I hear not the words of the prophet, if I neglect his warnings,
then I stone the prophet, and do my best to kill him, since I listen not to
his words, as if he were dead. And again, it is the cry of God lamenting
over mankind, when the prophet says, 'Woe is me, for I am like one
who gathers stubble in harvest and as a grape cluster in the vintage,
because there is no ear, nor first-born cluster for eating! Ah, woe is me,
my soul, for the godly man has perished from the earth and there is
no one among men to chasten them!'[4] These are the cries of the Lord,
grieving for mankind. . . . Now all these passages where God is said to
lament, or rejoice, or hate, or be glad, are to be understood as spoken by
Scripture in metaphorical and human fashion. For the divine nature is
remote from all affection of passion and change, remaining ever unmoved and untroubled in its own summit of bliss.

† *Hom. in Numeros*, xxxiii. 2

[1] Ps. lxxxvi. 15.   [2] ? Deut. i. 31.   [3] Gen. vi. 8.   [4] Mic. vii. 1, 2 (LXX), loosely quoted

(d) God and Matter

This matter can suffice for the creation of all bodies in the world, as many as God wills to exist, and can serve the Creator in the fashioning of all the forms and kinds which he wishes to create, by receiving the qualities which he wishes to impose upon it. Yet somehow many men of standing have considered it to be uncreated—and have called its existence and power accidental. And I marvel how they can blame those who deny the existence of a creator God or any design in the universe . . . when they themselves incur a similar accusation of impiety in saying that matter is uncreated and co-eternal with God the uncreated. According to this reasoning, if we assumed, for the sake of argument, that matter had not been in existence, God would have been without activity, not having matter with which he could begin his operations; for they allege that he could not make anything out of nothing, and that matter came to hand accidentally and not by his design; and they imagine that this accidental find could be sufficient for the mighty work of creation. . . . But let them concede for a moment that matter did not exist, and that God made out of nothing the things which he willed to exist: shall we suppose that God would have made a better or a different kind of matter . . . or a worse? Or exactly the same kind as that which they allege to be uncreated? I think it will be abundantly plain to anyone, that neither a better nor an inferior kind of matter could have taken on the forms and kinds which are in the world; it would have to be the kind of matter which in fact did so assume them. Therefore it must be considered impious to call that uncreated which, if it were believed to be the creation of God, would undoubtedly be found to be of the same kind as the allegedly uncreated. † *De Principiis*, II. i. 4

(e) Creation. The Cause of Diversity

When God in the beginning created all things which he wished to create, that is, rational beings, the only cause he had for creating was his own nature, that is, his goodness. Since, then, he himself was the cause of this creation, and in him was no variety, nor change, nor impossibility,[1] he created all beings equal and the same, since he had no cause for variety and diversity. But since those rational beings themselves . . . were given free will, this freedom either stirred each one to make progress by imitating God, or led him to deteriorate through

[1] We should perhaps read *possibilitas*, 'potentiality'.

ignoring God. And this was the cause of diversity among rational
creatures. . . . But God thought it just to deal with his creation according to desert; and as a house has to have within it 'not only vessels of
gold and silver, but also of wood and clay, and some are vessels for
honourable and some for dishonourable use';[1] so God drew together
these diversities of character into the organization of one world, so that
he might equip it as one house, as it were, with different vessels, that is,
with different characters or minds. Such, in my view, are the reasons
for the diversity which the world displays; for the divine providence
deals with each individual in accordance with the different motions of
each, and the different bent of their characters. On this principle the
Creator will not seem unjust in assigning a place to each individual
according to his desert in consequence of preceding causes; nor will the
good or ill fortune of each individual at his birth be regarded as
accidental . . . nor will men suppose that there are different creators or
differences in the nature of souls.   † Ibid. II. ix. 6

(f) A Series of Worlds

Although the world is composed of a diversity of functions, the constitution of the whole is not to be thought of as discordant and incoherent. As a body is an organism made up of many members, and it is
held together by one soul, so, in my opinion, the whole world is a
kind of huge and immense living creature which is united by one soul,
namely the power and reason of God. . . . Inasmuch as . . . the
different motives and various purposes of rational creatures have caused
diversity in the world, it may well be that the final issue of the world
may be in conformity with its beginning. For there is no doubt that
its end is to be found in the great diversity and variety which has arisen;
and just this variety which will be discerned in the end of this world
will supply the causes and occasions of diversities in another world
which is to follow this. The end of this world will thus be the beginning
of another.   † Ibid. II. i. 3

God cannot be called 'omnipotent' without the existence of subjects
over which he may exercise his power; and therefore in order that God
may be displayed as 'omnipotent' it is essential that everything should
subsist. . . . [2]Since 'all-sovereign' entails 'subjects' it follows of necessity that God created these subjects in the beginning, and that there was

---

[1] 2 Tim. ii. 20.   [2] This is taken from a quotation in Photius of a passage from Methodius
(Bishop of Olympus *c.* 310) which may well be—or be based on—the original Greek
of Origen which was ruthlessly condensed by Rufinus.

no time when they did not exist. If there were such a time . . . it would
follow that the unchangeable and unalterable God would be altered
and changed. For if he made everything later on it is clear that he
would change from not-making to making.¹   † *De Principiis*, I. ii. 10

[*To the question, What was God doing before this world began, if this world
had a beginning in time?*] We reply . . . that God did not begin his
activity with the creation of this visible world, but just as after the dissolution of this world there will be another world, so also before this
world there were, we believe, other worlds.   † Ibid. III. v. 3

(g) *God's power is not boundless*

Since God who is by nature good wishes to have those who might
receive his benefits and rejoice in their reception, he made creatures
worthy [*of himself*], that is, creatures who might worthily apprehend
him; so he speaks of himself as having 'begotten them as sons'.² But
he made all things in number and measure. For with God nothing is
without limit or without measure. For by his excellence he comprehends all things while he himself is comprehended by the conception of
none of his creatures.   † Ibid. IV. iv. 8

We must suppose that in the beginning God by his will appointed such
a number of rational beings as should suffice; for we must say that the
power of God has a limit and we must not, under pretext of honouring
God, annul this limitation. For if the power of God were infinite, it
would follow inevitably that it would not know itself; for the infinite is by nature incomprehensible. Therefore he made as many as
he could grasp and hold under his hand, and control beneath his providence; just as he prepared so much matter as he could set in order. . . .
                                              Ibid. II. ix. 1
                (Greek in Justinian, *Ep. ad Menam* [Mansi, IX. 489].)

(h) *Creation by Descent*

Since the end and consummation of the holy will be in 'those things
which are not seen and are eternal'³ . . . we must reckon that rational
beings had a similar origin. . . . If this is so, there was a descent from a
higher to a lower state not only on the part of those souls which had
deserved it by the various motions [*of their will*] but also on the part of
those who were brought down from the higher and invisible to this

¹ See note 2, p. 189.   ² Isa. i. 2.   ³ 2 Cor. iv. 18.

lower and visible realm, for the service of the whole world, although they did not wish it. 'For creation was made subject to vanity, not willingly, but by reason of him who subjected it in hope.'[1] In this way, the sun, moon, stars, and angels carry out obedient service to this world and to those souls which, because of the excessive failings of their intelligences, had need of these grosser and more palpable bodies; and on account of those for whom this was needful, the visible world was constituted. Therefore according to this significance [*of the word* constitutio *which in Greek is* καταβολή, *meaning also 'downfall'*] there seems to be indicated a bringing down of all alike from the higher to the lower realm. . . . The world must be supposed to have been made of a nature and a size to contain all the souls which were appointed to be trained therein, and all those powers which were provided to be with them to look after them and help them. All rational creatures have the same nature . . . the justice of God in all his dispensations can only be maintained by the assumption that each rational creature has in itself the cause for its assignment to one station of life or another. (5) . . . Those who do not understand . . . that the variety of God's dispensation is due to the preceding causes of free-will have thought that all things come about by chance, or fate. . . . Hence they have not been able to exonerate God's providence from blame.   † Ibid. III. v. 4–5

II. The Origin of Evil

(a) Not from God, nor from Matter

Celsus says that 'it is enough for the common people to be told, concerning the origin of evil, that it does not come from God, but is attached to matter, and is naturalized among mortals'. Well, it is true that evil does not come from God. . . . But . . . the rest of his statement is not true, according to our way of thinking. For the natural soul of each being is the cause of the wickedness which exists in him, and this is the real evil; and the acts that arise from this wickedness are the real evils. And, in our view there is nothing else that is evil, in the strict sense of the term.   *Contra Celsum*, iv. 66

(b) Good out of Evil

We say that by the providence and wisdom of God all things are so ordered in this world that nothing, whether good or evil, is utterly useless with God. But we will develop this assertion more clearly.

[1] Rom. viii. 20–21.

God does not create evil; still, he does not prevent it when it is displayed by others, although he could do so. But he uses evil, and those who exhibit it, for necessary purposes. For by means of those in whom there is evil, he bestows honour and approbation on those who strive for the glory of virtue. Virtue, if unopposed, would not shine out nor become more glorious by probation. Virtue is not virtue if it be untested and unexamined. . . . If you remove the wickedness of Judas and annul his treachery you take away likewise the cross of Christ and his passion: and if there were no cross then principalities and powers have not been stripped nor triumphed over by the wood of the cross.[1] Had there been no death of Christ, there would certainly have been no resurrection and there would have been no 'firstborn from the dead';[2] and then there would have been for us no hope of resurrection. Similarly concerning the devil himself, if we suppose, for the sake of argument, that he had been forcibly prevented from sinning, or that the will to do evil had been taken away from him after his sin; then at the same time there would have been taken from us the struggle against the wiles of the devil, and there would be no crown of victory in store for him who rightly struggled.

† *Hom. in Numeros*, xiv. 2

What are we to say in reply to this question: 'How can God create evil?' . . . Now in the full sense only virtue is good . . . and the opposite is evil. . . . (55) But one might find the terms 'good and evil' applied by a loose use of words to things which affect the body and to external circumstances; those things which contribute to physical welfare being accounted 'good', those which hinder such welfare being reckoned 'evil'. Thus Job says to his wife, 'If we received the good from the hand of the Lord, shall we not endure the evil?'[3] There is found in the Scriptures the saying of God himself, 'I am he who makes peace and creates evil'.[4] . . . Now God has not created evil if by this is understood evil properly so called: but some evils, though really they are few by comparison with the order of the whole universe, followed as a secondary consequence upon his primary work, just as spiral shavings and sawdust follow as a consequence upon the primary activity of a carpenter, and as builders seem to 'make' the waste stone and mortar which lie beside their buildings. (56) It may be granted that God sometimes creates some of these 'evils' in order that he may correct men by these means. If we are told that certain unpleasant experiences—so-called 'evils'—are inflicted by parents, teachers, and pedagogues, or by surgeons who use cautery or the knife for purposes of healing, we say that parents [&c.] inflict 'evil'; but that would not be an accusation against them; in just the same way God is said to inflict such 'evils' for purposes of correction and healing.   *Contra Celsum*, vi. 54–56

(c) *Evil and Non-entity*

'Without him nothing came into being.' . . . 'All things came into being through him.'[1] . . . We need to know what we are to understand by 'all things' and 'nothing'. For if the two statements are not elucidated one might infer that evil and all the abundance of sin and all wickedness came into being through the Word, since they are included in 'all things'. But this is false; for while there is no incongruity in ascribing the existence of created things to the agency of the Word; and while we must also consider that all the virtues and achievements of the blessed are due to his activity; we must not go on to make him responsible for sins and failures. Some have therefore laid it down that evil has no real existence; that therefore it never existed and never will exist; and that evil things are 'non-entity'. And, like certain Greek thinkers, who assert that there are genera and species of 'non-entities', so they suppose that 'nothing' really denotes the whole class of what has attained apparent subsistence, but not from God nor through the Word. . . . 'Nothing' and 'non-entity' would seem to be synonymous, etymologically, and interchangeable. And the Apostle clearly applies the term 'non-entity' not to things that have no sort of existence at all but to worthless things [Rom. iv. 17]. . . . And the contention that the wicked are called 'non-existent' can be supported by the name attributed to God in Exodus; for 'the Lord said to Moses: "He that is", that is my name'.[2] In relation to us, who claim to be of the Church, the good God makes this same statement; and in giving glory to him the Saviour says: 'No one is good except God, the Father'.[3] Thus 'he that is good' is the same as 'he that is', but evil is the opposite of good and 'non-entity' the opposite of 'being'; it follows that evil is 'non-entity'. And this perhaps has confounded those who say that the devil is not the handiwork of God; for *qua* devil he is not, but as a derivative being, who is the devil *per accidens*, he is a creation of God, since no creature exists apart from our God. We might, for example, say that 'a murderer, as such, is not of God's making', without denying that as man he has been made by God.   *Comm. in Ioannem*, ii. 13 (7)

[1] John i. 3.   [2] Exod. iii. 14.   [3] Mark x. 18.

III. Providence

(a) God's Care for Individuals

Celsus may say that 'creation was not for man, as it was not for lions, eagles, dolphins. . . .' We say that the Creator did not create these things for lions, [&c.]; but that all creation was for the sake of the rational creature and (as Celsus says) 'that this universe might become an entire and perfect unity of all its parts, as the work of God'. This is well said, and we must subscribe to it. But God is not concerned only with the whole, as Celsus thinks, but, besides the whole, with every rational being individually. And yet 'his providence for the whole never fails', for if the whole deteriorates through the transgression of a rational creature who is a part of the whole, he takes care to provide a corrective, and 'in time he brings back the whole to himself'. But 'he is not angry with apes or flies', yet he does bring punishment and chastisement on *men*, because they fail to fulfil the purposes for which they were made, and he warns them by the prophets, and by the Saviour who sojourned with the whole human race.   *Contra Celsum*, iv. 99

If anyone raise the objection, 'Why does some portion of the seeds fall into a soul which, like a rock, has only a shallow covering of soil?' the reply must be that it is good for such a soul as this, which impulsively desires the better things, yet does not take the road towards them, to have what it desires; that it may thus learn the truth about its natural tillage, and thereafter persevere to attain [*a good crop*] at long last. For the number of souls is, as far as we can see, infinite; and the same is true of their characters, and they have innumerable motions, projects, purposes, and impulses. There is one alone who can manage all these for the best,[1] since he knows the fitting times, the appropriate assistance to be given, the ways of training and direction. And he is the God and Father of the whole universe. He knows the way by which he led Pharaoh, through all those chastisements and through drowning in the sea. And in this drowning it is certainly not to be supposed that the providence[2] of God towards Pharaoh was finished; for it is not to be supposed that because he was drowned he was annihilated. 'For in the hand of God are both we and our words and all understanding and knowledge of works.'[3]

                    De Principiis, iii. i. 14 (Greek in *Philocalia*, xxi. 13)

[1] 'the best manager' (*oikonomos*).   [2] 'Management', 'economy' (see note on p. 75).
[3] Wisd. vii. 16.

(b) God's Providence and God's Will

We propose as our fixed and unchangeable belief that God is in-corporeal, omnipotent, and invisible; and at the same time that he cares for mortal affairs, and that nothing takes place without his providence, either in heaven or on earth. But note that we have said 'without his providence', not 'without his will'. For many things take place without his will, nothing without his providence. For providence is that by which God administers and disposes and watches over events as they happen. But his will is that by which he decides that something should or should not happen. . . . It follows, since we profess belief in God as administering and disposing all things, that he should reveal his will and show men what is for their good. For if he did not he would not be showing concern for men, nor should we believe in his care for mortal affairs.   † *Hom. in Genesin*, iii. 2

(c) Foreknowledge and Freedom

[*Foreknowledge of Judas's treachery.*] Celsus thinks that what is fore-told by the foreknowledge of someone happens *because* it has been fore-told; but we do not grant this. We aver that the foreteller is not the cause of the future event because he foretold that it was going to happen; but that the future events would have happened even if it were not foretold and that it provided the cause of the prophet's fore-telling it. And in the foreknowledge of the prophet the whole situa-tion is actually this, viz.: there is something that may happen or not but *this* alternative will happen. And we deny that the man with fore-sight removes the alternative possibility, as if he said something like this, 'This will certainly happen and it cannot happen otherwise'.

Contra Celsum, ii. 20

'Set apart for the gospel of God.'[1] And in the epistle to the Galatians he says this about himself: 'But when God, who separated me from my mother's womb, was pleased to reveal his Son in me.'[2] Such passages as these are seized on by those who do not understand that the man who is foreordained by the foreknowledge of God is really responsible for the happening of what is foreknown; and they imagine that God introduces men into the world who are already equipped by nature for salvation. . . . [Rom. viii. 28 ff]. (2) Let us observe the order of the words. . . . It is not foreordination that is the start of calling and justification. If this were so, a more convincing case could be put by

[1] Rom. i. 1.   [2] Gal. i. 15.

those who bring in the absurd argument about 'salvation by nature'. But in fact foreknowledge *precedes* foreordination. . . . God observed beforehand the sequences of future events, and noticed the inclination of some men towards piety, on their own responsibility, and their stirring towards piety which followed on this inclination; he sees how they devote themselves to living a virtuous life, and he foreknew them, knowing the present, and foreknowing the future. . . . And if anyone in reply asks whether it is possible for the events which God foreknew not to happen, we shall answer, Yes, and there is no necessity determining this happening or not happening. . . .[1] (3) . . . 'We know that all things work together for good for those that love God.[2]' This text clearly makes us responsible causes of the predestination and foreknowledge of God. For it is as much as to say that all things work together for good because those who love God are worthy of this co-operation. . . . If we grant that God foreknows, we ask our opponents, 'If we grant human responsibility, is God's foreknowledge the *cause* of future events? Or did he foreknow because it will happen thus?' In this case his foreknowledge is not the cause of what happens as a result of the responsible actions of each individual. Therefore the freedom bestowed by the Creator is able to choose which to realize, of various possibilities which arise.

Comm. in Ep. ad Romanos, i (Greek in *Philocalia*, xxv. 1)

IV. Man

(a) The Pre-existence and Fate of the Soul

Origen taught the pre-existence of the soul; see *De Principiis*, II. ix. 2 and many other passages. He was accused of teaching a Pythagorean metempsychosis—the transference of the soul to another human body, or to the body of an animal or vegetable. Justinian and Jerome based this charge on a passage at the end of *De Principiis*, I, which in the extant Latin version has been modified by Rufinus. But Justinian gives a fragment of the original Greek, and Jerome a Latin paraphrase.

We consider that the speculation and constructions put forward gratuitously by certain people are in no way to be accepted. According to these, souls may reach such degradation that forgetting their rational nature and dignity they sink down to the order of irrational beings and brutes.   † *De Principiis*, I. viii. 4 (*ad fin.*)

---

[1] As Origen justly observes in what follows, 'this subject requires considerable logical acumen and metaphysical speculation (θεωρία).'   [2] Rom. viii. 28.

The soul when it deviates from the good and inclines to wickedness and becomes more and more involved in it is brutalized through its folly and bestialized through its iniquity. [*And, a little later*] It is borne along towards loss of its rationality and to what may perhaps be called a 'watery' life, and soon, as its increasing degradation deserves, it puts on the 'watery' bodies of evil appropriate to such an irrational creature.

Justinian, *Ep. ad Menam*[1] (Mansi, ix. 529)

At the end [*of* De Principiis, I] he put forward the view that an angel or a soul or at any rate a demon (all of which he alleges to be of the same nature but of different wills) could become an animal in proportion to the magnitude of its insensibility and folly; and in view of the pain of punishment and the heat of the fire could rather choose to be a brute creature, and live in the waters and the waves, and to take on the body of some beast or other; and therefore we should fear [*to eat*] the bodies not only of quadrupeds but also of fishes. After putting forward this detestable view, by which he has wounded the feelings of the reader, he seeks to avoid the imputation of holding the opinion of Pythagoras (who taught *metempsychosis*) by adding at the end, 'These views are not doctrines, according to our opinion, but they are put forward only for discussion, lest they should seem to have been utterly neglected'.

Jerome, *Ep.* (cxxiv) *ad Avitum*.

The last sentence is important, for it seems to cancel Jerome's accusation. Pamphilus[2] (Rufinus, *Apologia Pamphili*, ix, Migne, *P.L.* xxii. 608) alleges that the objectionable speculations were put into the mouth of an interlocutor of Origen.

Many passages in Origen wholly reject any such doctrine, e.g.

We do not allege any re-embodiment of the soul, or any fall of the soul down to the level of the irrational creatures; and so it is clear that if we abstain from animal food it is not for the same reason as Pythagoras that we do not eat the flesh of beasts. *Contra Celsum*, viii. 30

['*Elias has already come.*'[3]] I do not think that this means that the soul [*of John the Baptist*] was [*the soul of*] Elias; lest I should fall into the doctrine of re-embodiment which is alien from the doctrine of the Church of God. It is not the tradition of the Apostles; it does not appear anywhere in Scripture. And indeed it is repugnant to . . . [*the passages foretelling the end of the world*]. For if, by hypothesis, the same soul may

[1] Menas was Patriarch of Constantinople, 536–552.   [2] Pamphilus of Caesarea, martyred 309, wrote an *Apology for* (Defence of) *Origen*, of which we have the first of the five books in an inaccurate translation by Rufinus.   [3] Mat. xvii. 12.

be embodied twice, under the conditions which obtain from the beginning to the end of the world, what is the reason for this second embodiment? If it is because of the sins committed in the first embodiment,
why should it not happen three times, or more, if punishment for sins
committed in this life can only be paid by this method of re-embodiment? If this follows, then there will be no speedy end to the process,
for the soul will have continually to sojourn in the body on account of
its former sins, and thus there will be no chance for the end of the
world. . . . [*And even if we may suppose the gradual purification of all souls
after countless ages this would not agree with the dominical prophecies of the
end which speak of sinners being surprised by the final catastrophe*: Matt.
xxiv. 37–39.] Then either there must be two kinds of punishment . . .
or else those who are surprised at the end of the world will not be
punished, as having cast away their sins altogether; or (and this is
better) there is one type of punishment . . . which takes place outside
of the conditions of this present life.   *Comm. in Matthaeum*. xiii. 1

(b) Image and Likeness

The fact that after God has said, 'Let us make man in our image and
likeness', the narrator goes on to say, 'In the image of God he made
him' and is silent about the likeness, indicates just this: that in his first
creation man received the dignity of the image of God, but the fulfilment of the likeness is reserved for the final consummation; that is,
that he himself should appropriate it by the eagerness of his own efforts,
through the imitation of God having the possibility of perfection given
to him at the beginning by the dignity of the image, and then in the
end, through the fulfilment of his works, should bring to perfect
consummation the likeness of God. The Apostle John defines this state
of things more clearly when he thus declares: 'My little children, we do
not yet know what we shall be but if it shall be revealed to us concerning the Saviour, without doubt ye will say: We shall be like him.'[1]

† *De Principiis*, III, iv. 1

[*Celsus had compared Christians and Jews to bats, ants, frogs, or worms,
ridiculing their pretensions to the divine favour. Origen retorts, Why should
Christians be thus scornfully spoken of, rather than men in general? Or
should not such contumely be reserved for the wicked?*] And yet it would be
wrong to liken to a worm any rational creature who has possibilities of
virtue. . . . It is clear that men in general could not be worms in rela-

[1] Cf. 1 John iii. 2.

tion to God. Reason takes its origin from the Logos that is with God, and this reason precludes a rational creature from being regarded as completely alien to God.   *Contra Celsum*, IV. 25

The Son in his kindness generously imparted deification to others . . . who are transformed through him into gods, as images of the prototype . . . the Word is the archetype of the many images.

Comm. in Ioannem, ii. 2

(c) Natural Law—Conscience

It is certain that when 'the Gentiles who have not the law' are said to 'do by nature the things of the law'[1] this does not refer to the sabbath and new moons and sacrifices which are prescribed in the law. For this law is not 'written in their hearts'. What is there written is what they are able to perceive by nature; as, for example, the prohibition of murder, adultery, theft, false witness, the duty of honouring father and mother, and the like. Perhaps also it is written in their hearts that there is one God who created all things. Yet these things which are said to be written in the heart seem to me to correspond more to the laws of the gospel, where all things are referred to natural equity. For what is closer to natural feelings than the command 'not to do to others what you would not that others should do to you'?[2] . . . The Apostle says that those who keep the law written in their hearts enjoy the testimony of a sound conscience.[3] Hence it seems necessary to discuss what this is which the Apostle calls conscience. . . . I observe an independence in conscience, in that it rejoices and exults in good acts, while it is not convicted in bad, but reprehends and convicts the soul, with which it is closely connected. Hence my opinion is that the conscience is the same as the spirit. . . . [Cf. 1 Cor. ii. 11 *and* Rom. viii. 12.] If the soul is disobedient and contumacious towards the spirit, the spirit will be divided and separated from the soul after death. And this, I think, is the meaning of the saying in the Gospel about the unsatisfactory steward: 'The Lord will divide him and appoint his portion with the unfaithful'[4] . . . and this following saying may be applied in the same sense: 'There will be two in a field, one shall be taken and one shall be left; and two women at a mill; one shall be taken and one shall be left.'[5]   † *Comm. in Ep. ad Romanos*, ii. 9

---

[1] Rom. ii. 14.   [2] Tobit iv. 15; Matt. vii. 12 gives the positive form.   [3] Rom. ii. 15
[4] Luke xii. 46.   [5] Matt. xxiv. 40–41.

No one, Jew or Gentile, is devoid of this law, which is in men by
nature. . . . It will be found that God gave to man all the feelings and
all the impulses by which he could strive and progress towards virtue;
and besides that he implanted in him the power of reason, by which he
might recognize what he ought to do and what to shun. God is found
to have bestowed all this on all men alike. Now if a man had neglected
to walk the way of virtue . . . in judgement on such a man God is
rightly said to 'prevail and to be justified in his words'.[1]

This natural law, then, speaks to all who are subject to law; it seems
to me that only infants, who have not yet acquired the power of distinguishing right from wrong, are exempt from the commandment of
this law.   † *Comm. in Ep. ad Romanos*, iii. 6

'Glory and honour and peace to every man whose deeds are good, to
the Jew first and afterwards to the Greek.'[2] Meaning by this, as I understand it, the Jews and Gentiles who do not yet believe. For it may be
that even one of those under the law, without believing in Christ,
may yet do good works, may keep justice and love mercy, preserve
chastity and continence, keep modesty and gentleness, and do every
good work; though he has not eternal life, because while believing in
'the only God' he has not believed also in 'his Son, Jesus Christ whom
he had sent',[3] still the glory and peace and honour of his works will be
able to survive death. And the Greek also, that is the Gentile, although
he had not the law, is 'a law unto himself, having the works of the law
in his heart'[4] and remaining true to his natural reason, as we see some
of the Gentiles do. If he keep justice or preserve chastity, or maintain
prudence, temperance, and modesty; although he be alien from eternal
life, because he does not believe in Christ, and cannot enter the kingdom of heaven, because he has not been 'born again of water and the
Spirit';[5] still it seems, according to the Apostle's words, that the glory
and honour and peace of his good works cannot perish utterly.
                                                          †Ibid. ii. 7

(d) Man in Relation to God: Faith, Works, Justification

Now certainly you will consider whether, as it was said of faith that it
was 'reckoned to him for righteousness',[6] so it might be said of other
virtues, e.g. that mercy can be reckoned to anyone for righteousness;
or wisdom, or knowledge, or kindness, or humility; or whether faith

[1] Ps. l. 6 (51. 4), cf. Rom. iii. 4.   [2] Rom. ii. 10.   [3] John xvii. 3.   [4] Rom. ii. 15.
[5] John iii. 5.   [6] Rom. iv. 9.

is reckoned for righteousness in the case of every believer. Now, when I return to the Scriptures, I do not find that for all believers faith is reckoned for righteousness. . . . For this reason I think that those other believers had not, as we have taught that Abraham had, a perfection of faith, an accumulation of many instances of faith, which deserved to be reckoned for righteousness. Now when St. Paul says, 'But to the man who works the reward is not reckoned as of grace, but of debt. But to the man who does not work, but believes on him who justifies the ungodly, his faith is reckoned for righteousness';[1] it seems as if he is showing that in respect of faith we find the grace of him who justifies, whereas in respect of works we find the justice of him who repays. But when I consider the apparent meaning of the passage in which he says that recompense is given as of debt to him who works, I can scarcely persuade myself that there can be any work which can claim remuneration from God as a debt, since even the very ability to do, or think, or speak, comes to us from the generous gift of God. How then can he be in debt to us, who has first put us in his debt?   † Ibid. iv. 1

But if perhaps it seems that what is said to come by faith is not given by free grace, on the ground that faith is first offered by men and thus grace is earned from God, listen to the Apostle's teaching about this in other passages. For when he enumerates the gifts of the Spirit, which he says are given to believers 'according to the measure of faith'[2] he there asserts that among other things the gift of faith also is bestowed by the Holy Spirit. For after many other things he says also on this point, 'To another faith, by the same Spirit'; so that he may show that 'even faith is given by grace'. And in another place his teaching is the same: 'because to you it has been granted not only to believe in Christ, but even to suffer on his behalf.'[3] You find it pointed out in the gospels also; when the Apostles say to the Saviour 'increase our faith';[4] thus recognizing that the faith which comes from man cannot be perfect, unless it has added to it the faith which comes from God. . . . That very faith by which we seem to believe in God is confirmed in us by the gift of grace.   † Ibid. iv. 5

[1] Rom. iv. 4, 5.   [2] 1 Cor. xii. 7, 8.   [3] Phil. i. 29.   [4] Luke xvii. 5.

V. Sin

(a) A Perversion of Man's Nature

'They have all gone out of the way. . . .'[1] I suppose that a man cannot
be said to have 'gone out of the way' unless he has at some time been
on the right way. Hence it is clear that the rational creature, the work of
God, was created aright, and set on the right way . . . but since he has
diverged along the path of sin he is rightly said to have 'gone out of the
way'.

The Apostle adds (from the Psalm), 'there is none that doeth good';[1]
a heavy saying. . . . How can it seem possible that no one at all can be
found, whether among Jews or Gentiles . . . who has sometime given
hospitality to a stranger, or bread to the hungry . . . or performed
some such action? I cannot think that the Apostle Paul intends to
make so incredible an assertion. . . . I think that he means something
like this. If a man lays the foundations of a house and builds two or three
walls, and collects a certain amount of material, he surely could not be
said to have 'made' a house; although he has engaged in building operations. A man is said to have 'made' a house when he has brought every
component part of the building to completion. This is what I think the
Apostle is saying here, that no one has 'done good', that is that no one
has brought goodness to complete fulfilment. If we ask who is truly
good and who has brought goodness to perfection we shall find only
the one who says 'I am the good shepherd'.[2]

† *Comm. in Ep. ad Romanos*, iii. 3

Celsus says . . . 'It is a very difficult thing to change a nature completely'. But we know that there is one nature which belongs to every
rational soul, and we assert that no nature was made evil by him who
created the universe, but that many have become wicked through
upbringing, through perversion, or the influence of environment, so
that wickedness has become second nature in some men; but we are
persuaded that for God's Logos to change inveterate wickedness is not
only not impossible but not even very difficult, if only a man accept
the duty of entrusting himself to God the ruler of all things, and of
acting always with a view to pleasing him. . . . But if there are some
for whom this conversion is hard, we must suppose that the reason lies
in their refusal to accept the fact that God the ruler of all is a just judge
of every man concerning all the actions of his life. For deliberate

[1] Rom. iii. 12 (quoting Ps. xiv).   [2] John x. 11.

choice and discipline have great effect even when faced with tasks which seem difficult, and indeed (to speak with some exaggeration) practically impossible. Human nature by the exercise of will has acquired the ability to walk on a tight-rope suspended high in the theatre . . . and it has achieved this ability by practice and application: are we to suppose that it is impossible for human nature to live virtuously, if it so wills, even if it has formerly sunk very low? A man who says this is surely bringing an indictment against the character of the Creator of the rational being rather than against the creature. For he is suggesting that he has made human nature competent to achieve things that are difficult but of no use, but incompetent to attain his own true blessedness. *Contra Celsum*, iii. 69

(b) The Instability of Rational Creatures

Since these rational beings . . . were created, and did not exist before their creation, they must needs be liable to change and variation just because they came into being from non-existence, since whatever value there was in their being was not there by nature, but was effected by the bounty of the Creator. Therefore their being is not theirs in their own right, nor is it eternal; it is given them by God. For it did not always exist, and everything which is given can be taken away and depart. Now there will be a reason for its departure, if the movement of their mind is not rightly and properly directed. For the Creator granted to the intelligences which he created the power of movement at their own free will, and that was in order that the good done in them might be their own, by being maintained by the use of their own will. But sloth and distaste for the effort involved in maintaining the good, and dislike and disregard for the better, cause the start of departure from the good. . . . Now to depart from the good means just this, to be established in evil. For it is certain that evil is the lack of good. The result was that each advanced in wickedness to the precise extent that he declined from good. . . . It seems that it was from this source that the Creator of all things received the seeds, as it were, and causes of variety and diversity so that in accordance with the diversity of intelligences, that is, of rational creatures (and they are to be supposed to have acquired this diversity from the cause above mentioned), his creation was various and diverse. †*De Principiis*, ii. ix. 2

Cf. above, pp. 188 f.

(c) Original Sin. Inherited from Adam by Imitation

... 'Therefore death reigned from Adam until Moses' (not over all but) 'over those who sinned in the likeness of Adam's transgression.'[1] For death entered in the world, and passed to all, but it did not reign over all. . . . For sin passed even to the just and touched them as it were with a light contagion. But it holds sway over the transgressors, that is over all who subject themselves to sin with whole-hearted devotion. . . . Thus the death of sin 'reigned from Adam until Moses', that is until the coming of the Law. . . . But when he says, 'Death reigned over them who sinned [&c.]' the meaning does not seem to me to be (unless there be here an indication of some mystery) that he makes a special class of certain individuals over whom death reigned. It may perhaps be that there were some within that period . . . who acted in much the same way as did Adam in paradise, according to the scriptural narrative, who took of the tree of knowledge of good and evil, who blushed at their nakedness and were cast out of paradise in which they dwelt. But I prefer to take it as meaning simply . . . all who were born of Adam the transgressor and who have in themselves the likeness of his transgression, having received it not only from his seed but also from his instruction. For all who are born in this world receive not only nourishment from their parents but also their early impressions; they are not only the sons but also the pupils of sinners. But when they are grown up and are free to follow their own sentiments, then each of them either 'walks in the way of his fathers'[2] . . . or proceeds along 'the way of the Lord his God'.[3]

† *Comm. in Ep. ad Romanos*, V. 1

(d) Sin perhaps Inherited by Generic Identity—'In Adam's Loins'

God cast Adam out of paradise and established him in this earth, in contrast with the paradise of delights; and this was the condemnation of his sin, which has undoubtedly come down to all men.[4] For all have been set in this place of humiliation and this vale of tears: either because all who were born of him were in the loins of Adam and were cast out of paradise together with him; or else it means that in some other mysterious way which is known to God alone each individual has been thrust out of paradise and has received condemnation.

† *Comm. in Ep. ad Romanos*, V. 4 (*ad fin.*)

[1] Rom. v. 14.   [2] 1 Kings xv. 26, &c.   [3] Cf. Gen. xviii. 19, &c.   [4] Cf. Rom. v. 18.

(e) Innate Sin

If the Apostle, in speaking of 'this body of sin'[1], is to be understood as meaning this body of ours [*rather than any body, being sinful because of its corporal nature*] he will be interpreted as meaning the same as David when he said of himself, 'I was conceived in sin, and in sin my mother conceived me'.[2] . . . Again the Apostle calls our body a 'body of humiliation':[3] and in a certain place he says of the Saviour that he came 'in the likeness of sinful flesh'[4] . . . thus showing that while our flesh is sinful flesh, the flesh of Christ is *like* 'sinful flesh'. For Christ was not conceived by means of the seed of a man. . . . Our body therefore is the 'body of sin' because, the Scripture relates, Adam did not know Eve his wife, and beget Cain, until he had sinned. . . . [*By the Law a sin-offering had to be made for a new-born child, who could not have sinned.*] And yet he had sin, and it is said that 'no one is clean from sin, even if his life has only been for one day'.[5] . . . It is for this reason that the Church has received from the Apostles the tradition of giving baptism to infants. For they were entrusted with the secrets of the divine mysteries, and they knew that there were in all mankind innate stains of sin which had to be washed away by water and the Spirit. It is because of these stains that the body is called 'the body of sin', not—as some of those think who bring in the transmigration of souls into different bodies—because of the sins which the soul has committed while in another embodiment, but because of this fact, that the soul has been established in a body 'of sin',[6] 'of death',[7] 'of humiliation'.[8] . . .

† Ibid. v. 9

(f) Sins of the Flesh

[*Even without the devil men would sin. The natural desires are not given by the devil.*] For my part I do not think that all men could be kept from exceeding moderation and restraint in taking food even if there were no instigation of the devil to urge them on . . . [*similarly in respect of drink, sexual intercourse, and other natural passions*]. It is evident that just as in respect of good actions man's purpose by itself is not competent to achieve the highest good, for it is only by God's aid that it is enabled to perfect each good design; so also in matters of evil, we receive as it were the beginning, the seeds, so to say, of sins, from those things which are an essential part of our natural life. But when we indulge

[1] Rom. vi. 6.   [2] Ps. l (51), 5.   [3] Phil. iii. 21.   [4] Rom. viii. 3.   [5] Job. xiv. 4–5 (LXX).
[6] Rom. vi. 6.   [7] Rom. vi. 24.   [8] Phil. iii. 21.

beyond what is enough, and do not resist the first motions of intemperance, then the hostile power [the devil] seizes the chance offered by this first wrongdoing, and incites us, and urges us on . . .

† *De Principiis*, III. ii. 2

(g) Pollution of Birth

[*Why should childbirth make a woman unclean, requiring sacrifice?* Lev. xii. 7.] You may see that there is here something inexplicable but important, from the fact that you will never find any of the saints celebrating his birthday, or holding a birthday party; nor keeping his son's or daughter's birthday as an occasion of rejoicing. Only sinners celebrate birthdays with rejoicing [*e.g.* Pharaoh (Gen. xl. 20) *and* Herod (Mark vi. 21)]. † *Hom. in Leviticum*, viii. 3

Everyone who enters the world is said to be affected by a kind of contamination. . . . [Job xiv. 4–5, *see above*, p. 205.] By the very fact that he is placed in his mother's womb, and that the source from which he takes the material of his body is the father's seed, he may be said to be contaminated in respect of father and mother. . . . Thus every man is polluted in father and mother and only Jesus my Lord came to birth without stain. He was not polluted in respect of his mother, for he entered a body which was not contaminated.

† Ibid. xii. 4

(h) The Infection of the First Sin

The serpent which seduced Eve and by his persuasive suggestions poured the poisons of sin into her and infected all her posterity with the contagion of the transgression . . .

† *Comm. in Canticum Canticorum*, iii (ed. Lommatzsch, xv, p. 54)

There is in each soul the power of choice, and freewill, by which it can perform all that is good. But this good thing which belongs to human nature has been spoiled by occasion of the transgression and inclined to shame or wantonness. Ibid. iv (xv, p. 72)

(j) The Curse of Adam Allegorized

'Adam' in Hebrew means 'man'; and in the narrative which purports to be about 'Adam' Moses is giving an explanation of the character of 'man'. 'In Adam all die'[1] and all were condemned 'in the likeness of Adam's sin';[2] these inspired utterances are not about one man but

[1] 1 Cor. xv. 24.   [2] Rom. v. 14.

rather about the whole human race. For the curse of Adam, which in the ensuing narrative is concerned with one man, is common to all men; and the expulsion of the man from paradise, clad in 'leather aprons' . . . has a hidden, mystical significance, excelling the myth of Plato[1] in which the soul loses its feathers and is borne hither and thither until it finds *terra firma*.   *Contra Celsum*, iv. 40

These aprons were made of skins taken from animals. For it was right that the sinner should put on such garments, of skins of beasts, which symbolized the mortality which he had received as a result of his sin, and of the frailty which resulted from the corruption of the flesh.
† *Hom. in Leviticum*, vi. 2

(k) A Speculation: The Soul as Fallen Mind

We may perhaps hazard a guess that the soul, or *psyche*, received its name from the fact that it grew cool [*psychros*] when it lost its participation in the divine fire . . . without, however, losing its ability to restore itself to the state of heat in which it was in the beginning. . . . All this points to the conclusion that mind, falling from its own estate and dignity, was made or called soul. And if soul be amended and corrected it returns to its condition of mind. . . . But our suggestion of the conversion of mind into soul, and any other remarks which seem to have the same bearing . . . are not to be thought of as put forward by us as dogma, but as treated by way of discussion and inquiry.
† *De Principiis*, II. viii. 3, 4

(l) Freedom

Origen never tires of asserting human responsibility and resisting any doctrine of arbitrary predestination. *De Principiis*, III, deals with this topic at length and discusses various passages of Scripture which seem to assert a divine foreordaining. Origen interprets many of these as meaning predestination *ex praevisis meritis*; other passages referring to 'hardening of hearts' by God he explains as describing a temporary remedial withholding of salvation until such time as men shall be able to appropriate it. This topic gives rise to further speculation on man's destiny.

In discussing such important and difficult topics, which relate to the manifold foreknowledge of God in his providence over immortal souls, we must be careful always to strive to preserve reverence, in respect to God and his Christ, and to avoid subordinating reverence to intellectual inquiry. There were some who were reproached for

[1] *Phaedrus* 246 c.

their failure to take advantage of their seeing miracles and hearing divine discourses, whereas the Tyrians would have repented, if such things had happened, and such discourses had been delivered, among them.[1] This might raise the question, 'Why then did the Lord preach to such men, for their undoing, to aggravate the sin laid to their charge?' To which it must be replied that God understood the intentions of those who arraign his providence; who excuse their unbelief on the grounds that his providence did not grant to them the sight of the events which others were privileged to behold, and did not arrange that they should hear the words which others heard to their advantage: and he wished to remove any plausibility from such an excuse. That is why he gives such an opportunity, which forms the basis of the charge against him for those who find fault with his government of events. His purpose being that after men have received their chance and in spite of that have been proved irreligious by the failure to take advantage of this proffered help, they may abandon their rash confidence, and, being set free by this very fact, may learn that it is for men's benefit that God sometimes delays and lingers in his dealings with men, in not granting them to see and hear such things; for when men have seen and heard them and yet have not believed it is a graver and heavier sin that is proved against them.

De Principiis, III. i. 17 (Greek in *Philocalia*, xxi. 16)

[*On* Rom. ix. 19 ff.—'vessels for honour and dishonour from the same lump of clay'.] If men bring in the consideration of different natures of different persons, and interpret the passage in this way, there is this to be said. If they maintain that the saved and the lost are 'from the same lump', and the Creator of the saved is the Creator also of the lost, and if he is good who made the 'earthy' as well as the 'spiritual' (and this follows from their premises); it still remains possible that one who was made into a 'vessel of honour' in this life, as a result of good conduct in a former existence, may now behave differently, in a way inappropriate to a 'vessel of honour', and thus for a future life become a 'vessel of dishonour'. On the other hand, it is possible that a 'vessel of dishonour' in this life, so made on account of an earlier existence, may amend in the 'new creation'[2] and become a 'vessel of honour, consecrated, and useful to his owner, ready for any good work'.[3] . . . Thus some through their deliberate acts advance from a worse to a better state; others fall from a better to a worse; others are kept in a

[1] Matt. xi. 21.   [2] Gal. vi. 16; 2 Cor. v. 17.   [3] 2 Tim. ii. 2.

state of good, or even progress beyond this, while some remain in a
state of evil, or deteriorate still further as wickedness spreads in them.

Hence I must needs think it possible that there are some who began
with small sins and advanced so far in evil that they have come to be
ranked with the hostile powers; conversely, they may . . . apply
healing medicine to their wounds and pass over to a state of good.
Wherefore, in my opinion, since the soul (as I have often said) is immortal and eternal, it is conceivable that in the passage of successive
measureless ages . . . souls may descend from the highest good to the
lowest evil, or from the extreme of evil may be restored to the highest
good.   Ibid. III. 21 (*Philocalia*, xxi. 22)[1]

(m) Freedom and Grace

Let us examine the saying, 'Then it is not the result of man's will, or effort
[running], but of God's mercy'.[2] The objectors say, 'In that case our
salvation is in no way our responsibility, it is a matter of our constitution, for which the Creator is responsible, or it arises from the decision
of one who shows mercy when he so pleases'. . . . 'If the Lord does
not build the house, the builders have laboured in vain; if the Lord
does not guard the city, the guard has kept vigil in vain'.[3] This is not
meant to deter us from building, or to counsel us not to be vigilant in
guarding the city which is in our soul. . . . We should do right in
calling a building a work of God, rather than of the builder, and the
preservation of a city from hostile attack we should rightly call an
achievement of God rather than of the guard. But in so speaking we
assume man's share in the achievement, while in thankfulness we
ascribe it to God who brings it to success. Similarly man's will is not
sufficient to attain the end [*of salvation*], nor is the running of the metaphorical athletes competent to attain 'the prize of the upward summons
of God in Christ Jesus'.[4] This is only accomplished with God's assistance. Thus it is quite true that 'It is not the result of man's will [&c.]'
. . . Our perfection does not come about by our remaining inactive,
yet it is not accomplished by our own activity; God plays the greater
part in effecting it. . . . We will take an illustration from navigation.
How small is the part played by nautical skill in a successful voyage
compared with the contribution made by wind, weather, and visi-
bility of the stars, to the safety of the voyagers! The helmsmen them-

---

[1] The passage in the *Philocalia* ends at '. . . spreads in them', but Rufinus's translation
continues and its faithfulness to Origen's Greek is here vouched for by Jerome's version
of it in *Ep.* (cxxiv) *ad Avitum*, 8.   [2] Rom. ix. 16.   [3] Ps. cxxvi (127), 1 f.   [4] Phil. iii. 14.

selves do not generally go so far as to claim credit for their alertness as
having ensured the ship's safety; they ascribe it all to God. Not that they
have had no hand in it; but providence has played an immeasurably
greater part than skill. The same is true in respect of our salvation . . .
(19) 'The will and the activity come from God'.[1] This leads some to say,
'If this is so, then God is the source of our evil willing and doing; and
we have no free-will. On the other hand, if our will is good, and our
acts are excellent . . . there is no virtue in it; our achievement is an
illusion, since it is imposed by God; and we have no free-will. The
answer to this is that the Apostle does not say that willing good or
willing evil comes from God . . . but willing in general. . . . Just as
our existence as animals, and our existence as men, is derived from
God, so is our power of willing in general, and our power of motion
in general. Because, as animals, we have the power of motion. e.g. of
moving our hands or feet, it would not be plausible to say that any
particular movement, striking, say, or destroying, or stealing, is derived
from God. The general power of motion comes from him, and we
employ it for ends good or bad. Thus we have the power of will and
activity from God, and we employ it for good or bad purposes.

De Principiis, III. i. 18–19 (*Philocalia*, xxi. 17–18)

[*The incarnation was not a sudden intervention of a God hitherto negligent,
like Zeus awaking from sleep.*] God had always been working for the
good of the human race. For nothing good has happened in men
except by the indwelling of the divine Logos in the souls of those who
were capable of receiving, if only for a short time, such workings of
the divine Logos . . .   *Contra Celsum*, vi. 78

VI. The Incarnation

(a) The Logos

If by participation [*in the Word*] we are raised from the dead, and enlightened, and also, it may be, shepherded by him and ruled over, it is
clear that through him we are made rational by divine inspiration, since
he does away with the irrationality and deadness in us, inasmuch as he
is the Word [reason] and the resurrection. But we must attend to this
point: whether all men in some way participate in him, inasmuch as
he is the Word [reason]. It is for this cause that the Apostle teaches
that he is sought, by those who elect to find him, not outside of the

[1] Phil. ii. 13.

seekers: 'Do not say in your heart, Who shall ascend to heaven? (that is, to bring Christ down), Who shall descend into the abyss? (that is, to bring Christ up from the dead). But what does the Scripture say? The word[1] is very near, in thy mouth and in thy heart.'[2] For Christ is the same as this word[1] which is sought.

Again, when the Lord himself says, 'If I had not come and spoken to them they would not have had sin; but now they have no excuse concerning their sin',[3] it is to be understood as meaning just this, that there are some by whom the Word is not yet so completely assimilated that sin ceases, and to them he speaks, saying that they are responsible for being involved in sin, if, after having participated in him, they act contrary to the ideas whose fulfilment results in his being completely assimilated by them. And only in this way is it true that 'If I had not come [&c.].' For suppose it said of the visible Jesus, as the majority will assume, then inquire, 'How can it be true that those to whom he has not come have not sin?' For in that case all who preceded the sojourn of the Saviour will be released from their sins, since Jesus who was observed in the flesh had not come. And besides, those to whom the tidings of him have never come will all be free from sin; and it is obvious that those who have not sin are not liable to judgement.

The truth is that reason[4] which is in men, of which, as we have said, the whole human race partakes, has two significations. Either it refers to the aggregate of ideas which is the portion of every normal man who has passed beyond childhood; or it refers to the highest pitch of rationality which is found only in the perfect. Now the saying 'If I had not come [&c.].' has reference to the first signification: while the second is implied in, 'All who came before me are thieves and robbers, and the sheep did not listen to them'.[5] For before the complete reception of the Word all human faculties are blameworthy as deficient and inadequate, and our irrational elements do not render them complete obedience; and these irrational elements are metaphorically called 'the sheep'. And, I suppose, 'the Word was made flesh' refers to the first meaning; 'the Word was God' to the second. . . .

(38) The Word can also be a son, in regard to his proclamation of the hidden things of his father, as a man's word may be called the son of his mind. For just as our word is the messenger of what is seen by the mind, so the Word of God knows the Father and reveals the Father whom he knows, since no created being can approach him without a guide. For

[1] ῥῆμα.   [2] Rom. x. 6 ff., cf. Deut. xxx. 12 ff.   [3] John xv. 22.   [4] λόγος (also 'word').
[5] John x. 8.

'No one knows the Father except the Son, and he to whom the Son
has revealed him',[1] and in that he is Word he is the 'Angel [messenger]
of mighty counsel' and 'the rule came upon his shoulder'.[2] For he ruled
as king[3] through his suffering the cross.

Comm. in Ioannem, i. 37–38 (42)

(b) The Incarnation Contingent on Man's Sin

God, then, is utterly one and uncompounded; but our Saviour, when
God sent him forth to be a propitiation[4] and the firstfruit of all creation,[5]
became many because of the many; or rather perhaps, he became all
things, inasmuch as all creation has need of him; all creation, that is,
that is capable of receiving freedom. And therefore he becomes the
light of men, when men who had been plunged in darkness by wickedness, need 'the light that shines in darkness and is not overcome by
darkness'.[6] He could not have become the light of men if men had not
been in darkness. Similarly we must suppose in regard to his being the
'first begotten of the dead'.[7] For if we suppose that the woman had not
been deceived, and Adam had not fallen, but man who was 'created
for incorruption'[8] had kept hold of incorruption, the Saviour would
not have gone down 'to the dust of death',[9] nor would he have died,
had there been no sin, nor would he have had to die because of his love
of man. . . . [*If man had not sinned*] we may suppose that he would have
remained Wisdom and Word and Life; and certainly Truth. But he
he would not have all the other attributes which he took upon himself
for our sake.   *Comm. in Ioannem*, i. 20 (22)

(c) The Subordination of the Son

We have said that all souls who lived in this world needed many
helpers, or rulers, or assistants; so in these last times when the end of
the world was already imminent, and the whole human race was ap-
proaching final perdition, and when not only those who were ruled
but also those to whom the responsibility of ruling had been entrusted
had grown weak; men at this time needed 'not such help as this nor
defenders'[10] of the same nature as themselves, but they implored the aid
of the very Author and Creator of their being, that he might restore to
men the discipline of obedience, to the ruling powers the discipline of
ruling; for this discipline had been broken and infringed. Hence the

---

[1] Matt. xi 27.   [2] Isa. ix. 6 (LXX).   [3] Presumably referring to the variant reading found
in that Old Latin version of Ps. xcvi. 10, 'The Lord hath reigned from the tree'.   [4] Rom.
iii. 25.   [5] Col. i. 15.   [6] John i. 5.   [7] Col. i. 18.   [8] Wisd. ii. 23.   [9] Ps. xxii. 15.
[10] A reminiscence of Virgil, *Aeneid*, ii. 521 f.

only begotten Son of God, who was the Word and Wisdom of God, though he was 'with the Father in the glory, which he had before the world was,'[1] 'abased himself and taking the form of a servant was made obedient unto death'[2] that he might teach obedience to those who could not achieve salvation save through obedience; and he also restored the laws of ruling and reigning which had been broken, by 'subjecting all enemies beneath his feet'[3] . . . not only was he made obedient to the Father 'even to the death of the cross', but even in the consummation of the age when he gathers up all in himself, whom he subjects to the Father . . . with them and in them he himself is also said to be subjected to the Father. † *De Principiis*, III. v. 6

(d) Descent without Change of State

Though the God of the whole universe descends in his own power with Jesus to live the life of men, and the Word which 'was in the beginning with God and was himself God' comes to us; yet he does not leave his home or desert his state. The result is not that one place is emptied of him while another is full, which did not before contain him. The power and divinity of God takes his dwelling as he wills, and where he finds a place for himself: God does not change his place. . . . When we speak of his leaving one and filling another we shall not be speaking of locality but asserting that the soul of the worthless and utterly degenerate is deserted by God, while the soul of him who wishes to live according to virtue, either advancing towards this or already living a virtuous life, is filled with the divine spirit, or partakes of it. Therefore in respect of Christ's descent, or the sojourn of God with men, there is no need of his leaving his greater state. *Contra Celsum*, iv.

For this [*divine descent*] he had no need of change . . . for he remains unchanged in his essential being[4] while he descends to take part in human affairs by the providence and dispensation[5] [*of God*].

Ibid. iv. 14

[*Celsus maintains that the incarnation entails a change in God, or a deceitful appearance.*] One might answer this (a) concerning the nature of the Divine Word who is God, and (b) concerning the soul of Jesus. (a) We may say that as in nursing mothers the quality of food changes to milk, suitable to the nature of the child . . . so in dealing with men God changes the power of the Word, whose nature it is to nourish the

---

[1] John xvii. 5.   [2] Phil. ii. 7 f.   [3] I Cor. xv. 25.   [4] οὐσία, 'substance'.   [5] οἰκονομία (cf. note 6, p. 75).

human soul, in advance with the merit of the individual. And to one
he comes as 'the rational pure milk'[1] (in the scriptural phrase) . . . to
another he is imparted as 'solid food'.[2] There is no question of the
Word's being false to his own nature in becoming nourishment for
each man in accordance with his capacity to receive it. . . . (b) If one
takes the change to have reference to the soul of Jesus, in entering the
body, then we shall ask, 'What is meant by "change" '? If change of
essential being,[3] we do not admit it, either in respect of his soul or even
concerning any other rational soul. If it be meant that his soul is subject to limitations[4] from the body with which it was mingled, or
arising from the place to which it came, then we ask, 'Does any incongruity result for the Word in bringing down a Saviour for the
human race, because of his great love for man?' For none of those who
were before him proclaimed as healers had such powers as the soul of
Jesus displayed in its works, when it descended to the afflictions of men
on behalf of our race . . . [citing Phil. ii. 5–9].   Contra Celsum, iv. 18

(e) Radiance and Image of God

Let us see how we are to understand the saying of Paul concerning
Christ, that he is the 'radiance of God's splendour and the representation of his being'.[5] 'God is light' says John.[6] The radiance of this light
is the only begotten Son, who proceeds from the Father without
separation, as radiance from the light, and gives light to the whole
creation. . . . Through radiance men understand and experience what
the light itself is. This radiance presents itself gently to the feeble eyes
of mortal men and gradually trains and accustoms them, as it were, to
endure the full blaze of the light. It removes from them all that clogs
and impedes their vision, in accord with the word of the Lord, 'Cast
out the beam from your eye'.[7] Thus it makes them able to receive the
splendour of the light; and in this also it becomes a kind of mediator
between men and the light.

(8) . . . Let us employ an illustration so that we may more fully
understand in what way the Saviour is 'the representation of the being
of God'. The illustration does not fully or adequately express the
meaning of the phrase we are discussing; but it may be regarded as
adopted to make just this point: that the Son, when 'being in the form
of God he abased himself',[8] is concerned, through the 'self-abasement',

---

[1] λογικὸν . . . γάλα, 1 Pet. ii. 2 (the connexion with λόγος, 'Word', cannot be reproduced
in English).   [2] Heb. v. 12.   [3] See note 4, p. 213.   [4] πάσχει τι (lit. 'suffers in any way',
is passive in any respect).   [5] Heb. i. 3.   [6] 1 John i. 5.   [7] Luke vi. 42.   [8] Phil. ii. 8.

to display to us the fullness of godhead. Let us suppose a statue of such a size as to fill the whole world; of such immensity that no one could contemplate it; let us then suppose that another statue was made, identical with the first in respect of the shape of the limbs, the features, the whole outward appearance and the material; like to it in all respects apart from the immense size. This would be made with this object; that those who could not contemplate and behold the enormous statue might look at the small copy and claim that they had seen the original, inasmuch as the copy, being a complete likeness, preserved all the lines of the limbs and the features, in fact the whole appearance and the actual material of the other.   † *De Principiis*, I. ii. 7–8

(f) Jesus and the Word

If 'God commanded and created things were established',[1] who would there be who could fulfil so great a command of the Father but he who is animate reason,[2] if I may so call him, and truth? For he who says in Jesus, 'I am the way, the truth, and the life',[3] did not, as the Gospels know, become as it were circumscribed, as if he had no actual existence outside the soul and body of Jesus. There are many passages to prove this, but we will establish the point by quoting a few. John the Baptist, when he prophesies that the Son of God will be present before long, speaks of him not as being in that particular body and soul, but as extending everywhere when he says of him, 'He who is coming after me is standing among you, but you do not know him'.[4] Now if he thought the Son of God was present only when the visible body of Jesus was there he surely would not have said, 'There stands among you he whom you do not know'. Again, Jesus himself, when he is stimulating the imagination of his disciples to higher ideas of the Son of God, says, 'Where two or three are assembled in my name, I am there in their midst'.[5] . . . In saying this we do not make a separation between the Son of God and Jesus. For after the incarnation[6] the soul and body of Jesus have become one, in a special sense, with the Word. For if 'Everyone who is joined to the Lord is one spirit'[7] . . . surely in a higher and diviner fashion that which was once compounded[8] with the Word of God is one with him?   *Contra Celsum*, ii. 9

---

[1] Ps. cxlviii. 5.   [2] ἔμψυχος λόγος.   [3] John xiv. 6.   [4] John i. 26.   [5] Matt. xviii. 20
[6] οἰκονομία, 'dispensation': cf. n. 6, p. 75, above.   [7] I Cor. vi. 17.   [8] σύνθετος—a word employed by Origen several times to express the union of the divine and human nature in Jesus.

If you are able to conceive of the Word as having been restored, after he had become flesh and all that he became for the benefit of mortal men,[1] becoming, that is, for them what each of them needed to become; having been thus restored, I say, that he might become what he was 'in the beginning with God', existing as God the Word in his own glory; then you will see him sitting on the throne of his glory, the very same Son of man who was known as the man Jesus; for he is one with the Word in a far different sense from that in which those who cleave to the Lord are of one spirit with him.

Comm. in Matthaeum, xv. 24

[*Plato calls the Demiurge—the agent of creation—the son of God.*] But if we say that the soul of Jesus is united with this great Son of God in the closest unity so that they are inseparable, this assertion need cause no surprise. For the sacred narratives know of other examples of things which are two in their own nature which are reckoned as one, and are one. For example, it is said of a man and wife, 'They are no longer two, but one flesh'[2] and . . . 'He who is joined to the Lord is one spirit'.[3] And who is joined to the Lord more than the soul of Jesus, nay, who in equal manner is joined to the Lord, the absolute Reason, Wisdom, Truth, Righteousness? If this be so, there is no duality between the soul of Jesus and God the Word, the 'firstborn of all creation'.[4]   *Contra Celsum*, vi. 47

To provide a fuller explanation of the matter it seems not inappropriate to use a simile, although in so hard and difficult a matter there are no adequate parallels to employ. . . . Iron is capable of cold and heat. If then some mass of iron is put into the fire it receives heat in all its pores and veins, and becomes wholly fire, if it never leaves the fire or is taken from it. Now shall we say that this mass, which is by nature iron, when placed in the fire and burning ceaselessly, is capable of cold? Nay rather we say . . . that it has become wholly fire, since we discern nothing but fire in it. In the same way that soul which is always in the Word, in Wisdom, in God, as the iron is in the fire, *is* God in all that it does and feels and knows . . .   † *De Principiis*, II. vi. 6

(g) The Sinlessness of Christ

It cannot be doubted that his soul was of the same nature as other souls . . . but whereas all souls have the power of choosing good and evil, the soul which belonged to Christ so chose to love righteousness that

---

[1] τοῖς γεννητοῖς.   [2] Matt. xix. 6, cf. Gen. ii. 24.   [3] Cf. 1 Cor. vi. 17.   [4] Col. i. 15.

because of the boundlessness of this love it cleaved to righteousness without possibility of change or separation, so that ... what was dependent on free choice became 'second nature'. Thus we must believe that there was in Christ a human rational soul, but we must think of it as having no possibility of sin.   Ibid. II. vi. 5

(h) The Two Natures

See *De Principiis*, I. ii. 1, quoted under 'The Trinity', p. 230, below.

Therefore with this soul[1] acting as connecting link between God and flesh – for it was not possible for the nature of God to be mingled with flesh without a mediator—there was born the God-man, that 'substance' being the connecting link which could assume a body without denying its own nature. . . . The Son of God by whom all things were created is called Jesus Christ, the Son of man. For the Son of God is said to have died in respect of that nature which was certainly capable of death; and he is called the Son of man who is proclaimed about to come 'in the glory of God the Father with the holy angels'.[2] And for this cause through the whole of Scripture the divine nature is spoken of in human terms, and at the same time the human nature is accorded the distinctive epithets proper to the divine. For the saying, 'The twain shall be in one flesh, and they are now not two but one flesh,'[3] is more applicable here than in any other reference.   † Ibid. II. vi. 3

Celsus thinks that the assumption by the immortal divine Word of a mortal body and a human soul entails a change and alteration in time. Let him learn that the Word remains the Word in his essential being[4] and does not suffer what the body or soul suffers; that he comes down at a certain time to be with him who cannot behold the splendour and brightness of his godhead, and as it were becomes flesh, uttered in bodily terms,[5] until he who has received him in this shape, being gradually raised to a higher level by the Word, may be able to gaze upon what I may call his primary form.

Contra Celsum, iv. 15 (*ad fin.*)

Some of the utterances of Jesus are those of 'the first-born of all creation'[6] who was in him, for example; 'I am the way, &c.'[7] Some were utterances of his perceptible human nature, for instance, 'Now

---

[1] *substantia animae*—by which, says Origen, the Son was united to the Father so that they were 'one spirit' (cf. 1 Cor. vi. 17).   [2] Matt. xvi. 27 (cf. Mark viii. 38).   [3] Matt. xix. 5–6, cf. Gen. ii. 24.   [4] τῇ οὐσίᾳ (cf. n. 4, p. 213).   [5] σωματικῶς λαλούμενος, cf. Col. ii. 9 (Greek).   [6] Col. i. 15.   [7] John xiv. 6.

you seek to kill me, a man who has told you the truth which I heard
from my Father'.[1] So in this place [*the agony in Gethsemane*] he displays,
in his human nature, both the weakness of human flesh and the willingness of spirit: weakness in 'Father, if it is possible let this cup pass away
from me'; willingness of spirit in 'But not as I will, as thou wilt'.[2]

Contra Celsum, ii. 25

The Saviour sometimes speaks concerning himself as a man, sometimes
as concerning a more divine nature, a nature which is one with the
uncreated nature of the Father. When he says 'Now ye seek to kill me,
a man who has spoken the truth to you', he says this knowing that what
they sought to destroy was not God, but man. But in saying, 'I and
the Father are one', 'I am the truth and the life', 'I am the resurrection',[3]
he is not teaching them about the man whom the Jews sought to destroy . . . 'You know me and know whence I am'[4] is said of himself as
man; while 'You know neither me nor my Father'[5] of his godhead.

Comm. in Ioannem, xix. 2 (1)

A tradition has come down to us that not only were there two outward forms in Jesus, one in which he was seen by all, another in which
he was transfigured before his disciples . . . but also that he appeared
to individuals in the form in which each deserved [*to see him*]. . . .
[*Like the manna which adapted itself to every taste*, cf. Wisdom xvi. 20.]
And this tradition does not seem incredible to me . . . [Hence John
xviii. 4–6, *and the need for the traitor's sign.*]

* *In Matthaeum Commentariorum Series*, 100

Origen uses this tradition in *Contra Celsum*, ii. 64. But the real humanity of
Christ is constantly asserted:

(j) The Reality of the Human Nature
The Temptation

The Lord when he took flesh was tempted by every temptation by
which men are to be tempted. He was tempted for this purpose, that
we might overcome through his victory. . . . [*From the fact that he says*
'*thou shalt not live by bread alone, &c.*'] we may see that it is not the Son of
God [i.e. *in his divine nature*] that speaks but the human nature which the
Son of God deigned to assume; . . . it is clear that it was not God but
man who was tempted.   ‡ *Hom. in Lucam*, xxix

[1] John viii. 40.   [2] Matt. xxvi. 39.   [3] John x. 30, xiv. 6, xi. 25.   [4] John vii. 28.   [5] John
viii. 19.

The Agony

When he took upon him the nature of human flesh he fully accepted all the characteristic properties of humanity, so that it should be realized that he had a body of flesh in reality and not in mere appearance; hence it was that in this place he prayed that the cup of suffering might pass from him. . . . It is noteworthy that the account of the agony is given in Matthew, Mark, and Luke who also tell of the temptation of Jesus by the devil. Whereas John, while giving an account of the passion in the same way as the others, omits the prayer of Jesus that the cup might pass from him, as he also gives no account of the temptation. I think the reason for this is that the first three evangelists are giving an account of Jesus rather in respect of his human than his divine nature; whereas John's interpretation has more regard to his divine nature. . . . So the first three relate the prayer of Jesus that the cup might pass from him, since to wish to avoid suffering is a human characteristic, arising from the infirmity of the flesh. John's purpose is to display Jesus as God the Word, and therefore, knowing that he is the life and the resurrection, he cannot admit that the impassible God shrank from the passion.   * *In Matthaeum Commentariorum Series*, 92

Limitations of Christ's Knowledge

'But concerning the day and hour no one knows, neither the angels of heaven nor the Son, save the Father only.'[1] According to this passage the Saviour joins himself with those who do not know that day and hour. . . . Some will go so far as to say that the Saviour, as man, 'increased in wisdom &c.'[2] . . . and did not reach the perfection of knowledge before he had completed his appointed work for man. . . . But when that work was completed, after 'God had highly exalted him'[3] . . . not only the Father knew but the Son also. . . . In the Acts . . . he says, 'It is not *for you* to know.'[4] . . . And further, since the Father 'put it in his own power' no one could know, because it had not yet been fixed by God. . . . [*The consummation had been fixed in principle, but not the actual time*.] God made the time of the judgement to depend on the conduct of humanity in the exercise of their free-will. . . . There is another and more famous interpretation than any of these . . . [*similar to the interpretation of* 1 Cor. xv. 28; *the subjection of Christ means the subjection of Christians in Christ*]. So long as the Church, which is the body of Christ, does not know the day and the hour, the Son himself

[1] Matt. xxiv. 36.   [2] Luke ii. 52.   [3] Phil. ii. 9.   [4] Acts i. 6, 7.

is said not to know it; that he may be understood to know it when all his members know. . . . [*Origen goes on to argue that 'know' means 'experience'.*] But the consummation of each individual . . . the Father alone knows; for the Son, while he accompanies and leads his followers, deliberately, so to say, delays his future coming, so that those who are striving to follow him may be able to do so, and may be found with him in 'that day and hour'.

* *In Matthaeum Commentariorum Series*, 55

[*Jer. i. 6. 'I do not know how to speak, for I am too young', to be applied to Christ.*] Jesus, before he became a grown man, while still a little child, since he 'abased himself',[1] made progress; for no one makes progress if he is already perfect—progress implies the need of progress . . . having 'abased himself', he then took back the things of which he had stripped himself, for he had done this as a voluntary act . . . [*thus Isa. vii. 15, 16 apply to him*].   ‡ *Hom. in Jeremiam*, i. 7

   Contrast *Contra Celsum*, iv. 15, quoted p. 217.

(k) Deification of Christ's Humanity

He whom we confidently believe to be God and Son of God from the beginning is the absolute Reason [*Logos*], Wisdom, Truth. We affirm that his mortal body and the human soul in it, by virtue not merely of association but of unity and commixture with the Logos, has become possessed of the highest powers and, partaking in the divinity of the Logos, has become divine . . . [*Greek philosophy speaks of changes of quality*]. If such assertions are sound, is there anything irrational in the supposition that the quality of the mortal body of Jesus changed to a heavenly and divine quality through the providence of God who so willed it?   *Contra Celsum*, iii. 41

VII. The Atonement

(a) Sacrifice: of Animals, of Men, of the Lamb of God

[*On the sacrifices at the several feasts.*] At the feast of the Passover it is written that it is a lamb which purifies the people, at other feasts a bullock, at others a goat or a ram or a she-goat or a heifer. . . . Our Lord and Saviour himself is said to be the lamb . . .; and if the lamb . . . is referred to the person of our Lord it seems to follow that the other animals which are appointed to the same purposes of purification

[1] Phil. ii. 8.

should be likewise referred to persons who [through the merit of the
purifications of the blood of Christ][1] confer some boon on the human
race. It may well be that as our Lord and Saviour . . . bestowed remission of sins on the whole world, so also the blood of others, holy
and righteous men . . . has been shed for the expiation, in some part, of
the people. . . . Christ is spoken of as a lamb because his willingness
and his goodness, by which he made God again propitious to men and
bestowed pardon for sins, stood for the human race as a lamb, a spotless and innocent victim, a victim by which heaven is believed to be
reconciled to men. So then it may be that any angel, or any of the
heavenly powers, or a righteous man, or even one of the holy prophets
or Apostles, who intercedes more strenuously on behalf of the sins of
men; such a one, as restoring the divine propitiation, may be thought
of as a ram, or bullock, or goat, offered in sacrifice to achieve purification for the people. . . . [Cf. Paul in Rom. ix. 3, 2 Tim. iv. 6.] While
there are sins there must needs be required sacrificial victims for sins.
For suppose, for argument's sake, that there had been no sin. Had there
been no sin the Son of God would not have been constrained to become
a lamb, nor would there have been need for him to be incarnate and to
be put to death; but he would have remained what he was in the
beginning, God the Word; but since sin entered into this world, and
sin of necessity requires propitiation, and propitiation cannot be
effected save by a sacrificial victim, such a victim had to be provided for
sin. And inasmuch as there were different and various kinds of sin,
sacrifices of diverse animals were enjoined, to fit the various types of
sin. . . . Besides things on earth, things in heaven also stand in need of
propitiation. For the heavens are threatened with destruction: as the
prophet says, 'The heavens will perish; and they shall grow old, like a
garment, and thou shalt fold them up like a robe, and they will be
changed'.[2] Think, therefore, of the purification of the whole universe,
the things in heaven, things on earth, and things beneath the earth:
What great numbers of victims all these would need! What bullocks,
rams, and goats! But for all these, there is one Lamb, who could 'take
away the sin of the whole world [universe]'.[3] Therefore the other
victims ceased; for this victim was such that it alone sufficed for the
salvation of the whole universe. For all others brought forgiveness of
sins by their prayers, he alone by his authority. . . . Thus the world is
inspired first to seek remission of sins by means of diverse victims, until
it should come to a perfect victim, a consummate victim, a lamb of a

[1] Omitted in some MSS.   [2] Ps. ci. 27 (102, 26).   [3] John i. 29.

year old, a perfect lamb, to take away the sins of the whole world; by
means of which it should celebrate spiritual festivals, not for the satisfaction of the flesh, but for the increase of the spirit, by the offering
of spiritual sacrifices in pureness of mind. For it is seemly that to God
should be offered the sacrifice of the heart, the victim of a contrite
spirit; not the slaughter of flesh and blood.

‡ *Hom. in Numeros*, xxiv. 1

(b) The Sacrifice of the Saints, Supplementing Christ's Sacrifice

[*On* Num. xviii. 1: 'And the Lord said unto them, You and your sons
shall bear the sins of the saints.'] Everyone who believes in Christ knows
that our Lord Jesus Christ came to take away the sin of the world, and
that he has wiped out our sins by his death. But now we shall attempt to
prove, if we can, from the divine Scriptures how his sons, that is, the
Apostles and martyrs, take away the sins of the saints. First, listen to
Paul when he says: 'I will gladly spend and be spent for your souls';[1]
and in another place: 'For I am already being offered and the time of
my departure [*or* release] is at hand'.[2] Thus the Apostle speaks of himself as being spent and offered on behalf of those to whom he was
writing. Now when a victim is offered it is offered for this end, that
the sins of those for whom it is slaughtered may be purged. And concerning the martyrs the Apostle John writes in the Apocalypse that
the souls of those who were slaughtered because of the name of the
Lord Jesus stand at the altar;[3] now he who stands at the altar is displayed as fulfilling the function of a priest; and it is the function of a
priest to offer supplication for the sins of the people. Hence I fear lest
it may be that since the time that the martyrdoms have ceased and the
sacrifices of the saints are no longer being offered for our sins we may
fail to win remission of our transgressions . . . for we are not worthy
to suffer persecutions because of Christ, nor to die because of the
name of the Son of God. And therefore also the devil, knowing that
remission of sins comes through the suffering of martyrdom, does not
wish to stir up against us the public persecutions of the Gentiles.

† Ibid. x. 2

[*Celsus puts forward the 'scandal of particularity': Why only one incarnation, in an obscure corner of the world?*] If anyone longs to see many
bodies filled with divine spirit and working for the salvation of men
everywhere, following the example of the one Christ, let him con-

[1] 2 Cor. xii. 15.   [2] 2 Tim. iv. 6.   [3] Cf. Rev. vi. 9 ff.

sider that those who everywhere teach the word of Jesus in sincerity and with right living are themselves called 'Christs' by the divine Scriptures, in the verse, 'Touch not my Christs [anointed] and do no evil to my prophets'.[1] And as we are told that 'Antichrist is coming', and at the same time we have learnt that there are many antichrists in the world;[2] in the same way we know that Christ has dwelt among men, and we observe that through him many Christs have come into being in the world, who like him have 'loved righteousness and hated iniquity'; and therefore God, the God of Christ, 'anointed them also with oil of rejoicing'.[3] *Contra Celsum*, vi. 79

As those who attended on the altar of sacrifice according to the law of Moses seemed to minister remission of sins by means of the blood of bulls and goats, so the souls of these who have been executed for the witness of Jesus, if their attendance on the heavenly altars be not in vain, minister remission of sins to those who pray. And at the same time we rejoice that as the high priest Jesus the Christ has offered the sacrifice of himself, the priests of whom he is high priest offer the sacrifice of themselves.

. . . Perhaps also as we are bought 'by the precious blood of Jesus'[4] . . . so by the precious blood of the martyrs certain have been bought.
Exhortatio ad Martyrium, 30

(c) The Value of Human Self-sacrifice

The disciples proclaimed that he who was but recently crucified had willingly accepted that death on behalf of mankind, on the analogy of men who have died for their country to put an end to visitations of plague or famine or tempests. For it seems to be part of the natural order of things that, according to certain recondite principles which are not easy for ordinary men to grasp, the death of one righteous man, voluntary undertaken for the general good, is effective to avert the power of impious spirits which produces pestilence, dearth, tempests, and the like. Therefore if men deliberately refuse to believe that Jesus died for man by way of the cross they should tell us whether they also refuse to accept the many stories from Greece and from the East which tell of men who died for the general good to free their cities and nations from disasters which had come upon them. Or do they regard these as facts and yet find it incredible that he who was accounted man should

[1] Ps. cv. 15. [2] 1 John ii. 18. [3] Ps. xlv. 7. [4] 1 Pet. i. 19.

have died to destroy the power of the great evil spirit, who is the ruler of the evil spirits, who had subjected all the souls of men which have come upon the earth?   *Contra Celsum*, i. 31

(d) A Ransom: The Devil Deceived

['A ransom for many'.[1]] To whom was it paid? Certainly not to God; can it then be to the evil one? For he had power over us until the ransom was given to him on our behalf, namely the life[2] of Jesus; and he was deceived thinking that he could keep his soul[2] in his power; not seeing that he could not reach the standard required so as to be able to keep it in his power. So also Death thought that it had him in its power, but it had no power over him who became 'free among the dead'[3] and stronger than the authority of death, and so much stronger, that all who wish to follow him can do so, though overcome by death, since death has now no strength against them: for no one who is with Jesus can be seized by death.   *Comm. in Matthaeum*, xvi. 8

(e) A Cosmic Sacrifice

[*The instruction to offer the sacrifice at the door of the tabernacle and also to sprinkle the blood on the altar at the door*, Lev. i. 3, 5] is perhaps meant to be taken as signifying that the blood of Jesus was not only shed at Jerusalem, where there was the altar . . . and the tabernacle . . . , but also sprinkled on the altar above, the 'altar in heaven', where is also the 'church of the first-born':[4] as the Apostle says, 'He made peace through the blood of his cross, whether things on earth or things in the heavens'.[5] . . . Jesus was offered as a sacrifice not only for things in earth but also for things in heaven: here for men he shed his material, physical blood; while for the priests—if such there be—who minister in heaven he offered up in sacrifice the vital power of his body, as a kind of spiritual sacrifice.   † *Hom. in Leviticum*, i. 3

But if one should carry this inquiry [*sc. the parallel between the heavenly and the Mosaic law, and between the 'everlasting gospel' of the Apocalypse and the temporal gospel on earth*] as far as the passion he might seem temerarious in looking for a passion in respect of the heavenly places. And yet if there are 'spiritual powers of wickedness in the heavenly places',[6] then, just as we are not ashamed to acknowledge him crucified

---

[1] Matt. xx. 28.   [2] ψυχή, meaning 'life' or 'soul'.   [3] Ps. lxxxviii. 5.   [4] Heb. xii. 23 f.
[5] Col. i. 20.   [6] Eph. vi. 12.

here for the destruction of that which he destroyed by his suffering, so we shall have no fear in assuming a similar passion there also at the end of time.   *De Principiis,* iv. 25
(Greek in Justinian, *Ep. ad Menam* [Mansi, ix. 532])

Christ is a great high priest, who has offered himself as the sacrifice once offered not only on behalf of men but also for every rational being. . . . For it would be absurd to say that he has tasted death for the sins of men and not also for anything else besides man that is involved in sin; the stars for example, which, as we read in Job, are not completely 'pure in sight of God'.[1]   *Comm. in Ioannem,* i. 40 (35)

(f) Vicarious Punishment

The Greeks and the barbarians have many traditional stories of occasions when such afflictions as plagues, noxious calms, or famines have been prevalent among mankind and when release has come through a man's self-sacrifice for the common weal, by which, as it were, the evil spirit is frustrated who produces their distress. And they do not scorn or reject the notion [*sc. of the efficacy of self-sacrifice*] in the case of such a man. Now it is not to our present purpose to sift the truth or falsehood of such tales. But no story is ever told, nor can have been told, of one who was able to accept death on behalf of the whole world, that all the world should be purified; that is, for the purification of a world which was doomed to perish had he not accepted death on its behalf. For Jesus alone has been able, by his great power, to take himself the burden of the sin of all and to carry it on the cross on which he hung 'apart from God'[2] on behalf of all. . . . The Father offered this Jesus for our sins, and because of them 'he was led as a sheep to the slaughter' . . . 'In his humiliation' (in which 'he abased himself, becoming obedient unto death, even the death of the cross') 'the judgement is taken away'.[3]   Ibid. xxviii. 19 (14)

Cf. *Contra Celsum,* i. 31, quoted pp. 223–4 above.

(g) God Reconciled to Man

'God set him forth to be a propitiation through faith in his blood',[4] that is, that by his blood, through the sacrifice of his body, he might make God propitious to men. . . . God is just, and the just cannot

---

[1] Job xxv. 5.   [2] Heb. ii. 9 (with variant χωρὶς for χάριτι Θεοῦ).   [3] Isa. liii. 7–8; Phil. ii. 8.   [4] Rom. iii. 25.

justify the unjust. Therefore he willed the intervention of a propitiator, that those who could not be justified by their own works might be justified by faith in him.   † *Comm. in Ep. ad Romanos*, iii. 8

Christ the true high priest who by his own blood made God propitious to you and reconciled you to the Father . . .
                    † *Hom. in Leviticum*, ix. 10

(h) Man Reconciled to God

'We have peace with God',[1] but it is through our Lord Jesus Christ who reconciled us to God through the sacrifice of his blood. . . . Christ came that he might destroy the enmities and make peace, and reconcile us to God when we were separated because of the barrier of wickedness which we set up by sinning.   † *Comm. in Ep. ad Romanos*, iv. 8

Therefore if Celsus asks us how we suppose we can know God and how we think to be saved by him, we reply that the Word of God, coming to those who seek him, or to those who receive him when he is manifested, is able to make known the Father and to reveal him who was not seen before his coming. Who can save the soul of man and bring it to God who is over all, except God the Word? He, being 'in the beginning with God', became flesh because of them that were bound to the flesh; that he might be comprehended by those who could not see him in so far as he 'was word, and was with God, and was God'. And being uttered in bodily form and proclaimed as flesh, he calls to himself them that are flesh, that he may make them, first, to be conformed to the Word which was made flesh, and, afterwards, raise them up to see him as he was before he became flesh, that they may rise above their contact with him after the flesh to say, 'If also we once knew Christ after the flesh, we now know him so no longer'.[2]
                    Contra Celsum, vi. 68

(j) The Deification of Humanity

[*They believed*] that from Jesus began a weaving together of the divine and human nature in order that human nature, through fellowship with what is more divine, might become divine, not only in Jesus but also in all those who, besides believing in Jesus, take up the life which he taught; the life which leads everyone who lives according to the precepts of Jesus to friendship with God and fellowship with him.
                    Ibid. iii. 28 (*ad fin.*)

[1] Rom. v. 1.   [2] 2 Cor. v. 16.

VIII. The Holy Spirit

(a) Personality

'The Spirit blows where it wills.'[1] This signifies that the Spirit is a substantial being.[2] It is not, as some imagine, an activity[3] of God without individual existence. And the Apostle, after enumerating the gifts of the Spirit, proceeds thus; 'And all these things come from the activity of the one same Spirit, distributing to each individually as he wills';[4] if he 'wills' and 'is active' and 'distributes', he is therefore an active substance[2] not a mere activity. [*Cf.* Acts xv. 21: 'It seemed good to the Holy Spirit and to us'; Acts xiii. 2: 'The Holy Spirit said'; Acts xxi. 10: 'This is what the Holy Spirit says'.]   *In Ioannem Fragmenta*, 37

(b) Divinity

The washing in water [*sc. in Baptism*] is a symbol of the cleansing of the soul by the washing away of all the filth that comes from wickedness; it is likewise in itself the origin and the source of divine gifts to him who presents himself to the divinity of the power of the invocations of the adorable Trinity.   *Comm. in Ioannem*, vi. 33 (17)

Basil, *De Spiritu Sancto*, xxix. 73, quotes the last phrase as 'to the divinity of the adorable Trinity through the power of the invocations'.

The passage seems ambiguous as to the divine personality of the Holy Spirit. But Basil quotes it with approval as a sign of grace in Origen who 'was not always quite sound in his ideas about the Spirit'.

The Spirit himself is in the law and in the gospel; he is ever with the Father and the Son; like the Father and the Son he always is, and was, and will be.   † *Comm. in Ep. ad Romanos*, vi. 7 (*ad fin.*)

Then [*after the Ascension*] the Holy Spirit is associated with the Father and the Son in honour and dignity. Concerning whom it is not yet clearly decided whether he is to be regarded as begotten or unbegotten[5] or even as the son of God, or not.   † *De Principiis*, praef. 4

(c) Relation to Father and Son

Now we must examine this question: Since it is true that 'All things come into being through'[6] the Word, did the Holy Spirit come into

---

[1] John iii. 8.   [2] οὐσία.   [3] ἐνέργεια.   [4] 1 Cor. xii. 11.   [5] Rufinus evidently read γεννητὸς ἢ ἀγέννητος, which Origen could hardly have meant (cf. the next passage here quoted). Jerome (*Ep. Ad Avitum*, 2) says 'created or uncreate', reading γενητὸς ἢ ἀγένητος.
[6] John i. 3.

being through him? For I suppose that if anyone asserts that the Spirit has derivative being[1] and puts forward the text 'All things came into being through him' he is forced to admit that the Holy Spirit came into being through the Word, the Word being anterior to the Spirit. While if a man refuses to admit that the Holy Spirit has come into being through Christ it follows that he must say that the Spirit is unbegotten,[2] if he judges that the statements in this Gospel are true. There will be then . . . [*these two positions*] and a third, that of the man who lays it down that there is no personal being[3] of the Holy Spirit distinct from the Father and the Son. But perhaps, if he holds the Son to be distinct from the Father he will favour the identification of the Spirit with the Father, since a clear distinction is made between the Holy Spirit and the Son [Matt. xii. 32: *blasphemy against the Son and the Spirit*]. We however, are persuaded that there are really three persons,[4] the Father, the Son, and the Holy Spirit, and we believe that only the Father is unbegotten; and we posit as true, and as the most reverent proposition, that all things came into being through the Word, and that of all these things the Holy Spirit is the most honourable, ranking first of all that have been brought into being by God through Jesus Christ. And it may be that this is the reason why the Holy Spirit is not given the title of very son of God, that the only-begotten Son alone is by nature the original Son, and it is probable that the Holy Spirit depends on him to minister to his person not only existence but wisdom and rationality and righteousness, and all other qualities which we must suppose him to possess by participation in the functions[5] of the Son of which we have spoken before.

And I suppose that the Holy Spirit provides, as it were, the matter for the spiritual gifts of God to those who receive the name of saints through him and through participation in him; this matter being put into operation from God, but ministered by the Word, and being in existence because of the Holy Spirit. I am moved to suppose this situation by St. Paul's writing in such terms concerning spiritual gifts: 'There are differences of gifts but the same Spirit; and differences of ministrations, and the same Lord; and differences of operations, and it is the same God who makes all things operative in all'.[6]

Comm. in Ioannem, ii. 10 (6)

Up to the present I have been able to find no passage in the Scriptures to suggest that the Holy Spirit is a created being; not even in the sense

---

[1] γενητόν.   [2] ἀγέννητον.   [3] οὐσία ἰδία.   [4] τρεῖς ὑποστάσεις.   [5] ἐπίνοιαι.   [6] I Cor. xii. 4 ff.

in which, as I have shown, Solomon speaks of Wisdom as created[1] or
that in which, as I have maintained, such appellations of the Son as
'life' or 'Word' are to be understood. I take it then, that the Spirit of
God which 'moved over the water'[2] is none other than the Holy Spirit.
This seems the reasonable interpretation, as I have demonstrated in my
exposition of the passage; but it is derived not directly from the narrative, but from the spiritual understanding of it.

† De Principiis, I. iii. 3

(d) Sanctification

The grace of the Holy Spirit is added that those creatures which are
not holy by virtue of their own being may be made holy by participation in the Spirit. Thus they derive existence from God the Father,
rationality from the Word, sanctity from the Holy Spirit. Again when
they have once been sanctified through the Holy Spirit they are made
capable of receiving Christ, in respect that he is 'the righteousness of
God'[3], and those who have deserved to advance to this stage through
the sanctification of the Holy Spirit will go on to attain the gift of wisdom through the power of the Spirit of God and his operation in
them'. . . . Thus the operation of the Father, which bestows existence
on all, proves more splendid and impressive when each person advances
and reaches higher stages of progress through participation in Christ
as wisdom, and as knowledge and sanctification; and as a man has become purer and cleaner by participation in the Holy Spirit he is made
worthy to receive, and receives, the grace of wisdom and knowledge.
Then, when all the stains of pollution and ignorance have been removed and purged away, he receives such advancement in purity and
cleanness, that the being which was given by God becomes worthy of
God, who bestowed it in order that it might attain its purity and perfection: so that the being is as worthy as is he who gave it existence.

† Ibid. I. iii. 8

I suppose that the clause in the psalm of Habakkuk 'in the midst of
two living beings (or "two lives") thou shalt be known'[4] should be
understood to refer to Christ and the Holy Spirit. For all knowledge of
the Father is attained by the revelation of the Son and in the Holy
Spirit; so that these two 'living beings' (or 'lives') are the cause of the
knowledge of God the Father. . . . [Cf. Matt. xi. 27, 1 Cor. ii. 10, John
xvi. 12, 13.]

† Ibid. I. iii. 4

---

[1] Cf. Prov. viii. 22.   [2] Gen. i. 2.   [3] 1 Cor. i. 30.   [4] Hab. iii. 2 (LXX).

(e) He works only in the holy

It is written in the Psalms, 'Thou shalt take away their spirit and they shall fail, and be turned again to their earth. Thou shalt send out thy spirit and they shall be created, and thou shalt renew the face of the earth'.[1] . . . Thus it is clearly stated that the Holy Spirit will dwell not in all, nor in those who are flesh, but in those by whom the earth shall be renewed. Above all, this was the reason for the bestowal of the grace and revelation of the Holy Spirit by the laying on of the Apostles' hands after baptism. Furthermore, after our Saviour's resurrection, when 'the old things had passed away, and all things had been made new'[2] being himself a 'new man'[3] and the 'first-begotten from the dead',[4] when the Apostles also had been 'renewed' through faith in his resurrection, he said to them 'Receive the Holy Spirit'.[5]

† *De Principiis*, I. iii. 7

See also p. 238 f.

IX. The Trinity

(a) The Eternally Begotten Son

We must first recognize that there is a distinction between the nature of the deity in Christ, as the only-begotten Son of the Father, and his human nature, which he took in these last times in fulfilment of God's purpose.[6] And first we must examine the nature of the only-begotten Son. . . . (2) . . . The only-begotten Son of God in his Wisdom existing substantially. . . . How could anyone believe that God the Father could have existed at any time without begetting Wisdom? . . . For that would be to say either that God could not beget Wisdom before he begot . . . or that he could but did not wish to; . . . and either supposition is patently absurd and impious. . . . We must believe that Wisdom is without any beginning. . . . (3) . . . He is called the Word because he is as it were the interpreter of the secrets of the mind of God.

(4) . . . We are forbidden the impiety of supposing that the way in which God the Father begets and sustains his only-begotten Son is equivalent to the begetting of man by man or animal by animal; there must needs be a great difference; and it is fitting that this should be so, since

[1] Ps. ciii (104), 29, 30.   [2] 2 Cor. v. 17.   [3] Eph. iv. 24.   [4] Col. i. 18.   [5] John xx. 22
[6] *pro dispensatione* = κατ᾽ οἰκονομίαν; see p. 75, note 6.

nothing can be found in existence, or conceived or imagined, to compare with God. Thus human thought cannot apprehend how the unbegotten God becomes the Father of the only-begotten Son. For it is an eternal and ceaseless generation, as radiance is generated from light. For he does not become the Son externally, by the adoption of the Spirit, but he is by nature the Son. (5) . . . [Col. i. 15; Heb. i. 3; Wisdom vii. 25]. He is the radiance of the eternal light, the unblemished mirror of the activity of God, and the image of his goodness. And Wisdom, as we said before, we speak of as deriving its existence only from him who is the beginning of all things; and from all wisdom has its origin, for he alone is Son by nature; and therefore he is called 'only-begotten'.

(6) . . . The existence of the Son is generated by the Father. This must be accepted by those who profess that nothing is ungenerate,[1] that is with underived existence,[2] except only God the Father. For caution is needed lest anyone should fall into those absurd fables invented by those who picture for themselves some kind of 'prolations', so as to assign parts to the divine nature and to divide the essential being of God the Father. . . . Rather as an act of will proceeds from the mind without cutting a part off the mind or being separated or divided from it; in some such way the Father is to be thought of as 'begetting' the Son.   † *De Principiis*, I. ii. 1–6 (abridged)

A different meaning seems to be given to 'prolation' in the next extract, where the doctrine combated is based on the distinction between λόγος ἐνδιάθετος, 'conception' and λόγος προφορικός, 'expression'. In this context the unsatisfactory doctrine is very like the suggestion put forward ('will proceeding from mind') by Origen himself in the last quotation.

They continually quote 'My heart has disgorged a good word',[3] thinking that the Son of God is a 'prolation'[4] of the Father consisting as it were of syllables; and on this showing they do not give individuality[5] to him, if we are to take them literally, nor do they clearly indicate his separate existence[6]—and we do not mean a particular mode of existence, but any separate existence at all. For the plain man finds difficulty in understanding the description of the Son as a 'Word'. Let them describe God the Word as such a word as has a life of its own: and either not distinct from the Father and by that token not really a son (because possessing no individuality[7]) or else distinct and endowed with concrete existence.[8]   *Comm. in Ioannem*, i. 24 (25)

---

[1] *ingenitum* = ἀγέννητον.   [2] *innatum* = ἀγένητον.   [3] Ps. xliv. (45), 1.   [4] προφορά.
[5] ὑπόστασις (hypostasis).   [6] οὐσία.   [7] ὑπόστασις (hypostasis).   [8] οὐσία.

John tells us that 'God is light'[1] and Paul calls the Son 'the radiance'of
eternal light.[2] Therefore, as light can never be without radiance, how
can it be said that there was a time when the Son was not? For that is
as much as to say that there was a time when Truth was not, when
Wisdom was not, when Life was not. . . . But we have to apologize
for using such phrases as 'there was never a time when he was not'.[3]
For these words have a temporal significance; but when they are used
of the Father and the Son and Holy Spirit, they are to be understood
as denoting something 'supra-temporal'.   † De Principiis, iv. iv. 28

(b) The Subordination of the Son

No one can be a father without the existence of a son . . . the title of
'Omnipotent' cannot be older than that of 'Father'; for it is through
the Son that the Father is omnipotent . . . [because the Son, as Wisdom,
was the agent of creation. And it is because all things are subjected to him
through Christ that the Father enjoys the glory of omnipotence.] All things
were subjected by means of wisdom, that is, word and reason. . . . This
is the fairest and clearest glory of omnipotence, when all things are subjected by reason and wisdom, not by force and constraint. . . . The
existence[4] of the Son derives from the Father, but not in time, nor does
it have any beginning, except in the sense that it starts from God
himself.   † Ibid. i. ii. 10

The external subordination of the Son, as derivative, is emphasized in a Greek
fragment preserved in Justinian's Epistle to Menas, which seems to be taken from
De Principiis, I. ii. 13 where the translation of Rufinus has diverged widely from
the original in the interests of orthodoxy:

[Origen says:] Therefore I think that we should be right in saying of the
Saviour that he is the image of the goodness of God, but not that goodness itself.[5] And perhaps we may say that the Son is good, but not
absolutely good. And as he is the image of the invisible God he is by
that token God, but not the God of whom Christ himself says 'That
they may know thee, the only true God'.[6] Thus he is the image of
goodness but not unconditionally[7] good, as is the Father.

Justinian, Ep. ad Menam (Mansi, ix. 525)
(? = De Principiis, I. ii. 13)

---

[1] 1 John i. 5.   [2] Heb. i. 3.   [3] οὐκ ἔστιν ὅτε οὐκ ἦν ('there is no when he was not'), the
formula used against the Arians, seems to have been invented by Origen. It occurs also at
De Principiis, I. ii. 9, and Comm. in Rom. i. 5. The substantial accuracy of Rufinus's paraphrase seems to be warranted by the quotation from Origen in Athanasius, De Decretis
Nicaenae Synodi, 27. (The Greek, unlike the English rendering in the text, does not contain a word for 'time'.)   [4] substantia = ὑπόστασις.   [5] αὐτοαγαθόν.   [6] John xvii. 3.
[7] ἀπαραλλάκτως.

But, on the other hand, compare:

While in respect of the Father he is the image of goodness, in respect of all others he is as the Father's goodness is in respect of him.

Comm. in Matthaeum, xv. 10

He himself is wisdom itself and righteousness itself and truth itself; is he not also sovereignty itself? * Ibid. xiv. 7

But not, Origen implies by silence, goodness itself.

If the Father comprehends [*i.e. holds in his grasp*] all, and the Son is included in that 'all', then the Father comprehends the Son. But someone will raise the question whether the only-begotten Son's knowledge of the Father is identical with the Father's self-knowledge, and will demonstrate that the saying 'The father who sent me is greater than I'[1] is true in all respects. So that in respect of knowledge the Father is known by himself more fully and clearly and completely than he is known by the Son.

De Principiis, IV. 35

(Greek in Justinian, *Ep. ad Menam* [Mansi, ix. 525])

But contrast the following:

If anyone inquires if our Saviour knows all that is known by the Father . . . it must be understood that he is the Saviour because he is the Truth, and further that if he is the whole Truth, he knows everything that is true.

Comm. in Ioannem, i. 27

[*On* John xiii. 31, 'Now is the Son of Man glorified, and God is glorified in him] . . . I ask: Is it possible for God to be glorified . . . when he has greater glory in himself? . . .

Ibid. xxxii. 28 (18)

In more than one place Origen uses the proportion, the Father: the Son (and the Holy Spirit) :: the Son (and the Holy Spirit): all created beings, e.g.:

We say that the Son and the Holy Spirit excel all created beings to a degree which admits of no comparison, and are themselves excelled by the Father to the same or even greater degree.

Ibid. xiii. 25

In *De Principiis*, I. iii. 5. below, p. 238–9, the Holy Spirit is said to be inferior to the Son.

Those who entertain false notions about Christ under pretence of doing him honour are not to be thought of as 'for' him:[2] such are they

---

[1] Cf. John x. 29 and xiv. 28.   [2] Matt. xii. 30.

who confuse the conception of Father and Son and who suppose that the Father and Son are one in individual being[1] and only admit distinctions of function[2] in the identical subject.[3]

Comm. in Matthaeum, xvii. 14

In his use of the article and in the omission of it John displays great care and an accurate knowledge of Greek idiom. He adds the article to 'Word'. but to the appellation 'God' he sometimes prefixes it, sometimes omits it. He prefixes the article when the name 'God' is applied to the absolute being,[4] the author of all things; he does not use it when the Word is named 'God'. But while 'the God' is distinguished from 'God' in these contexts, there is probably a similar distinction between 'the Word' and 'Word'. For just as the supreme God is 'the God' and not simply 'God', so the Word [*Logos*] who is the source of the reason [*logos*] which is in every reasonable being, is called 'the Word', a title which would not rightly be applied to the reason in each individual. Hence we can resolve a difficulty which troubles many who claim to be devout. In their anxiety to avoid designating two gods they became involved in false and impious doctrines; for either they deny the individuality[5] of the Son, as something distinct from that of the Father, while they confess the divinity of him whom they call, as far as the name goes, the Son; or they deny the divinity of the Son while asserting his individuality and personality[6] as really separate and distinct from that of the Father. To such people we must say that sometimes 'God' means 'God-in-himself';[7] thus it is that the the Saviour, in his prayer to the Father, says, 'That they may know thee, the only true God'.[8] Everything which, without being 'God-in-himself' is deified by participation in his godhead should strictly be called 'God', not 'the God'. The 'firstborn of all creation',[9] since he by being 'with God' first gathered godhead to himself, is therefore in every way more honoured than the others besides himself, who are 'gods' of whom God is the God, as it is said, 'God the Lord of gods spoke and called the world'.[10] For it was through his ministry that they became gods, since he drew divinity from God for them to be deified, and of his kindness generously shared it with them. God, then, is the true God, and those who through him are fashioned into gods are copies of the prototype. And, again, the copy which is the archetype of the many copies is the Word which was 'with God' who was 'in the beginning'. He remains God

---

[1] ὑπόστασις.　[2] ἐπίνοια.　[3] τὸ ἕν ὑποκείμενον.　[4] ἀγένητος.　[5] ἰδιότης.　[6] οὐσία.　[7] αὐτόθεος.
[8] John xvii. 3.　[9] Col. i. 15.　[10] Ps. xlix (50), 1.

by being with God: but he would not have had this status had he not
been with God; and he would not have remained God had he not persisted in the unremitted vision of the depth of the Father's being.

Comm. in Ioannem, ii. 2

(c) Degrees of Divinity

The Father, then, is proclaimed as the one true God; but besides the
true God there are many who become gods by participation in God.
No doubt some will take offence at these statements, being anxious to
avoid equating the glory of him who surpasses the whole creation
with the others who are given the title of gods. Therefore we must add
a further distinction besides that which we have assumed in our assertion that God the Word is the minister of godhead to the other gods.
For the reason [*logos*] in each natural being is in the same proportion to
the Word [*Logos*] which 'was in the beginning', 'was with God' and
'was God', as God the Word is to God: for as the Father is God-in-
himself and true God compared with his image and images of that
image (and therefore men are said to be 'after the image of God', and
not 'images of God'), so is the Word-in-himself compared with the
reason [*logos*] in the individual. For each is in the position of a fountain-
head: the Father the spring of godhead; the Son the spring of reason.
As therefore 'there are many gods',[1] but for us there is one God, the
Father; and many lords, but for us there is one Lord, Jesus Christ; so
there are many reasons [*logoi*], but for us we claim that there exists the
Word [*Logos*] which was in the beginning, which was with God, the
God-Word. . . . Now the God of the universe is God of the elect,
and much more of the Saviour of the elect. After that he is God of
those who are truly gods, and in general he is God 'of the living and
not of the dead'.[2] The God-Word is God perhaps of those who rely
utterly upon him and of those who think of him as father.

The sun, moon, and stars, as some of our predecessors have explained,
were allotted to those who were not worthy to claim the God of gods
as their God . . . [Deut. iv. 19]. Thus some have as their God the God
of the universe; in the second place come those who get no farther than
the Son of God, his Christ: and in the third degree those others who
have as their gods the sun, moon, and stars and all the army of heaven.
These 'stray from God', but their error is far other and better than that
of those who give the name of gods to the 'works of men's hands, gold
and silver, the product of craftsmanship'.[3] And lastly there are those

[1] 1 Cor. viii. 6.   [2] Matt. xxii. 32. [3] Wisd. xiii. 10.

who are devoted to so-called gods which are no gods at all. Correspondingly then some have a share in the Word 'which was in the
beginning, was with God, and was God'—as Hosea, Isaiah, Jeremiah,
and any others who showed themselves such that the 'word of the
Lord' or 'the Word' came to them. There are others who have 'known
nothing except Jesus Christ and him crucified',[1] thinking the Word
made flesh to be the whole of the Word, knowing Christ only 'after
the flesh';[2] such is the generality of those who are reckoned as believers.
And in the third place are those who have applied themselves to reasonings [logoi] which have some share in the Word, since these reasonings
surpassed all other; and it may well be that such are the followers of
the sects which are renowned and eminent in philosophy among the
Greeks. In the fourth place are those who have believed in reasonings
which are utterly corrupt and godless.   *Comm. in Ioannem*, ii. 3

(d) Distinction between Father and Son

Some are confused on the subject of the relation between the Father
and Son: they take the text 'We are found false witnesses of God, because we testified of God that he raised the Christ, whom he did not
raise',[3] and similar passages which clearly show a distinction between
raiser and raised; and with these they compare 'Destroy this temple and
I will raise it in three days',[4] and take this as proving a numerical
identity between the Son and the Father, so that the two are spoken of
as really one subject,[5] not just one in essence,[6] and Father and Son differ
in certain functions[7] and not in individual existence.[8] To such men one
must first quote the dominant, systematic statements of the distinction
between the Father and the Son; and point out that the Son must be in
the relation of son to the Father and *vice versa*. And besides, Jesus admits that he 'can do nothing save what he sees the Father doing' and he
says that 'whatever the Father does, these things the Son does likewise'.[9] It is not then incongruous that he should have raised the corpse,
which was his body, if his Father granted him to do this, though strictly
speaking the Father should be said to have raised Christ from the dead.
                                                    Ibid. x. 37 (21)

(e) Prayer is addressed to the Father, not to the Son, but with and through him

'I exhort therefore, first of all, that petitions, supplications, requests,
thanksgivings, be made for all men.[10] In my opinion a petition[11] is a

---

[1] 1 Cor. ii. 2.   [2] 2 Cor. v. 16.   [3] 1 Cor. xv. 15.   [4] John ii. 19.   [5] $ὑποκείμενον$—subject
of accidents or predicates.   [6] $οὐσία$.   [7] $ἐπίνοιαι$.   [8] $ὑπόστασις$.   [9] John v. 19.   [10] 1 Tim.
iii. 1.   [11] $δέησις$.

prayer sent up with entreaty for the obtaining of something which a man lacks; a supplication[1] is another sort of prayer which a man sends up more solemnly, combined with praise, concerning great matters; a request[2] is a claim for certain things addressed to God by one who has, as it were, greater freedom of speech; while thanksgiving is the acknowledgement, with prayer, of benefits received from God. . . . Well, then, it is not improper to address petitions, requests and thanksgivings [*not only to God but*] also to saints; while two of these, requests and thanksgivings, may be addressed not only to saints but also to ordinary men; but petitions to saints only, if some Paul or Peter may be found, that they may help us by making us worthy to benefit from the authority given them for the remission of sins. . . . If these prayers are to be addressed to holy men, how much more should thanksgivings be offered to Christ who has bestowed such benefits on us through the will of the Father. And requests also are to be addressed to him . . .

(15) But supplicatory prayer, if we rightly understand the nature of prayer, is never to be offered to any derivative being,[3] not even to Christ himself, but solely to the God of the whole universe, the Father, to whom also our Saviour himself prayed, as we have before set out, and teaches us to pray. For when he is asked 'Teach us to pray'[4] he does not teach prayer to himself but to the Father. . . . For if the Son is distinct from the Father[5] in person as a different subject,[5] then either prayer must be addressed to the Son and not to the Father, or to both, or to the Father only. Now it will be admitted universally that 'pray to the Son and not to the Father' is most absurd and would be a proposition contrary to the obvious nature of the case; while 'pray to both' would clearly imply the use of the plural in our requests . . . a thing in itself incongruous and for which one could not show precedent in the Scriptures.

It remains then to pray only to God the Father of the whole universe; but not apart from the high priest. . . . A man who is exact about his prayers should not pray to him who himself prays, but to the Father whom our Lord has taught us to call upon in prayers. But at the same time no prayer should be addressed to the Father apart from the same Jesus. He himself clearly shows this when he says 'Verily, verily I say unto you, if you ask anything of my Father he will give it to you in

---

[1] προσευχή.   [2] ἔντευξις.   [3] γεννητός [? γενητός].   [4] Luke xi. 1.   [5] κατ' οὐσίαν καὶ ὑποκείμενον. [It seems unlikely that οὐσία can here mean 'essence'. See preceding extract.]

my name'.[1] . . . Jesus said, 'Why do you call me good? There is none
good but one, God'[2] the Father. Would he not have said accordingly,
'Why do you pray to me? Prayer ought only to be made to the
Father, to whom I also pray. . . . For you ought not to pray *to* a high
priest who has been set up for you by the Father, and to an advocate
who receives his being from the Father, but *through* a high priest and
advocate "who is able to be touched with the feeling of our infirmities,
tempted in all points as we are but" (because the Father granted this to
him) "without sin".[3] Learn then how great a gift you have received
from my Father in having received the "spirit of adoption"[4] through
the resurrection in me, in order that you may be called sons of God
and my brothers. For you have read the utterance concerning you
which was addressed by me through David to the Father; "I will declare thy name to my brethren: in the midst of the congregation I will
sing of thee".[5] It is not seemly to pray to a brother, for you claim to be
sons of the same Father: your prayer should be offered up only to the
Father, with me and through me.'

(16) . . . Are we not divided if some of us pray to the Father, some
to the Son? It is a foolish error they commit who pray to the Son,
whether with the Father or apart from the Father: an error arising from
excessive simplicity and due to a lack of examination and inquiry. Let
us therefore address supplications to the Father as God: let us make
request to him as Father: let us offer petitions to him as Lord: let us
give thanks to him as God and Father and Lord: but as being the Lord
of those who are not utterly slaves. For the Father would rightly be
considered also the Lord of the Son, and the Lord of those who become
sons through him.   *De Oratione*, 14–16

(f) The Distinct Spheres of the Three Persons

It seems right to inquire why a man who is born again to salvation
through God has need of the Father and the Son and the Holy Ghost,
and would not be destined to attain salvation if there were not the
whole Trinity. In discussing this it will doubtless be necessary to define
the particular operations as well of the Father and the Son as of the
Holy Father. In my judgement, then, the operations of the Father and
the Son extend not only to saints but also to sinners, to rational men
and likewise to dumb animals; and further to inanimate things; in fact
to all that exists; whereas the operation of the Holy Spirit in no way
affects inanimate things, nor yet those which are animate but dumb;

[1] John xxi. 23 f.   [2] Matt. xix. 7.   [3] Heb. iv. 15.   [4] Rom. viii. 15.   [5] Ps. xxi. (22), 22.

nor even can it be found in those who while possessed of reason are
set in wickedness and in no measure turned towards better things. I
conclude that the work of the Holy Spirit is confined to those who are
already turning themselves to better things, and are walking in the
ways of Christ Jesus; those, namely, who are engaged in good actions
and who are abiding in God.   † *De Principiis*, I. iii. 5

Rufinus seems here to have modified the original in the interests of orthodoxy.
According to the quotation in Justinian, Origen gave here a bold statement of
the subordination of the Son and the Holy Spirit. 'Subordinationism', it is true,
was pre-Nicene orthodoxy; but it was not generally so frankly expressed. The
substantial accuracy of Justinian's quotation seems to be guaranteed by Jerome,
Ep. (cxxiv) *ad Avitum.*

[*Origen said:*] God the Father, since he embraces all things, touches each
thing that exists, since he bestows on all existence from his own existence; for he is 'He who is'.[1] The Son is inferior in relation to the
Father, since he touches only things endowed with reason; for he is
subordinate to the Father. The Holy Spirit is still lower in degree, per-
taining only to the saints. So then the power of the Father is superior
to the Son and the Holy Spirit, while the Son's power is greater than
the Holy Spirit; and again the power of the Holy Spirit excels all other
holy things.   Justinian, *Ep. ad Menam* (Mansi, ix. 524)

We have said that the Holy Spirit is granted only to the holy, while the
benefits, or operations, of the Father and the Son extend to the good
and the bad, the righteous and the unrighteous. Let none therefore
suppose that we have thereby raised the Holy Spirit above the Father
and the Son, or are asserting that he is of higher rank; such an inference
is utterly illogical. For we have restricted his grace and work to a particular sphere. And, besides this, there must be no question of lesser or
greater in the Trinity, since the source of the one godhead holds sway
over all things by his Word and Reason and sanctifies by the 'Spirit of
his mouth' all that is worthy of sanctification; as the Psalm says, 'By the
word of the Lord the heavens were set fast, and the whole power of
them by the spirit [breath] of his mouth'.[2] There is also a certain operation of God the Father in his creatures besides that by which of his own
nature he bestows existence on all. There is also a certain special
ministry of our Lord Jesus Christ towards those on whom from his own
nature he confers rationality; a ministry through which he bestows
well-being on those that are in being. There is also another grace of

[1] Exod. iii. 14.   [2] Ps. xxxii (33), 6.

the Holy Spirit which is bestowed on the deserving, a grace which is ministered through Christ while it is made effective by the Father according to the desert of those who are made able to receive it [*or* him]. This is most plainly shown by the Apostle Paul when he describes the power of the Trinity as one and the same and says: 'There are differences of gifts, but the same Spirit; differences of ministrations, but the same Lord; and differences of operations, but the same God who makes all things operative in all. But to each is given the manifestation of the Spirit, according to what is profitable.'[1] Hence it is most plainly laid down that there is no divergence in the Trinity; what is called the gift of the Spirit is ministered through the Son and made operative through God the Father. 'But all these things are made operative by one and the same Spirit, distributing to each as he wills.'[2]

† *De Principiis*, i. iii. 7

Compare the passages quoted under 'The Holy Spirit', pp. 227-9, above.

That the operation of the Father and the Son is concerned as well with sinners as with saints is clear from this fact; that all rational creatures are partakers in the Word (for 'word' means 'reason') and thus possess seeds, as it were, of wisdom and righteousness implanted in them; and Christ is 'Wisdom' and 'Righteousness'. And all partake of him who truly 'is'; who said through Moses 'I am He who is'.[3] . . . Further, it is said in the gospel, 'If I had not come and spoken to them, they would not be guilty, but now they have no excuse for their sins'.[4] . . . This means that they have no excuse from the time when the divine reason or discourse has begun to show them in their heart the distinction between right and wrong. . . . Again, the gospel teaches that mankind as a whole is not without a share in God, when the Saviour says, . . . 'The kingdom of God is within you'.[5]   † Ibid. 1. iii. 6

(g) *Logos and Wisdom in Creation*

'All things came into being through him.'[6] The agent 'through whom' never has the first place but always the second. . . . Thus if all things were brought into being *through* the Word, it was not *by* him but by one greater and mightier than the Word. And who would this be but the Father?   *Comm. in Ioannem*, ii. 10 (6)

Just as a house or ship is built according to the principles of architecture or shipbuilding, and the house or ship has as its beginning the principles

---

[1] 1 Cor. xii. 4-7.   [2] 1 Cor. xii. 11.   [3] Exod. iii. 14.   [4] John xv. 22.   [5] Luke xvii. 21.
[6] John i. 3.

and reasons which are in the craftsmen; so I suppose that all things came into being in accordance with the reasons of things which were to be, which were revealed before by God; for 'in wisdom he has made all things'.[1] And we must say that having created, so to speak, an animate Wisdom, God gave to this Wisdom the task of imposing shape and form on existing things and on matter, from the principles inherent in wisdom. . . . And if we carefully examine all the functions [*of the Word*], he is the beginning only in respect of being Wisdom; it is not in respect of his being Word [reason] that he is really the beginning if, that is, the Word 'was *in* the beginning'. So that one may make bold to say that the most fundamental of all the functions designated by the names of the 'firstborn of all creation' is wisdom.   Ibid. i. 19 (22)

(h) The Source of Being

God does not 'partake of being'.[2] He *is partaken of*—by those who have the spirit of God. And our Saviour does not 'partake of' righteousness; he *is* righteousness, and is partaken of by the righteous. But the question of 'being' is extensive and difficult, and especially if 'being' properly so called is motionless and unembodied being. The problem is whether God 'is transcendent over "being" in dignity and power',[3] and imparts 'being' to those to whom he imparts it according to his own principle,[4] and to the Word[4] himself; or whether he *is* himself 'being', though he is described as invisible by nature in the saying about the Saviour which calls him 'the image of the invisible God'.[5] 'Invisible' means 'unembodied'. And we have to inquire whether we should apply to the 'only-begotten, the firstborn of all creation'[5] the titles 'being of beings', 'idea of ideas', and 'the source' [*sc. of 'being' and 'ideas'*], while we speak of God the Father as transcending all these.

Contra Celsum, vi. 64

(j) The Son is not a new God

[*Unlike the Egyptian Serapis*] the Son of God, the 'first-born of all creation',[5] though he seemed to become man but recently, is not for that reason a 'new God'. For the sacred Scriptures know that he is older than all created things; and that it was to him that God said, concerning the creation of man, 'Let us make man after our image and likeness'.[6]   Ibid. v. 37 (*ad fin.*)

---

[1] Ps. civ. 24.   [2] οὐσία—meaning also 'substance'.   [3] Plato, *Republic*, 509 B.   [4] λόγος.
[5] Col. i. 15.   [6] Gen. i. 26.

(k) But, in a sense, a 'second God'

To Celsus we Christians seem reprehensible, since we are taught . . . to worship and honour virtue, as the product of God, and as being the Son of God . . . as his genuine disciple affirmed when he said of him, 'who became for us wisdom from God, and righteousness and sanctification and redemption'.[1] And if then we call him a 'second God',[2] it must be realized that by a 'second God' we mean just this: the virtue that includes all virtues, the reason [logos] that includes every kind of reason. . . . And we say that this virtue and reason is uniquely associated and made one with the soul of Jesus, since he alone has been perfectly capable of the utmost participation in absolute Reason, absolute Wisdom absolute Righteousness.   *Contra Celsum* v. 39

(l) Unity of Will between Father and Son

Jesus says to them, 'My food is that I may do the will of him who sent me and complete his work'[3]—fitting food for the Son of God, when he is a doer of the Father's will, making the willing in himself just what it was in the Father, so that the will of God is in the will of the Son, and the will of the Son is inseparable from the will of the Father, so that there are no longer two wills but one. And this unity of will is the reason for the saying of the Son 'I and my Father are one';[4] and because of this unity of will, he who has seen him has seen the Son, and has also seen him who sent him.[5] . . .   *Comm. in Ioannem*, xiii. 36

'Now if they worshipped one God only they would perhaps have a forceful argument against the rest; but, as it is, they give excessive adoration to him who appeared just lately. Yet they suppose that they are committing no offence concerning God, even if a servant of God be worshipped.'—There might seem to be some plausibility in this charge against us. But we must reply that if Celsus had considered the saying, 'I and my Father are one',[4] and what the Son said in his prayer to the Father: 'As I and thou are one',[6] he would not suppose that we worship any but the supreme God. 'For the Father is in me' he says, 'and I am in the Father'.[7] But if anyone be disturbed by these considerations, wondering whether we are deserting to those who reject

---

[1] 1 Cor. i. 30.   [2] Origen calls the Logos 'a second God' in two other places in *Contra Celsum*, vi. 61, and vii. 57. '. . . He died for all mankind . . . yet Celsus would not think him worthy of the second degree of honour after the God of the whole universe, which in his in virtue of his mighty deeds in heaven and on earth. . . .'   [3] John iv. 34.   [4] John x. 30.   [5] Cf. John xiv. 9.   [6] John xvii. 22.   [7] John xiv. 11.

the existence of two persons,[1] the Father and the Son, he should observe this saying; 'All the believers were of one heart and soul',[2] in order to understand 'I and my Father are one'. . . . And we do not 'give excessive adoration to him who has appeared just lately' as to one who did not exist before that appearance. For we believe him when he said 'Before Abraham was, I am',[3] and 'I am the truth'.[4] None of us is so stupid as to suppose that truth had no existence before the time of Christ's appearing on earth. We worship, then, the Father of truth, and the Son who is the truth. And they are two separate persons,[5] but one in unity and concord of mind and in identity of will; so that he who has seen the Son, 'radiance of the glory' and 'expression of the being'[6] of God, has seen God in him who is the image of God.

Contra Celsum, viii. 12

According to Theodoret (II. viii. 45) the Council of Sardica in 343 condemned as 'blasphemous and corrupt' the interpretation of the unity of Father and Son in terms of 'unity and concord of mind'.[7] Athanasius (*Oratio contra Arianos*, iii. 10) attacks this doctrine of 'moral unity'.

X. The Church

(*No Salvation outside the Church*

. . . [*Rahab* (Josh. ii) *mystically represents the Church, the scarlet thread the blood of Christ: and only those in her house are saved.*] If anyone wishes to be saved . . . let him come to this house where the blood of Christ is for a sign of redemption. For that blood was for condemnation among those who said, 'His blood be on us and on our children'.[8] Jesus was 'for the fall and resurrection of many';[9] and therefore in respect of those who 'speak against his sign' his blood is effective for punishment, but effective for salvation in the case of believers. Let no one therefore persuade himself or deceive himself: outside this house, that is, outside the Church, no one is saved. . . . The sign of salvation [*sc. the scarlet thread*] was given through the window because Christ by his incarnation gave us the sight of the light of godhead as it were through a window; that all may attain salvation by that sign who shall be found in the house of her who once was a harlot, being made clean by water

---

[1] ὑποστάσεις. [2] Acts iv. 32. [3] John viii. 58. [4] John xiv. 6. [5] δύο τῇ ὑποστάσει πράγματα. [6] Heb. i. 3. [7] ὁμόνοια καὶ συμφωνία. [8] Matt. xxvii. 25. [9] Luke ii. 34.

and the Holy Spirit, and by the blood of our Lord and Saviour Jesus
Christ, to whom is glory and power for ever and ever. Amen.

† Hom. in Lib. Iesu Nave, iii. 5

(b) The Destiny of those Outside

[*On* Jer. 1. 25 (LXX), 'The Lord has opened his treasury and has
brought forth vessels of his wrath' . . .] I will say with confidence that
the treasury of the Lord is his Church, and in that treasury, that is, in
the Church, there often lurk men who are vessels of wrath. Therefore
a time will come when the Lord will open the treasury of the Church:
for now the Church is closed and 'vessels of wrath' are in it together
with 'vessels of mercy',[1] and chaff as well as grain, and, besides good
fish, there are fish to be cast away and destroyed, which have all been
caught in the net.[2] . . . Outside the treasury the sinful vessels are not
vessels of wrath: they are less culpable than those. For they are servants
who do not know their Lord's will and do not do it.[3] Now he that
enters the Church is either a 'vessel of wrath' or a 'vessel of mercy': he
that is outside the church is neither. I need another name for the man
who stays outside the church; and as I confidently declare that he is not
a vessel of mercy, so on the other hand I openly give my opinion, based
on common sense, that he cannot be called a 'vessel of wrath', but a
vessel reserved for something else. Shall I be able to support this opinion from Scripture . . .? The Apostle says: 'Now in a great house there
are not only golden and silver vessels, but also vessels of wood and
earthenware: some for honour, some for contempt. . . .'[4] Now is this
great house, do you suppose, an existing house, in which are vessels for
honour and others for contempt? Or is it that, in that house which is
to be, the vessels of gold and silver, which are for honour, will be
found to be vessels of mercy: while the rest, that is ordinary men, who
are outside the treasury, though neither vessels of wrath nor of mercy,
will yet be able to be vessels in the great house, according to the same
mysterious dispensation of God: vessels which have not been cleaned
but are vessels of pottery, for contempt, and yet necessary for the
house?

‡ Hom. in Ieremiam, xx. 3

(c) The Church as Old as Creation

I would not have you suppose that the 'bride of Christ'[5] or the Church
is spoken of only after the coming of the Saviour in the flesh: but rather

---

[1] Rom. ix. 22–24.   [2] Cf. Matt. xiii. 47 ff.   [3] Cf. Luke xii. 27.   [4] 2 Tim. ii. 20.   [5] Cf.
Rev. xxi. 2.

from the beginning of the human race, from the very foundation of the world; nay, I may follow Paul in tracing the origin of this mystery even further, before the foundation of the world. For Paul says: 'He chose us in Christ before the foundation of the world, that we should be holy. . . .'[1] The Apostle also says that the Church is built on the foundation not only of Apostles but also of prophets.[2] Now Adam is numbered among the prophets, and he prophesied the 'great mystery in respect of Christ and the Church' when he said: 'For this reason a man shall leave his father and his mother and shall cleave to his wife, and the two shall be in one flesh'.[3] For the Apostle is clearly speaking of these words when he says: 'This mystery is great; but I am speaking in respect of Christ and the Church'.[4] Further the Apostle also says: 'For he so loved the Church that he gave himself for her, sanctifying her with the washing of water'.[5] And in this he shows that it is not the case that she did not exist before. For how could he love her if she did not exist? Without doubt she existed and so he loved her. For the Church existed in all the saints who had been from the beginning of time. Thus, loving the Church, he came to her. And as his 'children share in flesh and blood, so he also was made partaker of these'[6] and gave himself for them. For these saints were the Church, which he loved so as to increase it in numbers, to improve it with virtues, and by the 'charity of perfection'[7] transfer it from earth to heaven.

† *Comm. in Canticum Canticorum* ii (Lommatzsch 14, p. 418)

(d) The Promise to Peter

'Simon Peter answered and said, You are the Christ, the Son of the living God.'[8] If, with Peter, we also say, 'You are the Christ' [&c.], when this is not revealed to us by flesh and blood, but when the light from the Father in heaven has shined in our hearts,[9] and we become Peter, then to us may be said, 'You are Peter'. For every disciple of Christ is a rock, after drinking of 'that spiritual rock which followed';[10] and on every such rock is built the whole principle [*logos*] of the Church and the corresponding polity. For the perfect possess the sum of the things which bring the full blessedness of words, deeds, and thoughts; and in each of them is the Church built by God.

* *Comm. in Matthaeum*, xii. 10

---

[1] Eph. i. 4, 5.   [2] Eph. ii. 20.   [3] Gen. ii. 24.   [4] Eph. v. 32.   [5] Eph. v. 25, 26.   [6] Heb. ii. 14.   [7] Cf. Col. iii. 14.   [8] Matt. xvi. 16.   [9] 2 Cor. iv. 6.   [10] 1 Cor. x. 4.

(e) The Ministry

The Priesthood

[*The two divisions of the tabernacle.*] You have heard of the two sanctu-
aries: one as it were visible and open to the priests; the other invisible,
to which the High Priest alone had access, while the rest remained outside. The first sanctuary, I suppose, may be taken to represent the
Church in which we are now placed, while we are in the flesh: in
which priests minister at the altar of whole burnt-offerings, when that
fire has been kindled of which Jesus spoke when he said: 'I have come
to send fire on the earth, and how I wish that it were kindled'.[1] And
pray do not marvel that this sanctuary is open only for priests. For all
who have been anointed with the unction of the sacred chrism have
been made priests [*cf.* 1 Pet. ii. 9] . . . [*and offer the sacrifice of themselves*].

† *Hom. in Leviticum*, ix. 9

The People's Share in Ordination

'Moses called the congregation and said to them. This is the word
which the Lord commanded.'[2] Although the Lord had given commands about the appointment of the chief priest and had chosen him,
still the congregation is also summoned. For in the ordination of a
priest the presence of the people is also required that all may know for
certain that the man elected to the priesthood is of the whole people
the most eminent, the most learned, the holiest, the most outstanding in
every kind of virtue. And this must be done in the presence of the
people to avoid any subsequent change of mind or lingering doubt.

† Ibid. vi. 3

XI. The Sacraments

(a) Baptism

Renunciation of the Devil

Let every one of the faithful recall the words he used in renouncing the
devil when first he came to the waters of Baptism, when he took upon
himself the first seals[3] of faith and came to the saving fountain; he proclaimed that he would not deal in the pomps of the devil, nor his
works, nor would he submit to his servitude and his pleasures.

† *Hom. in Numeros*, xii. 4

[1] Luke xii. 49.   [2] Lev. viii. 5.   [3] *signacula*, or 'tokens'.

Chrism

[*On* Exod. xii. 7: *The Passover*: 'They shall take of the blood and put it upon the door posts . . .']. We sacrifice and anoint our houses with the blood. I mean by this our body, if the anointing is our faith in him who annihilates the power of the destroyer; and after our anointing, that is our believing in the Anointed, i.e. Christ, then we are bidden to come to the meal.   *Selecta in Exodum*

[*On* Ezek. xvi. 9.] 'I washed you in water.' The washing and the grace of the Holy Spirit and the sanctifying Word. 'I washed you in oil.' The chrism is the indwelling of the Holy Spirit in knowledge of the truth.[1]   *Selecta in Ezechielem*

So when one is converted from sin, purification is granted. . . . But the gift of the Spirit is represented under the figure of oil; so that he who is converted from sin may not only achieve purification but also be filled with the Holy Spirit, whereby he may also receive his former robe [*i.e. the prodigal's*] and the ring, be reconciled completely to his father, and restored to the status of a son.   † *Hom. in Leviticum*, viii. 2

Outward Sign—Inward Grace

'For not all those are Israelites who are of Israel'[2] nor are all those straightway washed with the Holy Spirit who are washed with water; just as, conversely, those who are numbered among the catechumens are not all deprived and bereft of the Holy Spirit. For I find in the divine Scriptures several catechumens who were held worthy of the Holy Spirit and that others after receiving baptism were unworthy of the grace of the Holy Spirit. Cornelius was a catechumen and before he came to the water he desired to receive the Holy Spirit.[3] Simon [Magus] had received baptism but he was refused the gift of the Holy Spirit because he approached the grace with hypocrisy.[4]
                                     † *Hom. in Numeros*, iii. 1

Although in accordance with the prescribed form which has been handed down in the Church we have been baptized in those visible waters and with the visible chrism, he only is truly baptized 'from above' in the Holy Spirit and in water who has 'died to sin' and is truly 'baptized in the death of Christ' and is 'buried with him in baptism unto death'.[5]   † *Comm. in Ep. ad Romanos*, v. 8

[1] Chrism to Origen seems symbolic rather than fully sacramental.   [2] Rom. ix. 6.   [3] Cf. Acts. x. 1–3, 44–48.   [4] Acts viii. 9–24.   [5] Rom. vi. 3, 4. 11.

The record in the Acts of the Apostles tells of the manifest indwelling of the Spirit in the baptized, when the water has prepared the way for those who approach with sincerity. . . . Baptism is called 'bath of re-birth'[1] which takes place with 'renewal of Spirit'. In these days also 'the Spirit', since it is from God, is 'borne above the water';[2] but the Spirit does not enter into everyone after the water.

Comm. in Evang. Ioannis, vi. 33 (17)

The Catechumenate

Many passages in Origen are addressed to catechumens, warning them against any confidence in an automatic bestowal of the Spirit in Baptism, and of the need for repentance and faith.

It is not all who are washed so as to attain salvation. We, who have received the grace of baptism in the name of Christ, have been washed; but I know not who of us has been washed unto salvation. Simon [Magus] was washed and was continuing in fellowship with Philip;[3] but he was not washed unto salvation. . . . To be washed unto salva-tion is a matter of enormous difficulty. Mark, catechumens, and listen, and, as a result of these warnings, prepare yourselves before baptism, while you are are still catechumens, and see that you come to the font and are washed unto salvation. . . . He who is washed unto salvation receives both water and the Holy Spirit. Simon was not so washed; he received water but not the Holy Spirit.   ‡ *Hom. in Ezechielem*, vi. 5

Union with Christ

[*A parallel between Joshua (in Greek 'Jesus')—the crossing of Jordan being his exaltation (Jos. iii. 7), and Jesus Christ—his baptism of death being his exaltation (Phil. ii. 9, 10).*] Jesus [Joshua] is not exalted before the mystery of baptism [*i.e. the crossing of Jordan*], but his exaltation, an exaltation in the sight of the people, thence takes its beginning. For if all who are baptized in Christ are baptized in his death, while the death of Jesus is completed in the exaltation of the cross, then Jesus is rightly exalted for each one of the faithful at that moment when each one comes to the mystery of baptism. For it is written 'God has exalted him and has given him a name which is above every name. . . .' [Phil. ii. 9 f.] . . .

† *Hom. in Lib. Iesu Nave*, iv. 2

---

[1] Tit. iii. 5.   [2] Gen. i. 3.   [3] Acts viii. 4 ff., 9 ff.

(b) The Eucharist

The Lord's Body

'Each one therefore as he has conceived in his heart.'[1] Ask yourselves if you are conceiving, or taking in; and if you are retaining: lest what is said should flow away and perish. . . . You who are wont to take part in the divine mysteries know how carefully and reverently you guard the body of the Lord when you receive it, lest the least crumb of it should fall to the ground, lest any thing should be lost of the hallowed gift. For you regard, and rightly regard, yourselves as culpable if any part should fall to the ground through your carelessness. When you show, and rightly show, such care in guarding his body can you suppose it less blameworthy to neglect the word of God than his body?

‡ *Hom. in Exod.* xiii. 3

Right Reception

That which is 'sanctified through the word of God and prayer'[2] does not of its own accord sanctify the recipient; for if this were so it would sanctify him who eats the bread of the Lord unworthily and no one through this food would become 'ill or weak' or 'sleep'.[3] Thus even in respect of the bread of the Lord the advantage to the receiver depends on his partaking of the bread with a pure mind and a clear conscience. We are not deprived of any good merely by not eating of the bread sanctified by the word of God and prayer; neither do we abound in any good by the mere eating. What causes our deprivation is wickedness and sin; what causes our abundance is righteousness and well-doing. . . . [Cf. 1 Cor. viii. 8.] The food which is 'sanctified' . . . 'goes into the belly', in respect of its material nature, and is 'discharged into the privy'.[4] But in respect of the prayer which is added to it it becomes profitable, 'according to the proportion of faith',[5] and is the cause of spiritual discernment in the mind which has an eye to its spiritual profit. It is not the material bread that profits the man who eats the bread of the Lord not unworthily; rather it is the word which is spoken over it. *Comm. in Matthaeum*, xi. 14

The 'Spiritual' Interpretation of Body and Blood

[*Allegorizing* Num. xxiii. 24 (LXX), 'He will not sleep until he devours his prey and drinks the blood of the wounded'.] What people is this,

---

[1] Exod. xxxv. 5 (LXX). [2] 1 Tim. iv. 5. [3] 1 Cor. xi. 30. [4] Matt. ix. 17. [5] Rom. xii. 6.

which practises the drinking of blood? When the Jewish followers of
the Lord heard such words in the gospel they were offended, and said
'Who can eat flesh, and drink blood?'[1] But the Christian people, the
faithful people, hears this and eagerly welcomes it, and follows him who
says, 'Unless you eat my flesh, and drink my blood, you will not have
life in yourselves. For my flesh is really food, and my blood is really
drink.'[1] And, to be sure, he who said this was *wounded* for men; for
'he was wounded for our sins' as Isaiah says.[2] Now we are said to drink
the blood of Christ not only in the way of sacraments, but also when we
receive his words, in which life consists; as he himself says, 'The words
which I have spoken are spirit and life'.[3] Therefore he is 'the wounded'
whose 'blood we drink,' that is to say, we receive the words of his
teaching.   † *Hom. in Num.* xvi. 9

[*John* xiii. 26–30: *The departure of Judas after receiving the morsel of
bread.*] The morsel which Jesus gave to Judas was of the same kind as
that which he gave to the rest of the Apostles when he said, 'Take, eat'.
But to them the result was salvation; to Judas it was condemnation, so
that 'after he had received the morsel Satan entered him'. Let this bread
and the cup be understood by the simpler folk according to the more
general acceptation of the Eucharist; but by those who have been
schooled to a profounder apprehension let it be interpreted in reference
to the diviner promise, the promise of the nourishing word of truth.
I might illustrate the point by the physical effect of the most nutritive
bread, which aggravates a latent fever, although it is conducive to
health and well-being. Thus a true word supplied to a sick soul, which
does not require such nourishment, often irritates it, and becomes the
occasion for its deterioration: in such a case it is dangerous to speak the
truth.   *Comm. in Ioannem,* xxxii. 24 (16)

That bread which God the Word proclaims as his body is the word
which nourishes our souls. . . . That drink which God the Word proclaims as his blood is the word which 'so wonderfully refreshes and
inebriates'.[4] . . . For the body and blood of God the Word can be
nothing else than the word which nourishes and the word which 'makes
glad the heart'.[5] He said, 'This is my blood of the new covenant'. Why
did he not say, 'This is the bread of the new convenant'? Because the
bread is the word of righteousness by eating which our souls are nourished, while the drink is the word of the recognition of Christ according to the mystery of his birth and passion. Since therefore the coven-
_____
[1] John vi. 52 ff.   [2] Isa. liii. 5.   [3] John vi. 63.   [4] Ps. xxii (23), 5   [5] Ps. civ. 15.

ant of God is set before us in the blood of the passion of Christ, that believing the Son of God to have been born and to have suffered in the flesh we may be saved—not through righteousness, for there could be no salvation through righteousness alone without faith in the passion of Christ; therefore it is only of the cup that it is said, 'This is the cup of the new testament'.   * *In Matthaeum Commentarorium Series*, 85

The Sacrifice of the Priestly Church

He has given instructions so that we may know how we ought to approach God's altar. For it is an altar upon which we offer our prayers to God. That we may know, then, how we ought to offer them, he bids us put aside our soiled garments—the uncleanness of the flesh, the faults of character, the defilements of lust. Or do you not recognize that the priesthood has been given to you also, that is to the whole Church of God and the nation of believers? . . . [1 Pet. ii. 9). You have therefore a priesthood, being a priestly nation. Therefore, you ought to offer to God a sacrifice of praise, of prayers, of pity, of purity, of righteousness, of holiness. To offer this aright you have need of clean garments, of vestments kept apart from the common clothing of the rest of mankind; and you must have the divine fire, God's own fire which he gives to men, of which the Son of God says, 'I have come to send fire on earth'.[1]   ‡ *Hom. in Leviticum*, ix. 1

[Lev. xxiv. 5–9: *the shewbread* 'for a memorial'.] If these things are interpreted with reference to the greatness of the mystery, you will find that that memorial effects an immense propitiation. If you come to that 'bread which comes down from heaven and gives life to the world';[2] that 'bread of setting forth' [LXX *for* 'shewbread'] which 'God set forth as a propitiation through faith in his blood',[3] and if you have regard to that memorial of which the Lord says, 'Do this for a memorial of me', you will find that this is the only memorial which makes God propitious to men. If therefore you recall more attentively the Church's mysteries, you will find in these writings of the Law the prefiguration of the truth to come.   ‡ Ibid. xiii. 3

[1] Luke xii. 49.   [2] John vi. 33.   [3] Rom. iii. 25.

XII. The Discipline of the Church

(a) Penance

The 'Power of the Keys'

Those who lay claim to the position of bishops avail themselves of the saying 'You are Peter . . .';[1] as having received, like Peter, the keys of the kingdom of heaven from the Saviour; and they teach that what is bound, that is, condemned, by them is bound in heaven also, and what has received from them remission is loosed also in heaven. Therefore it must be said that the claim is sound if there is in them that which was the ground for the saying to Peter, 'You are Peter'; and that this saying may rightly be extended to them if they are such that Christ can build the Church upon them. But the gates of hell ought not to prevail against him who wishes to bind and loose: and if he is 'held fast by the cords of his sins',[2] then it is in vain that he binds and looses.

Comm. in Matt. xii. 14

Cf. above, p. 245.

Among the Christians there are men appointed to make careful scrutiny of the life and conduct of those who seek admission to the Church, to prevent those of infamous behaviour from coming into their assembly. They have a method of dealing with sinners and especially with the incontinent. . . . They mourn for them as lost and dead to God. . . . If they show a genuine reformation they regard them as risen from the dead and admit them again after a period longer than their original probation. But they do not appoint them to office or positions of authority in the Church when they have fallen into sin after having come to the Word.   *Contra Celsum,* iii. 51

Only One Penitence for Grave Sins

In more serious offences opportunity for penitence is granted only once; but those common offences which we frequently incur always admit of penitence and are redeemed continually.

‡ *Hom. in Leviticum,* xv (*ad fin.*)

Some Sins Irremissible

The Apostles and those who are like the Apostles, being priests after the fashion of the great high priest, who have gained knowledge of the

[1] Matt. xvi. 18.   [2] Prov. v. 22.

service of God; all these know, through the instruction of the Spirit, what are the sins for which one should offer sacrifice . . . and what sins admit of no sacrifice. . . . I do not know how certain men, arrogating more than the priestly right, perhaps not fully versed in priestly knowledge, can claim the power to condone idolatry, to forgive adultery and fornication; as if, through their prayers on behalf of those who have not shrunk from such enormities, even the 'sin unto death'[1] is pardoned. *De Oratione*, 28

Confession

['That the thoughts out of many hearts may be revealed', Luke ii. 35.] There were evil thoughts in men, and they were revealed for this reason, that being brought into the open they might be destroyed, slain and put to death, and cease to be, and that he who died for us might kill them. For while these thoughts were hidden and not brought into the open they could not be utterly done to death. Hence if we have sinned we also ought to say, 'I have made my sin known to thee, and I have not hidden my wickedness. I have said I will declare my unrighteousness to the Lord against myself.'[2] For if we do this and reveal our sins not only to God but also to those who can heal our wounds and sins, our wickedness will be wiped out by him who says, 'I will wipe out your wickedness like a cloud'[3] . . .

‡ *Hom. in Lucam*, xvii

[*The various sin-offerings.*] Perhaps the members of the Church who listen to this may say, 'Those men of Old Testament times had the better of it, compared with us. In those days pardon was offered to sinners on the performance of various rites of sacrifice. With us there is only one pardon for sins, and that is given at the outset through the grace of the font; and after that there is no mercy for sinners, and no pardon is granted.' Certainly the Christian should be under stricter discipline, since Christ died for him. For the men of old there were slain sheep, goats, oxen, and birds, and meal was sprinkled; for you the Son of God was slain, and do you delight in sinning again? And yet, lest these thoughts should rather cast you down in despair than stimulate you to virtue, having heard of all the sacrifices for sins under the Law, now listen to all the ways of remission of sins in the Gospels. First, we are baptized for remission of sins. Secondly, there is the remission in the suffering of martyrdom. Thirdly, the remission

[1] I John v. 15.   [2] Ps. xxxi (32). 5.   [3] Isa. xliv. 22.

given in return for works of mercy . . . [Luke xi. 44]. Fourthly, the forgiveness through our forgiveness of others . . . [Matt. vi. 14, 15]. Fifthly, the forgiveness bestowed when a man 'has converted a sinner from the error of his ways' [Jas. v. 20]. Sixthly, sins are remitted through abundance of love . . . [Luke vii. 47, 'because she loved much' *and* 1 Pet. iv. 8]. Besides these there is also a seventh way of forgiveness, hard and painful though it is, namely the remission of sins through penitence, when 'the sinner washes his bed with tears, and tears are his bread, by day and night',[1] and when he does not hold back in shame from declaring his sin to the priest of the Lord and asking for medicine . . . [*cf.* Jas. v. 14].   † *Hom. in Leviticum*, ii. 4

(b) Marriage

Rigorous Monogamy

In these days we meet with second, third, and fourth marriages, to say nothing of larger numbers; and we are well aware that such wedlock will cast us out of the kingdom of God. For as such marriages, and not merely fornication, are a bar to office in the Church, for neither bishop, priest or deacon nor widow can be digamists: so also, it may be that the digamists will be cast out from the society of the 'church of the firstborn [2] and the undefiled which has 'neither spot or wrinkle'.[3] Not that such a man may be sent to eternal fire, but that he may have no part in the kingdom of God. Remember my interpretation of 1 Corinthians i. 2, 'The church of God in Corinth, together with those who call on his name'. I distinguished the church from those who invoke the name of the Lord. For I suppose the monogamous, the virgin, the perpetually chaste, to belong to the Church of God; while the digamist, however moral his behaviour, however strong in virtues he may be, is yet not of the Church . . . but of the second grade, of 'those who call on the name of the Lord'.[4] Such are saved in the name of Jesus Christ, but they are in no way crowned by him.

‡ *Hom. in Lucam*, xvii

Concession in Practice

[*The ideal of monogamy and the principle of indissolubility of marriage.*] But by this time some of the leaders of the Church have contravened the scriptural injunctions in allowing a woman to marry again while her husband is alive. This is against the letter of Scripture . . . [1 Cor. vii.

[1] Pss. vi. 6, xlii. 3. [2] Heb. xii. 23. [3] Eph. v. 27. [4] Rom. x. 13; Joel ii. 32.

39, Rom. vii. 3] but it is not an utterly unreasonable concession; for it is probable that the indulgence is granted in consideration of the worse evils [*that a rigorous policy would produce*], though it contravenes the law laid down in the Scriptures.   *Comm. in Matthaeum*, xiv. 23

XIII. The Last Things

(a) The Resurrection Body

How can men suppose that our animal body is to be changed by the grace of the resurrection and become spiritual . . .? It is clearly absurd to say that it will be involved in the passions of flesh and blood . . . [1 Cor. xv. 50, 51, 37, 38.] By the command of God the body which was earthly and animal will be replaced by a spiritual body, such as may be able to dwell in heaven; even on those who have been of lower worth, even of contemptible, almost negligible merit, the glory and worth of the body will be bestowed in proportion to the deserts of the life and soul of each. But even for those destined for eternal fire or for punishment there will be an incorruptible body through the change of the resurrection.   † *De Principiis*, II. x. 3

[2 Cor. v. 1.] From this then we can conjecture what will be the purity, the fineness, the glory of that body if we compare it with those present bodies which though celestial and most brilliant are yet 'made with hands' and 'visible' [*cf.* 2 Cor. iv. 18] . . . . We cannot doubt that our body's nature can be changed into such a quality . . . by the will of God, the creator . . . as the worth of rational nature shall demand.
                                         † Ibid. III. vi. 4

(b) Free Will in the Future Life

If material substance were annihilated [sc. *in the consummation*] it would have to be restored and created again. For it is evidently possible that rational natures, who are never deprived of free will, may be able again to be liable to change; for God grants them this privilege, lest if their condition were unchangeable they should fail to recognize that this condition of happiness was owing to the grace of God and not to their own virtue. The result of these changes would doubtless be once more the variety and diversity of bodies.   † Ibid. II. iii. 3[1]

[1] Jerome's Latin quotation (in *Ep. ad Avitum*) and part of the original quoted by Justinian (*Ep. ad Menam*) show that Rufinus here, as elsewhere, sits very loosely to the Greek in his translation. But he does not seem here to have altered the general sense as he does in other places.

But contrast the following:

We do not deny that material nature retains free will: but such is the power of Christ's cross . . . that it suffices for the healing not merely of the present and the future but even of past ages; and not only for this human order of ours but also for heavenly powers and orders . . . [Col. i. 20]. And we learn from the Apostle what it is that restrains free will in the ages to come, when he says 'Love never fails'.[1] . . . And John says 'He who abides in love abides in God'.[2] Thus love, which is the greatest of all things, will restrain every creature from falling. Then God will be all in all.[3]   † *Comm. in Ep. ad Romanos*, v. 10

(c) The Final Consummation

We speak on this subject very cautiously and diffidently, rather by way of discussion than coming to definite conclusions. . . . The end and consummation of the world will be granted; and then each being will undergo the punishment which his sins have merited. God alone knows that time. . . . We suppose that the goodness of God will restore the whole creation to unity in the end, through his Christ, when his enemies have been subdued and overcome . . . (2) . . . The human race . . . will be restored to that unity promised by the Lord Jesus . . . [John xvii. 22, 23] . . . (3) . . . Whether any of those orders [*viz. the opposing powers*] who act under the devil's leadership . . . will be able in some future ages to be converted to goodness, inasmuch as they still have the power of free will; or whether a persistent and inveterate evil becomes from long habit their very nature, I leave to the reader's judgement: whether that part of creation will be utterly sundered from that final unity and harmony and not be restored in these present ages of time 'which are seen' nor in the ages of eternity 'which are not seen'.[4] Meanwhile both in time and in eternity all these beings are dealt with in due order and proportion according to their deserts; so that some are restored in the first ages, some in later, some even in the last times; restored through greater and heavier punishments, and penalties of long duration which are endured perhaps through many ages . . . (4) . . . [*The end of matter.*] If the 'heavens will be changed',[5] what is changed certainly does not perish; and if 'the fashion of the world passes'[6] this does not mean utter annihilation but a kind of change of quality . . . [*cf.* Isa. lxvi. 22] . . . In the end 'God will be all and in all'.[7]

[1] 1 Cor. xiii. 8.   [2] 1 John iv. 16.   [3] 1 Cor. xv. 28.   [4] Cf. 2 Cor. iv. 18.   [5] Cf. Ps. cii (103), 26.   [6] 1 Cor. vii. 31.   [7] 1 Cor. xv. 28.

If anyone thinks that matter will be utterly destroyed, it passes my comprehension how all these substances can live and exist without material
bodies, since to live without material substance is the privilege of God
alone. . . .[1] Another perhaps may say that in the consummation all
matter will be so purified that it may be thought of as a kind of
ethereal substance. . . . But only God knows.[1]

† De Principiis, I. vi. 1–4

(d) The End of the Devil

When it is said that 'the last enemy[2] shall be destroyed',[3] it is not to be
understood as meaning that his substance, which is God's creation,
perishes, but that his purpose and hostile will perishes; for this does not
come from God but from himself. Therefore his destruction means not
his ceasing to exist but ceasing to be an enemy and ceasing to be death.
Nothing is impossible to omnipotence; there is nothing that cannot be
healed by its Maker; the Creator made all things in order that they
might exist; and if things were made that they might exist they cannot
become non-existent.

† Ibid. III. vi. 5

Cf. section 3 in the last extract, and also the following passage:

(e) Progress in Future Life

The restoration to unity must not be imagined as a sudden happening.
Rather it is to be thought of as gradually effected by stages during the
passing of countless ages. Little by little and individually the correction
and purification will be accomplished. Some will lead the way and
climb to the heights with swifter progress, others following hard upon
them; yet others will be far behind. Thus multitudes of individuals and
countless orders will advance and reconcile themselves to God, who
once were enemies; and so at length the last enemy will be reached. . . .
When all rational beings have been restored then the nature of this
body of ours will be changed into the glory of the spiritual body.

† Ibid. III. vi. 6

(f) Punishment

[Isa. l. 11 . . . 'the fire which you have kindled'.] This seems to indicate
that the individual sinner kindles the flame of his personal fire and that
he is not plunged into some fire kindled by another. . . . As excess of

---

[1-1] The sense of the original Greek seems to have been different, if Jerome (*Ep. ad Avitum*) is right in saying that Origen taught 'that corporal substances will utterly perish or at last become ethereal'. [2] i.e. the devil: cf. *Hom. in Iesu Nave*, viii. 4 . . . 'Speaking of the devil he says, "The last enemy, death" . . .' [3] 1 Cor. vi. 26.

food generates fevers . . . so the soul collects abundance of sins and in due time this collection of evils boils up to make the sinner's punishment and catches fire for his retribution. This is when the mind itself, or the conscience, which through divine power keeps record of all things, . . . sees displayed before its eyes the story of its misdeeds . . . [*cf.* Rom. ii. 15, 16].

(6) . . . God acts in dealing with sinners as a physician . . . the fury of his anger is profitable for the purging of souls. Even that penalty which is said to be imposed by way of fire is understood as applied to assist a sinner to health . . . [*cf.* Isa. xlviii. 14, 15, x. 17, lxvi. 16; Mal. iii. 3]. † *De Principiis,* II. x. 4, 6

XIV. Miscellaneous

(a) A Summary of the Christian Faith

Let the teaching of the Church be preserved which has been handed down from the Apostles through the order of succession, and has persisted in the churches down to the present day. That alone is to be believed as truth which in no point conflicts with the tradition of the Church and the Apostles.

(4) The following are examples of the doctrines which are clearly handed down through the apostolic preaching. First, that God is one; and that he created and ordered all things, and when nothing existed brought into existence the whole universe . . . and that this God in the last days sent our Lord Jesus Christ, as he had before promised by his prophets, first to all Israel, then, after the unfaithfulness of the people of Israel, to all the Gentiles. This just and good God, the Father of our Lord Jesus Christ, himself gave the Law and the Prophets and the Gospels. He is the God of the Apostles, of the Old Testament and of the New.

Next, that this same Jesus Christ who came into the world was begotten of the Father before all creation; he assisted the Father in the creation of all things (for 'through him all things were made');[1] and then in the last days he 'abased himself';[2] he was made man and became incarnate, being God; and when made man, remained God. He assumed a body like ours, differing only in this, that it was born of a virgin and the Holy Spirit. This Jesus Christ was truly born and truly

[1] John i. 13.   [2] Phil. ii. 8.

suffered; it was by no mere semblance that he underwent the death which is the common lot of man. He really died; for he really rose from the dead; and after his resurrection he had intercourse with his disciples and then was taken up to heaven.

Then the tradition teaches that the Holy Spirit is associated with the Father and the Son in honour and dignity. It is not yet clearly decided whether or not the Spirit is to be thought of as begotten or unbegotten,[1] or even as the Son of God; this question needs careful investigation, based on Holy Scripture, and is to be examined with prudent inquiry. This at least is indubitable; that the teaching in the churches declares that this Spirit has inspired every saint, prophet and apostle; and that the selfsame Spirit was in those of old as in those who have been inspired after the coming of Christ.

(5) Further, that the soul has its own existence and life, and when it has departed from this world it will be dealt with according to its deserts, either to enter on the inheritance of eternal life and bliss, if its deeds have earned this destiny; or to be consigned to eternal fire and punishment, if the guilt of its crimes has twisted it in that direction. Also that there will be a time of resurrection of the dead, when the body which is 'sown in corruption will rise in incorruption'.[2] . . . It is also laid down in the doctrine of the Church that every rational soul is possessed of free choice and will; and that it has to struggle against the devil and his angels and the opposing powers. . . .

(7) It is also contained in the Church's teaching that the world was made and came into being at a certain time, and is to be dissolved because it is of itself subject to corruption. But what existed before the world and what will exist after it has not yet been clearly demonstrated; for there is no definite pronouncement on this in the teaching of the Church.

(8) Lastly, that the Scriptures were composed through the agency of God's Spirit; and they have not only the meaning which is clear on the surface but another meaning also which is hidden from most people, whereby the narrative presents types of certain mysteries and images of divine matters.[3] Herein the whole Church is united in believing that the whole 'Law [*i.e. the Old Testament*] is spiritual';[4] but this spiritual law is not perceived by all, but only by those on whom is bestowed the grace of the Holy Spirit in the word of wisdom and knowledge.

† Ibid. praef. 2, 4–5, 7–8

[1] See note on p. 227 f.   [2] I Cor. xv. 42.   [3] Cf. below, p. 261.   [4] Rom. vii. 14.

(b) Reason—Revelation—Faith

Let us not suppose that these physical eyes give faith its strength; this strength is provided by the intellect and the reason. Let the unfaithful put their trust in signs and portents which human sight gazes upon: the faithful man should rather be sensible and level-headed. Let him take reason and argument for his guide and so discriminate between true and false.   ‡ *Hom. in Lucam*, i

But we would not seem to make assertions on such important and difficult questions on the basis of mere logic; nor would we appear to compel the assent of our readers by bare conjecture. Let us see then if we can call to our aid some statement of the Holy Scriptures to support the credibility of our arguments by their authority.

† *De Principiis*, I. v. 4

We maintain that human nature is of itself utterly incompetent to seek God and find him without the aid of him who is sought; of him who is found of them that acknowledge, after all their best efforts, that they have need of his help, who reveals himself to those to whom he deigns to be manifested; since it is natural for God to be known by man, and natural for the soul of man to know God while still in the body.

Contra Celsum, vii. 42

It is indeed distressing to find a man in error in respect of morality; but in my opinion it is far worse to go astray in matters of belief. For if men are to be punished for moral offences, those who offend through false beliefs are still more culpable. If morality were sufficient for salvation, how is it that philosophers among the heathen, and the many among the heretics who live disciplined lives, fail to attain salvation because the falseness of their belief as it were darkens and defiles their conduct? This, in my view, is the intention of the 23rd Psalm, where it says 'Who shall ascend into the hill of the Lord . . .? He whose hands are innocent, and his heart pure'.[1] To be 'pure in heart', I take it, means just this; to keep the heart clean from all false belief. But it must be understood that it is really impossible for a man's hands to be innocent unless his heart is pure; and, conversely, a man cannot be innocent in heart and pure from false beliefs if his hands be not innocent and pure from sin. Each entails the other, and innocent thought in the soul and irreproachable living are inseparable.

* *In Matthaeum Commentariorum Series*, 33

[1] Ps. xxiii (24). 3, 4.

(c) Toleration

[*Celsus speaks of bitter hate between Christian sects.*] When the heterodox will not be persuaded we follow the injunction 'An heretical man, after a first and second admonition, avoid, knowing that such a man is perverse, and a sinner, self-condemned'.[1] Nevertheless, those who bear in mind the sayings, 'Blessed are the peacemakers', 'Blessed are the meek',[2] would bear no malice towards those who falsify the teachings of Christianity; and when men have been led astray they would not call them 'sorcerers' or 'malignant trouble-makers'. *Contra Celsum*, v. 63

(d) Interpretation of Scripture. 'Body', 'Soul', and 'Spirit'

There are three ways in which the meaning of the Holy Scriptures should be inscribed in the soul of every Christian man. First, the simpler sort are edified by what may be called the 'body' of scripture; this is the name I give to the common acceptation. Secondly, those who have made some progress are edified by, as it were, the 'soul'. Thirdly, the perfect . . . [*cf.* 1 Cor. ii. 6, 7] are edified by the 'spiritual' Law, which has the shadow of the good things to come'.[3] Thus as a man consists of body, soul, and spirit, so also does the Scripture which is the gift of God designed for man's salvation . . . (12) Some parts of scripture have no 'body'; and there we must look only for the 'soul' and 'spirit'. Perhaps this is the point of the description in John's gospel of the water-pots 'for the purifying of the Jews, holding two or three measures';[4] the Apostle enigmatically implying that the Jews are purified through the word of the Scripture which sometimes holds two measures, i.e. what one may call the 'soul' and 'spirit'; sometimes three, i.e. the 'body' as well. . . . The usefulness of the 'body' is testified by the multitude of simple believers and is quite obvious. Paul gives us many examples of the 'soul' . . . [e.g. 1 Cor. ix. 9, 'Thou shalt not muzzle the threshing ox'], to which he adds the explanation . . . (13) The spiritual interpretation belongs to him who is able to explain the way in which the worship of the 'Jews after the flesh'[5] yields images and 'shadows of heavenly things'[6] and how the 'Law had the shadow of good things to come' . . . [e.g. 1 Cor. x. 11, x. 4 (the 'spiritual rock'), Gal. iv. 21–24 (Hagar and Sarah)].

De Principiis, IV. ii. 4 (Greek in *Philocalia* I. 11)

[1] Tit. iii. 10 f. [2] Matt. v. 9, 5. [3] Heb. x. 1. [4] John ii. 6. [5] Cf. 1 Cor. x. 18. [6] Heb. viii. 5.

(e) The Spiritual and the Carnal Gospel

As there is a law which contains a 'shadow of the good things to come'[1] which are revealed by the law which is proclaimed according to truth, so also there is a gospel which teaches a shadow of the mysteries of Christ which is thought to be understood by all the ordinary folk. But John speaks of an everlasting gospel',[2] which should properly be called a spiritual gospel. This gospel clearly displays face to face, to those who understand, all things concerning the very Son of God, and the mysteries propounded by his words; and the realities of which his doings were enigmas. . . .

Thus it is necessary that there should be both a 'carnal' and a 'spiritual' preaching of Christianity. We must preach this 'carnal' gospel, when we have to, with the determination 'to know nothing, for those who are carnal, except Jesus Christ and him crucified'.[3] But when men are found who are well equipped in the spirit and fruitful in it, who love the heavenly wisdom, they must be made to participate in the Word who has ascended from the incarnate state to the state in which he was 'in the beginning with God'.

Comm. in Ioannem, i. 7 (9)

---

[1] Heb. x. 1.   [2] Rev. xiv. 6.   [3] Cf. 1 Cor. ii. 2.

Thascius Caecilius Cyprianus (Cyprian)

Bishop of Carthage 248–58.—EDITION: W. Hartel in *Corpus Scriptorum Ecclesiasticorum Latinorum* (Vienna, 1868–71).

I. The Church and Ministry

(a) The Unity of the Church

The complicated manuscript tradition of the treatise *On the Unity of the Catholic Church*, c. 4, has been intensively studied in the last fifty years. It is clear that there are two different versions, found separately in some MSS., conflated in others, set end to end in others. The older view, that the 'episcopalian' text of Cyprian was interpolated by a 'papal' forger (Benson), is now generally abandoned, and it is generally supposed that both versions are the work of Cyprian. Many scholars have thought that the 'papal' version ('Primacy Text') was a revision of the original 'episcopalian' ('*Textus Receptus*'), adapting it in view of the Novatianist schism at Rome (Chapman, followed by many others); or the 'Primacy text' may have been written first and later revised for more general consumption (Batiffol). The dominant view at present seems to be that the 'Primacy Text' was altered by Cyprian to the *Textus Receptus* as a result of the controversy about baptism with Stephen, Bishop of Rome. M. Bévenot, S.J., by a diligent examination of the MSS., has succeeded in establishing the two distinct texts, here given successively. Bévenot maintains that the 'papalism' of the 'Primacy Text' is more apparent than real, Peter's 'primacy' being emphasized to support the apostolic authority of bishops, not the pre-eminence of the Bishop of Rome.

. . . The Lord says to Peter, 'I say unto you, that you are Peter, and upon this rock I will build my church . . .' [Matt. xvi. 18 f.]

['Primacy Text']

Again, after his resurrection he says to him, 'Feed my sheep'.[1] He 'builds his church' on him, and to him he gives his sheep to be fed: and although he confers an equal power on all the Apostles, yet he has appointed one throne and by his authority has ordained the source and principle of unity. The other Apostles were, to be sure, what Peter was, but primacy is given to Peter, and the Church and the throne are shown to be one. And all are pastors, but one flock is indicated, which is fed by all the Apostles with unanimous consent. If a man does not

[1] John xxi. 17.

hold this unity of Peter, does he believe himself to hold the faith? If a man deserts the throne of Peter, on whom the Church is founded, is he confident that he is in the Church?

[*Textus Receptus*]

He builds his Church on one man; and although after his resurrection he confers an equal power on all the Apostles and says, 'As my Father has sent me . . .' [John xx. 21–23], yet, in order to display the unity, he has by his authority ordained the source of the same unity, which originates from one man. The other Apostles were, to be sure, what Peter was, endowed with an equal share in honour and power, but a beginning is made from one man that the Church of Christ may be shown to be one. This church the Holy Spirit points to in the Song of Songs, speaking in the person of the Lord, 'My dove is one . . . the favourite of her mother' [Cant. vi. 9]. If a man does not hold this unity of the Church, does he believe himself to hold the faith? If a man withstands and resists the Church, is he confident that he is in the Church? For the blessed Apostle Paul has the same teaching, and sets forth the sacrament of unity, when he says, 'There is one body, one Spirit, one hope of our calling, one Lord, one faith, one baptism, one God'.[1] (5) This unity we ought firmly to hold and defend, especially we who preside in the Church as bishops that we may prove the episcopate also to be itself one and undivided. Let no one deceive the brethren by falsehood; let no one corrupt the truth of our faith by faithless transgression.

[*Common text, continued*]

The episcopate is one; the individual members have each a part, and the parts make up a solid whole. The Church is one; yet by her fruitful increase she is extended far and wide to form a plurality: even as the sun has many rays, but one light; and a tree many boughs but one trunk, whose foundation is the deep-seated root; and as when many streams flow down from one source, though a multitude seems to be poured out from the abundance of the copious supply, yet in the source itself unity is preserved. Cut off a ray from the sun's orb; the unity of light refuses division: break a branch from the tree; the broken member cannot bud: sever the stream from its fount; once severed it is dried up. So also the Church, flooded with the light of the Lord, extends her rays over all the globe: yet it is one light which is diffused everywhere and the unity of the body is not broken up. She stretches

[1] Eph. iv. 4 ff.

forth her branches over the whole earth in rich abundance; she spreads far and wide the bounty of her onward-flowing streams; yet there is but one head, one source, one mother, abounding in the increase of her fruitfulness. Of her womb are we born, by her milk are we nourished, and we are quickened from her breath.

(6) The spouse of Christ cannot be made an adulteress; she is undefiled and chaste. She knows but one home, and guards with virtuous chastity the sanctity of one chamber. She it is who preserves us for God, who enrols into the Kingdom the sons she has borne. Whoever stands aloof from the Church and is joined to an adulteress is cut off from the promises given to the Church; and he that leaves the Church of Christ attains not to Christ's rewards. He is an alien, an enemy. He cannot have God for his father who has not the Church for his mother. If any one was able to escape outside of Noah's ark, then he also escapes who is outside the doors of the Church.

(7) This sacrament of unity, this bond of peace inseparable and indivisible, is indicated when in the Gospel the robe of the Lord Jesus Christ was not divided at all or rent, but they cast lots for the raiment of Christ, to see who should put on Christ for clothing; and so the raiment was received whole and the robe was taken unspoilt and undivided. Divine Scripture speaks, and says, 'But as for the robe, since it was seamless, woven throughout, from the part above, they said among themselves: "Let us not rend it, but cast lots for it to see whose it shall be." ' That garment stood for the unity which comes 'from the part above', that is, from Heaven and from the Father, a unity which could not be rent at all by him that received it and had it in possession; he took it indivisibly in its unbreakable entirety. He who rends and divides the Church of Christ cannot possess the clothing of Christ. . . .

The Lord warns us of this when he says, 'The man who is not with me is against me . . .'.[1] The man who breaks the peace and harmony of Christ is acting against Christ; he who 'gathers' anywhere but in the Church is 'scattering'. The Lord says, 'I and the Father are a unity'.[2] Again, it is said of Father, Son, and Spirit, 'The three are a unity'.[3] Does anyone suppose that this unity, deriving from the divine stability, and cemented by heavenly mysteries, can be broken in the Church, and sundered by the separation brought about by conflicting purposes? He who does not keep this unity does not keep God's law, does not hold the faith of the Father and the Son, does not keep hold on life and salvation.   *De Catholicae Ecclesiae Unitate*, 4–7

[1] Matt. xii. 30.   [2] John x. 30.   [3] John v. 7.

CYPRIAN

(b) The Episcopal Office

Note that 'priest', *sacerdos*, normally means 'bishop' in Cyprian.

We are bound to observe the precepts and admonitions of our Lord; and he ordained the high office of bishop and the principle of his Church when in the gospel he spoke these words to Peter, 'You are Peter, and on this rock I will build my church . . .'. [Matt. xvi. 18 f.] Thereafter, age has succeeded age, bishop has followed bishop, and the office of bishop and the principle of church government has been handed down, so that the Church is established on the foundation of bishops, and every act of the Church is directed by those same presiding officers. Since this has been laid down by divine institution, I am amazed that certain persons [sc. *who had lapsed in persecution*] should have the temerity to elect to write to me in such a fashion as to end their letter in the name of the Church; seeing that the Church consists of the bishop, the clergy, and all the faithful. *Epistle* xxxiii. 1

[*In saying* 'Lord, to whom shall we go?' (John vi. 67–69)] Peter speaks as representing the Church, for our instruction; since the Church was to be built on him. He shows us here that, although the proud and arrogant multitude of those who refuse to obey may take themselves off, still the Church never departs from Christ; and the Church is made up of the people united to their priest, the flock cleaving to its shepherd. Hence you should know that the bishop is in the Church, and the Church in the bishop, and that if anyone is not with the bishop he is not in the Church; and that those people are vainly beguiling themselves who, not being at peace with the priests of God, creep up stealthily, and trust by underhand means to enter into communion with certain persons: seeing that the Church is catholic and one, and may not be sundered or divided, but should assuredly be kept together and united by the glue which is the mutual adherence of the priest. Ibid. lxvi. 7

(c) Choice of Bishops; Made by Bishops, with Approval of Clergy and Laity

In appointments of priests we ought to choose none but men of spotless and upright character as our leaders, that when they worthily offer sacrifices to God they may be heard in the prayers which they make for the safety of the Lord's people . . .

. . . The people, in obedience to the Lord's commands and in fear of

God, ought to separate from a ruler who is a sinner and not to be associated with the sacrifices of a sacrilegious priest, since the people especially have the power of choosing worthy priests or refusing the unworthy. (4) The practice of choosing a priest in the presence of the people and before the eyes of all, and requiring that he should be approved as fit and worthy by the general decision and testimony, evidently comes to us with divine authority; just as in Numbers the Lord commanded Moses: 'Take Aaron your brother and Eleazar his son and set them on the mount in the sight of the whole congregation, and take off Aaron's vestment and put it on Eleazar'.[1] . . . Thus God shows that appointments to the priesthood should only take place with the cognizance of the people and in their presence, that, the people being at hand, the faults of the wicked may be revealed, the merits of the good proclaimed, and the appointment may be valid and regular, as having been tested by the vote and decision of all [*cf. the election of Matthias* (Acts i. 15), *and the appointment of 'deacons'* (Acts vi. 2)] . . .

(5) Therefore we should be careful to observe and keep the procedure we have received from the divine tradition and from the practice of the Apostles, which is kept among us and in practically all the provinces: namely, that for the appointment of priests in due form the neighbouring bishops of the same province should assemble with the people for whom a ruler is to be appointed, and the bishop be chosen in the presence of the people who have the fullest knowledge of the manner of life of individuals and are acquainted with the behaviour of each from having lived with them. We observe that this was done among you in the appointment of Sabinus our colleague; as a result of the vote[2] of the brethren and the decision of the bishops who had met and who had submitted letters to you about him, the episcopal office was conferred on him, and the hand was laid upon him, to take the place of Basilides.   Ibid. lxvii. 2, 3–5

Cornelius was made bishop by many of our colleagues, who were then in Rome . . .; on the decision of God and Christ,[3] with the

---

[1] Num. xx. 25 f.   [2] The people's suffrage was evidently limited to the ratification of the choice made by the bishops; and the inferior clergy seem to have had no more voice in the election than the laity.   [3] Cf. *Epistle* lxvi. 1 . . . [*To criticize the character of a bishop*] is to disbelieve in God, to show oneself a rebel against Christ and his gospel. He says, 'Are not sparrows sold at two a penny? And yet not one of them falls to the ground without the Father's will' [Matt. x. 29]. . . . Are you going to suppose that the priests [bishops] of God are appointed in the Church without his cognizance? To imagine that those who are appointed are unworthy and immoral is to imagine that God's priests are not set up in the Church by God and through God.

testimony of almost all the clergy, by the vote[1] of the people who
were present, and by the consent of ancient priests [*bishops*] and good
men.   *Epistle* lv. 8

The invariable source of heresies and schisms is in refusal to obey the
priest of God [the bishop], the failure to have one in the church who is
looked upon as the temporal representative of Christ as priest and
judge. If the whole brotherhood obeyed the bishop in this way, according to the divine instructions, no one would move against the college
of priests [bishops], no one, after the divine decision,[2] the vote[1] of the
people, the consent of his fellow-bishops, would set himself up as a
judge, not of the bishops [*who elected him*] but of God himself.[2]
                                                     Ibid. lix. 5

(d) Unworthy or Irregular Ministrations Invalid

[Rev. xiv. 9 ff.] How can a man suppose himself capable of acting as
God's priest [*bishop*] if he has obeyed and served the priests of the
devil? . . . Those who have offered sacrilegious sacrifices cannot claim
the priesthood of God, nor offer prayer for their brethren in his sight,
since it is written in the gospel, 'God does not listen to a sinner . . .'
[John ix. 31].

(4) . . . The oblation cannot be consecrated where there is not the
Holy Spirit, nor does the Lord grant grace to anyone through the
prayers and intercessions of one who himself has done wrong to the
Lord.   Ibid. lxv. 2

Cf. lxvii. 4, above. Cyprian does not say how the existence of an unworthy bishop is to be reconciled with his claim that God guides the
election.

II. Christian Initiation

(a) Infant Baptism and Original Sin

If remission of sins is granted even to the worst offenders, and to those
who have previously committed many sins against God, when they
have afterwards believed, and if no one is shut out from baptism and
grace; how much less ought an infant to be shut out, who being newly
born has committed no sin, except that being born of Adam's line
according to the flesh he has at his first birth contracted the contagion

[1] See n. 2, p. 267.   [2] See n. 3, p. 267.

of the ancient death? Indeed the infant's approach to the reception of remission of sins is the easier from the very fact that the sins remitted are another's, not his own.   Ibid. lxiv. 5

(b) Baptism: The Chrism

The baptized person must also be anointed, that by receiving the *chrism*, that is, the unction, he may be God's anointed and have in himself the grace of Christ.   Ibid. lxx. 3

(c) The Seal of the Laying on of the Hand

[*After the baptisms by Philip in Samaria*] Peter and John supplied what was lacking; prayer was made for the baptized, the hand laid upon them, the Holy Spirit was invoked and was poured upon them. The same practice is observed among us now; those baptized in the church are brought to the officers of the church and by our prayer and imposition of the hand they obtain the Holy Spirit and are perfected by the seal of the Lord.   Ibid. lxxiii. 9

Men can only be fully sanctified and sons of God if they are born of both sacraments; since the Scripture says, 'Unless a man is born again of water and spirit he cannot enter the kingdom of God'.[1]

                                    Ibid. lxii. 1

(d) The Gift of the Spirit: Contradictory Statements

A man is born not by imposition of the hand, when he receives the Holy Spirit, but in baptism. Thus he is born first and then receives the Holy Spirit. This is what happened with the first man, Adam. God fashioned him, then breathed into his face the breath of life. The Spirit cannot be received unless the person is already there to receive it.

                                    Ibid. lxxiv. 7

It is through baptism that the Holy Spirit is received, and those who have been baptized and have obtained the Holy Spirit are admitted to drink the cup of the Lord.   Ibid. lxii. 8

(e) Heretical Baptism: The Issue between Rome and Africa

This decision on the baptism of those who join the Church from heresy is no new or sudden departure. A long time has passed since Agrippinus, of honoured memory, presided over a meeting of a large number of

[1] John iii. 3. 5.

bishops, which came to this decision.[1] From that time to this the many thousands of heretics in our provinces who have been converted to the Church have not scorned or hesitated to attain the grace of the life-giving bath and of saving baptism; rather they have embraced the opportunity rationally and gladly . . .

(4) In a letter, of which you sent me a copy, I find it clearly stated that 'no enquiry is to be made about the minister of baptism, since the baptized may have received remission of sin in virtue of his own faith', This is a topic which, I feel, must not be passed over: especially as in the same letter I noted a mention of Marcion, with the instruction that not even those who come into the Church from his heresy should be baptized in the name of Jesus Christ. We must there-fore examine the faith of those who hold a belief outside the church, and consider whether they can obtain any grace in virtue of sharing the same faith . . .

(5) . . . The Lord instructed his disciples to baptize . . . 'In the name of the Father, and of the Son, and of the Holy Ghost'[2] . . . Does Marcion hold this Trinity? . . . How can one baptized among such heretics be considered as having obtained remission of sins and the grace of divine mercy through his faith, seeing that he has not the truth of the Faith itself?   *Epistle* lxxiii. 3–5

I send you a copy of our brother Stephen's answer. When you read it you will be all the more cognizant of his error, for he tries to maintain the cause of heretics against Christians and the Church of God. For among arrogant claims, irrelevancies, and inconsistencies—he is an inexpert and careless writer—he goes so far as to add; 'If anyone comes to you from any heresy whatever, let there be no novel additions to the traditional procedure, namely the imposition of hands for repentance; since the heretics themselves do not baptize those who come to them from other sects, but merely admit them to communion'. . . . Thus he had judged the baptisms of all heretics to be valid and regular.

                                                       Ibid. lxxiv. 1

If any one objects that Novatian observes the same rule as the Catholic Church, and baptizes with the same creed as we do, acknowledges the same God the Father, the same Christ the Son, the same Holy Ghost, and therefore can lay claim to the power of baptizing, because he does not appear to differ from us in the baptismal interrogation—if anyone

[1] The First Council of Carthage, 215–17.   [2] Matt. xxviii. 19.

thinks this a valid objection, let him know in the first place that the schismatics have not one and the same rule of the creed as ours, nor the same interrogation. For when they ask, 'Dost thou believe in the remission of sins and eternal life through the holy Church?' there is a lie in their interrogation, seeing that they do not have the Church. Moreover, they admit, by their own words, that remission of sins can only be given through the holy Church; and since they do not have this they show that sins cannot be remitted among them.   Ibid. lxix. 7

(f) No Validity Outside the Church

Some of our colleagues, by a curious presumption, are led to suppose that those who have been dipped among the heretics ought not to be baptized when they join us; because, they say, there is 'one baptism'.[1] Yes, but that one baptism is in the Catholic Church. And if there is one Church, there can be no baptism outside it. There cannot be two baptisms: if heretics really baptize, then baptism belongs to them. And anyone who on his own authority concedes them this privilege admits, by yielding their claim, that the enemy and adversary of Christ should appear to possess the power of washing, purifying, sanctifying a man. Our assertion is that those who come to us from heresy are baptized by us, not re-baptized. They do not receive anything there; there is nothing there for them to receive. They come to us that they may receive here, where there is all grace and truth; for grace and truth are one.   Ibid. lxxi. 1

The Church is one and indivisible: therefore there cannot be a Church among the heretics. The Holy Spirit is one, and cannot dwell with those outside the community; therefore the Holy Spirit has no place among heretics. It follows that there can be no baptism among heretics; for baptism is based on this same unity and cannot be separated either from the Church or from the Holy Spirit.

(5) . . . It is ridiculous to assert that spiritual birth—that second birth of ours in Christ through the bath of regeneration—can take place among the heretics where, it is admitted, the Spirit has no place. Water cannot of itself purify and sanctify, unless it is accompanied by the Holy Spirit.   Ibid. lxxiv. 4–5

[1] Eph. iv. 5.

III. The Eucharist

(a) The Sacrifice

If Christ Jesus, our Lord and God, is himself the high priest of God the Father, and first offered himself as a sacrifice to the Father, and commanded this to be done in remembrance of himself, then assuredly the priest acts truly in Christ's stead, when he reproduces what Christ did, and he then offers a true and complete sacrifice to God the Father, if he begins to offer as he sees Christ himself has offered.

Epistle lxiii. 14

(b) The Presence flees an unworthy recipient

[*One who had been guilty of apostasy*] could not eat or handle the holy things of the Lord. He found himself holding a cinder in his open hands. By the instance of this one man it was shown that the Lord departs when he is denied, and that what is taken does not benefit the undeserving unto salvation, seeing that the saving grace is changed into a cinder on the departure of the holy thing.　　　*De Lapsis*, 26

IV. The New Life in the Spirit. A Personal Confession

I was myself so entangled and constrained by the very many errors of my former life that I could not believe it possible for me to escape from them, so much was I subservient to the faults which clung to me; and in despair of improvement I cherished these evils of mine as if they had been my dearest possessions. But when the stain of my earlier life had been washed away by the help of the water of birth, and light from above had poured down upon my heart, now cleansed and purified; when I had drunk the Spirit from heaven, and the second birth had restored me so as to make me a new man; then straightway in a marvellous manner doubts began to be resolved, closed doors to open, dark places to grow light; what before had seemed difficult was now easy, what I had thought impossible was now capable of accomplishment. So that I could now see that what had been born after the flesh and lived at the mercy of sin belonged to the earth, while that which the Holy Spirit was enlivening had begun to belong to God. You know, to be sure, and are as aware as I am of all that this death of sin and new life of virtue has removed from us, and all that it has conferred upon us. You yourself know, and I do not hold forth about it. Boasting directed to one's own praise is odious; and yet it may be a sign of gratitude rather than boasting if it is proclaimed as due to the gift of God and not ascribed to a man's virtue, so that freedom from sin is derived from God, the former sin from human error. All our power for good is derived from God. From God, I say; for he is the source of our life and our strength; from him we gain vitality so that in our present position we recognize beforehand the signs of things that are to come. Only let fear be the guardian of innocence, so that the Lord, who in his kindness has streamed into our minds with the inflowing of his heavenly mercy, may through righteous activity be retained as a guest of the soul that delights in him, lest the security we have received should produce heedlessness and the old enemy creep in unawares once more.   *Ad Donatum*, 4

Athanasius

c. 296–373. Bishop of Alexandria 328–373.—Edition: Migne, *Patrologia Graeca*, xxv–xxviii (reprinting Benedictine text of 1698).

I. God and Man

(a) Creation and the Fall: Man Mortal by Nature, Immortal by Grace

[*Three erroneous views of creation are rejected:* (i) *the Stoic 'spontaneous generation';* (ii) *the Platonic notion of pre-existent matter;* (iii) *the Gnostic idea of the 'Demiurge', the agent of creation, other than the Father. In contrast to these is the Christian doctrine:*] The godly teaching and the faith according to Christ . . . knows that God made the whole order of things and brought it into being out of nothing . . . [Gen. i. 1; Heb. xi. 3 *and* 'the most useful book of the Shepherd', *i.e. Hermas* (Mandate i)]. For God is good, or rather he is in himself the source of goodness. Being good, he could not grudge anyone anything; therefore he did not grudge existence to any; and so he made all things out of nothing through his own Word, our Lord Jesus Christ. And among created things he felt special concern for the race of men, and since he observed that according to the condition of their birth men were incapable of permanence, he bestowed on them a further gift. He did not merely create man in the same way as he created all the irrational creatures on earth; he made men 'after his own image', giving them a share even in the power of his own Word,[1] so that they might have as it were shadows of the Word, and thus becoming 'rational',[2] might be able to continue in blessedness and live the true life, which is the life of the saints in paradise.

But God also knew that man's will could incline either way, and therefore in his providence he safeguarded the grace given to man by imposing a condition and putting him in a certain place. For he brought them to his own paradise, and laid down this condition; that if they preserved the grace and remained good, they should have a life in paradise free from trouble, pain, and care, besides having the promise

---

[1] Cf. *Contra Arianos*, iii. 10 (*ad fin.*) . . . We are called 'the image and glory of God' not on our own account; it is on account of the image and true glory of God that dwells in us, namely his Word who later became flesh for us, that we have the grace of this designation.' [2] By a share in *Logos* ('word', 'reason') men became *logikoi* ('rational'). 'Spiritual' might be nearer the meaning but would miss the connexion.

of immortal life in heaven: but if they transgressed and turned away
and became evil, they should know that they would suffer that corruption in death which was natural to them, and then they would no
longer live in paradise, but outside it thereafter would remain in death
and corruption when they died . . .

For to 'die in death'[1] surely means just this, not merely to die but to
remain in the corruption of death.   *De Incarnatione*, 3

Adam before the transgression received the grace from outside himself;
it was not bound up with his physical nature.   *Contra Arianos*, ii. 68

Our guilt was the cause of the descent of the Word, and our transgression called forth his loving-kindness, so that he came to us, and the
Lord was displayed among men. For we were the occasion of his
embodiment, and for our salvation he went so far in his love for man as
to be born and to be displayed in a human body.

In this way then God made man, and wished him to remain in immortality; but men despised and rejected the contemplation of God,
and devised and planned wickedness for themselves . . . and received
the threatened condemnation of death. Thenceforth they no longer
remained as they had been made but became corrupted by their
devices, and death reigned over them as king. For the transgression of
the commandment was turning them back to their natural state, so
that having come into being out of non-existence they should rightly
suffer disintegration into non-existence in the course of time. For if
their natural condition was once non-existence and they were summoned into being by the presence and loving-kindness of the Word,
it followed that when men were deprived of the knowledge of God
and turned back to non-existence (since evil is not-being, good is
being) they should for ever be deprived even of being, seeing that
they have their existence from God 'who is':[2] that is, that they should
disintegrate and remain in death and destruction. For man is by
nature mortal, in that he came into being from non-entity; but because
of his likeness to 'him who is' he would have lived henceforth as God
(for that is the meaning of the scriptural passage, 'I said, You are
Gods . . ., but you die like men . . .'[3]) had he preserved that likeness by
contemplation of God and thus blunted the power of disintegration
which is natural to him. As Wisdom says, 'Observance of the laws [*of
Wisdom*] is the confirmation of immortality.'[4]

[1] Gen. ii. 16.   [2] Cf. Exod. iii. 14.   [3] Ps. lxxxi (82), 6 f.   [4] Wisd. vi. 18.

(5) For God has not only made us out of non-entity but also bestowed upon us a life like the life of God, by the grace of the Word. But men turned away from eternal things . . . and became the authors of their own destruction in death. For by nature they were subject to destruction; but by grace of participation in the Word they would have escaped this natural condition, had they remained good; for because of the presence of the Word with them their natural corruption was kept away from them; 'God created man for incorruption &c. . . .' [Wisd. ii. 23 f.]. But [after the fall] men began to die, and henceforward destruction prevailed against them and had greater power over the whole race than it had by nature, inasmuch as, because of the transgression of the commandment, it had over men the advantage also of the threat of the deity. . . .

(6) . . . The human race was being destroyed; man, as endowed with reason[1] and made after God's image, was disappearing; and the work of God was perishing. . . . The situation was in truth at once paradoxical and unseemly![2]

On the one hand it would be paradoxical for God to lie . . . and God would be untrue if man did not die when God had pronounced sentence of death. On the other hand it would be unseemly that beings who were once made rational and partaking in his Word should perish and turn back again to non-existence through disintegration. For it would be unworthy of God's goodness that his created beings should perish. . . . It had been better not to have come into being than, having come into being, to perish through neglect.

De Incarnatione, 4–6

II. God the Son

(a) Eternal Generation

It is right to call the Son the eternal offspring of the Father. For the substance of the Father was never imperfect, so that what belonged to it might be added later. To beget in time is characteristic of man: for man's nature is incomplete; God's offspring is eternal, for his nature is always perfect.

Contra Arianos, i. 14

---

[1] *logikos*, see note [2], p. 274.   [2] i.e. presented a dilemma; *either* God could allow man to live, and so be inconsistent—a paradox; *or* God could be consistent and allow his creation to perish—unseemly, because unworthy of his goodness.

(b) Identity of Substance

Your assertion that 'the Son is from nothing' and 'did not exist before he was begotten' implies that the names 'Son', 'God', 'Wisdom' are given him in virtue of participation. . . . Participation in what? . . . In the Spirit? No, the Spirit 'takes from the Son'.[1] . . . Therefore it is of the Father that 'he partakes', for this is the only remaining possibility. But of what does he partake, and from whence? If it is something external, provided by the Father, he no longer partakes of the Father, nor can he be called the Father's Son. . . . Therefore what he partakes is 'of the substance of the Father'. And if this be something other than the substance of the Son . . . there will be something intermediate between this that is from the Father and the substance (whatever that be) of the Son . . .

(16) . . . We are forced to say that the Son is entirely that which is 'of the substance of the Father'.   Ibid. i. 15–16

(c) Creation and Co-eternity

If God is Maker and Creator, and creates his works through the Son, and we cannot but regard things which came to be as having existence through the Word, is it not blasphemous, since God is the maker, to say that his craftsman, his Word and Wisdom, 'once was not'? This is as much as to deny that God is the maker, if he has not, as his own, his craftsman, that is, his Word, derived from himself. For then the Word through whom he fashions his work is adventitious, alien, essentially unlike. . . . If the Word is not eternally with the Father, then the Trinity is not eternal; there was first a unity which later has become a trinity by addition. . . . And, what is worse, the Trinity is found to be disparate, consisting of alien and different natures and substances. . . . It may conceivably receive further addition, *ad infinitum.* . . . It may diminish; for clearly what is added may be subtracted.

Ibid. i. 17

(d) Eternal Father implies Eternal Son

Was God, 'who is' ever without reason [Word]? Was he, who is light, without radiance? Or was he always the Father of the Word? . . . Who can endure to hear them say that God was ever without reason [Word] . . . or that God was not always Father?

(25) . . . God is, eternally; then since the Father always is, his brightness exists eternally; and that is his Word. Again, God 'who is' has,

[1] John xvi. 14.

derived from himself, the Word who also is. The Word has not super-vened from previous non-existence, nor was the Father once without reason [Word] . . . If a man looked at the sun and asked about its radiance, 'Did that which is make something which did not exist before, or something which already existed?'[1] he would not be re-garded as reasoning sensibly; he would in fact be crazy in supposing that what comes from the light is something external to it and asking when and where and whether it was made. Such reasoning and such questions about the Son and the Father would display a greater degree of insanity; for this is to make the Word an external addition to the Father and to speak erroneously of a natural offspring as a created thing, by saying, 'He did not exist before he was begotten'.

Contra Arianos, i. 24–25

(e) Perfect and Unchangeable

It is superfluous to examine their question 'Is the Word capable of change?' It is enough merely to write down the kind of things they say, to show their reckless impiety. They ask such nonsensical questions as, 'Has he free will, or not?' 'Is he good from choice, of free will, and can he change, if he so will, being by nature capable of change?' . . . It is blasphemy even to utter such things. For if the Word be capable of change and alteration, where will he come to a stop, and what will be the end of his development? And how will the changeable possibly be like the changeless? In which of his states will a man be able to 'see the Father' in him?[2] . . . And how can he be wholly 'in the Father'[3] if his moral decision is undetermined? Perhaps he is not yet perfect, since he is changeable, and is developing day by day! . . . But he must needs be perfect, if he is equal with God.

Ibid. i. 35

(f) Certain Texts Considered: Christ 'Exalted' as Man, and for Man.

['God highly exalted him,' Phil. ii. 9.] 'Highly exalted' does not signify the exaltation of the substance of the Word; that was and is always equal with God. The exaltation is of the manhood. It is said *after* the incarnation of the Word, to make it clear that 'humbled' and 'exalted' refer to the human nature. . . . The Word, being the image of the Father, and immortal, 'took the form of a servant', and as man endured death for our sake in his own flesh, that thus he might offer himself to the Father on our behalf; therefore also as man he is said to

---

[1] A question the Arians asked about the relation of Father and Son.   [2] Cf. John xiv. 9.
[3] John x. 38, &c.

be highly exalted because of us and on our behalf, that as by his death we all died in Christ, so also in Christ himself we may all be exalted, being raised from the dead and ascending into heaven 'whither Jesus the forerunner has entered for us . . .' [Heb. vi. 20]. And if it is now *for us* that Christ has entered into heaven itself, though he was before and always is the Lord and the maker of the heavens, it is therefore *for us* that Scripture speaks of his being exalted. Just as He who himself sanctified all says also that he sanctifies himself to the Father *for our sakes*;[1] not that the Word may become holy, but that he himself may sanctify all of us in himself. Ibid. i. 41

(g) Christ is not deified: humanity is deified in him

The Scripture says 'gave him' [*sc.* 'a name above all names', Phil. ii. 9]: but this does not refer to the Word himself; for as we have said, even before he became man he was worshipped by the angels and by the whole creation in respect of his unique heritage. It was because of us and for us that this also is written of him. For as Christ died and was exalted as man, so, as man, he is said to receive what, as God, he always had, in order that this great gift might extend to us. For the Word was not degraded by receiving a body, so that he should seek to 'receive' God's gift. Rather he deified what he put on; and, more than that, he bestowed this gift upon the race of men. Ibid. i. 42

(h) He 'rose' as man, and for man. Redemption and Victory

The Scripture speaks of the exaltation of the Word 'from the lower parts of the earth',[2] since the death is also ascribed to him. Both events are spoken of as his, since it was his body, and not another's, which was exalted from the dead and taken up into heaven. Again, since the body was his body, and since the Word was not external to it, it is natural that on the exaltation of his body he, as man, should be said to be exalted, on account of the body. If then he did not become man let this not be said of him. But if 'the Word was made flesh', then resurrection and exaltation must be ascribed to him, in respect of his manhood, that the death ascribed to him may be a redemption for the sins of men and an annihilation of death, and that the resurrection and exaltation may because of him be kept secure for us. He who is the Son of God himself became the Son of man. As Word, he gives from the Father; for all that the Father does and gives he does and supplies through him. As the Son of man he himself is said, humanly, to receive what proceeds from

[1] John xvii. 19.   [2] Eph. iv. 9.

himself. For he received it according to the exaltation of human nature; and this exaltation was its deification, an exaltation which the Word himself always had in respect of the godhead and perfection which was his own as inherited from his Father.   *Contra Arianos*, i. 45

(i) 'Anointed' with the Spirit, as Man and for Man

['Thy throne, O God, is for ever . . . God anointed thee . . . above those who share in thee' (Ps. xliv (45) 6 f.)]. Kings of Israel became kings on being anointed . . .; the Saviour on the contrary, though he was God, and always reigned with his Father's sovereignty, and though he was himself the supplier of the Holy Ghost, is nevertheless said on this occasion to be 'anointed'; that here again, as he is said to be anointed, as man, with the Spirit, so he might provide for us men, besides exaltation and resurrection, the indwelling and personal possession of the Spirit.   Ibid. i. 46

Before he became man he, as the Word, supplied to the saints the Spirit, as being his own; so when he was made man he sanctified all by the Spirit, and says to his disciples 'Receive the Holy Spirit.'[1] . . .

It is not the Word, as Word, that is advanced, for he has all things, eternally; but men, who have in him and through him the source of their receiving these things. For when he is said to be anointed as man, it is we who are anointed in him; when he is baptized, it is we who are baptized in him . . . [*cf.* John xvii. 22].   Ibid. i. 48

(j) The Son Contrasted with Creation, Compared with the Father

['. . . they shall perish, but thou remainest' (Heb. i. 8, 10, 11).] From this passage even the Arians might realize, if they were willing, that the Maker is different from his works; he is God, while they come into being, made out of nothing. For 'they shall perish' does not mean that creation was destined for destruction; it is designed to show the nature of created things by expressing their end. For things capable of destruction have come from nothing, and of themselves testify that once they did not exist—and that even though because of the grace of their maker they do not in fact perish. Therefore . . . it is said of the Son 'thou remainest', to show his eternity; for he is incapable of destruction . . . , 'he did not exist before his generation' is a statement alien to him; it is proper to him to exist always, and to 'remain', together with

[1] John xx. 22.

the Father. . . . He is proper to the Father's substance and one in nature with it. For that reason the Son himself said not 'my Father is *better* than I', lest anyone should suppose him to be foreign to the Father's nature, but '*greater* than I';[1] greater, that is, not in size or in virtue of duration but because of his begetting from the Father himself; in fact, in saying 'greater' he again shows that he is proper to the substance of the Father.   Ibid. i. 58

(k) The Robe of Flesh

Aaron was not born a high priest, but a man, and in course of time, when God willed, he became a high priest . . . putting on over his usual clothes the ephod, breastplate, and robe . . . and thus clad he entered in to the holy place and offered the sacrifice for the people. . . . So the Lord 'in the beginning was the Word . . .'; but when the Father willed that ransoms should be given for all and grace bestowed on all, then indeed, just as Aaron put on his robe, so the Word took earthly flesh, having Mary for the mother of his body, to correspond to the virgin soil [*from which Adam was made*];[2] that as a high priest, himself having an offering, he might offer himself to the Father and cleanse us all from sins . . . As Aaron remained the same and did not change by assuming the high priest's dress . . . so the Lord did not become another by taking the flesh, but remained the same and was clothed in it.   Ibid. ii. 7, 8

(l) The creative Word is not created

Let us look at the replies which the Arians gave to Alexander[3] (who is now in peace) at the beginning, when their heresy was being formed. They wrote, 'He is a creature, but not as one of the creatures; a work, but not as one of the works; an offspring, but not as one of the off-springs'. . . . What is the use of this disingenuous talk, saying that he is 'a creature and not a creature'? . . . (20) Let the Word be excepted from the works, and be restored to the Father as being the Creator, and be acknowledged to be Son by nature; or, if he is merely a creature, let him be acknowledged to have the same status as the other creatures have in relation to each other; and let each of them, as well as he, be said to be 'a creature, but not as one of the creatures, &c.' For you Arians have said that 'offspring' is the same as 'work' in writing

---

[1] John xiv. 28.   [2] The same parallel is drawn by Irenaeus, Tertullian, and later writers. See p. 82.   [3] Archbishop of Alexandria 313-26; convened a council at Alexandria, 321, which excommunicated Arius.

'generated or made'.[1] For though the Son may excel the rest by comparison, yet he remains a creature like them; for among those who are by nature creatures one may find some excelling others. 'Star excels star in glory.'[2] . . .

But if the whole earth sings the praises of the Creator and the truth, and blesses him and trembles before him; and if its Creator is the Word, and he himself says 'I am the truth',[3] then it follows that the Word is not a creature, but alone is proper to the Father, and in him all things are set in order, and he himself has his praises sung by all, as Creator. For he himself says, 'I was by his side, ordering';[4] and 'My Father works hitherto, and I work'.[5]

Contra Arianos ii. 19–20

(m) He is worshipped as God

He would not have been thus worshipped, nor thus spoken of [*as in* Heb. i. 6; Isa. xlv. 14; John xii. 13, xx. 28], if he belonged merely to the creatures. But as it is, since he is not a creature, but the offspring of the God who is worshipped, an offspring proper to his substance, and a Son by nature, therefore he is worshipped and is believed to be God, and is Lord of hosts, and has authority and is all-sovereign, as the Father is; for he himself says 'All things which belong to the Father are mine'.[6] For it is proper to the Son to have all that the Father has, and to be such that the Father is beheld in him, and that through him all things were made and that in him the salvation of all is brought about and is established.

Ibid. ii. 24

(n) The Father's Word and Will

Created things have come into being by God's pleasure and by his will; but the Son is not a creation of his will, nor has he come into being subsequently, as the creation; but he is by nature the proper offspring of the Father's substance. He is the proper Word of the Father and we cannot therefore suppose any will existing before him; since he is the Father's living Counsel and Power, fashioning what the Father had decided upon.

(66) . . . By the act of will by which the Son is willed by the Father, the Son himself loves and wills and honours the Father.

Ibid. iii. 63, 66

---

[1] γεννηθέντα ἢ ποιηθέντα as if they were synonymous: *contra*, Nicene creed, γεννηθέντα, οὐ ποιηθέντα, 'begotten, not made'.   [2] I Cor. xv. 41.   [3] John xiv. 6.   [4] Prov. viii. 30.   [5] John v. 17.   [6] John xvi. 15.

(o) Not Brought into Being as Agent of Creation

The Word of God was not made for us; rather we were made for him and 'in him all things were created'.[1] Nor is it true that because of our weakness[2] he, the strong, was brought into being by the Father (who then existed alone), in order that he might fashion us through him as by an instrument. Nothing could be further from the truth! For even if God had decided not to make created things, still the Word would have been 'with God' none the less, and the Father in him. While created things could not have come into being without the Word . . . For as the light enlightens all things with its radiance, and without that radiance nothing would be illuminated, so the Father wrought all things through the Word, as by a hand.[3] For instance, God said, 'Let there be light'.[4] . . . And he did not speak in order that some sub-ordinate might hear, understand what the speaker wanted, and go and perform the task. This is what happens in human affairs. But the Word of God is creator and maker, and he *is* the Father's will.

Ibid. ii. 31

(p) The Analogy of Light

. . . We see that the radiance from the sun is integral to it, and that the substance of the sun is not divided or diminished; but its substance is entire, and its radiance perfect and entire, and the radiance does not diminish the substance of the light, but is as it were a genuine off-spring from it. Thus we see that the Son is begotten not from without, but 'from the Father', and that Father remains entire, while the 'stamp of his substance'[5] exists always and preserves the likeness and image without alteration.

Ibid. ii. 33

(q) The Eternal Son: the Substantial Word

The Arians say, 'How can the Son exist eternally with the Father? For human beings are born as sons of men in course of time. The father is, say, thirty years old, and the son is begotten then and starts his existence. In fact, every human son "did not exist before he was begotten".' And again they whisper, 'How can the Son be the Word, or the Word be the image of God? For human speech is a combina-tion of syllables which merely signifies the speaker's meaning, and immediately ceases and disappears.'

[1] Col. i. 16.   [2] The Arians contended that God created through a subordinate Son because the created order could not tolerate the direct action of the Almighty.   [3] Cf. Irenaeus, p. 85. The same figure is used by Tertullian, Cyprian, Cyril of Alexandria, and other Fathers.   [4] Gen. i. 3.   [5] Heb. i. 3.

(35) Now if they are discussing a *man*, then they may argue about his word and his son on the human level. But if they are talking of God, man's creator, they must not think of him on the human level. The character of the parent determines the character of the offspring. Man is begotten in time and begets in time; he comes into being from non-existence, and therefore his word ceases and does not remain. But 'God is not like man',[1] as the Scripture has said; but he is 'he who exists'[2] and exists for ever; therefore his Word is 'that which exists', and exists eternally with the Father, as radiance from a light. A human word is a combination of syllables, and has no independent life or activity; it merely signifies the speakers' meaning, and just issues and passes away and disappears, since it had no existence at all before it was uttered; therefore a man's word has no independent life and activity; in short it is not a man. But God's word is not merely 'emitted',[3] as one might say, nor is it just an articulate noise; nor is 'the Son of God' just a synonym for 'the command of God'; but he is the perfect off-spring of the perfect. The words of man have no power to effect any thing; hence man works by means of hands, not words; for hands have substantial existence, but a word has not. But 'the Word of God', as the Apostle says, 'is living, and effective . . .' [Heb. iv. 12 f.].

Contra Arianos, ii. 34–35

(r) Improper Questions

We must not inquire, 'Why is the Word of God not like our word?' since 'God is not like us',[1] as we have said before. Nor is it right to inquire, 'How is the Word from God?' 'How is he God's radiance?' 'How does God beget?' 'What is the manner of his begetting?' Such presumption would be madness, for it is a demand to have explained in words something ineffable and proper to God's nature, known only to him and to the Son. It is equivalent to asking 'Where is God?' 'How does God exist?' 'What is the nature of the Father?' Such questions show a lack of reverence and an ignorance of God; and in the same way we are not permitted to ask such presumptuous questions about the begetting of the Son of God nor to make our nature and our limitations the measure of God and of his wisdom.

Ibid. ii. 36

(s) Begotten as Son—'Created' as Man

[*Athanasius has dealt at some length with* Prov. viii. 22, 'The Lord created me the beginning of his ways, for his works', *which the Arians*

---

[1] Judith viii. 16.   [2] Exod. iii. 14.   [3] προφορικός. See note 2, p. 297.

used to support their contention that the Son was created. He maintains that this refers to his incarnation] . . . If he is before all things, yet says, 'he created me'—not 'that I might make the works' but—'for the works', then either 'he created' refers to something later than himself, or he will clearly be later than the works, finding them already in existence when he is created, and created 'for' them. If so, how can he be before all things? And how were all things 'made through him'[1] and 'are established in him'?[2] . . . The Word of God is not a creature, but creator, and says in the fashion of proverbs[3] 'he created me' at the time when he put on created flesh. There is something else which may be understood from the passage itself. . . . He calls the Father *Lord*: not because he was a servant, but because he 'took the form of a servant.[4] For it was right for him on the one hand to call God Father, as being the Word from the Father; on the other hand to call the Father Lord, since he came 'to finish the work',[5] and took a servant's form.

(51) . . . If he says that he was 'created for the works' it is clear that he means to signify not his substance but the dispensation[6] which happened 'for his works', and this dispensation is subordinate to[7] being.

Ibid. ii. 50–51

God is first the Creator of men and then becomes their Father by virtue of his Word that dwells in them. With respect to the Word this is reversed; God is by nature his Father and later becomes his Creator and Maker when the Word assumes flesh that is created and made, and becomes man . . . Since he assumed created nature and became like us in respect of his body it is reasonable for him to be called our 'brother' and 'firstborn'. For though it was after us that he became man for us and our brother by likeness of body, he is still called, and is, the firstborn in this, that when all men were perishing according to Adam's transgression, his flesh was the first of all to be saved and set free, since it had become the body of the Word; and we henceforth are saved as his body was saved, by becoming 'incorporate' with it . . . (62) . . . He is 'only-begotten' because of his begetting from the Father; 'firstborn' because of his coming down to creation and his making many brothers.

Ibid. ii. 61–62

[1] John i. 3.   [2] Col. i. 17.   [3] Athanasius has previously pointed out that one expects to find the meaning of proverbs *beneath* the surface.   [4] Phil. ii. 7.   [5] John, iv. 34.   [6] 'Economy'—the Incarnation, see note 6, p. 75.   [7] Or 'later than'—δεύτερον.

(t) Coinherence of Father and Son

'I in the Father and the Father in me'[1] does not mean (as the Arians
suppose) that they are decanted into each other, being each filled from
the other, as in the case of empty vessels, so that the Son fills the
Father's emptiness, and the Father the Son's, each of them separately
not being full and perfect . . . ; for the Father is full and perfect, and
the Son is 'the fulness of the godhead'.[2] Again, God is not in the Son in
the same way as he comes into the saints and thus strengthens them.
For the Son is himself the 'power and wisdom'[3] of the Father; it is by
partaking of him that created things are sanctified in the Spirit; but he
himself is not Son by participation, but he is the Father's proper offspring. Nor is the Son in the Father in the sense that 'we live and move
and exist in him'.[4] For he is the Life, as being from the fount of the
Father, in which all things are brought to life and have substantial
existence. The Life does not live in Life; for then it would not *be*
life; but rather he brings all things to life.   *Contra Arianos*, iii. 1

For this inseparable activity of the Three Persons, by which, in the words of
Bishop Bull, 'they exist One in the Other, and so to speak mutually run into
and penetrate Each Other' (*Defensio Fidei Nicaenae*, II. ix, 23), later theologians
coined the technical term περιχώρησις, represented by the English 'coinherence'.

The whole being of the Son belongs to the Father's substance, as
radiance from light, and stream from source; so that he who sees the
son sees what belongs to the Father; and knows that the Son's being is
in the Father just as it is *from* the Father. For the Father is in the Son as
the sun is in its radiance, the thought in the word, the source in the
stream.

Having said 'I and the Father are one thing'[5] he adds 'I in the Father
and the Father in me'[6] to show the identity of the godhead and the
unity of the substance.

(4) For they are 'one thing', not in the sense of a thing divided into
two parts, these being nothing but one thing; nor in the sense of one
thing with two names, so that the Son is at one time Father, at another
time his own Son. Sabellius held this opinion and was condemned as a
heretic. But they are two, in that the Father is father and not also son;
the Son is son and not also father; but the nature is one (for the offspring
is not unlike the parent, being his image), and all that is the Father's is

[1] John xiv. 10.   [2] Col. ii. 9.   [3] 1 Cor. i. 24.   [4] Acts xvii. 28.   [5] John x. 30.   [6] John
xiv. 10.

the Son's. The Son is not another God, for he was not devised from outside [*the Father*]; for then there might surely be many gods, if we assume a godhead besides the Father. For even if the Son is distinct from the Father, as his offspring, still as God he is identical with him; he and the Father are one by specific and proper nature, and by the identity of the one godhead. For the radiance also is light, not a second light besides the sun, nor a different light, nor a light by participation in the sun, but a whole proper offspring of it. No one would say that there are two lights, but that the sun and its radiance are two, while the light from the sun, which illuminates things everywhere, is one. In the same way the godhead of the Son is the Father's. Hence it is undivided, and 'God is one, and there is none other besides him'.[1] Thus, since they are one, and the godhead itself is one, the same things are predicated of the Son as of the Father, except the title of 'Father'; for instance, 'God'— 'The Word was God';[2] 'All-sovereign'—'Thus says he who was and is and is coming, the all-sovereign';[3] 'Lord'—'One Lord, Jesus Christ';[4] 'Light'—'I am the light'.[5]   Ibid. iii. 3–4

The Son is implied with the Father; for one cannot use the title 'father' unless a son exists; whereas in calling God 'maker' we do not necessarily signify the things which come into being; for a maker is before his works. But in calling God 'Father' we at once intimate the Son's existence. Therefore whoever believes in the Son believes in the Father; for he believes in what belongs to the Father's substance; and thus there is one faith in one God. And whoever worships and honours the Son worships and honours the Father; for the godhead is one; and therefore there is one honour and one worship which is given to the Father in and through the Son. And he who worships thus worships one God.   Ibid. iii. 6

(*u*) *He 'became man', not 'came to a man'*

He became man, and did not come into a man. We must be clear about this, to avoid the notion . . . that the Word dwelt in a man, hallowing him and displaying himself in him, as in earlier times the Word came to each of the saints. In that case there would have been no paradox, and those who saw him would not have been startled, as when they said, 'Where does this man come from?'[6] and, 'You are a man. Why do you make yourself God?'[7] They are quite accustomed to the idea,

[1] Mark xii. 32.   [2] John i. 1.   [3] Rev. i. 8.   [4] 1 Cor. viii. 6.   [5] John viii. 12.   [6] Mark iv. 41.
[7] John x. 33.

as in the words, 'The Word of the Lord came', to the various prophets. But in fact the Word of God, through whom all things came into being, endured to become also Son of man, and 'humbled himself', taking the form of a servant';[1] and for this reason the cross of Christ is 'a scandal to the Jews, but to us Christ is God's power and God's wisdom'.[2] For 'The Word became flesh'[3] as John says, and in Scripture 'flesh' is commonly used for 'man' . . . [Cf. Joel ii. 28.]

Contra Arianos, iii. 30

(v) The Word Incarnate yet Omnipresent

The Word was not confined within his body; nor was he there and nowhere else; he did not activate that body and leave the universe emptied of his activity and guidance. Here is the supreme marvel. He was the Word and nothing contained him; rather he himself contained all things. He is in the whole creation, yet in his essential being he is distinct from it all, while he is in all things in the activities of his power, ordering all things, extending over all things his universal providence, quickening each and every thing at once, containing the universe and not contained by it, but in his Father alone existing wholly and entirely. So also when he was in the human body he himself gave that body life; and at the same time he was of course giving life to the whole universe, and was present in all things; and yet distinct from and outside the universe. And while being recognized from his body, through his actions in the body, he was also manifest in his working in the universe.

De Incarnatione, 17

(w) The Divinity and the Humanity in the Incarnate Christ

Now in the past he used to come to individual saints, and to hallow those who genuinely received him. But when they were born it was not said that 'he had become man', nor when they suffered was it said that 'he had suffered'. He was always God, and hallowed those to whom he came, and set all things in order in accordance with the Father's will. Later he became man, for our sakes, and, as the Apostle says, 'the godhead dwelt' in the flesh 'in bodily fashion'.[4] This is as much as to say, 'Though he was God he had a body for his own, and using it as an instrument he had become man for our sakes'. Thus it is that the properties of the flesh are said to be his, since he was in that flesh; hunger, thirst, pain, weariness, and the like, to which the flesh is liable: while the works belonging to the Word himself (raising the dead, restoring sight to the blind, curing the woman's haemorrhage)

[1] Phil. ii. 7 f.   [2] 1 Cor. i. 23 f.   [3] John. i. 14.   [4] Col. ii. 9.

he himself did through his own body. The Word 'bore the weakness'[1] of the flesh as his own; for the flesh was his flesh: the flesh assisted the works of the godhead, for the godhead was in the flesh; the body was God's.

(32) . . . Certainly, when the need arose to raise Peter's mother-in-law, who had a fever, he stretched out his hand as a human action, but stopped the illness by a divine act. In the case of 'the man born blind'[2] the spittle from his material body was human, but the opening of the eyes by means of the clay was a divine act. In the case of Lazarus he ut⁺ered, as man, a human cry;[3] but it was as God, by a divine act, that he raised Lazarus from the dead. These things happened in this way, and were thus demonstrated, because he had a body not by way of an illusion, but in reality.   *Contra Arianos*, iii. 31–32

Being God, he became man: and then as God he raised the dead, healed all by a word, and also changed the water into wine. These were not human acts. But as wearing a body he felt thirst and weariness and suffered pain. These experiences are not appropriate to deity. As God he said, 'I in the Father, the Father in me';[4] as wearing a body he thus attacked the Jews, 'Why do you seek to kill me, when I am a man who has told you the truth, which I heard from my Father?'[5] And yet these are not events occurring disconnectedly, distinguished according to their quality, so that one class may be ascribed to the body, apart from the divinity, the other to the divinity, apart from the body. They all occurred inseparably conjoined, and the Lord, who marvellously performed those acts by his grace, was one. He spat in human fashion; but his spittle had divine power, for by it he restored sight to the eyes of the man blind from birth. When he willed to make himself known as God, he used his human tongue to signify this, when he said, 'I and the Father are a unity'.[6] He cured by his mere will. Yet it was by extending his human hand that he raised Peter's mother-in-law when she had the fever, and raised up from the dead the daughter of the synagogue-ruler, when she had already passed from life.
                                              Ep. ad Serapionem, iv. 14

(*x*) *Human Nature Deified by the Incarnation*

. . . If the works of the godhead had not taken place by means of the body, man would not have been made divine. If the properties of the flesh had not been ascribed to the Word, man would not have been

[1] Isa. liii. 4. [2] John ix. 6 f. [3] John xi. 45. [4] John xiv. 11. [5] John viii. 40. [6] John x. 30.

thoroughly freed from them. But as it is the Word became man and took as his own the properties of the flesh. Thus, because of the Word which has come in the body, these attributes [*i.e. death and corruption*] no longer adhere to the body, but have been destroyed by the Word. Henceforth men no longer remain sinful and dead according to their own attributes, but they rise in accordance with the Word's power, and persist immortal and incorruptible. Whence also as the flesh is said to have been begotten from Mary, the mother of God, he himself is said to have been begotten, he who bestows birth on all others so that they come into being. This is in order that he may transfer our birth to himself, that we may no longer return as earth to earth, but, as being joined with the Word from heaven, may be carried up with him into heaven.   *Contra Arianos*, iii. 33

(γ) *Limitations of Knowledge, as Man*

The flesh is ignorant, but the Word, as Word, knows everything, even before it comes to be. For when the Word became man he did not cease to be God; nor because he is God does he avoid what is human. Far from it; rather, being God, he has taken the flesh to himself, and, in flesh, deified the flesh. In the flesh he asked questions; in the flesh he raised the dead; he knew where Lazarus lay; but he asked. . . . The all-holy Word of God bore our ignorance so that he might bestow on us the knowledge of his Father.   Ibid. iii. 38

Why did he say 'Not even the Son knows',[1] when in fact he knew? I think every believer knows the answer; that he spoke, as elsewhere, as man, because of the flesh. This does not show a defect in the Word, but of the human nature, of which ignorance is a characteristic. Since he was made man he is not ashamed to profess ignorance because of the ignorance of flesh; to show that though knowing as God he is ignorant according to the flesh.   Ibid. iii. 43

(z) *Christ's human Weakness*

['Let this cup pass, &c.'.] He willed what he begged to be spared, for that was the reason for his coming; the willing was his . . . the cowardice belonged to the flesh. . . . Because of the flesh he mingled his will with human weakness, that by abolishing this he might make man stout-hearted in the face of death.   Ibid. iii. 57

[1] Mark xiii. 32.

III. The Work of Christ

(a) The Twofold Task, i. To Annul Death's Dominion, ii. To Restore the Image of God

What then had to be done in this situation?[1] What action must God take? Should he demand of men repentance for the transgression? For this, someone might say, would be worthy of God; that as man went over to destruction as a result of the transgression, so he might come back to immortality as a result of repentance. But repentance will not safeguard the honour of God's character; for he would still be inconsistent if man did not remain under death's dominion; and further, repentance does not recall men from their natural condition but merely makes them cease from their sins. Repentance would have been quite enough, had there been just a transgression without consequent disintegration. . . . But now men were deprived of the grace of being 'after the image'. . . . What was needed to restore that grace and to recall man? Surely the Word of God who at the beginning had made the universe out of nothing. . . . Since he was the Word of the Father and above all, it follows that he alone was able to recreate the universe and was alone worthy to suffer on behalf of all, and to be ambassador for all men with the Father.   *De Incarnatione*, 7

(b) Victory over Death for Men

To this end the incorporeal and immortal and immaterial Word of God comes to our place, though to be sure he was not remote from it before. For no part of the creation has been bereft of him, for he had filled all things completely, while remaining with his own Father. But he comes down to dwell among us through his love for us and in his manifestation to us. And seeing the human race perishing, though with reason . . . he pitied our weakness . . . and so that the work of his Father for men should not be frustrated he takes to himself a body, a body like our own . . . and since we were all liable to the disintegration of death he surrendered his body to death in the place of all men, and presented it to the Father . . . that by all dying in him the law of disintegration to which men were subject might be annulled (seeing that its power reached its end in the Lord's body, and it no longer has scope against men who are like him) . . . and that he might revive men from death by their appropriation of his body and by the grace of the resurrection.   Ibid. 8

[1] Described in the previous chapter, quoted above, p. 276.

(c) Vicarious Sacrifice and the Gift of Immortality

The Word takes a body that is capable of death, that by partaking in the Word, who is above all, that body might be sufficient to die instead of all, and might remain indestructible through the indwelling Word, and that henceforward by the grace of the resurrection, destruction should cease from all men. Hence by offering to death the body which he assumed, as a sacrifice and oblation free from any blemish, he did away with death forthwith for all those who are like him, by the offering of a substitute. . . . For he fulfilled all the liability in his death, being the Word of God, supreme over all men; and as the immortal Son of God, dwelling with all men in virtue of his likeness to them, he naturally clothed all with immortality in the assurance of the resurrection. For disintegration in death no longer has scope because of the Word dwelling in them through the one body. Just as when a great prince enters into a great city . . . no enemy or robber now attacks it because the prince has taken his abode in one of the houses; so it is in the case of the Prince of all mankind.   *De Incarnatione*, 9

(d) The Renewal of God's Image

[(10)–(12) *Man by sin forfeited the knowledge of God and the 'image', the Word, so as to become 'irrational'.*] What was God to do? Could he acquiesce in man's being deceived by the devil and losing the knowledge of God? If so, what was the use of his having been made after the image of God? Better to have been made an irrational creature than to be created rational and live the life of irrational creatures. . . . Or what profit to God . . . if men, his creatures, do not worship him? . . . What then was God to do? . . . Surely to renew the state of being 'in the image'. . . . And how could this happen, except by the coming of our Saviour Jesus Christ, the very image of God?   *Ibid.* 13

(e) Salvation by Revelation

If a portrait on wood has been obliterated as a result of adventitious dirt the subject of the portrait must present himself in order that the likeness may be renewed in the same material. . . . In the same way the all-holy Son of the Father came to our parts, that he might renew man who was made after his likeness. . . .

Wishing to help men he lives with men as man, taking a body like theirs; and through things of this world (I mean through the activities of his body) he teaches them, so that they who were unwilling to know him from his universal providence and guidance may, from his

actions performed through the body, come to know the Word of
God in the body, and through him may know the Father.   Ibid. 14

(*f*) *The Incarnation Necessary for Salvation*

[*God could have forgiven without the Incarnation.*] The reasonableness of
what actually happened can be seen in this way; if God had merely
spoken and the curse had been annulled there would have been a display
of the power of him who uttered the command, but man would only
have been restored to the condition of Adam before his sin, receiving
grace from outside, and not having it united with the body; for that
was man's state when he was set in paradise. He might perhaps have
been in a worse state, because he had learned to sin. Then being in such
a condition he might have been seduced by the serpent, and then there
would have again been need for God to command and annul the
curse, and this would have gone on endlessly.   *Contra Arianos*, ii. 68

(*g*) *Redemption and Deification*

He assumed a created human body, that, having renewed it as its
creator, he might deify it in himself, and thus bring us all into the
kingdom of heaven through our likeness to him. . . . We should not
have been freed from sin and the curse, had not the flesh which the
Word assumed been by nature human (for we should have nothing
in common with what was alien to us); so too humanity would not
have been deified, if the Word who became flesh had not been by
nature derived from the Father and his true and proper Word. For it
was for this reason that the conjunction was of this kind, that he might
join him who by nature was man to him who naturally belonged to
the godhead, that his salvation and deification might be sure. . . .
There would have been no profit to us men if either the Word had not
been truly and by nature the Son of God, or the flesh which he assumed
had not been real flesh.   Ibid. ii. 70

The Word was made man in order that we might be made divine. He
displayed himself through a body, that we might receive knowledge
of the invisible Father. He endured insult at the hands of men, that we
might inherit immortality. In himself he suffered no injury, being impassible and immortal and very Word of God: but in his impassibility
he was guarding and saving suffering men, for whose sake he endured
this treatment.   *De Incarnatione*, 54

The themes of salvation and deification are also treated in passages given
under *God the Son;* see pp. 278–80.

IV. The Holy Spirit and the Trinity

(a) The Spirit Uncreated

[*The 'Tropici',*[1] *while resisting the Arian degradation of the Son into a 'creature', speak of the Spirit as 'created'.*] They refuse to suppose the Son of God a creature; how can they endure even to hear the Spirit of the Son so spoken of? If they refuse to class the Son with created things, because of the unity of the Word with the Father . . . how can they dare to call the Spirit a created thing, when he has the same unity with the Son as the Son with the Father? They safeguard the unity of God by not dividing the Son from the Father: how is it that they fail to understand that by thus dividing the Spirit from the Word, they no longer safeguard the one godhead in trinity; for they tear it apart and mix with it an alien and different element . . . by making the Spirit of different essence? What kind of divine life is this, compounded of Creator and created? . . .   *Ep. ad Serapionem,* i. 2

(b) Yet not Begotten

'If', say the Tropici, 'the Spirit is not a created being nor one of the angels, but proceeds from the Father; then he is a Son also, and there are two Sons, the Spirit and the Word, and if so, how is the Word the only-begotten? The Word and Spirit must be equal. . . . Why is the Spirit not said to be begotten if he is "from the Father"? Why is he not called Son, but simply Holy Spirit? But if he is "of the Son" then the Father is the grandfather of the Spirit!' Such are the jests of these dishonourable men who attempt too curiously to search out 'the deep things of God, which no one knows except the Spirit'[2] whom they blaspheme. . . . God is not as man, and man should not dare to raise such questions about him [*i.e. arguments on the analogy of human relationships*].   Ibid. i. 15

(c) The Trinity Indivisible and Consubstantial

In Scripture the Spirit is nowhere called Son [of God] nor the Son's son. But the Son is the Father's Son; the Spirit, the Father's Spirit; and thus there is one godhead of the Holy Trinity, and one faith in the Holy Trinity.

[1] Athanasius so nicknames the party who were commonly called Pneumatomachi ('those who fight against the Spirit'), apparently because they explained away all passages of Scripture which did not suit their views as mere figures of speech, or 'tropes'. They had given trouble to Serapion, bishop of Thmuis in the Nile delta.   [2] 1 Cor. ii. 10.

(17) . . . If the Spirit were a creature, he would not be included in the Trinity; for the whole Trinity is one God. Nothing alien is mingled in the Trinity, it is indivisible and of the same nature.   Ibid. i. 16–17

(d) The Mutual Relations of the Persons

Such being the co-ordination and unity in the Holy Trinity, who would divide the Son from the Father, or the Spirit from the Son or the Father himself? Who would dare to say that the Trinity was internally 'dissimilar' or 'heterogeneous'? Or to speak of the Son as 'of alien essence' from the Father, or of the Spirit as 'foreign' to the Son? But if anyone asks how this happens, how the Son can be said to be in us when the Spirit is; or the Father, when the Son is; or how the whole Trinity is implied in the mention of one Person, or is said to be in us when one Person is—if anyone asks such questions, let him first himself divide brightness from light, or wisdom from a wise man, or explain how such things can be. If he cannot do this, much more mad is the presumption in making such inquiries about God; for [*the truth about*] the godhead is not given by a display of arguments, as has been said,[1] but by faith, and reason exercised with reverent caution. . . . Yet such perplexity may be remedied, firstly and chiefly by faith, but in the second place by such analogies as those of image, brightness, the source and the river, of substance and [*specific*] character. For as the Son is in the Spirit as in his own image; so the Father is in the Son. The Scriptures have supplied us with such comparisons . . . so that we may believe that there is one sanctification, *from* the Father, *through* the Son, *in* the Holy Spirit. For as the Son is only-begotten; so the Spirit, who is given and sent by the Son, is one. . . . For since the Son is one, who is the living Word, he must be one who is the Son's complete and perfect sanctifying and illuminating living energy and gift, which is said to proceed from the Father, because it shines forth from the Son who is acknowledged to be 'from the Father'; and it is sent out and given by the Son. The Son is sent by the Father; . . . [John iii. 16]; the Son sends the Spirit . . . [John xvi. 7]; the Son glorifies the Father . . . [John xvii. 4]; the Spirit glorifies the Son . . . [John xvi. 14]. The Son says, 'I speak to the world what I have heard from the Father';[2] while the Spirit receives from the Son: 'He will receive of mine and will proclaim [*it*] to you.'[3] And the Son came in the Father's name; so the Son says, 'The Spirit, whom the Father will send in my name'.[4]

[1] Cf. 1 Cor. i. 17 and ii. 4.   [2] John viii. 26.   [3] John xvi. 14.   [4] John xiv. 26.

(21) Thus the Spirit is to the Son, in order and nature, as the Son is to the Father; therefore if anyone calls the Spirit a creature, he must needs say the same of the Son. For as the Son, who is 'in the Father and the Father in him',[1] is not a created being but belongs to the essence of the Father . . . so it is not legitimate to class with creatures the Spirit, who is in the Son and the Son in him, nor to separate him from the Word and thus to render the Trinity imperfect.

Ep. ad Serapionem, i. 20–21

(e) Sanctification

If we are made sharers of the divine nature through our partaking of the Spirit, it would be only a madman who would say that the Spirit is of created nature and not of the nature of God.

(25) . . . (*ad fin.*) [The Spirit] in whom created beings are deified could not himself be outside of the deity of the Father.   Ibid. i. 24–25

(f) The Spirit of Creation

It is written in the 103rd Psalm: 'Thou shalt take away their spirit [breath] and they shall fail, and return to their dust. Thou shalt send forth thy Spirit and they shall be created'.[2]

Hence it is clear that the Spirit is not a creature but shares in the work of creation. The Father creates all things *through* the Word, *in* the Spirit; for where the Word is, there is the Spirit also; and things created through the Word have their being from the Spirit by means of the Word: 'By the word of the Lord the heavens were set fast: and by the spirit of his mouth all the power of them'.[3]   Ibid. iii. 4

(g) The Eternal Trinity

The Lord founded the faith of the Catholic Church on the Trinity . . . [Matt. xxviii. 19].

(7) . . . If the Trinity exists, and the faith is founded in the Trinity, let [*our opponents*] say whether the Trinity always was or whether 'once there was not a Trinity'. If the Trinity is eternal, then the Spirit is not a creature, because the Spirit eternally exists with the Word, and is in the Word. . . . They [the Tropici] say that the Trinity came to be constituted as a result of evolution and development; first there was a duality which awaited the production of a creature which could be

---

[1] John x. 38, &c.   [2] Ps. ciii (104), 29 f.   [3] Ps. xxxii (33), 6.

joined with the Father and the Son so that the Trinity might come into being. No such thought should ever enter the mind of a Christian. The Trinity is now, as it ever was; and as it is, so it always was.

Ibid. iii. 6, 7

(h) The Spirit in Relation to Christ, and to Man

Because of the grace of the Spirit which has been given us we come to be in him, and he in us; and since the Spirit is God's spirit it is reasonable that we, having the Spirit, should be considered to be 'in God' through the Spirit which has been given to us. Not that we come to be in the Father in the same way as the Son is in him. For the Son does not merely partake of the Spirit so as to come to be in the Father by reason of the Spirit: nor does he receive the Spirit, but rather he himself supplies it to all. And the Spirit does not unite the Son to the Father, but rather the Spirit receives from the Word. The Son is in the Father, as being his own Word and radiance; but we, apart from the Spirit, are alien and remote from God, and are united with the Godhead by participation in the Spirit; so that our being in the Father does not belong to us, but to the Spirit, which is in us and dwells in us.   *Contra Arianos*, iii. 24

(i) The Holy Trinity: Summary[1]

We believe in one unbegotten God, the Father almighty, maker of all things, visible and invisible, whose being is derived from himself; and in one only-begotten Word, Wisdom, Son begotten of the Father without beginning, and eternally; a Word not as expressed[2] or as conceived,[3] not an effluence[4] from the perfect, not a section[5] of the impassible nature, not an emanation[6] from it; but a Son perfect in himself, living and acting, the real image of the Father, equal in honour and glory . . . [John v. 23] true God of true God . . . [1 John v. 20] omnipotent from the omnipotent; for all things which the Father rules and commands, the Son rules and commands likewise, for he is entire from the entire, like to the Father . . . [John xiv. 5–7]. He was begotten in a way inexplicable and incomprehensible . . . [Isa. liii. 8]. He also in the end of the ages came down from the Father's bosom, and from the undefiled virgin Mary took upon him our humanity,[7] Christ Jesus, whom [which] on our behalf he allowed to suffer, of his own choice . . . [John x. 18]. In which humanity[7] he was crucified and died for us, rose from the dead, and was taken up to heaven. He also was 'made

[1] See note at end of this passage, p. 298. [2] προφορικός—Word as uttered. [3] ἐνδιάθετος—Word as mental conception. [4] ἀπόρροια. [5] τμῆσις—a part cut off. [6] προβολή—something projected. [7] lit. 'man'.

the beginning of ways'[1] for us, when he was on earth; he showed us light out of darkness, salvation out of error, life from the dead, entrance into paradise. . . . He has also prepared the ascent to heaven, whither as precursor the Lord's humanity[2] has entered for us, the humanity in which he is to judge the living and the dead.

(2) We believe likewise in the Holy Spirit . . . [1 Cor. ii. 10]. We do not think of a 'Son-Father'[3] (as do the Sabellians who call him 'unisubstantial' not 'consubstantial', thus destroying his sonship). Nor do we ascribe to the Father the passible body which the Son bore for the salvation of the whole world: nor may we suppose three 'hypostases' divided from each other, as three men are corporally separate: this would introduce the many gods of the heathen. Rather, as a river is generated from its source, and is not separated from it, although there are two forms and two names. . . . As the source is not the river, nor the river the source, but each is one and the same water . . . ; so the godhead flows from the Father to the Son without change or separation. . . . Nor do we think of the Son of God, who is God the creator of all things, as 'created' or 'made' or 'coming from non-existences';[4] he is existent from the existent.   *Expositio Fidei*, 1

['Athanasian', though, probably not by Athanasius

There is one form of godhead, which is also in the Word; one God the Father, existing by himself in respect that he is above all, and appearing in the Son in respect that he pervades all things, and in the Spirit in respect that he acts in him in all things through the Word. Thus we acknowledge God to be one through the Trinity.

Contra Arianos, iii. 15

V. The Eucharist

(a) The Heavenly Feast

My beloved brethren, it is no temporal feast that we come to, but an eternal, heavenly feast. We do not display it in shadows; we approach it in reality. The Jews had their fill of the flesh of a dumb lamb, and when their feast was finished they anointed their door-posts with the blood, to beg for aid against the destroyer. But the food that we partake of is the Father's Word; we have the lintels of our hearts sealed with the blood of the new covenant; and we acknowledge the grace bestowed on us from our Saviour.   *Epistolae Festales*, iv. 3

[1] Prov. viii. 22.   [2] 'the dominical man'.   [3] υἱοπάτωρ.   [4] ἐξ οὐκ ὄντων.

(b) Spiritual Nourishment

'Does this scandalize you? What if you see the Son of Man ascending to where he was before? It is the Spirit who gives life; the flesh is of no avail. The words which I have spoken to you are spirit and life.'[1] Here he has employed two terms about himself, flesh and spirit; and he has distinguished spirit from flesh, so that they might believe not only in so much of him as was apparent to sight, but also in what was invisible, and thus might learn that what he was saying was not fleshly but spiritual. For how many would his body suffice for food, so as to become the nourishment of the whole world? The reason for his mention of the ascension into heaven of the Son of man was in order to draw them away from the material notion; that thenceforward they might learn that the flesh he spoke of was heavenly food from above and spiritual nourishment given from him. For he says, 'What I have spoken to you is spirit and life', which is as much as to say, 'What is displayed and given for the world's salvation is the flesh which I wear: but this flesh and its blood will be given to you by me spiritually as nourishment, so that this may be bestowed spiritually on each, and may become for individuals a safeguard to ensure resurrection to eternal life.'   *Ep. ad Serapionem*, iv. 19

[1] John vi. 61 ff.

Appendix

Works cited, with translations of Latin titles

CLEMENT OF ROME (see pp. 1-3, and Irenaeus, p. 91)

  [*First*] *Epistle to the Corinthians* (The so-called 'Second Epistle to the Corinthians' attributed to Clement is not genuine)

IGNATIUS (see pp. 3-5)

  Epistle to the Ephesians
  Epistle to the Magnesians
  Epistle to the Philadelphians
  Epistle to the Romans
  Epistle to the Smyrnaeans
  Epistle to the Trallians

THE DIDACHE (see pp. 5-7)

THE EPISTLE TO DIOGNETUS (see pp. 7-9)

JUSTIN MARTYR (see pp. 9-10)

Apologia I	Apology (*or* Defence of Christianity)
Apologia II	Second Apology (*or* Second Defence of Christianity)

IRENAEUS (see pp. 12-13)

Adversus Haereses (or Ἔλεγχος καὶ Ἀνατροπὴ τῆς Ψευδωνύμου Γνώσεως)	Against Heresies (*or* Refutation and Overthrow of False Gnosis *or* '. . . of Knowledge Falsely so Called')
Demonstration of the Apostolic Preaching (Εἰς ἐπίδειξιν τοῦ ἀποστολικοῦ Κηρύγματος)	The title is quoted by Eusebius (H.E. v. 26), but the work is extant only in an Armenian version, discovered 1904

TERTULLIAN (see pp. 14-16)

Ad Martyres	To the Martyrs (an appeal to stand firm)
Ad Uxorem	To his Wife (a dissuasive against second marriages)
**Adversus Hermogenem*	Against Hermogenes (a Gnostic heretic)
**Adversus Marcionem*	Against Marcion (see p. 15)
*Adversus Praxean	Against Praxeas (see p. 15)
Apologeticus	Defence of Christianity (see p. 15)
*De Anima	On the Soul
De Baptismo	On Baptism
*De Carne Christi	On Christ's Human Nature

* Works written as Montanist, or during Tertullian's transition to Montanism (*c.* 203).

TERTULLIAN—*Continued*

*De Corona Militis	On the Soldier's Wreath (arising from a Christian soldier's refusal to accept the laurel crown awarded by the Emperor. Tertullian defends his action, and discusses the participation of Christians in traditional customs which, in his view, were essentially pagan)
*De Exhortatione Castitatis	On the Exhortation to Chastity (the same theme as *Ad Uxorem*)
*De Fuga in Persecutione	On Flight in Persecution (the moral question whether a Christian might flee from persecutors and so avoid the ultimate choice between apostasy and martyrdom)
De Idololatria	On Idolatry (a protest against any connexion of Christians with heathen practices)
*De Ieiunio [*adversus Psychicos*]	On Fasting [against the Worldly (i.e. the orthodox Churchmen, see p. 116)]
*De Monogamia	On Monogamy (the same theme as *Ad Uxorem*)
De Oratione	On Prayer
De Patientia	On Contentment (see note, p. 114)
De Poenitentia	On Repentance
De Praescriptione Haereticorum	A Demurrer to the Heretics' Plea (the title employs a legal metaphor)
*De Pudicitia	On Modesty (asserting that sexual sins are unpardonable)
*De Resurrectione Carnis	On the Resurrection of the Body
De Spectaculis	On Public Shows (i.e. games and shows in the arena, heathen and immoral in Tertullian's view)
*De Virginibus Velandis	On the Veiling of Virgins (whether 1 Cor. xi. 1–16 means that all women should at all times wear veils)
*Testimonium Animae (or *De Testimonio Animae*)	On the Evidence of the Natural Christianity of the Soul (the full title is *de Testimonio Animae naturaliter Christianae*. Cf. 'testimonium animae naturaliter Christianae': 'the testimony that the soul is naturally Christian', *Apologeticus*, 17, pp. 103–4)

* Works written as Montanist, or during Tertullian's transition to Montanism (*c.* 203).

CLEMENT OF ALEXANDRIA (see pp. 16–18)

Paedagogus	An Introduction to Christianity (lit. 'The Tutor': a *paedagogus* was a chosen slave charged with the duty of looking after the master's children, especially taking them to school—the word used in Gal. iii. 24)
Protrepticus	An Invitation (lit. [Speech of] Exhortation [to the heathen to come into the Church])
Quis Dives Salvetur?	The Question of the Rich Man's Salvation (lit. 'Who is the Rich Man who is saved?')
Stromateis	Miscellanies (lit. 'Patchwork Quilt')

ORIGEN (see pp. 18–22)

Commentarii:	*Commentaries:*
In Canticum Canticorum	On the Songs of Songs
In Matthaeum	On St. Matthew's Gospel
In Matthaeum Commentariorum Series	Series of Comments on St. Matthew
In Ioannem	On St. John's Gospel
In Ep. ad Romanos	On the Epistle to the Romans
Contra Celsum	Against Celsus (who had written a comprehensive work in opposition to Christian claims, no longer extant as such, though much of it is included, with the Christian answers, in this work of Origen's)
De Oratione	On Prayer
De Principiis	On First Principles (see p. 21)
Exhortatio ad Martyrium	A Call to Martyrdom
Homiliae:	*Homilies* (Sermons):
In Genesin	On Genesis
In Exodum	On Exodus
In Leviticum	On Leviticus
In Numeros	On Numbers
In Librum Iesu Nave	On the Book of Joshua. (Hebrew 'Joshua' = Greek and Latin 'Iesus' (cf. Hebrews iv. 8, A.V.). The O.T. leader is distinguished as 'Iesus Nave', i.e. 'son of Nun'.)
In Ieremiam	On Jeremiah
In Ezechielem	On Ezekiel
In Lucam	On St. Luke
In Ioannem Fragmenta	Notes on St. John's Gospel (separate from the Commentary listed above)

ORIGEN—*Continued*

  Selecta: *Selected Comments:*
    In Exodum   On Exodus
    In Ezechielem   On Ezekiel

CYPRIAN (see pp. 22–24)

  Ad Donatum   To Donatus
  De Catholicae Ecclesiae Unitate On the Unity of the Catholic Church
  De Lapsis   On the Lapsed (see pp. 22–3)
  Epistolae   Letters

ATHANASIUS (see pp. 24–27)

  [*Orationes*] *Contra Arianos*   [Orations] against the Arians (see p. 26)
  De Incarnatione   On the Incarnation
  Ep. ad Serapionem   Letter to Serapion (bishop of Thmuis)
  Epistolae Festales   Pastoral Letters at Easter (an annual series)
  [*Expositio Fidei*   Exposition of the Faith]
                          ('Athanasian', though probably not by
                              Athanasius)

Index